YAGARA DICTIONARY AND SALVAGE GRAMMAR

YAGARA DICTIONARY AND SALVAGE GRAMMAR

KAREN SULLIVAN AND GLENDA HARWARD-NALDER

Australian
National
University

ANU PRESS

ASIA-PACIFIC LINGUISTICS

Australian
National
University

ANU PRESS

Published by ANU Press
The Australian National University
Canberra ACT 2600, Australia
Email: anupress@anu.edu.au

Available to download for free at press.anu.edu.au

ISBN (print): 9781760466176
ISBN (online): 9781760466183

WorldCat (print): 1416932553
WorldCat (online): 1417107717

DOI: 10.22459/YDSG.2024

Cover design and layout by ANU Press

This book is published under the aegis of the Asia-Pacific Linguistics editorial board of ANU Press.

Contents

List of illustrations

Figures

Tables

Abbreviations and conventions

Abbreviations of sources

AIAS Australian Institute of Aboriginal Studies

AIATSIS Australian Institute of Aboriginal and Torres Strait Islander Studies

B Birch 1873

Ba Bannister 1986

Bd Ballard 2007

Be Bell 1934

Bl Blackman 1900

Bn Bensted 1924

Bu Bunce 1846–47

Ca Cadell c.1900

Cl Clunie 1839

Cu Curr 1887

CW Colliver & Woolston 1975, 1978

D Donovan 1877, 1888a–d, 1895

DF Darragh & Fensham 2013

E Eipper 1841a–c, 1986

F Flint 1960

Fi Finch 1842

FNSI Stephens & Sharp 2009

G Gibson 1863, 1882

Ga Gardner 1854

H Holmer 1983

Ha Hardcastle 1946–7

Hi Hinchcliffe 1890

Hk Hockings 1884

Hn Hanlon 1931

Hp Harper 1894

Hw Howitt 1904; Pitt Rivers Museum 2012

J Jefferies 2011

Ja Jackson 1937

K Kite & Wurm 2004

Kd Kidd 2001

L Lauterer 1891, 1895

La Latham 1852

Le Leichhardt 1842–44

Lg Lang 1846, 1847

Ln Lenet 1904

M Meston 1867–1960, 1894, 1895, 1923a–c, 1931a–b, 1984, 1986a, 1986b

Ma Mathew 1910

Mac Macarthur & Moore 1867

MB Moreton Bay 1838

MMEIC Minjerribah Moorgumpin Elders in Council

N NNW 1868

P Petrie 1902, 1904,

Q State of Queensland 2022

QYAC Quandamooka Yoolooburrabee Aboriginal Corporation and Queensland Parks and Wildlife Service and Partnerships 2021

R Ridley 1855, 1875, 1887, 1986

RB Radcliffe-Browne 1930

Ro Roth 1897, 1910

S Steele 1984

Sh Sharpe 2020

Su Suttor 1897

T Turner 1861

Th Threlkeld 1846

Ti Tindale 1974

TK Tennant-Kelly 2011

W Watkins 1891, 1984, 1986; Watkins & Hamilton 1887

Wa Watson 1943

We Welsby 1916

Wi Winterbotham 1950, 1957

Wu Wurm 1960

Linguistic abbreviations

1 first person

2 second person

3 third person

ABL ablative case

ACC accusative case

ALL allative case

ATEL atelicity-marking suffix

BACK suffix indicating motion back the way one came

C consonant

CAUS causative suffix

CHARACT nominalising suffix

CONT continuative suffix

DEST suffix describing motion to a location

DIST distal

DU dual

DUR durative case

EMPH emphatic

ERG ergative case

EXCL exclusive

F feminine suffix

FUT future tense

IMP imperative

INCH inchoative verbalising suffix

IPA International Phonetic Alphabet

IPFV imperfective

LOC locative case

MED medial

NEG negation

NOM nominative case

NP noun phrase; syntactic phrase headed by a noun

OBLG suffix indicating obligation

PL plural

POSS possessive case or determiner

PROX proximal

PRS present tense

PST past tense

PURP purposive suffix

Q interrogative particle marking questions

REFL reflexive suffix

RNP NP relativising suffix

RTP clause relativising suffix

SAE Standard Australian English

SBJV subjunctive suffix

SG singular

SONG particle in songs

STATE suffix that forms stative verbs

V vowel

VERY suffix adding emphasis

Linguistic conventions

/ / Slashes indicate phonological representation (the underlying sounds of a word).

[ ] Square brackets indicate phonetic representation (how a word sounds acoustically).

- The hyphen marks morpheme boundaries. That is, it separates stems from suffixes and appears between morphemes in compounds and reduplicated forms. In Part 2: Dictionary, hyphens are not used with suffixes or compounds and only appear in reduplicated forms.

= The equal sign marks a clitic boundary and occurs before the clitics =*bu* and =*gu*.

Part 1. Grammar

1.1. The Yagara language

1.1.1. Yagara dialects

Yagara is a Pama-Nyungan language traditionally spoken in what is now South East Queensland. Yagara, which is sometimes spelled *Yuggera*, *Jagera* and other variations, is traditionally spoken from the Great Dividing Range in the west, to Stradbroke Island in the east, encompassing present-day Ipswich and Brisbane, and extending down into the Fassifern Valley in the south (Bell 1934, 13; see Figure 1.1). Yagara is the source of the Australian English words *yakka* 'work' (from *yaga*), *dilly* 'dilly bag' (from *dili*), *humpy* 'traditional temporary shelter' (from *ngumbi*);[1] and possibly *jackaroo* 'cattle/ sheep station worker' (from *dagairu* 'stranger').

Though Yagara is linguistically one language, some of its dialects belong to distinct groups and are associated with particular Countries (O'Grady, Voegelin and Voegelin 1966; Wurm 1972, 1994; Oates 1975; Walsh 1981; Bowern and Atkinson 2012). The differences between the Yagara dialects are socially and politically important, but linguistically small. The dialects have fewer phonological and lexical differences than Australian English and New Zealand English, for example, and all seem to have identical morphosyntax.

---

1   Though the vowel in English *humpy* might be expected to originate from Yagara *a*, not *u*, three sources record *ngumbi* with *oo*, which indicates Yagara *u*.

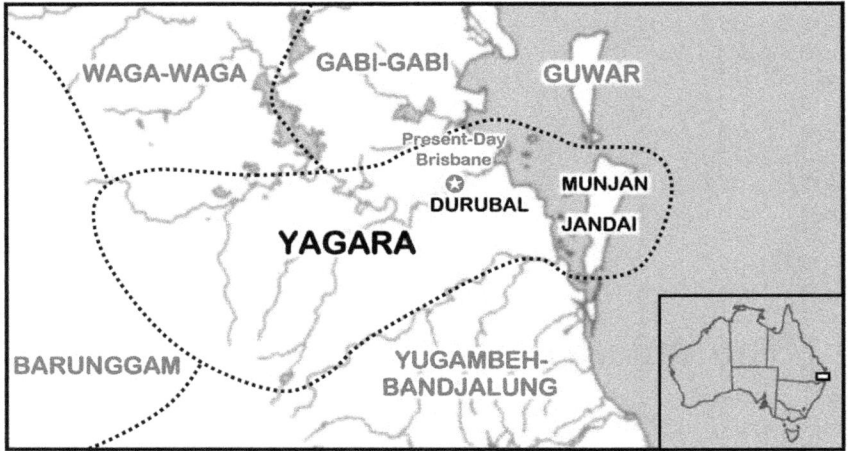

Figure 1.1: Yagara (in black font) and surrounding languages (in grey).

Dialects are not shown, with the exception of the Durubal dialect traditionally spoken around the present-day Brisbane CBD, and the Yagara saltwater dialects Jandai and Munjan (small black font).

Source: Authors' approximation based on Birch (1873), Watkins and Hamilton (1887), Watkins (1891), Harper (1894), Welsby (1916), Bensted (1924), Bell (1934), Meston (1894, 1923a–c), Watson (1943), Hardcastle (1946–7), and Holmer (1983). This map is hesitant and relevant only to the discussion of this section. As highlighted by Aird (2020) and Aird et al. (2020), concepts of language and tribe are less reliable for Native Title Claim purposes than research based on visible (photographic) evidence of real-life events and people.

It is unclear whether the mainland Yagara-speaking clans considered themselves speakers of the same language. All recorded mainland Yagara speakers used the word *yagara* to mean 'no', for example. A different word for 'no' can be a signal that a dialect is considered a distinct language, so it is possible that all the mainland Yagara-speaking clans identified as speakers of the same language despite belonging to socially distinct groups.

The map in Figure 1.1 labels three Yagara dialects: Durubal, Jandai and Munjan (see Figure 1.1). These are the dialects for which we have the most information. Several other potential names for Yagara dialects are listed in Section 2.2.

The Durubal or *Turrbal* speakers are the traditional caretakers of the present-day Brisbane city centre, and their dialect differs from the saltwater dialects and potentially from the dialects farther south, as described later in this section. The Durubal dialect is also the main source of information on Yagara morphosyntax in the current grammar, due mainly to the Bible stories that Ridley elicited from the boy Tom Petrie in 1855 (see 1.1.4 and 3.5–3.7). Other dialects are represented by wordlists and short sentences.

Mainland dialects like Durubal can also be called freshwater dialects, whereas Jandai and Munjan are saltwater dialects, based on the language groups' traditional identities as inland (freshwater) people and coastal (saltwater) people (Jefferies 2011, 79).

The two documented saltwater dialects, Jandai and Munjan, have their own words for 'no'. Instead of *yagara* 'no' as in mainland Yagara, Jandai uses *jandai* 'no' and Munjan uses *munjan* 'no'. These two island dialects, while similar to each other, differ phonologically from all the mainland dialects in documented ways.

Jandai is traditionally spoken by the Jandaiwal people of central and southern Stradbroke Island (Watkins and Hamilton 1887, 222). Munjan or *Moondjan* is a northern Stradbroke dialect that belongs to the Nunagal or *Noonuckle* people (Tindale 1974; Watkins and Hamilton 1887, 222). The Guwanbal or *Gowanpul* people are a clan of the Nunagal, according to Holmer (1983, 405).

There is general agreement that the Jandai and Munjan dialects are extremely similar. Watkins (1891, 49) comments that Jandai and Munjan 'are very much alike and resemble the Yuggera of the Yerongpan tribe, south-west of Brisbane'. He observes that Guwar, the language spoken on Moreton Island, is in contrast 'very distinct' (1891, 49). When Watkins and Hamilton sent their Jandai and Munjan wordlists to Curr for publication in the volume *The Australian Race*, Curr agreed that the lists were highly similar. In fact, he declared that there was no need to publish the Munjan list, 'which much resembles Jandai' (1887, 221), and the Munjan list was discarded and lost.

The general similarity of Yagara dialects is also underscored by the claim from an 1894 observer that Yagara speakers had one name that referred collectively to their languages. Edward 'Old Ned' Harper writes in the *Queenslander* that 'The whole of the Blacks along the south side of Moreton Bay and all along its shores to Amity Point use the word Yug-ger-a-bool to signify their respective dialects' (Harper 1894, 410). Meston (1894) disagrees with Harper, writing:

the 'Yuggera' dialect was spoken nowhere in Moreton Bay, but began with the 'Coorpoóroo-jaggin' tribe of South Brisbane and the 'Yeerongpan' and Jeeparra tribes of the Eight-mile and Brown's Plains, and extended from there to Cunningham's Gap and the head of the Brisbane. Yuggera was spoken at Ipswich. (Meston 1894, 549)

Meston's characterisation of Yagara as a mainland language is corroborated by Holmer, who in 1983 observes that the language termed 'Yugarabul' by Watson (1943):

is a mainland language (or in any case one which comprises neither Stradbroke nor Moreton Island ...). Indeed, the term *jagarabal* (or *jagarabul*), that is Watson's 'Yugarabul', was not recognised on the island as a language name and the basic word from which the name is derived, *jagara* 'no', was hardly known at all by our island informants. (1983, 393)

As noted, the only recorded difference between the Jandai and Munjan dialects is the typical word for 'no', which is *jandai* in Jandai and *munjan* in Munjan. However, both saltwater dialects do seem to differ in several respects from the mainland freshwater dialects of Yagara. For example, *a* is raised to *i* in some words in the saltwater dialects. Holmer notes this process when he observes that unstressed /a/ is likely to be raised in Munjan, with the result that it is often written *i*. The language name *Waga-Waga* (Wakka-Wakka) was spelled *Waky-Waky* by Munjan speakers, reflecting their pronunciation of the name (Holmer 1983, 395). According to Nunagal and Badjala woman Myrtle Thompson, one of Holmer's informants, the word pronounced *dagai* 'flayed corpse; white man' on the mainland was *digi* in Munjan. The latter form was also supplied by Mabel Brown, a consultant on Nunagal living at Dunwich (Holmer 1983, 394). Holmer notes a similar dialectal contrast in words including 'moon', pronounced with *a* on the mainland (*gilan*) and *i* in Munjan (*gilin*); and the name Meeanjin (Brisbane), which is *Miganjin* or *Miyanjin* in mainland Yagara and *Miginjin* in Munjan. This name is also impacted by the lenition of unstressed intervocalic /g/ to /y/ in some dialects, resulting in *Miyanjin* rather than *Miganjin* (the lenition is discussed further in 1.3.2).

Hardcastle (1946–7, 22) claims that *malara* 'man' is *mallara* in the Brisbane area but *mullara* in the Boonah area; that *magil* 'water dragon' is *magil* in Brisbane but *muggil* in Boonah; and that 'in these and several other words it will be noticed that the Boonah dialect has a short "u" sound where the Brisbane dialect has a short "a" sound' (1946–7, 22). When Hardcastle read Petrie's transcriptions of Brisbane-area words aloud to Boonah-area Yagara speakers, they attributed the differences to Petrie being a 'salt water fella' (1946–7, 21). It is possible, however, that Hardcastle simply misread Petrie's transcriptions. Petrie spelled 'man' as *mallara* and 'water dragon' as *magil*, but Hardcastle may have read these words aloud with the vowels in Standard Australian English (SAE) *mall* or *mark*, for example, whereas Petrie doubtless intended a vowel closer to SAE *mull*. It is also possible that the southern Yagara pronunciation of words such as *magil* genuinely has a different first vowel than in northern dialects.

The differing words for 'no' in the freshwater and saltwater dialects may have been accompanied by other lexical differences. For instance, Petrie (1904, 106) writes that the mainland word for 'dilly bag' is *dili*, whereas the form used on Stradbroke Island is *gulai*. However, these words could also have referred to distinct types of bags. Meston writes that 'goanna' is *bara* on the mainland and *giwa* in Munjan, but other sources make it clear that *giwa* denotes a lace monitor and *bara* indicates a smaller species of monitor lizard.

In consideration of the incomplete data on all of the dialects, it is difficult to say whether the absence of a word in one dialect means that the word was not used, or that the word was simply not documented for that dialect. Readers are encouraged to check the reference list after each dictionary entry to see which researcher collected each word, and refer to section (1.1.4) to see where the data was gathered, in order to have greater certainty that a specific word belongs to a given dialect.

1.1.2. Previous linguistic studies

Revitalisation work on Jandai, traditionally spoken on Stradbroke Island (Minjerribah), has been led by the traditional owners of the language. Notably, the Minjerribah Moorgumpin Elders in Council (MMEIC) have produced a series of materials including the *Jandai Language Dictionary* (2011) with around 700 Jandai and Guwar words, compiled with the help of linguist Colleen Hattersley. A list of around 400 Yagara and Guwar words was self-published by Guwanbal and Gabi-Gabi woman Kerry Charlton and Barry Brown (Charlton and Brown 2019). Quandamooka artist and language advocate Sandra Delaney has created various Jandai reference materials.

In the past 20 years, several significant academic works have been published covering the languages traditionally spoken in the area around present-day Brisbane. In 1998 Margaret Sharpe published a dictionary of the northern varieties of Yugambeh-Bandjalang, which in 2020 evolved into a dictionary and grammar more accessible to the layperson. The Yugambeh-Bandjalang varieties described in Sharpe's volumes are traditionally spoken as far north as the Gold Coast area in southern Queensland, and belong to the Bandjalangic family, which is the grouping most closely related to Yagara, according to Bowern and Atkinson (2012). A more southern Yugambeh-Bandjalang language, Wangerriburra, is documented in a 2001 sketch grammar and dictionary compiled from data collected in 1913 (Kombumerri Corporation for Culture 2001; based on Allen and Lane 1914). Guwar, the traditional language of the Ngugi people of Moreton Island (Bannister 1982; Jefferies 2011), does not yet have a grammar, though Anthony Jefferies' 2011 Masters thesis considers the historical relationships between the Guwar, Yagara and Bandjalang languages and speakers. In 2004, Suzanne Kite published a grammar of the Duuŋidjawu language spoken to the north-west of Brisbane, based on data collected by Stephen Wurm in the mid-1900s. Duuŋidjawu is one of four mutually intelligible dialects belonging to a language that Kite and Wurm label as Waga-Waga following RMW Dixon (Kite and Wurm 2004, 3). Jeanie Bell, a Yagara and Dulingbara woman, compiled wordlists for Gabi-Gabi and Badjala in 1994, and wrote a sketch grammar of Badjala, traditionally spoken on K'Gari (Fraser Island), as her Masters thesis in 2003. Badjala artist Fiona Foley published a Badjala dictionary in 1996 (Foley 2019).

1.1.3. Language loss and reclamation

Proponents of language revitalisation such as the MMEIC are fighting a long history of Indigenous language suppression in the area. The Queensland government began legislating the destruction of Aboriginal culture and society in 1865, when the *Industrial and Reformatory Schools Act* allowed Indigenous children to be taken away to white-run missions. Government attacks on Indigenous culture and language continued to build for over a hundred years, culminating in the *Aborigines Act 1971* (Qld), which banned Aboriginal cultural customs, censored their reading material and devalued the work of Aboriginal people living on reserves. This Act was repealed in 1984.

Archibald Meston, who collected some of the Yagara words and sentences used in this grammar, led early legislation that was devastating for the Yagara language and its speakers. Meston's *Report on the Aboriginals of Queensland*, written in his capacity as the government-appointed Special Commissioner, was presented to the two Houses of Parliament in 1896. The report made the case for the containment of Aborigines in isolation from colonial settlements that were established on their lands, to contain 'remnant tribes' and 'half-caste children' away from towns in the south-east of the state. His report emphasised the need to restrict the movement of women and girls outside the confines of Deebing Creek and Myora Mission Stations so as to avoid 'a permanent increase of half-caste population' (Meston 1896, 9). Meston described Deebing Creek as 'a home and a refuge for the scattered remnants of tribes within a radius of thirty or forty miles', and Myora's purpose as 'chiefly to provide protection and education for aboriginal and half-caste children scattered about Moreton Bay' (1896, 12). His use of terms such as 'remnant' and 'scatter' allude euphemistically to the ongoing genocide, removal and imprisonment of Aboriginal people to clear the way for land theft. Meston's recommendations led to the implementation of the *Aboriginal Protection and Restriction of the Sale of Opium Act 1897* (Qld), which enforced control by state and church authorities over every aspect of the lives of Aboriginal people or any 'half-caste' individuals who associated with them.

Subsequently, the Queensland *Aboriginals Preservation and Protection Act* and *Torres Strait Islanders Act* (both 1939) legalised the forced removal of people from their homelands to distant reserves; the abduction of children from their families (the stolen generations); restrictions on movements; the destruction of language and kinship groups; the compulsion to work for low wages; the withholding of wages without consent (stolen wages); the random seizure of property; exclusion from voting; and curtailment of access to processes of justice that were available to the rest of the community.

Despite the imposition of these instruments of control, traditional languages continued to be spoken in secret by older members of the community. They were reluctant to pass on their linguistic knowledge, however, because their children and grandchildren could be seized and sent away. As a result of this suppression, later generations of Indigenous language owners have worked hard to revive the languages that are their birthright, both through private transmission of cultural and linguistic knowledge, and through public endeavours such as the MMEIC's publications.

There is undoubtedly private language knowledge that has not been included in the present volume. The private language knowledge that has been passed down through families and communities, sometimes at great risk to themselves, is an irreplaceable resource. We hope that the current volume will in no way be taken to supersede or supplant the vocabulary, meanings, pronunciations and spellings that are the heritage of language owners whose knowledge has been handed down from native speakers.

This volume is primarily an attempt to collect all publicly available language information in one place as an easily accessible resource. In Part 2: Dictionary and Part 3: Texts, the original source materials are presented in two formats: (1) their original spellings, word boundaries and translations; and (2) spellings, morpheme breakdowns and glosses as analysed and standardised by the authors. Though the standardised versions may be more accessible to some readers, the inclusion of original materials will make it easier, in the future, to correct the authors' inevitable mistakes or adapt the work for other purposes. Our goal is not to present an authoritative volume, but rather to provide access to comprehensive textual resources to be used as a tool in the ongoing struggle for language preservation.

1.1.4. List of sources

As a result of the suppression of Indigenous languages in the area, there are presently no fluent native speakers of Yagara. The current grammar is therefore based on a corpus of vocabulary lists (which form the basis of Part 2: Dictionary) and longer written texts (all of which are included in their entirety in Part 3: Texts) rather than direct elicitation from native speakers.

First Nations scholars seek to decolonise research by adopting an 'Indigenist' methodology (Rigney 1997), which is distinguished by its reconceptualist intent. Reconceptualism 'focuses on and learns from the array of cultural knowledge, skills, abilities and contacts possessed by socially marginalised groups that often go unrecognized and unacknowledged' (Yosso 2005, 69). This section provides brief contextual information about the sources on which this volume is based, to facilitate viewing the source material through the lens of our distinct historical experiences of colonisation (Harward-Nalder and Grenfell 2012).

Habitually, colonial collectors established their authority by presenting 'scientific' papers in the Western tradition or publishing their wordlists in the newspapers of the day, usually without acknowledgement of their Indigenous informants. Several engaged in arguments through letters to editors in attempts to correct each other and thereby re-establish their authority. In line with a critical approach to these texts, this section provides contextual information about the authors of the major sources of information on Yagara, without reference to subsequent debates about their reliability by non-Indigenous writers. For example, the authors' cultural backgrounds provide information about their reasons for collecting specific words or texts, and offer insight into why they might have understood and translated these words and texts in particular ways. Their language backgrounds and habits of transcription shed light on how they might have heard and written Yagara words.

The list below is organised in roughly chronological order of the language data collection, with relevant information about the context to assist readers to form their own opinions of the sources.

Threlkeld, Lancelot (1788–1859). A London-born Congregational minister, Threlkeld was appointed as missionary in January 1825 at Reid's Mistake (Belmont) on Lake Macquarie (Awaba). He kept a handwritten journal of his time at Lake Macquarie covering the period 1828–1846.

Clunie, James Oliphant (1795–1851). Born in Scotland to a minister and his wife, Clunie served in the 17th Regiment, seeing conflict in the War of 1812. His regiment served in Australia from 1830 to 1836, after which he was appointed Commandant of the Moreton Bay Convict Settlement. Clunie provided a list of 107 words for publication in Major Thomas Mitchell's (1792–1855) *Journal of Three Expeditions*, first published in 1838. In this list, a silent final *e* on words is used to modify the quality of the previous vowel.

Lang, John Dunmore (1799–1878). Scottish-born Lang was a Presbyterian evangelist and Scottish migration advocate. He arrived in Australia in 1823 and brought a large contingent of German Lutheran missionaries to Queensland in 1838, including Eipper (see entry below). Lang first visited Moreton Bay in 1845. He appears to be the author of a 404-word 'anonymous' wordlist from 1846, since the first page of the manuscript records the maritime birth of Lang's son. In 1847, Lang published *Cooksland* which contained 'a specimen of the Moreton Bay dialect of the Aboriginal language'. Lang generally transcribes *oo* for /u/ and *u* for /a/; his final *-cre* indicates /gar/; and final *-are* may mean /ari/, though a final *-ere* often indicates /ir/ with no following vowel. Lang transcribes prestopping (see 1.3.2) more reliably than any other source.

Eipper, Christopher (Rev.) (1813–1894). German-born Eipper was a Presbyterian minister and missionary. He taught Christianity to Aboriginal people at the Zion Hill Mission in Nundah, translating biblical texts into Aboriginal languages. Eipper's 1841 publication *Mission to Aborigines* includes Yagara vocabulary and sentences from a Durubal consultant.

Leichhardt, FW (Ludwig) (1813–c.1848). A German explorer and naturalist, Leichhardt was famed for his exploration of northern and central Australia. After his arrival in Sydney in 1842, a specimen-collecting trip took him to Moreton Bay, following which he undertook his first epic journey from Moreton Bay to Port Essington, north of Darwin. In the rainforests of Moreton Bay, his botanical language was almost exclusively derived from the various dialects of Aboriginal informants. In addition to scientific data, his journals and lecture notes contain Indigenous knowledge he elicited about the ecology of the areas he explored.

Ridley, William (1819–1878). Reverend Ridley was born in Essex and was among the missionaries recruited by JD Lang (see entry above), arriving in Australia in 1850. After teaching at the Australian College for a short time, Ridley spent several years proselytising to First Nations peoples in the New England and Moreton Bay areas as an itinerant missionary for the Scots Church. In 1855, Ridley convinced 13-year-old Tom Petrie (see entry below) to translate three Bible stories into the Yagara dialect of the Durubal people (see 3.4–3.6), as recounted in *Tom Petrie's Reminiscences* (Petrie 1904, 143). In Ridley's transcriptions, the velar nasal *ng* is often accurately recorded, but the alveo-palatal nasal *ny* is usually written as *n*. Like most authors, Ridley alternately transcribes the same stops (*b, d* and *g*) as voiced and voiceless. He often writes *u* for *a*, though word-finally his *u* indicates *u*. He sometimes records *o* for *u*.

Petrie, Thomas (1831–1910). Petrie was brought to Australia from Edinburgh as an infant, and moved to Moreton Bay at age 6. Here, he played with the local Durubal children and became a fluent speaker of the Durubal dialect of Yagara. Petrie paraphrased Bible stories for the Rev. Ridley at age 13 (see entry above). A few additional Durubal words and phrases occur in the book *Tom Petrie's Reminiscences* penned by Petrie's daughter (Petrie 1904, 143) and in brief articles he authored in 1901 and 1902 (Petrie 1901; 1902).

Turner, George (1818–1891). Turner was a Scottish member of the London Missionary Society. In 1861 he published his recollections (*Nineteen Years in Polynesia*), which includes a list of words in a column headed 'Dialect spoken by the Aborigines of New Holland, near Moreton Bay' in a table of Eastern Polynesian dialects. Turner transcribes *r* with accuracy, but writes *m* for *ng*.

NNW. These initials represent an anonymous source who collected a wordlist from Turrbal man Nunungga in the Pine River area, 20 miles north of Brisbane, in an edition of *Our Paper* in 1868. NNW's list was collected at the time of the rush by colonists to the town of Gympie after reports that gold had been found. NNW likely spoke a non-rhotic dialect of English, because *r* is transcribed post-vocalically where it is not found in Yagara. NNW tends to write *oe* for *a*.

Watkins, George (1848–1916) and Hamilton, James (unknown–1891). Watkins was born in England and arrived in Queensland in 1867. Both Watkins and his ex-Scottish policeman co-author Hamilton were assigned to work at the Dunwich Benevolent Asylum on Stradbroke Island in 1868. Their transcriptions of the Jandai variety of Yagara usually omit initial *ny* and *ng*, though they sometimes write the latter sound as *gn*.

Finch, Charles Wray (1809–1873). An English-born Australian politician, Finch migrated to Sydney in 1831 as a soldier. Initially he farmed land near Wellington, while a police magistrate at Patrick's Plains. In the 1850s he settled a pastoral property in the Parramatta area, serving on the NSW Legislative Council and Assembly from 1853 to 1873. The Charles Wray Finch Papers held at the State Library of Queensland contain an Aboriginal wordlist that Finch's son, Edward, collected while droving stock to Moreton Bay, accompanied by Aboriginal stockman Jemmy Ruine.

Bunce, Daniel (1813–1872). An English botanist and gardener, Bunce emigrated to Tasmania in 1833. In 1839 in Port Phillip, he joined a party of Aboriginal people on a journey to Western Port, and made an intensive study of their spoken language. In 1846 Bunce joined Ludwig Leichhardt (see entry above) on his second attempt to cross Australia, leaving the Darling

Downs in December. Bunce's notebooks from the 1839 and 1846 journeys contain language data that form the basis of Bunce's 1859 *Language of the Aborigines* (Bunce 1859).

Latham, Robert Gordon (1812–1888). An English ethnologist and philologist, Latham was interested in tracing the origin of races through the genealogical relationships of languages. In 1852 he published *Man and His Migrations,* and in the same year provided an appendix to John Macgillivray's *Narrative of the Voyage of HMS Rattlesnake* listed as 'Remarks on the Vocabularies of the Voyage of the *Rattlesnake*'.

Birch, Gustavus (1820–1883). Birch was born in Australia as the eldest son of English migrants. He became a government agent and resident of Amity Point, Stradbroke Island, living as a recluse on the campgrounds of the Ngugi and Nunagal for over 30 years. Birch distributed supplies, recorded tribal names and kept track of the comings and goings of the families in his annual diaries, which also included words from the Munjan variety of Yagara. In his diary for 1873, Birch writes unstressed non-final *a* as *e*. His length marking on vowels is reliable. He writes *kg* for *g* and *dt* for *d*, presumably to show that he is unsure of voicing. He sometimes adds post-vocalic *r* when not present.

Meston, Archibald (1851–1924). Scottish-born Meston arrived in Australia in 1859. He framed the 1897 Queensland Act of Parliament that enabled the forced removal of Aboriginal people to white-run missions (see 1.1.3). As Protector of Aborigines for southern Queensland from 1898–1903 he interpreted the culture and languages of 'a dying race' for the state's white population, through articles and columns published in various newspapers. He also staged 'Wild Aborigine' performances using actors transported from the missions and reserves that he had established. Meston uses *h* after a vowel to indicate length. He writes *gn* for initial *ng*. His use of *r* is fairly accurate, and he identifies *ny* better than most sources. He appears to use *d, j* and *ch* interchangeably.

Curr, Edward Micklethwaite (1820–1899). Curr was the Australian-born son of English free settlers associated with the Van Diemen's Land Company. The company acquired large tracts of land for sheep raising during the frontier wars in Tasmania, and the family acquired additional runs through squatting in Victoria. Curr served as a member of the Board for the Protection of Aborigines from 1875. He compiled an *Australian Comparative Vocabulary* in 1881, drawing on information from a network of farmers and rural workers who provided him with Aboriginal words matching those on a list he circulated. In 1887, he published *The Australian Race: Its Origins, Languages, Customs and Place of Landing in Australia*.

Gibson, James (unknown–1908). Gibson's family moved from the UK to Queensland in 1864. Gibson farmed the property 'Stanmore' in the sugar cane growing district of Yatala. He was involved in local government and the debate led by Parliamentarian William Brookes about 'Coloured Labour' vs European immigration. In the 1850s he travelled around Queensland with the explorer William Landsborough. In 1882 Gibson wrote a letter to British anthropologist AW Howitt about the Chepara Tribe and their language, to accompany the artefacts that he also sent (see 3.2; Pitt Rivers Museum 2012). Howitt (see entry below) subsequently published this information in *The Native Tribes of South East Australia* (1904).

Harper, Edward (Ned) (1826–1896). Harper was a timber getter who arrived in the Tweed in 1845, subsequently establishing Harper's Wharf on the Nerang River. He penned an article under the heading 'Some Errors About the Blacks', published in *The Queenslander* newspaper of 1 September 1894 for a series entitled 'Early Days on the Tweed'. This article established his authority as a speaker of Aboriginal languages, coming from his nearly 60 years of experience with Aboriginal people, and corrected some of the many errors in articles on Aboriginal culture and language submitted by Archibald Meston.

Donovan, Dan (1828–1909). Australian-born Donovan was a member of the Natural History Society and attended their Laidley meetings. In the 1870s he contributed to local newspapers a series of columns on native timbers (Donovan 1888a–1888d). On 30 November 1895 it was reported in *The Queenslander* that Donovan had read a paper titled 'The Bora at Gatton' at a meeting of the Royal Society at the Queensland Museum, held on 8 November 1895. His paper described a corroboree held in the Gatton Scrub which he attended with a member of the Laidley tribe. The contribution of his paper was valued because it included a large number of 'native words'.

Suttor, John Bligh (Jr) (1859–1925). A descendant of the Suttor family of Bathurst who were known for their friendly relations with the Aboriginal people whose lands they occupied, Suttor provided a table entitled 'Linguistics' that was published in *The Australasian Anthropological Journal* in 1897. One column is a wordlist from Moreton Bay.

Blackman, Frederick Archibald (1835–1906). Blackman was a pastoralist, inventor, naturalist and author who provided commentary via letters to the editor on the article 'Aboriginal Names of Places, Etc., with their Meanings' published in the 21 June 1900 edition of *Science of Man*. Blackman based his authority on time spent growing up and living among Aboriginal people in the Wide Bay – Port Curtis area between 1850 and 1879.

Cadell, William Thomas (1845–1922). In the 1870s, Australian-born Cadell was a co-purchaser of 'Deepwater Station' in the highlands now known as Glen Innes, established on the lands of the Ngarabal people in 1839. Cadell was a successful sheep and cattle breeder and champion of agricultural shows. He travelled widely to provide expert advice to pastoralists in the New England and Darling Downs areas, keeping extensive records, including lists of Aboriginal words.

Watson, Frederic James (1868–1947). Watson arrived in Australia as a child in 1876. His obituary noted that he had worked as an 'officer of the Queensland Department of Agriculture and Stock' for 25 years (*Courier-Mail* 1947, 6), and that on retirement, he took an interest in the traditions and languages of the south-eastern Aboriginal tribes (Gabi-Gabi, Waga-Waga, Yugambeh and Yagara). He became a fellow and an associate member of the Queensland Place Names Committee. All of his Yagara data are apparently derived from other sources, but he sometimes adds observations that seem based on firsthand experience.

Howitt, Alfred William (1830–1908). An educated English migrant, explorer and natural scientist, Howitt came to Melbourne in 1852 to try his luck on the goldfields. After spending some time farming his uncle's property he took to the bush as a drover. He was also recruited to examine the pastoral potential of the Lake Eyre district, and to lead an expedition in search of missing explorers Burke, Wills and King. Following this, in 1863, he began a career as a public servant, travelling long distances on horseback in the state of Victoria as a magistrate, and publishing the results of his geological investigations. Influenced by the writings of Charles Darwin, Howitt developed an interest in Aboriginal society, and published substantial papers and books on the topic between 1880 and 1904.

Lenet, George William (1868–1960). English-born Lenet worked at the Mt Biggenden Mine. In 1904 he published Yagara wordlists from the Beaudesert District and Cleveland District.

Roth, Walter Edmund (1861–1933). A British colonial administrator, anthropologist and medical practitioner, Roth was appointed the first Northern Protector of Aboriginals in 1898 and was based in Cooktown, Queensland. From 1904 to 1906 he was chief protector and part of his duties was to record Aboriginal Australian cultures. He produced a series of articles that often include mainland Yagara words. Roth often omits unstressed vowels.

Hinchcliffe, Frederick William (1864–1934). An Australian-born printer and journalist, Hinchcliffe was the son of English migrants, and worked at his father's printing company in Brisbane, Logan and surrounds. Hinchcliffe was also among the critics of Meston's work, publishing a revised list of mainland Yagara words with corrections. Hinchcliffe omits all initial *ny* and *ng*, and generally uses English orthography, writing *gym* for the sequence *jim*, for example. He often adds extra post-vocalic *r*.

Radcliffe-Brown, Alfred Reginald (1881–1955). An English social anthropologist, Radcliffe-Brown developed the theory of structural functionalism and coadaptation. He arrived in Western Australia in 1910 and spent the next two years undertaking fieldwork on the workings of the societies there with biologist and writer EL Grant Watson and Australian writer Daisy Bates. His book, *The Social Organization of Australian Tribes* was published in 1930. An earlier (1914) presentation to the British Association for the Advancement of Science in Melbourne drew accusations of plagiarism from Daisy Bates who had sent an unpublished manuscript to Radcliffe-Brown for comment.

Lauterer, Joseph (1848–1911). Lauterer was a German-born medical practitioner who worked in South Brisbane for 25 years. He collected a 'Yerongpan' (mainland Yagara) wordlist. Lauterer writes *h* after vowels to show length.

Welsby, Thomas (1858–1941). Born in Ipswich, Queensland, Welsby was a businessman, parliamentarian, sportsman and historian who holidayed in Amity Point on Stradbroke Island. In the 1920s he published serialised newspaper columns containing factual and fictional historical accounts of the First Peoples and their families and of the seamen and public servants who frequented Amity Point. Welsby often adds an extra *r* or *h* at the end of a vowel-final word. Like other sources, he often writes *u* for *a*.

Hanlon, William Egan (1862–1941). An English migrant, WE Hanlon arrived in the Logan district as a one-year-old child with his parents in 1863. They were part of a contingent of cotton manufacturers encouraged to join the Manchester Cotton Company by the offer of land. In June 1931 he submitted a letter to *The Brisbane Courier-Mail* contributing to the discussion on Aboriginal placenames. He subsequently read a paper entitled 'The Early Settlement of the Logan and Albert Districts' before the Historical Society of Queensland on 27 March 1934, which contained Aboriginal placenames and stories.

Bell, Enid (1889–1965). Bell was born at Coochin Coochin near Boonah, Qld. She recorded the legends of the Yagarabal tribe in the 'Coochin' Valley, as told in language and song by her friend Susan, whose traditional name and status was Bunjoey daughter of Moolpaljo, Chief of the Yagarabal tribe. Bell contributed to *Aboriginal Language: Dialects of Vanished Tribes* published in 1934.

Jackson, George Kenneth (Ken) (1914–1943). Australian-born Jackson developed a keen interest in Aboriginal history and artefacts while working at Thylungra Station between Quilpie and Windorah in south-west Queensland as a jackaroo. He was appointed to the staff of the Queensland Museum as a cadet assistant in ethnology in 1937, in which role he developed a list of Durubal words. At the outbreak of World War II, Ken was among the first few hundred to enlist in Brisbane. He continued to collect materials while serving in the armed forces, but was killed in action.

Hardcastle, Thomas William (1885–1960). Hardcastle was an Australian-born farmer who lived at Dugandan in the Boonah district for most of his life. Hardcastle contributed an article on the vocabulary and accounts of events of the local Aboriginal tribe, the 'Ugarapuls' (Yagarabal), in 1947, for publication in the *Queensland Geographical Journal*. However, it is possible that Hardcastle's wife Maggie, a Queensland University graduate, may have written the article, due to its academic tone. Hardcastle writes a silent final *e* on words to indicate a difference in the quality of the previous vowel, as in the English spelling of words such as *mat* vs *mate*. As a speaker of a non-rhotic variety of English, Hardcastle adds an *r* post-vocalically where this sound is not present in Yagara. His double *ee* seems to indicate a long *ii* and never a short *i*, which is valuable, because this distinction is otherwise rarely recorded. He writes *j* as *tch*, which is a reasonable English-orthography approximation of what *j* probably sounded like in a stressed syllable.

Winterbotham, Lindsey Page (1887–1960). Australian-born Winterbotham, a medical practitioner, developed an interest in anthropology, and enjoyed talking to and corresponding with Aboriginal people. This led to his becoming a founding member of the Anthropological Society of Queensland and honorary curator of the Queensland University Anthropological Museum. In 1955 he recorded the stories of the Jinibara people and neighbouring groups in south-east Queensland, as told by Gaiarbau (Willie MacKenzie).

Flint, Elwyn Henry (1910–1983). Australian-born Flint, an ordained Anglican priest and army chaplain, learned Japanese to assist with intelligence work during World War II. This experience led to an academic career in linguistics, and his undertaking the Queensland Speech Survey during the 1960s. The survey comprised recordings and field notes in Aboriginal communities, including Stradbroke Island, where in 1960 he recorded stories and songs from Gaiarbau (Willie MacKenzie) and a Jandai speaker (references to the latter have been redacted from this volume at the request of a family member).

Wurm, Stephen (1922–2001). Hungarian-born Stephen Wurm was a Professor of Linguistics at The Australian National University from 1968 to 1987. His 1960 recordings from Woodenbong, NSW, included the elicitation of a few words and phrases in Yagara from a non-fluent anonymous consultant.

Tindale, Norman Barnett (1900–1993). An Australian anthropologist, archaeologist, entomologist and ethnologist, Tindale undertook fieldwork that aimed to map the various tribal groupings of Aboriginal Australians. While Tindale's collected works have status and value within academic disciplines, his methods continue to be criticised by descendants of his research subjects as contributing to racialised ideas about Australian Aboriginal people (Ah Kee 2012; Baker 2019) and as superficial and unreliable by comparison with the decades-long endeavours of those researching genealogies, tribal boundaries, and languages (Aird 2012, 2020). These criticisms are particularly concerning as Tindale's representations continue to inform judgements in contemporary legal contexts without serious examination, and are given precedence over evidence provided by Aboriginal knowledge-holders (Monaghan 2003; Aird 2020).

Bannister, Dennis Daniel (1917–1990). Bannister copied vocabularies and sentences recorded between 1838 and 1975, and consolidated those for languages in the Brisbane region into Turrubul–English and English–Turrubul wordlists, and Guwar, Njula, Gurai–English and reverse wordlists. These included wordlists from the Meston collection at Oxley Library. In some cases, Bannister attempted to analyse the languages' grammar and standardise their spelling.

Colliver, Frederick Stanley (1908–1991) and Frank Palmer Woolston (1911–1998). FS Colliver, a field naturalist for over 40 years, arrived in Brisbane in 1948 to fill the position of curator of the University of Queensland's Geology Museum. Woolston, an optometrist by profession, was an active member of the Anthropological Society of Queensland and an associate member of the Australian Institute of Aboriginal Studies. Woolston recorded and documented ethno-history and Aboriginal cultural heritage relating to North Queensland, establishing a long and valued relationship with rainforest area and Mornington Island Aboriginal groups. Their work, entitled *Aboriginals in the Brisbane Area*, was first published in *Brisbane Retrospect – Eight Aspects of Brisbane History*, by the Library Board of Queensland in 1978. It contained a table of Aboriginal placenames gleaned from sources dating from the time of first contact until the 1900s.

Holmer, Nils (1904–1994). Swedish-born Holmer was professor of linguistics at Lund University before undertaking field work in Australia 1980–1983, where he gathered linguistic data across the whole of south-east Queensland. Holmer collected Yagara data on Stradbroke Island, and therefore records mainly saltwater (i.e. Jandai and Munjan) forms. His transcriptions are fairly reliable, but the lateness of his data collection means that speakers were often less certain of word forms, meanings and origins than earlier generations.

Steele, John Gladstone (1935–2016). Steele was an Australian-born academic in Environmental Physics at the University of Queensland, with a passion for local history and bushwalking. Steele's *Aboriginal Pathways* (1984) includes Yagara vocabularies, mostly repeated from Meston, Watkins and Petrie, but with a number of placenames that Aboriginal informants may have provided directly to Steele. He saw *Pathways* as a companion volume to *Petrie's Reminiscences* (Petrie 1904).

1.2. Kinship

1.2.1. Moieties, sections and totems

Vocabulary related to family and marriage in Yagara relies on an understanding of *moieties*, the two groupings into which all members of the community are divided; and the two *sections* within each of these moieties. A four-section system of this general type is found across much of Australia and is the dominant system in Queensland (McConvell 2018).

Every individual in Yagara society belongs to one of the two moieties, either *Gabai* or *Gamil* (Clark 1916), with ramifications for kinship, marriageability and other social roles and obligations. The Gabai moiety is named for the small native bee *gabai,* a term which is cognate with moiety names across Queensland (McConvell 2018). The name *Gamil* has unclear origins and lacks cognates. The term does not refer to another bee species as might be expected based on the pattern found in other Queensland languages (McConvell 2018). One could speculate that it might be related to *gaming* 'mother's brother', which is recorded as *garnill* in an article in *The Queenslander* (Hinchcliffe 1890).

Moiety membership is inherited matrilineally (Mathews 1898, 83; Clark 1916, 8; Tennant-Kelly 1935, 471; Radcliffe-Browne 1930, 239; Winterbotham 1957, 21; cf. Howitt 1904, 230; Ridley 1855). Matrimoieties are common in Queensland and are found among speakers of the Waga-Waga and Gabi-Gabi languages (McConvell 2018, 255; Kite and Wurm 2004, 9).

Each moiety is divided into two *sections* (Tennant-Kelly 1935, 472), which are also called *skins* or *skin names* (Dousset 2011). The Gabai moiety is divided into the sections Banjur and Barang (for males) and Banjurgan and Baranggan (for females), whereas Gamil consists of Jarawany and Bunda (for males) and Jarawanygan and Bundagan (for females). Each female section name consists of the male name plus the feminine suffix *-gan.* The four section names are nearly identical to those in Duuŋidjawu, which for males are *Bandjur, Barang, Banda* and *Djoronj* (Kite and Wurm 2004, 9).

In addition to a section, every individual has a totem, or *yuri* 'meat' (Holmer 1983), which must be one of the *yuri* appropriate for their section (see Table 1.1 for examples). Totems and sections are similarly related in Duuŋidjawu (Kite and Wurm 2004), Gabi-Gabi (Meston 1893; Tennant-

Kelly 1935) and Jinibara cultures (Winterbotham 1957), for example. To illustrate, one of the *yuri* suitable for Barang is *gabai* 'small native bee', so this *yuri* could belong to a Barang man or Baranggan woman, but presumably not to a member of a different section. A woman's *yuri* could be passed on to descendants, particularly those who belonged to the same moiety or section (Howitt 1904, 230; Tennant-Kelly 1935, 471; Macdonald 2010, 49).

Yagara speakers' *yuri* are represented by native animal species. Members of the *yuri* are the spiritual brothers and sisters of the animal of their *yuri*, and they are not allowed to kill or eat this animal, or eat its products, such as honey (Roth 1910, 102; Winterbotham 1957). Anyone who wishes to hunt or eat the species represented by the *yuri* must ask the *yuri* members for permission, and it is considered bad form to kill an animal of a person's *yuri* in front of that person (Tennant-Kelly 1935, 469–70; Winterbotham 1957, 19–20). Members of a *yuri* are also responsible for performing increase rites for the animal represented by their *yuri*, which is done at special places that are important for the animal. These 'totem-centres' are called *jurbil* (Radcliffe-Browne 1930, 239).

In effect, people of a particular *yuri* have the job of overseeing the sustainable management of the species represented by their *yuri*. Speakers would commonly introduce themselves using their *yuri* and section as well as their names, which indicates the importance of these concepts to individuals' identities (Howitt 1904, 234; Tennant-Kelly 1935, 472; Winterbotham 1957, 12).

Though it is not recorded which animals are associated with which *yuri* specifically for Yagara speakers, Tennant-Kelly (1935) lists the Gabi-Gabi totems associated with the two Gabi-Gabi moieties, which are equivalent to the two Yagara moieties; Meston (1867–1960) lists a few Gabi-Gabi totems associated with the Gabi-Gabi sections, which also equate to the Yagara sections; and Winterbotham (1957, 14) includes a number of totems of the Jinibara people, whose sections likewise have one-for-one equivalents in the Yagara system. These are laid out in Table 1.1 in order to give an idea of the types of *yuri* that may be associated with each Yagara section.

Table 1.1: Yagara moieties and the totems of equivalent Gabi-Gabi and Jinibara moieties.

Yagara moiety	Yagara section	Jinibara totems (from Winterbotham)	Gabi-Gabi totems (from Meston)	Gabi-Gabi totems (from Tennant-Kelly)
Gabai	Banjur(gan)	possum	magpie lark	carpet snake, sweet-and-sour sugar bag, possum, turtle (two kinds), bunya nut, long eel, grass tree, cockatoo, turkey, wood duck, small owl, tree snake
	Barang(gan)	emu, bee	emu, mosquito	
Gamil	Jarawany(gan)	kangaroo, eaglehawk	hawk	brown snake, ground goanna, eaglehawk, turtle (two kinds, having distinct markings as opposed to the two kinds in the other moiety), eel (two kinds), porcupine, sand goanna, king parrot
	Bunda(gan)	brown snake	kangaroo, caterpillar	

Source: Authors' summary of Winterbotham (1957), Meston (1867–1960) and Tennant-Kelly (1935).

A person's section not only determined their *yuri*, but also delimited their marriage partners. In order for a marriage to be socially acceptable, or *straight*, a man or woman of a particular section needed to marry a partner of a specific other section, as listed in Table 1.2 (Radcliffe-Browne 1930, 238; Watson 1943, 90; cf. Meston 1893, 2). For example, a Bundagan woman would be expected to marry a Barang man. Note that a person's appropriate marriage partner is always of the opposite moiety. If a 'straight' marriage is not possible, the second-best option would be to marry the non-ideal section within the opposite moiety. For example, a Bundagan woman (who is Gamil) should marry a Barang man (who is Gabai), but the next-best option for her would be a Banjur man (Gabai), who is at least of the correct moiety.

Table 1.2: 'Straight' marriage moieties and sections.

Moiety and section		Moiety and section
Gamil; Jarawany(gan)		Gabai; Banjur(gan)
Gabai; Banjur(gan)		Gamil; Jarawany(gan)
Gabai; Barang(gan)	marries	Gamil; Bunda(gan)
Gamil; Bunda(gan)		Gabai; Barang(gan)

Source: Authors' summary of Radcliffe-Browne (1930) and Watson (1943).

Some people did not marry the appropriate section, or even the appropriate moiety. In the 1930s on the Cherbourg mission, 'wrong' marriages were frequent, according to Tennant-Kelly (1935, 470). The pressure to marry straight was doubtless much stronger among Yagara speakers who were not forcibly displaced to the mission. Marrying the correct moiety was of great importance among the neighbouring Jinibara, for example (Winterbotham 1957). It is noteworthy that even on the Cherbourg mission in the 1930s, it was considered 'incestuous' and 'unclean' to marry someone of the same *yuri* (Tennant-Kelly 1935, 471, 473; Winterbotham 1957, 12).

Moiety and section inheritance was matrilineal, in that a woman's children would receive the same moiety and section even if the woman did not marry straight (Mathews 1898, 83; Tennant-Kelly 1935, 470; Winterbotham 1957, 21). The moiety of children would always be the same as their mother. For example, the children of a Gamil woman would also be Gamil. However, the section of the children would always be the opposite section within the same moiety as the mother. For example, a Jarawanygan woman (who is Gamil) would always have Bunda sons and Bundagan daughters (who are also Gamil). Table 1.3 lists the moiety and section of children based on that of their mothers.

Table 1.3: Children's moieties and sections are based on those of their mothers.

Mother's moiety and section		Children's moiety and section
Gamil; Jarawanygan		Gamil; Bunda(gan)
Gabai; Banjurgan	gives birth to	Gabai; Barang(gan)
Gabai; Baranggan		Gabai; Banjur(gan)
Gamil; Bundagan		Gamil; Jarawany(gan)

Source: Authors' summary of Mathews (1898), Radcliffe-Browne (1930), Tennant-Kelly (1935), Watson (1943) and Winterbotham (1957).

As noted, totems were also inherited matrilineally (Tennant-Kelly 1935, 471; Howitt 1904, 230), commonly from a person's mother's mother, who would always share the person's section (Macdonald 2010, 49). Figure 1.2 illustrates how a granddaughter would share the section of her maternal grandmother. For example, a Bundagan woman's daughter would be Jarawanygan, and the Jarawanygan woman's daughter would be Bundagan, and so the cycle would continue, repeating every two generations.

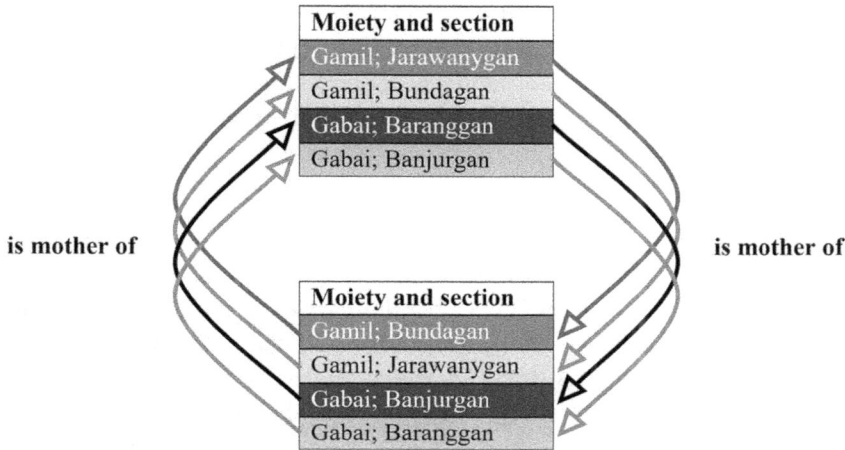

Figure 1.2: Alternate female generations have the same sections.

Source: Authors' summary of Mathews (1898), Radcliffe-Browne (1930), Tennant-Kelly (1935), Watson (1943) and Winterbotham (1957).

If straight marriages are assumed throughout, then a person's father's father would also share the person's section. For example, a Bunda man would ideally marry a Baranggan woman (see Table 1.2). Their son would be Banjur (see Table 1.3), and he should marry a Jarawanygan woman (Table 1.2). The son of the Jarawanygan woman then would be Bunda (Table 1.3) like his paternal grandfather.

A person's maternal aunt's children and paternal uncle's children would be their 'parallel cousins' and would share their own section. On the other hand, the person's maternal uncle's children and paternal aunt's children would be 'cross cousins', who would be of the appropriate section for the person to marry. For example, a Banjurgan woman's mother is Baranggan (see Table 1.3). The mother's brother is Barang, so he should marry a Bundagan woman (see Table 1.2). The sons of a Bundagan woman would be Jarawany, which is the appropriate section for the Banjurgan cousin to marry, though this marriage would be considered 'too close' and would be forbidden nonetheless (Howitt 1904, 232; Tennant-Kelly 2011). The distinction between parallel cousins and cross cousins is important in the kinship system, discussed in section (1.2.2).

A few Yagara-speaking individuals' totems have been recorded. Putingga (Sam), a Durubal man, stated that his family totem was *gabul* 'carpet snake' (Petrie 1904, 118). Gaiarbau (Willie MacKenzie), a Jinibara man who was familiar with Yagara, had the 'honey bee totem' and was of the Barang section (Winterbotham 1950, 1957).

Animal totems are associated with communities or regions as well as with moieties. According to Jefferies (2011), the totem of the Brisbane River is *muruguji* 'black swan', and the Nunagal totem is a red hawk with a white neck (2011, 78, footnote 72). Other Nunagal totems are the dolphin and the carpet snake, whereas Ngugi totems include the shark and the red-bellied black snake. A totem that is associated with a community can nonetheless be the family totem of an individual in a different community (Winterbotham 1957, 15). For example, even though *gabul* 'carpet snake' is a Nunagal totem, it was also the family *yuri* of Putingga, who was a Durubal man.

Finally, Petrie (1904) writes that among the Durubal people:

> [the] nighthawk had some connection with the origin of all the women, while a small bat held similar relationship to all the men. These hawks and bats might perhaps correspond with the so-called sex-totems in other parts of Australia. (1904, 118)

This hypothesis resembles Howitt's (1904, 110–11) claim that in a number of groups, including the Wotjobaluk of present-day Victoria, the bat was a 'brother' of all men and the owlet-nightjar a 'sister' of all women. The Yagara word *wumanggan* 'owlet-nightjar' also means 'mother-in-law'.

1.2.2. Kinship terms

As in most Australian languages, Yagara kinship terms obligatorily distinguish between relatives on the mother's side of the family versus those on the father's side, following the Dravidian kinship system (Dousset 2011, 45). For example, in Yagara, a person's maternal grandfather is their *najang* whereas their paternal grandfather has the entirely distinct name *yuguny*. Yagara also obligatorily distinguishes older and younger siblings. In Yagara, a person's younger brother is their *duwanggal*, whereas their older brother is their *ngabang*, for example.

In accordance with the Dravidian system, a person's relatives usually have the same term if those relatives are same-sex siblings. For instance, the sisters of a person's *bujang* 'mother' are also called *bujang* 'mother' (Ballard 2007, 39), and a person's father's brothers are also the person's *bing* 'father'. The same is true for grandparents' siblings, such that the sisters of a person's *baabang* 'mother's mother' are also their *baabang* 'mother's mother'. The equivalence between kin members and their same-sex siblings is shared by neighbouring languages Badjala, Duuŋidjawu and Duuŋibura, as set out in Tennant-Kelly (2011), and Yugambeh, as described in Sharpe (1998, 159), and is a standard feature of the Dravidian system that is 'identifiable in all Australian Aboriginal kinship terminologies' (Dousset 2008; 2011, 45).

Because of this convention regarding same-sex siblings, a person's parallel cousins (the children of their mother's sister or their father's brother) also have the same titles as the person's own siblings. For example, the person's younger brother is their *duwanggal* 'younger brother', and the son of their maternal aunt is also their *duwanggal* 'younger brother'. It is unclear whether a person's maternal aunt's sons would be *duwanggal* 'younger brother' or *ngabang* 'older brother' based on whether they are older or younger than the person themselves, or whether the status of *duwanggal* 'younger brother' versus *ngabang* 'older brother' would be determined by the relative ages of the maternal aunt and the mother. That is, if the maternal aunt is older than the mother, but her sons are younger than the mother's children, it is unclear whether the aunt's sons would be *duwanggal* 'younger brother' based on the children's ages or *ngabang* 'older brother' based on the mothers' ages. The latter system is found in Western Desert languages, for example (Dousset 2011).

Since siblings belong to the same section, a classificatory *bujang* 'mother' will generally belong to the same section as the biological *bujang* 'mother'. Likewise, a parallel cousin who is a classificatory *duwanggal* 'younger brother' (for example) will usually belong to the same section as a biological *duwanggal* 'younger brother', because the cousin's mother or father is generally of the same section as the person's own mother or father. Two persons who share a term such as *bujang* 'mother' will always belong to the same section if all the relevant marriages are 'straight' (see Table 1.2), though they may belong to different sections if marriages diverge from this pattern.

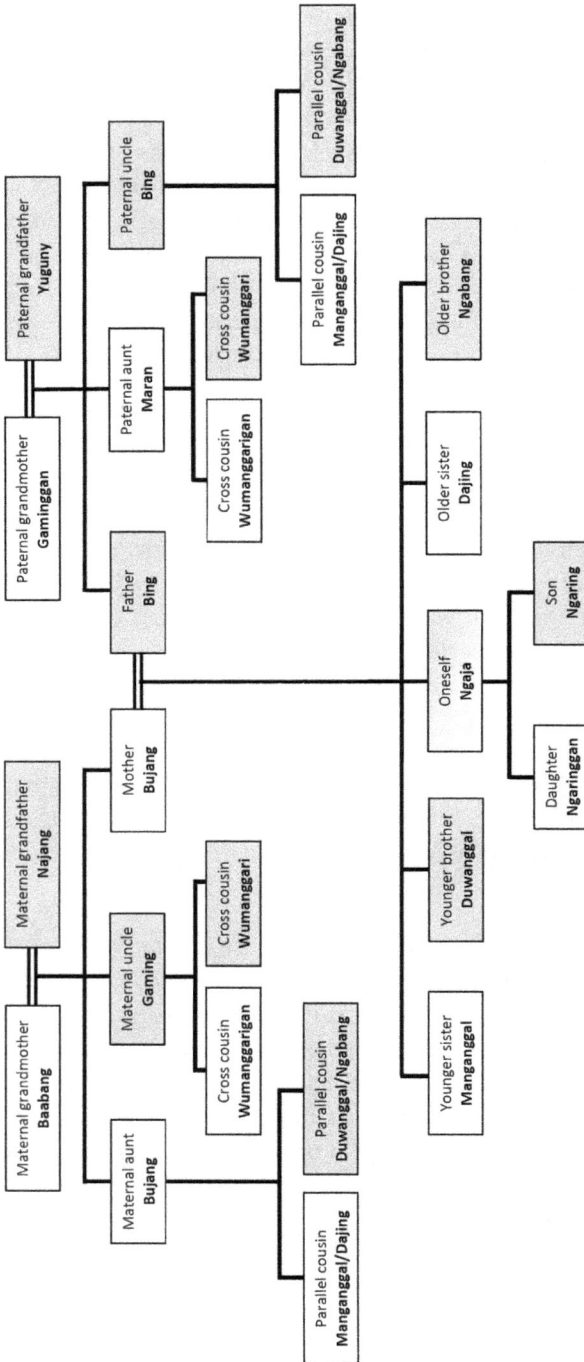

Figure 1.3: Selected kinship relations in Yagara.

Shaded boxes represent male individuals.

Source: Authors' summary based on sources listed in 2.2.

The children of a person's parents' opposite-sex siblings are their cross cousins, who belong to a different section and cannot be considered siblings. Specifically, a person's cross cousins belong to the section that they would be expected to marry, as in Table 1.2, though marriage to first cousins was forbidden (Howitt 1904, 232; Tennant-Kelly 2011). For example, a Bundagan woman's husband should be Barang. Her maternal uncles' children, and her paternal aunts' children, will likewise be Barang and Baranggan. Female cross-cousins are called *wumanggarigan* and male cross-cousins are *wumanggari*.

Parallel cousins, cross cousins and other basic family relations are shown in a family tree in Figure 1.3. Shaded boxes represent male individuals.

Figure 1.3 shows only a selection of the kin terms in Yagara. Certain other roles, not shown in Figure 1.3, share the names of the roles that are shown. For example, the wife of a person's *gaming* 'mother's brother' is their *maran,* the same word as *maran* 'father's sister', assuming that Yagara patterns like nearby languages (Tennant-Kelly 2011). It is likely that the husband of a person's paternal aunt (*maran*) is also their *gaming* 'mother's brother'.

A person's *baabang* 'mother's mother' will, like their *bujang* 'mother', belong to their own moiety. If all the marriages in a family are straight (see Table 1.2), their *yuguny* 'father's father' will also belong to the same moiety, as described in Section 1.2.1. However, there is no record of the term for same-moiety grandchildren. A strong possibility is that same-moiety grandchildren may be called by the same names as same-moiety grandparents, that is, *baabang* 'mother's mother' for 'daughter's daughter' and *yuguny* 'father's father' for 'son's son'. This pattern of reciprocal naming occurs in Yugambeh (Sharpe 1998, 43, 103) and other Pama-Nyungan languages (Dousset 2011).

Cross-moiety grandchildren may be labelled as cross cousins, as in Gabi-Gabi and Duuɲidjawu (Winterbotham 1957, 31; Tennant-Kelly 2011). In this case, a *gaminggan* 'father's mother' and *najang* 'mother's father' would call a female grandchild *wumanggarigan* 'female cross cousin' and a male grandchild *wumanggari* 'male cross cousin'.

A husband (*nyugunbing*) and wife (*nyugunbinggan*) use a different set of terms for each other's relatives than for their own. As in many societies around Australia, certain Yagara in-laws have a special status, which in Yagara is called *bugui* 'subject to the in-law respect relation'. For a male, his mother-in-law and brother-in-law are *bugui*, and he should not look at them, speak directly to them, nor should they touch each other's food (Ridley 1855; Winterbotham 1957, 22; Tennant-Kelly 2011).

For a male, the spouse's family includes the *wumanggan* 'mother-in-law', *wumang* 'father-in-law' and *gabagiri* 'brother-in-law'. The same word *gabagiri* 'brother-in-law' likely refers to either a wife's brother or a sister's husband, as in Duuŋidjawu (Winterbotham 1957, 31). This is consistent since these two individuals would have the same section as each other. For example, a Jarawany man's wife is Banjurgan and her brother is Banjur, while the man's sister is Jarawanygan and her husband is Banjur, so both the wife's brother and the sister's husband have the same section. The word for 'sister-in-law' is not recorded, but could be *gabagirigan,* the feminine form of *gabagiri* 'brother-in-law'. The term *wumang* 'father-in-law' is likely reciprocal, as in Yugambeh (Sharpe 1998, 167), meaning that a son-in-law would also be called *wumang*. The same stem *wumang* likely occurs in the terms for cross cousins, *wumanggari* and *wumanggarigan,* and may allude to the taboos regarding both in-laws (who are *bugui*) and cross cousins (whom one cannot marry).

For a female, the relationship with in-laws is less restrictive. A woman is the *nguwun.gin.gan* 'daughter-in-law' of her spouse's parents. This term is probably reciprocal, meaning that her husband's mother is also called *nguwun.gin.gan* 'husband's mother'. If the two feminine suffixes *-gin* and *-gan* are removed from *nguwun.gin.gan,* this results in *nguwun,* which could be the word for 'husband's father'. A woman's *wumang* 'son-in-law' is *bugui* 'subject to the in-law respect relation' and she may not speak to him.

1.3. Phonology

The Yagara corpus employed here consists of written texts and brief recordings. Phonetic and phonological analysis based on these limited resources necessarily leaves much to be desired. The texts in the corpus were, however, collected by a wide range of individuals, as described in 1.1.4, so words in the corpus are frequently transcribed in a number of different ways. These different perspectives can be helpful in reconstructing what the words actually sounded like. For example, *giba* 'initiated male youth' is written *kipper* (Birch 1873; Clunie 1839), *kippa* (Ridley 1875; Meston

1986a; Watson 1943; Hardcastle 1946–7), *gibar* (Holmer 1983), and *gip-pa* (Colliver and Woolston 1978). These variable spellings suggest several features of the original word that the authors were hearing.

Firstly, a comparison of the spellings of *giba* indicates that some researchers heard the first sound in the word as the voiced stop [g], whereas others heard the sound as the voiceless stop [k]. This variability suggests that [g] and [k] are underlyingly the same sound in Yagara. Since these sounds were phonologically the same, Yagara speakers could use a stop that was either more voiced (more like a [g]) or less voiced (more like a [k]) without being misunderstood. In other words, voicing of stops is not contrastive in Yagara. Secondly, when the spellings of *giba* are compared with other words transcribed by the same authors, it becomes apparent that certain authors tended to write a final 'r' when none was pronounced, on the basis of (non-rhotic) English spelling (see 1.1.4 for summaries of the authors' influences and transcription styles). The diversity of authors and spellings in the corpus therefore makes it easier to deduce the original phonology of *giba*. The full set of spellings found in the original sources, which together formed the basis of the reconstructed phonological forms, are listed following these forms in Part 2.

This volume employs the orthography developed by the Minjerribah Moorgumpin Elders in Council (MMEIC) as utilised in the Jandai Dictionary and other MMEIC publications. The current orthography differs from the MMEIC system in that the long vowels, which are not indicated in the Jandai Dictionary, are here represented as *ii, aa* and *uu*. In the tables, figures and descriptions in this chapter, phonemes are labelled in the International Phonetic Alphabet (IPA), with the MMEIC-based orthography (when different) in brackets. Elsewhere the MMEIC orthography is used.

In the MMEIC orthography, the stop series in Yagara is represented with the voiced segments /b/, /d/ and /g/, with the palatal stop written /j/. Voicing is not contrastive in Yagara, as noted above, so the choice to represent these sounds as voiced (as *b* rather than *p*, for example) is arbitrary.

The alveolo-palatal nasal /ɲ/, as in English *canyon*, is written *ny*. This nasal occurs in *ganyara* 'one' or *nyamal* 'child', for example.

The velar nasal /ŋ/ is written *ng*, whereas an alveolar nasal /n/ followed by a velar stop /g/ is written *n.g*. For example, *bing* 'father' ends in roughly the same sound as English *sing*, whereas in *bin.ging* 'short-necked turtle' the *n.g* is more like in English *ten grams*. A velar nasal followed by a velar stop is written *ngg*; the *ngg* in *bangga* 'quickly' is similar to the *ng* in English *stronger*.

The phonemic inventory of Yagara, as inferred from the source texts, consists of twelve consonants (Table 1.4) and three vowels with a length distinction (Table 1.5).

Table 1.4: The consonant inventory of Yagara.

	bilabial	alveolar	lamino-palatal	velar
Stop	b	d	ɟ (j)	g
Nasal	m	n	ɲ (ny)	ŋ (ng)
Tap	–	r	–	–
Glide	w	–	j (y)	–
Lateral	–	l	–	–

Source: Authors' summary, based on the source texts.

Table 1.5: The vowel inventory of Yagara.

		front	Central	back
high	short	i	–	u
	long	iː (ii)	–	uː (uu)
low	short	–	ʌ	–
	long	–	aː (aa)	–

Source: Authors' summary, based on the source texts.

1.3.1. Consonant inventory

Yagara resembles many Australian languages in having nasals, stops, glides, a lateral and a rhotic, as summarised in Table 1.4. Like most Australian languages, Yagara has both a nasal and a stop at each place of articulation. Yagara has four stops (/b/, /d/, /ɟ/ and /g/) and four nasals (/m/, /n/, /ɲ/ and /ŋ/).

The /ɟ/ stop, written here as *j*, was frequently perceived as an affricate. For example, *jugung* 'tongue' is recorded as *tsurugung* (Lauterer 1891), *djurgoom* (Curr 1887), *jurgan* (Welsby 1916), *ɟugen* (Holmer 1983) and *choorgoong* (Meston 1986a).

Somewhat unusually among Australian languages, Yagara appears to have only a single rhotic /r/. In this respect Yagara resembles the neighbouring languages Yugambeh (Sharpe 1998) and Gabi-Gabi (which likewise has only one rhotic according to Holmer [1983]). Holmer observed only a single rhotic in Yagara (in the Munjan dialect that he called 'Nunagal'; 1983, 395), and the MMEIC decided on a single rhotic for use in the 2011 Jandai Dictionary. Though some Yagara source texts include both single *r* and double *rr*, this choice seems based on English conventions. In the original spellings of the source texts in Part 3, all 161 tokens of *rr* are written between vowels, as are all 112 tokens of *ll*, for example, even though Yagara /r/ and /l/ occur in a wide range of positions (see 1.3.5). This suggests that transcribers simply tended to write double consonants between vowels. The choice of *r* versus *rr* in the source texts does not therefore seem to distinguish two different rhotics.

The Yagara rhotic /r/ is typically produced as a tap in the song recordings of Gaiarbau, a Jinibara man who was familiar with Yagara (Winterbotham 1950), though the rhotic is an approximant in a later Yagara recording from an unidentified non-fluent informant (Wurm 1960). Holmer describes the rhotic as a '(slightly) trilled continuant' (1983, 395).

Final vowels after /r/ were often dropped by speakers, particularly when the final vowel was the same as the vowel before the /r/. The word *jara* 'country', for example, is transcribed as *gera* (Finch 1842), *tsarra* (Lauterer 1891) and *djara* (Watkins and Hamilton 1887), but also is written as *dar* (Eipper 1841a, 10–12) and *ta* (Turner 1861, 537). Other sources list both variants. Verbs ending in the suffix *-ra* show the same variation as roots ending in /rV/. For example, Holmer (1983) transcribes *jabu-ra* 'be.frightened-NEG' as *ɡabur(a)* with brackets around the final vowel, perhaps indicating that the vowel was optional.

The lateral approximant /l/ is always voiced in the recordings of Gaiarbau and Wurm's informant, and seems to have been a 'light l' similar to the /l/ in the word *light* in Standard Australian English (SAE).

1.3.2. Phonological rules affecting consonants

Several environmental effects can be extrapolated from the text corpus. For example, unstressed intervocalic /g/ is often reduced or omitted entirely, particularly in southern dialects. This process has affected the name for Brisbane, *Miyanjin,* which evolved from *Migan-jin* 'point-place'. In the sources, lenited /g/ is frequently omitted in this name, as in Colliver and Woolston's (1978) *me-an-jin*; or it may be transcribed as *y*, such as when Watkins (1891) writes *Meeyantin*. The variation between *mulwara* 'ritual scar' and the variant *mulgara* may also be due to the lenition of *g* in *mulwara*; and the variation between *ngara-ngarawai* 'wild heather' and *ngara-ngaragai* could be attributed to the same process.

According to Meston (1867–1960), Brisbane was called *Meeannjin* in the south and *Maginchin* around Moreton Bay. However, Watkins (1891, 50) probably collected the lenited form *Meeyantin* on Stradbroke Island; Birch (1873, 20) and Holmer (1983, 406) collected lenited forms of *ngara-ngarawai* on the island; and Ridley (1875, 81) collected lenited *mulwarra* around Brisbane; so the process seems to have occurred in more northern areas as well. The same lenition process has affected Bandjalangic languages in which the shift has spread out from the coastal Mibiny-speaking area, which is adjacent to Yagara (Jefferies 2011, 82).

Prestopping of the nasals and the lateral in Yagara was noted by Holmer (1983, 395), Jefferies (2011, 74) and Bell (2003); and observed in Yugambeh-Bandjalang by Cunningham (1969, 78) and Sharpe (1998, 15). The process is evident in transcribers' tendency to write sequences such as *bm, dn* and *dl*, which are phonologically impossible in Yagara (see section 1.3.5). The Yagara word for 'two', for example, has been transcribed *budla* (Ridley 1875), *boodela* (Curr 1887) and *boodla* (Watkins 1891). Notations such as *dl* in *budla* appear to represent non-phonological prestopped nasals and laterals similar to those described in other Australian languages (Butcher and Loakes 2008; Round 2014). The *bm, dn* and *dl* sounds are therefore allophones of /m/, /n/ and /l/.

The prestopped allophones occur when /m/, /n/, /ɲ/ or /l/ follows a stressed short vowel, as in *bula* 'two'. The short /a/ in *wali* 'bad' similarly conditions prestopping and is transcribed *wadley* (Watkins and Hamilton 1887) and *wadli* (Ridley 1875). The same occurs for the /i/ in *bina* 'ear', which leads to the transcriptions *pitney* (Eipper 1841a), *pitney* (Lang 1847), *pidna* (Watkins 1891; Meston 1986a) and *bidna* (Clunie 1839). Prestopping of /ŋ/ was not observed in the current data, and only a single instance of /ɲ/ was found (*banyu* 'ridge, backbone' was recorded as *padnoo* in Lang 1846); however, the lack of documentation for prestopped /ɲ/ and /ŋ/ is likely due to the authors' general tendency to omit or misrepresent /ɲ/ and /ŋ/ rather than to an absence of prestopping in these contexts.

The degree of voicing of the laminal palatal stop /ɟ/ (written *j* in the orthography used elsewhere in this volume), along with its degree of frication, changes before /i/. In this environment, /ɟ/ becomes more affricated and less voiced. This encourages transcriptions that indicate a voiceless affricate such as *tch* or *ch* or even the fricative *s*. For example, *jina* 'foot' is transcribed as *chidna* (Clunie 1839; Meston 1986a), and *tchindna* (Watson 1943; Meston 1986a) as well as *cidne* (Lauterer 1897) and *sidney* (Lang 1847). (Note that the *d* in these examples is evidence of prestopping.) The effect of /i/ is even more pronounced in unstressed syllables with /ɟ/, which are five times more likely to be transcribed in the source texts as voiceless (*ch, tch* or *s*) than when followed by /a/ or /u/.

An epenthetic bilabial nasal *m* sometimes occurs before a bilabial stop. This is apparent in the name *Mulumba* 'Point Lookout' from *mulu* 'stone' and the suffix *-ba* 'place', which Colliver and Woolston (1978) write *Mooloomba* and Birch (1873) writes *Moodloomba*. Epenthetic *m* occurs in a similar context when Ridley (1875) writes *ngunu-bu* 'night-DUR' as *ɲūnŭmbo*, and when Lauterer (1891) writes *marumba-bany* 'good-INCH' as *marumbambanyi*, for example.

The source texts provide evidence of several morphophonemic rules that simplify sequences of sonorant consonants. The first rule affects the small set of Yagara verbs that end in /n/, /ɲ/, or /l/. (All other verbs end in vowels; see 1.3.5.) First, the final consonants of verbs ending in /n/, /ɲ/, or /l/ are lost before the four verbal suffixes beginning in /r/ or /l/ (that is, *–ra* 'DEST'; *–ri* 'PST'; *-la* 'OBGL'; and *-li* 'FUT'). For example, /garubabaɲ/ 'throng' with /ri/ 'PST' results in /garubabari/ 'throng-PST'; /ɲan/ 'go' with /ra/ 'DEST' results in /ɲara/ 'go-DEST'; /ɲan/ 'go' with /la/ 'OBLG' results in /nyala/ 'go-OBLG'; and /yagaɲ/ 'heal' with /li/ 'FUT' produces /yagali/ 'heal-FUT'.

The final consonants of verbs are retained in unsuffixed roots, as in /ɲan/ *nyan* 'go'; and before most suffixes, as in /wuɟanba/ *wujan-ba* 'give-SBJV', though they disappear in imperatives such as /wuɟa/ *wuja* 'give-IMP'. No nominal suffixes begin with /r/ or /l/, and free morphemes cannot begin with /r/ or /l/, so suffixed verbs such as *garubabany* and *nyan* are the only contexts in Yagara where a consonant precedes /r/ or /l/. Since /n/, /ɲ/, and /l/ disappear in these contexts, it would be accurate to say that all consonant clusters ending in /r/ or /l/ are reduced to /r/ or /l/.

Final /l/, on any part of speech, also disappears before the central nasals /n/ and /ɲ/, but not before the peripherals /m/ and /ŋ/. When verbs ending in /l/ take the present-tense suffix /ɲa/ -*nya*, the verb's final /l/ is omitted, as occurs with /galimal/ *galimal* 'punish' in /galimaɲa/ *galimal-nya* 'punish-PRS'. Similarly, the third-person singular pronoun /ŋuɲal/ *ngunyal* and the noun /ɟundal/ *jundal* 'woman' lose their final /l/ before accusative -*na*, in /ŋuɲana/ *ngunyal-na* '3.SG.ACC' and /ɟundana/ *jundal-na* 'woman-ACC', both occurring multiple times in Ridley (1875). Two other nouns ending in /l/, *Immanuel* and *Mumbal* (literally 'thunder', which Ridley uses to mean 'God'), occur several times with accusative -*na* in Ridley (1875) but never lose their final /l/; this may be because Reverend Ridley considered these to be holy names that should not be abbreviated. Elsewhere the loss of /l/ before /n/ and /ɲ/ is universal. The peripheral nasals /m/ and /ŋ/ do not cause /l/ to be lost. These nasals may occur following /l/ within a single morpheme, as in *Mugulngura* 'woman's name' and *walmuram* 'sand goanna', or in reduplicated morphemes, as in *ngal-ngal* 'dingo'. In sum, central nasals, but not peripheral nasals, condition the loss of /l/.

Finally, there is no evidence for long or geminate consonants in Yagara. When a lateral, rhotic or nasal would be followed by the same phoneme due to suffixing or compounding, the two identical consonants are simplified to a single segment. For example, *dany-nya* 'lie-PRS' is transcribed by Ridley (1875) as *daina*, who elsewhere writes *dany* as *dain*, with no indication that the /ɲ/ in *dany-nya* is longer than in *dany*.

The verb /daɲ/ *dany* 'lie' therefore loses its final /ɲ/ before /ɲ/, as well as prior to /l/ or /r/ as discussed previously. Other verbs with final consonants are similarly affected. An analogous situation may have led to the loss of verbs with final consonants in the neighbouring Yugambeh language, for which Sharpe identifies a set of verbs that previously ended in consonants (1998, 31). If these consonants disappeared in many contexts, as in Yagara, this may have contributed to their eventual loss in Yugambeh.

The possible sequences of consonants in Yagara and attested examples of each are shown in Table 1.7 in 1.3.5.

1.3.3. Vowel inventory

Yagara has a three-vowel system consisting of /i/, /a/ and /u/ with a phonological length distinction. As noted, though vowel length is not systematically represented in the original MMEIC orthography, here long vowels are indicated as *ii, aa* and *uu*. The length distinction is indicated by the minimal pairs *biigi* 'sun' and *bigi* 'Bangalow palm'; *jaan* 'Aboriginal man' and *jan* 'wet'; and *baguuru* 'tree' and *baguru* 'be amazed'.

Most written sources indicate vowel length in some way. Holmer rarely transcribes long vowels, but does so in *naara* 'black duck', for example, which he writes as *nár* (Holmer 1983). Several speakers of non-rhotic dialects of English transcribe length in Yagara using a post-vocalic *r*. For instance, Hinchcliffe (1890) writes *guwaa* 'cloud, rain' as *guwar*, and Hardcastle (1946–7) writes *jaraagil* 'frog' as *jerargil*. Other sources indicate length by adding *h* after a vowel. Lauterer (1897) transcribes *guwaa* 'cloud, rain' as *guwah*, and Meston (1867–1960) writes *jaraagil* 'frog' as *charáhgill*, for example. Vowel length distinction is also apparent in that short vowels condition the prestopped allophone of nasals and the lateral, as discussed in 1.3.2.

With the available data, diphthongs cannot satisfactorily be distinguished from vowel-glide sequences. Of the potential six diphthongs (/ai/, /ui/, /au/, /ia/, /ua/ and /iu/), /ai/, /ui/ and /au/ are here considered present in Yagara. This decision is informed by consideration of neighbouring languages. In Yugambeh-Bandjalang, all diphthongs end in /i/ (Sharpe 1998, 16), which supports the plausibility of the /ai/ and /ui/ diphthongs in Yagara. In Duuŋidjawu, which Kite and Wurm consider a dialect of Waga-Waga (2004), no diphthongs are identified (2004, 19). However, Holmer suggests that both Waga-Waga and Yugambeh-Bandjalang had /ai/ and /au/ sequences, but that these sequences became /e/ and /o/ in these languages (Holmer 1983, 15–19). If so, Yagara may have retained the /ai/ and /au/ formerly found in these languages and does not seem to have developed /e/ and /o/ (see Section 1.3.4). The presence of /ai/, /ui/ and /au/ in surrounding languages is only faint evidence for their presence in Yagara, and transcription of these sequences as /ayi/, /uwi/ and /awu/ (or of /iya/, /uwa/ and /iyu/ as /ia/, /ua/ and /iu/) may be found to be more accurate or desirable than the system used here.

1.3.4. How stress affects vowel quality

Unstressed vowels are significantly centralised (see Section 1.3.6), with the result that unstressed /u/ may sound more like [o], for example. The current section argues that the vowels transcribed as mid-central vowels in the corpus are not phonological vowels, but are allomorphs of /a/, /i/ and /u/ conditioned by a lack of stress.

In the source texts, unstressed vowels are sometimes transcribed as vowels that are neither low nor high, such as *e* and *o*, with *e* representing /i/ and /a/, and *o* often standing for /u/ and occasionally /a/. However, the vowels represented as *e* and *o* seem to be mid-centralised allomorphs of /a/, /i/ or /u/, as suggested by the absence of minimal pairs contrasting *e* or *o* with other vowels. The non-phonemic status of *e* and *o* is also indicated by their distribution in the corpus. For example, the authors in the corpus differ more in their use of *e* and *o* than they do in their choice of *a, i* or *u*. There is no word in the corpus that is consistently transcribed with *e* or *o* in all sources, whereas all sources frequently agree on *a, i* or *u*. In *waril* 'creek', for instance, all nine sources of the word transcribe both *a* and *i*; and in *mumbal* 'thunder', all five sources agree on the *u* and *a* (though Jackson 1937 transcribes the word as *moonbal*). If the sounds written as *e* and *o* are derived allophones of /a/, /i/ or /u/, their production might be expected to vary more than the basic allophones [a], [i] or [u], depending on the speed and care of the transcribed speech, for example, so the inconsistent transcription of *e* and *o* in the corpus is evidence that these vowels are allophones rather than phonemes.

In fact, the use of *e* and *o* can vary even between transcriptions of the same word by the same researcher. For example, Clunie (1839) writes *wali* 'bad' as both *wadle* and *wadly*, and Holmer (1983) transcribes *gurung* 'black' as both *gurung* and *gurong*. Throughout the texts, the sounds transcribed as *e* and *o* are mostly unstressed vowels, as in the second syllables of *wali* and *gurung*, which indicates that allomorphs written *e* and *o* tended to occur in this environment.

This trend emphasises the influence of stress on vowel quality and supports the analysis of *e* and *o* as mid-centralised allophones that occur in unstressed syllables.

There are doubtless other phonological rules affecting vowels. For example, Holmer (1983) observes that /a/ becomes more rounded when adjacent to /w/ and higher after /j/ (1983, 395). Place assimilation of the former type may have contributed to the transcription of *wana* 'do not' as *wonnah* (Clunie 1839), for example. However, there is only incidental evidence for these effects in the corpus.

1.3.5. Syllable structure and phoneme distribution

Syllables are CV(V)(C). That is, all syllables must have a consonant onset, followed by a short vowel, a long vowel, or a diphthong (see 1.3.3); optionally followed by a sonorant consonant coda. As in the neighbouring Badjala, Duuŋidjawu and Yugambeh languages (Bell 2003; Kite and Wurm 2004; Sharpe 1998), words may consist of a single syllable.

All consonant segments can be syllable onsets. Neither the lateral /l/ nor the rhotic /r/ can be word onsets, though four verbal suffixes begin with these phonemes. Closed syllables may end with a nasal, lateral or rhotic, but not a stop or glide. The above restrictions on onsets and codas appear identical to those in Duuŋidjawu (Kite and Wurm 2004, 21) and similar to those in Yugambeh-Bandjalang, though Yugambeh-Bandjalang suffixes can begin with vowels (Sharpe 1998).

Yagara differs from some of its neighbours in that it allows verbs to end in nasals or laterals. Badjala and Duuŋidjawu verb roots all end in vowels (Bell 2003, 87; Kite and Wurm 2004, 69), as do Yugambeh-Bandjalang verb roots (Sharpe 1998, 31), though Sharpe observes that 'a few, now irregular verbs, probably had stems ending in consonants' (1998, 31; see 1.3.2). Gabi-Gabi verbs may end in nasals or rhotics in addition to vowels (Bell 1994). The vast majority of Yagara verbs end in a vowel, as in *biya* 'throw'. However, a small number of verbs end in /n/, /ɲ/ or /l/.

The permissible segments at syllable- and word-boundaries are listed in Table 1.6. Morpheme boundaries have the same restrictions as syllable boundaries.

Table 1.6: List of consonant phonemes (in IPA) acceptable in various syllable and word positions.

Syllable-initial	b, d, g; ɟ; m, n, ɲ, ŋ; w, j; r; l
Word-initial	b, d, g; ɟ; m, n, ɲ, ŋ; w, j
Syllable-final	m, n, ɲ, ŋ; r; l
Word-final	m, n, ɲ, ŋ; r; l

Source: Authors' summary, based on the source texts.

Table 1.7 is a matrix of attested combinations of permissible syllable codas followed by permissible syllable onsets. Final consonants disappear before /l/ and /r/; final /l/ is lost before /n/ and /ɲ/; and sequences of the same consonant simplify (see 1.3.2). All other combinations are apparently possible.

Table 1.7: Attested combinations of permissible syllable codas followed by permissible syllable onsets.

	Nasal coda	Rhotic coda	Lateral coda
Stop onset	*mumbal* 'thunder' *jirban-di* 'bone-LOC' *bin.ging* 'short-necked turtle' *garang-garang* 'clothing' *wanji* 'when'	*jirban* 'bone' *dur-dur* 'nape' *gar-gar* 'type of gum' *bularju* 'swamp mahogany'	*ngunyal-ba* '3SG-ABL' *gudal-di* 'bushes-LOC' *dabil=gu* 'water=PURP' *jimbaljin* 'female friend'
Nasal onset	*nyan-ma* 'go-CAUS' *bugany-ma* 'sleep-CAUS' *nyalang-ma* 'lie-CAUS'	*miir-miir* 'full of holes'	*ngal-ngal* 'dingo' *walmuram* 'sand goanna'
Glide onset	*gun-gunwan* 'emerald dove' *bangwal* 'fern root'	*barwan* 'wide'	*bulwalam* 'nose piercing' *dalwalbin* 'cotton tree'
Rhotic onset	N/A (nasals are lost before /r/)	N/A (/rr/ simplifies to /r/)	N/A (laterals are lost before /r/)
Lateral onset	N/A (nasals are lost before /l/)	*bumagarla* 'kill'	N/A (/ll/ simplifies to /l/)

N/A: Not applicable.
Source: Authors' summary, based on the source texts.

Only one long vowel can occur within a single morpheme, as in the nearby language Badjala (Bell 2003, 24). Reduplicated words may have two long vowels, as in *buunyi-buunyi* 'bunya', *waa-waa* 'crow' or *biigi-biigi* 'regent bird'.

1.3.6. Stress

Stress is normally initial in Yagara, as in Duuŋidjawu (Kite and Wurm 2004, 22) and Yugambeh-Bandjalang (Sharpe 1998, 18). Watson notices the initial stress pattern in Yagara (1943, 8), which is confirmed by the Yagara words in Wurm's recording (Wurm 1960).

Prestopping, which occurs with stressed short vowels (see 1.3.2), also points to initial stress regardless of word length. For example, Ridley writes *ginabulum* 'tree species' as *kidnabullum* and *mulagu* 'next day' as *mŭdelago*, in which the *d* indicates prestopping after the first vowel.

Though stress is generally initial, long vowels in the second syllable attract stress, as occurs in the nearby Yugambeh-Bandjalang and Badjala languages (Sharpe 1998, 14; Bell 2003, 24). For example, Meston (1867–1960) places a stress mark over the second syllable of his notations of *magiiba* 'friend' and *jaraagil* 'frog', which would otherwise have initial stress. In Wurm's recordings, *diyiin* 'today' and *waliinggara* 'old woman' have stress on the second syllable rather than the first.

Compounded words keep the stress patterns of the component words. The compound *bina-wali* 'ear-bad; deaf' is transcribed by Ridley as *pidnwuddeli*, in which the *d* in *pidn* and the *dde* in *wuddeli* indicate prestopping and therefore stress. The placename *Guji-mulu* 'red-stone; Cuchiemudlo' is transcribed *Coochie Mudlow* by Lenet and *coodgee mudlow* by Watkins, with the prestopping in *mudlow* demonstrating that the third syllable in the compound is stressed. In these compounds, then, the first and third syllables appear to be stressed. These syllables correspond to the syllables that are stressed in each of the compounded words when they occur in isolation.

1.3.7. Phonological analyses in the sources

Four sources, Holmer, Ridley, Lauterer and Watson, provide phonological information about Yagara and attempt to transcribe the language systematically. This section will begin with Holmer (1983), move on to Ridley (1875) and Lauterer (1895), and then finish with Watson (1943). Unlike Holmer, Ridley and Lauterer, Watson confesses to having no personal experience with Yagara, so his analysis is given less attention here.

In Part 3 of his *Linguistic Survey of South-Eastern Queensland*, Holmer (1983) uses the same transcription system for numerous Queensland languages, so the system includes sounds found in Gunggari, for example, that are not present in Yagara. The Yagara dialect that Holmer analyses is Munjan, spoken by the Nunagal people of northern Stradbroke Island. Holmer calls this language 'Nunagal' (Holmer 1983, 398).

Table 1.8: Holmer's vowel transcriptions for Yagara and three other languages in Part 3 of his _Linguistic Survey_.

Holmer's vowel	Holmer's description
a	more or less as in (standard or Australian) English 'c**u**t'
e	more or less as in English 'b**e**d'
i	more or less as in English 's**i**t'
o	more or less as in (standard or Australian) English 'g**o**t'
u	more or less as in English 'p**u**t'
aa	more or less as in English 'f**a**ther'
ee	more or less as in English 'wh**ere**'
ii	more or less as in English 'b**e**'
oo	more or less as in (standard or Australian) English 'c**a**ll'
uu	more or less as in English 'd**o**'

Note: the various indications of length used in the sources are replaced here with the double vowels used elsewhere in the volume. The relevant sounds in English examples in the tables have also been underscored and boldfaced for clarity.

Source: Authors' summary of Holmer (1983).

As shown in Table 1.8, Holmer identifies five distinctive vowel qualities (a, e, i, o and u) whereas only three are posited here (a, i and u; see Table 1.5), for reasons outlined in Section 1.3.4. However, we will argue that Holmer's identification of the mid vowels /e/ and /o/ is rare and often tentative.

Though Holmer proposes a five-vowel system, whereas the current analysis suggests a three-vowel system, it should be noted that Holmer's vowels /e/ and /o/ occur rarely in his transcriptions. Holmer identifies no instances of long /ee/ or long /oo/ in the Munjan data he analyses, and uses short /e/ and short /o/ in only a few words. In fact, he includes /e/ or /o/ in the first (presumably stressed) syllable of only four words out of the 450 in his list: _bang_ 'dead' (Holmer's _boŋ_); _gung-gung_ 'egg', a loanword (Holmer's _goŋ-goŋ_), _gin-gin_ 'redbreast' _(gen.gin),_ and _Ngirubin_ 'a place name' _(ŋerobin)._ The /e/ and /o/ in unstressed syllables can be attributed to centralisation and can be considered a less significant point of disagreement than the occurrence of these vowels in stressed syllables (see Section 1.3.4).

Furthermore, of the instances of /e/ and /o/ that Holmer identifies, he designates about half of the instances of /e/ as variants of /a/, and attributes some of these variants to the saltwater trend of raising /a/ to a higher front vowel, as noted here in Section 1.1.1. Holmer also hypothesises that some instances of /u/ may be mispronounced due to 'features of Queensland pronunciation of English' (1983, 479), such that *jalu* 'fire' may sound more like *jalou*, he suggests. This may result in some instances of /u/ being pronounced more like /o/. In consideration of these factors, the choice of a three-vowel system, as described in 1.3.3, does not seem to deviate substantially from Holmer's phonology.

Holmer's list of around 450 words includes 16 vowel sequences, consisting of six instances of *ai*, eight tokens of *ua* and two of *ia*.

In contrast to Holmer's vowels, his consonants for Munjan align exactly with the system proposed here (see Table 1.4), though Holmer writes /ɟ/, /ɲ/ and /ŋ/ as *ɟ, ɲ* and *ŋ* rather than *j, ny* and *ng* as in the following sections of this volume. Holmer recognises that voicing on stops is not distinctive and uses the voiced forms *b, d, ɟ* and *g* throughout.

It is useful to note the consonants that Holmer did *not* find in Munjan. Holmer's list includes not only the consonants recognised in this volume (see Table 1.4), but also others found in the non-Yagara languages that Holmer examines. These include 'palatalised interdental' stops, a 'slightly retroflex' stop, two types of trills and a retroflex rhotic. Notably, Holmer never makes use of these symbols in his Munjan transcriptions. Instead, he limits himself to equivalents of the consonants included in the phonemic inventory in Table 1.4. This suggests that Holmer did not observe retroflex stops, multiple types of trills or a retroflex rhotic in Munjan, even though he was aware of these sounds and identified them in other languages.

Ridley's 1875 book *Kámilarói, and Other Australian Languages* presents the system in Table 1.9 for representing the vowels of the languages in the book, including the Durubal dialect of Yagara (Ridley 1875, 3).

Ridley uses all the vowels listed in Table 1.9 in his transcriptions of Durubal. He is inconsistent in his choices, however, writing *ngaja* 'I' as *yutta, ŋutta* and *atta*; *yaran* 'beard' as *yeren, yarran*, and *yurra*; and other variations. Ridley's use of *u* and *a* is particularly interchangeable. Though he typically writes *u* to indicate /a/, as suggested by Table 1.9, his *u* usually indicates /u/ word-finally, for example, based on comparison with other sources.

Table 1.9: Ridley's vowel transcriptions for Yagara and nine other languages in his *Kámilarói, and Other Australian Languages*.

Ridley's vowel	Ridley's description
a	as in m**a**t
e	as in n**e**t
i	as in **i**t
o	as in **o**n
u	as in t**u**n
aa	as in f**a**ther
ee	as in ob**ey**
ii	as in rav**i**ne
oo	as in t**o**ne
uu	as in m**oo**n
ai	as in w**i**ne
ao	as in h**ow**
oi	as in n**oi**se

Source: Authors' summary of Ridley (1875).

Ridley distinguishes voiced and voiceless stops even though these are not phonological in Yagara, and writes both *p* and *b*, for example. He consistently ignores initial /ɲ/ and omits or misrepresents initial /ŋ/ before /u/. His system of consonants otherwise is the same as in this volume (see Table 1.4).

Table 1.10: Lauterer's vowel transcriptions for Yagara in 'Outlines of a Grammar'.

Lauterer's vowel	Lauterer's description
a	as in f**a**ther
e	as in t**e**n
i	as in k**i**ss
o	as in g**o**
u	as in tr**u**e
æ	as in h**a**ppy
œ	as in b**u**t

Source: Authors' summary of Lauterer (1895).

Lauterer's (1895) pronunciation guide differs in several respects from Ridley's, which Lauterer attributes to dialectal difference between the 'Yaggara dialect, spoken in the "sandy country" (Yerongpan) between Brisbane and Ipswich', and 'the true Turrabul as it occurs in Ridley's grammar' (1895, 619). However, many of these purported differences are likely due to Ridley and Lauterer's individual abilities and methods, plus the 40 years between their times of data collection (see 1.1.1 on dialectal differences).

Lauterer lists the Yagara consonants as '*k, n, n', d, t, b, p, m, w, r, l, s*'. He also includes '*y* (as in yes)' but lists this glide with the vowels (1895: 619). Unlike Ridley, Lauterer recognises the palatals /ɲ/ and /ʝ/ (his *n'* and *s*) and observes that they 'have a sound not easily pronounced by an English tongue, being identical with the Slavonian *n* and *s* before *i*' (1895, 619). Though Lauterer does not directly recognise /ŋ/ as a separate sound from /n/ and /ɲ/, he nonetheless uses *ng* to represent a velar nasal in his transcriptions. Like Ridley, he distinguishes voiced and voiceless stops. In other respects, Lauterer's consonantal system is the same as the one used here.

Watson, in his volume *Four Representative Tribes of South Eastern Queensland*, includes a pronunciation guide to the languages (Watson 1943, 8). Though Watson collected data directly from consultants for other languages in the volume, he bases his 'Yuggerabul' wordlist mainly on Ridley and Petrie. 'The accentuation of word syllables in the Yugarabul vocabulary herewith is not recorded by the personal knowledge of the compiler, but on general principles of aboriginal practice', Watson writes (1943, 9). Watson's pronunciation guide is therefore not included here, except for his equivalents of vowels in the other transcription systems as listed in Table 1.11.

Across the various phonological descriptions, the vowels vary more than the consonants. Table 1.11 lists approximate equivalents in Holmer (1983), Lauterer (1895), Ridley (1875) and Watson (1943), along with the system employed here.

Table 1.11 is intended only to give an impression of equivalents across the various systems. In the rest of this volume, vowel transcriptions deviate from this table when they take into consideration contextual factors and transcriptions in sources other than Holmer, Lauterer, Ridley and Watson.

Table 1.11: Approximate correspondence of vowel transcriptions based on explanations in the sources.

Current volume	Holmer (1983)	Lauterer (1895)	Ridley (1875)	Watson (1943)
a	a, e, o	æ, œ, e	a, u, o	a, ŭ, o
aa	aa	a	aa	aa
ai	ai	–	ai, ee	ai, ee
au	–	–	ao	au
i	i, e	i, e	i, e	i, e
ii	ii	–	ii	ii
u	u, o, oo	u	o	u, â, o
uu	uu	u	uu	uu
ui	–	–	oi	–

Source: Authors' summary of Holmer (1983), Lauterer (1895), Ridley (1875) and Watson (1943).

1.4. Parts of speech

The limited scope of the Yagara text collection leaves room for varying interpretations regarding the parts of speech found in Yagara. For example, the sets of words here considered as 'adjectives' and 'nouns' occur in distinct contexts in the texts. However, it is possible that 'adjectives' can appear in all the positions that 'nouns' do, but that we simply lack the evidence for this in the texts. The parts of speech distinguished here are based on the available Yagara data and comparison with surrounding languages. In particular, the categories proposed here are functionally identical to the parts of speech identified by Kite and Wurm for Duuŋidjawu (2004, 23) and nearly the same as those distinguished for Badjala by Bell (2003, 26).

- Nominals:
  - Nouns
  - Adjectives
  - Quantifiers
  - Location and time words
  - Pronouns
  - Demonstratives
  - Interrogatives
- Verbs
- Particles and interjections

Several properties allow the above parts of speech to be distinguished. First, nominals are the only class that may be inflected for case, which is assigned on the basis of the nominal's role in an event (see 1.5.2). Each of the nominal types listed above (nouns, adjectives, etc.) is documented at least once in the texts with a case-marking suffix, whereas no verbs or particles have these suffixes. Moreover, certain derivational suffixes occur only on nominals (see 1.5.4). Nouns can additionally take plural suffixes. Nouns, pronouns, quantifiers and interrogatives may be arguments of verbs or other predicates. All classes of nominals may modify other nominals.

Verbs may be inflected for tense, aspect and mood, and also take inflections that change their valence (that is, whether they require an object or not) or mark the verb as being in a subordinate clause. Verbs also take a few derivational suffixes, though only the poorly attested negation suffix -*ra* is specific to verbs (see 1.6.9), so these do not generally help distinguish verbs from other classes.

Particles and interjections never inflect or undergo derivation. However, like the other classes, they may take clitics (see Section 1.8).

Words rarely belong to multiple classes. For example, few words in the texts function as both a nominal and a verb. The clearest examples in the data are *bina*, which numerous sources attest as meaning both 'ear' and 'hear'; *yigil*, which indicates both 'cold' and 'be cold'; and *baan*, which means both 'nasty; angry' and 'be nasty; be angry'. Both *yigil* and *baan* occur as a modifier of nouns and with verbal inflections. Though few words are found as both a nominal and a verb in the texts, many words function as more than one type of nominal, such as an adjective and a noun. In addition, words can change their grammatical category through the addition of derivational suffixes (1.5.4 and 1.6.9).

The parts of speech and their morphological properties are described in the following sections.

1.5. Nominal morphology

1.5.1. Nouns

Yagara nouns in the text collection have the following structure:

ROOT – (DERIVATION) – (INFLECTION) = (CLITICS)

Inflection consists of case marking (Section 1.5.2) and plural marking (1.5.3). Derivational suffixes change the meaning of a stem and often change its part of speech (1.5.4). Clitics occur on any type of phrase or clause (1.8).

1.5.2. Noun cases

The Yagara noun cases are listed in Table 1.12. Following the table are descriptions and examples of each case.

Table 1.12: Noun cases.

Case	Case suffix	Abbreviation
nominative	*-Ø*	-NOM
ergative	*-du*	-ERG
accusative	*-na*	-ACC
possessive	*-nuba*	-POSS
locative	*-di*	-LOC
allative	*-nga*	-ALL
ablative	*-ba*	-ABL
durative	*-bu*	-DUR
accompaniment	*-ba-nga*	-ABL-ALL
colocalisation	*-ba-di*	-ABL-LOC

Source: Authors' summary, based on the source texts.

The core cases (nominative, accusative and ergative) indicate subjects and objects. Ergative case, which is always optional in Yagara, marks the subject of a transitive verb. Accusative case, which is optional on nouns but obligatory on pronouns (Section 1.5.10), marks the object of a transitive verb. Nominative case marks the subject of an intransitive verb.

The optional ergative and accusative case marking in Yagara is echoed by neighbouring languages. Yugambeh similarly allows both accusative and ergative case marking on nouns (Sharpe 1998, 34), whereas Duuŋidjawu and Badjala both have obligatory ergative marking on nouns but a split system with nominative, accusative and ergative marking on pronouns (Bell 2003, 30; Kite and Wurm 2004, 25).

The subject of an intransitive clause in Yagara has nominative case and is always unmarked, such as *guiyar* 'fish' in (1).

(1) **guiyar**   yara-dunga   dabil-di
     fish   swim-IPFV   water-LOC
     fish were swimming in the water.
     kuïyŭr yŭrŭdunga tabbilti. (Ridley 1875)

Most subjects of transitive clauses are also unmarked, though a few have the optional ergative marker *du*. All six examples with *du* are shown in (2)–(7). Subjects seem to be ergative marked when the subject is unexpected, such as when it previously had a non-subject role, as in (2); or when the subject is not human, as in (3)–(5). It is not clear why the subject in (7) is marked, though this sentence is also unusual in that the subject comes after the verb. All examples except (7) are from Ridley (1875).

(2) barany   ngunyal   banman
     then   3SG.NOM   pluck
     Then she plucked;
     Burru wunnal pŭnmān;

     nga   da-ri   nga   dagai-na   wujan
     and   eat-PST   and   white.man-ACC   give
     and ate, and gave to the white man;
     ŋa turri, ŋa dugganu widdan;

     dagai-**du**   da-ri
     white.man-**ERG**   eat-PST
     The white man ate.
     duggaidu turri.

(3) yuwan-**du**   ngana   nyalang-ma-ri   yaa-ri
     serpent-**ERG**   1SG.ACC   tell.lie-CAUS-PST   say-PST
     'The serpent told lies to me and spoke;
     'Yŭndu ŋunna nulluŋmurri yari;

(4) magui-**du**   bargil   ngunyal-ba-di   nyinyi-du
     devil-**ERG**   a.long.time   3SG-ABL-LOC   dwell-ATEL
     An evil spirit had been living in him for a long time;
     Maguïkŭ barkil wunnalpuddi ŋinedu;

(5) nga   magui-**du**   ngunyana   gawany   gadigal-di
     and   devil-**ERG**   3SG.ACC   drive   forest-LOC
     and the demon drove him into the forest.
     Ŋa maguïdu wunnana kawāne kŭdigulti.

(6)   magui-**du**   yaa-ri   gurumba   milin
        devil-**ERG**   say-PST   great   many
        The demon said, 'We are a great many.'
        Maguidu yari, 'Kurumba mulla.'

(7)   da-ma-nya   malar-jin-**du**
        eat-CAUS-PRS   man-PL-**ERG**
        People are eating it.
        Junmino Ma-lardino.

Objects of transitive clauses are usually unmarked, but sometimes take the accusative *na*, as in (8)–(9). There are 24 instances of accusative *na* in Ridley (1875), though none in the other texts.

(8)   imanuwal   wana   dagai-jin-**na**
        Immanuel   forbid   white.man-PL-**ACC**
        Immanuel forbade the white men
        Immanuel wunna duggatina

        balga-du   ngumbi-nga
        come-ATEL   house-ALL
        going into the house;
        bulgutu ūmpiŋga;

(9)   guna   muya   danga   baguur-**na**
        heart   desire   that.DIST   tree-**ACC**
        her heart desired that fruit.
        kudna muïya dūŋa bagūrnu.

In addition to the core cases, Yagara has non-core cases that indicate possession, location and other relations. A noun that refers to an owner or recipient can take the possessive suffix *-nuba*, as in example (10) in which *yairu* 'Jairus' is the owner of the *ngumbi* 'house', or (11) where the *dagai-jin* 'white men' belong to the Commandant.

(10)   barany   dagai-jin
        then   white.man-PL
        Then the white men
        Berren duggatin

ngumbi-nga yairu-**nuba** balga-ri
house-ALL Jairus-**POSS** come-PST
came to the house of Jairus;
umpiŋa Yāirūnubba bulkurri;

(11) dagai-jin gamandan-**nuba** wira ngumbi-nga
white.man-PL Commandant-**POSS** return house-ALL
The Commandant's men returned to the house;
Duggatin Kommandantnūbba wirreni ūmpiŋa;

The locative -*di* is used for meanings similar to English *in, into, at* or *on,* as in the three instances in (12).

(12) miir mara-**di** bimba-ri
hole hand-**LOC** pierce-PST
They pierced holes in his hands;
mīr murradi bimberri;

nga miir jina-**di** bimba-ri
and hole foot-**LOC** pierce-PST
and pierced holes in his feet.
ŋa mīr tjidnendi bimberri.

nga ngunyali imanuwal baguur-**di** wura
and 3PL.NOM Immanuel tree-**LOC** put
and they put Immanuel on the trees:
Ŋa wunnale Imanuel bāgūrti wune: (Ridley 1875)

The allative -*nga* usually resembles English *to,* as in examples (13)–(14).

(13) dagai-jin gamandan-nuba wira ngumbi-**nga**
white.man-PL Commandant-POSS return house-**ALL**
The Commandant's men returned to the house;
Duggatin Kommandantnūbba wirreni ūmpiŋa; (Ridley 1875)

(14) wanya-**nga** nginda
where-**ALL** 2SG.NOM
Where are you going?
Woon-nanta-Intair? (Hardcastle 1946–7)

The ablative -*ba* can be glossed as *from* or *out of* as in (15) or (16).

(15) ngunyali   balgal-**ma-ri**   baguuru-**ba**
     3PL.NOM   arise-CAUS-PST   tree-**ABL**
     They lifted him from the trees;
     Wunnale bulgunmurri bagūrubba; (Ridley 1875)

(16) barany   ngambila   magui   nyan-dunga   dagai-**ba**
     at.once   all   devil   go-IPFV   white.man-**ABL**
     At once all the demons are leaving the white man
     Berren ŋāmbille maguï yeatunga duggaipa (Ridley 1875)

The durative *-bu* occurs only on measures of time, and is similar to English *for/at/on/during* preceding a unit of time, as in (17)–(18).

(17) imanuwal   ngunu-**bu**   ganggir   dany-dunga
     Immanuel   night-**DUR**   dead   lie-IPFV
     That night Immanuel lay dead;
     Imanuel ŋūnūmbo kungīr daieduŋa; (Ridley 1875)

(18) nga   nginda   ngundu   baluny   biigi-**bu**
     and   2SG.NOM   surely   die   day-**DUR**
     and on that day you will surely die.
     Ŋa ŋinda ŋūndu balluia bigibu. (Ridley 1875)

The ablative-allative sequence *-ba-nga* indicates accompaniment, and is used when someone is going somewhere with the referent of the suffixed nominal, as in (19). This sequence is only found on the pronoun *ngunyali* in the texts, as in (19).

(19) imanuwal   nyan-dunga   ngunyali-**ba-nga**
     Immanuel   travel-IPFV   3PL-**ABL-ALL**
     Immanuel was travelling with them.
     Imanuel yeatūŋa ŋulle buggā. (Ridley 1875)

The ablative-locative sequence *-ba-di* indicates that someone is in the same location as the referent of the suffixed nominal, as in (20)–(21). The colocalised participants are not in motion, as with *-ba-nga*, but are static in a shared location. The sequence *-ba-di* indicating colocalisation is found on a wide range of pronouns and nouns.

(20) yaa-ri   ngaja   nginda-**ba-di**   nyinyi
     say-PST   1SG.NOM   2SG-**ABL-LOC**   dwell
     He said, 'I'm staying with you.'
     Yari, 'ŋutta ŋintapuddi ŋinne.' (Ridley 1875)

(21) nga   dagai-jin-**ba-di**   ngambila=bu   yaa-ri
     and   white.man-PL-**ABL-LOC**   all=EMPH   say-PST
     and in front of all the white men, said;
     ŋa duggatin buddi ŋambillabo yari; (Ridley 1875)

The sequences -*ba-nga* and -*ba-di* may be considered compound cases, since their meaning is not strictly predictable from that of the component cases.

The locative cases (locative -*di*, allative -*nga* and ablative -*ba*) occur in sequences other than the ablative-allative -*ba-nga* as in (19) and the ablative-locative -*ba-di* as in (20)–(21). However, the other sequences seem to be relatively compositional. For example, when God takes a bone out of Adam's side, the locative-ablative sequence -*di-ba* in (22) compositionally describes this spatial movement, insofar as bone is moved from its position inside the body (locative) away from the body (ablative).

Note that Ridley uses the word *mumbal* 'thunder' to refer to God.

(22) mumbal   jirban   guda-**di-ba**   banman
     thunder   bone   side-**LOC-ABL**   pluck
     God plucked a bone from his side;
     Mumbal tirben kŭttādibēr pŭnmān; (Ridley 1875)

Case marking, when present in a noun phrase, always occurs on the head noun. Case marking is also found on possessive pronouns and adjectives (see 1.5.10 and 1.5.7), but it is impossible to say if it is obligatory in these instances, as discussed in the relevant sections. Case is optional on adnominal demonstratives (see 1.5.11). Yagara may follow the pattern of neighbouring language Duuŋidjawu, where case marking is obligatory on a head noun but optional on all other elements in a noun phrase (Kite and Wurm 2004, 96). In Yugambeh-Bandjalang and Badjala, on the other hand, case marking is obligatory on adjectives as well as nouns and pronouns (Sharpe 1998, 34; Bell 2003, 136). It is possible that Yagara, like Badjala and Yugambeh-Bandjalang, requires case agreement on adjectives that modify a case-marked noun. The text collection contains too few relevant examples to indicate which elements in a noun phrase (other than the head noun) are required to have case marking.

The same set of cases found on common nouns and proper nouns, as shown in Table 1.12, also occur on pronouns (see 1.5.10) and interrogatives (see 1.5.13), with minor differences in form.

1.5.3. Plural marking

Plural marking of any kind occurs only on nouns in the text collections. On some nouns, plurality is indicated by reduplication, as noted in Section 1.5.5. More typically, plurality is indicated with the suffix *-jin*, as in *malara-jin* 'men'. This marker is not obligatory and plurals are usually not overtly marked. The plural marker occurs inside case marking, as in *malara-jin-du* 'man-PL-ERG' or *dagai-jin-na* 'white.man-PL-ACC'; but outside derivation, as in *wali-bany-jin* 'bad-INCH-PL; blind people'. The plural *-jin* may indicate a wide range of quantities, from the small but indeterminate number of pig-keepers in (23), to everything in existence in (24). The suffix is not limited to human referents, though (24) is the only example in the texts that includes inanimate referents.

(23) dagai-**jin**   biing-biing   nyundal-dany
      white.man-**PL**   pig   keep.animals-RNP
      The pig-keeping men
      Duggatin pigpig inēlta

      nyigiran   Miyanjin-di   ngambila   yaa-ri
      run   Brisbane-LOC   all   say-PST
      run to the city; they told everything.
      Īgeren mientjinti; ŋambilla yari. (Ridley 1875)

(24) mumbal   ngambila=bu   nana-**jin**   yaga-ri
      thunder   all=EMPH   thing-**PL**   make-PST
      God made everything.
      Mūmbāl ŋāmbillebu nunāntjin yugāri. (Ridley 1875)

In addition to the plural *-jin*, Yagara has two other nominal suffixes indicating quantity. Of these, *-bajagan* indicates a smaller number than *-jin*, and *-jangil* indicates a larger number. Both of these suffixes are mentioned only by Lauterer (1891, 1895). Lauterer (1895, 619) defines *-bajagan* as 'more than one', *-jin* as 'many' and *-jangil* as 'plenty'. Later on, he claims that *-jangil* is appropriate for numbers 'over five' (1895, 621). However, other sources show that *-jin* may be used for quantities greater than five, as in (24).

All three morphemes appear to be suffixes, rather than quantifiers such as *milin* 'many' or *bula* 'both'. Quantifiers typically precede the nouns they modify (see 1.5.8), whereas *-bajagan*, *-jin* and *-jangil* always follow nouns, as in Lauterer's examples with *bing* 'father', *bingpas'agan (bing-bajagan)*, *bingds'in (bing-jin)* and *bingds'angil (bing-jangil)* (1895, 619).

With the available data, it is impossible to conclude whether *-bajagan* is a dual or a paucal. Lauterer's definition of *-bajagan* as 'more than one' rather than 'two' suggests a paucal, however.

The suffix *-jangil*, which indicates more referents than the plural *-jin*, must be considered a type of greater plural. The suffix *-jangil* could be specifically a 'global plural', as in the Arandic language Kaytetye (Corbett 2000, 33), which indicates all members of a category. Holmer (1983, 398) claims that *-jin* indicates 'some', which suggests that *-jangil* may mean 'all'. However, the plural *-jin* can unambiguously mean 'all', as in (24), which makes a global plural interpretation of *-jangil* less probable. More likely, *-jangil* fulfils a different function of greater plurals, which is to signal an unexpectedly high number of referents. On this interpretation, *bing-jangil* might be roughly translated as 'a whole lot of fathers' or 'heaps of fathers'.

Greater plurals, also called 'plurals of abundance', do not seem particularly common in the world's languages. However, they are found in several languages besides the Kaytetye language mentioned above (Corbett 2000, 33), including Syrian Arabic (Cowell 1964, 369); Bangun and Fula, two Niger-Kordofanian languages (Corbett 2000, 31); and Hamer, a South Omotic language (Corbett 2000, 32).

1.5.4. Derivational suffixes

Derivational suffixes change the meaning, and often the part of speech, of the stems they attach to. Most derivational suffixes in Yagara take a nominal stem (a noun or sometimes an adjective), though a few are found on verbs.

Yagara suffixes are agglutinative, so they can combine in long sequences with each suffix remaining recognisable and unchanged (except when affected by the phonological rules in Section 1.3.2). Though inflectional suffixes are limited in which suffixes may follow others (see Sections 1.5.2, 1.5.3 and 1.6.2), derivational suffixes' only requirement is that they attach to a stem of a particular grammatical category.

Derivational suffixes are summarised in Table 1.13. In the second column of the table, the first abbreviation (N, etc.) indicates the type of stem the suffix attaches to. If the suffix apparently takes any sort of stem, this is indicated by 'X'. This designation is followed by an arrow and another abbreviation noting the sort of stem that results. For example, 'X → N' means that the suffix can attach to any stem type but results in a noun.

Table 1.13: Derivational affixes.

Derivational suffix	Grammatical categories of stem (before suffix is added) and word (after suffix is added)	Approximate meaning (where 'X' stands for the meaning of the stem)	Abbreviation (if used in Texts)
-ba	N → N	'place of X'	–
-ban	N → N	'product of X'	–
-bany	Adj/N → V	'be or become X'	INCH
-bila	Adj/N → V	'state typified by X'	STATE
-bin	N → N	'place of X'; -bin is also in plant names	–
-bira	N → N	'people of X'	–
-gaba	N → N	'item(s) for X'	ITEM
-gali	X → Adj/N	'very X'; 'person who is very X'	VERY
-gan	X → N	'characterised by X'	CHARACT
-gan/-gin	N → N	'female X'	F
-wal/-bal/-bul	X → N	'those who say X'	–

Source: Authors' summary, based on the source texts.

Descriptions and examples of each of the suffixes in Table 1.13 are listed below.

-ba

The best-known Yagara suffix might be -ba 'place of X'. This suffix is found in many present-day placenames, such as *Gurilba* 'Kurilpa; West End; place of rats', from *guril* 'water rat' and -ba 'place of X', or *Bulimba* 'Bulimba; place of peewees', from *bulim* 'peewee' and -ba 'place of X'. This suffix is probably related to the locative suffix -bah in Yugambeh-Bandjalang (Sharpe 1998, 35), which is also frequent in placenames.

-ban

The suffix -*ban* 'product of X' attaches to nouns, and results in a noun. It indicates an object or substance that is made from the referent of the stem. A headband made of the *bara* vine is a *baraban* 'product of the vine', for example, and milk is *ngamuban* 'product of the breast'.

-bany

The inchoative suffix -*bany* 'become X' indicates the onset of a state. The suffix attaches to both nouns and adjectives and results in a verb, as in (25)–(26). In (25), it changes *jan.gali* 'very wet' into the verb *jan.galibany* 'become very wet'.

(25) jan-gali-**bany**
      wet-VERY-**INCH**
      I've become thoroughly wet.
      Jungul-pun. 'I'm a wet fellow.' (Hardcastle 1946–7)

In (26), the suffix -*bany* changes the noun *dagai* 'white man' into the verb *dagaibany* 'become a white man'.

(26) ngunyal   dagai-**bany**
      3SG.NOM   white.man-**INCH**
      He became a white man
      Wunnal duggai punni (Ridley 1875)

-bila

The verbalising suffix -*bila* 'state typified by X' indicates that the subject is afflicted, infested or typified by the referent(s) of the suffixed noun, as in (27)–(28). In (27), the suffix forms the verb *banybila* 'be sick' from the adjective *bany* 'sick'.

(27) jundal   bany-**bila**
      woman   be.sick-**STATE**
      A woman was sick;
      Jūndāl paiïmbila; (Ridley 1875)

In (28), the suffix *-bila* makes a verb *garang-garangbila* 'wear clothes' from the noun *garang-garang* 'clothes'.

(28) garang-garang-**bila**
clothes-**STATE**
He is wearing clothes,
geraŋ geraŋ pilla, (Ridley 1875)

-bin

The suffix *-bin* resembles *-ba* in that it appears in placenames. For example, it is found in *Jin.gilingbin* 'Bulimba ferry', from *jin.gilinggan* 'willie wagtail', or *Murumurulbin* 'ibis place (sandbank below Hamilton)' from *murumurul* 'ibis'.

Another apparent suffix *-bin* is common in the names of plants, as in *dagabin* 'grass tree' and *durbin* 'bracken fern', for example.

-bira

A few names for Aboriginal groups and placenames incorporate the suffix *-bira*, meaning 'people of' or 'place of'. The suffix does not seem productive. It is found in *Winyambira* 'people of the soldier crab' and in five group names with stems of unknown meanings.

-gaba

Terms for tools and clothing often incorporate the suffix *-gaba* 'item(s) for X'. For example, *magulgaba* 'hat' consists of *magul* 'head' and *-gaba* and could be glossed as 'item for the head'. The suffix *-gaba* occurs in several lexical innovations for European items, as in *biigigaba* 'thing for the sun; clock'.

In two examples, *-gaba* apparently has the form *-ba*. In Yugambeh the cognate suffix *-gubi* 'pertaining to' is frequently shortened to *-bi* or *-ba* (Sharpe 1998, 39), and intervocalic /g/ in Yagara is frequently reduced (see 1.3.2), so this alternation seems plausible. This usage of *-ba* occurs in *bibaba* 'waistcoat' and *wanganba* 'traditional upper-body garment'. The usage may however involve a distinct morpheme *ba* related to upper-body garments.

-gali

Hardcastle glosses the suffix *-gali* as an adverb, *kully* 'very'. The morpheme is most common in the word *milin.gali* 'very many' as in (29). When the suffix occurs on nouns, the resultant meaning is not always predictable from that of the noun stem, as in *digirgali* 'big eater' from *digir* 'belly', or *gingali* 'little girl' from *gin* 'girl; woman'. The suffix also occurs on verbs (see 1.6.2).

(29) biing-biing   milin-**gali**   bibu-di   da-ma-nya
     pig   many-**VERY**   hill-LOC   eat-CAUS-PRS
     Many pigs are feeding on the hillside.
     Pigpig millenkolle bippudi tanmunna. (Ridley 1875)

-gan

The suffix *-gan* takes a nominal as input and produces a noun, and is found in *nyanggagan* 'summer' and *yigilgan* 'winter', which are derived from *nyangga* 'hot' and *yigil* 'cold' respectively. Many animal names end in *-gan*, which suggests that these nouns are derived from adjectives that are not otherwise attested; *jin.gilinggan* 'willie wagtail' is one such example. The suffix is also present in *gujalgan* 'mischief' which comes from *gujal* 'gammon'. In one instance, *-gan* appears to attach to a verb stem (see 1.6.3).

-gan/-gin

The *-gan/-gin* suffix attaches to a noun, results in a noun, and indicates a female. The suffix is shared by surrounding languages (*-gan* in Duuŋidjawu [Kite and Wurm 2004, 36] and *-gan* or *-gunn* [/gʌn/] in Yugambeh [Sharpe 2020, 38; Kombumerri Corporation for Culture 2001, 18]). It seems much more productive in Yugambeh than in Yagara, for example, so it may be a borrowing. In Yagara it is found mainly in kinship and moiety terms, as in *Bundagan* 'female member of the Bunda section group' or *nyaringgan* 'female offspring; daughter'.

-wal/-bal/-bul

The various allomorphs of a suffix that appears on group names, *-wal,* *-bal* and *-bul,* seem to be lexicalised as part of language and group names such as *Yagarabal* 'Yagara speakers' and *Jandaiwal* 'Jandai speakers'. These group names can often be analysed as comprising a word that typifies the language spoken by the group, usually the word for 'no', followed by *wal-/bal/-bul*. This is the case for *Yagarabal* and *Jandaiwal*, which indicate people who say *yagara* 'no' and *jandai* 'no', respectively. Though this suffix usually attaches to interjections meaning 'no', it may attach to other parts of speech.

For example, Watson (1943, 5) claims that *Durubal* 'Turrbal people' comes from the noun *darau* 'loose stones' due to the 'geological nature of the Brisbane area' for which the Durubal are the traditional caretakers.

1.5.5. Reduplication

Nouns frequently reduplicate in Yagara, as do adjectives and at least one verb. All reduplication is complete reduplication and generally involves an identical base and reduplicant. Nonetheless, reduplicated words are subject to the deletion rules described in Section 1.3.2. For example, *nyamal-nyamal* 'children' becomes /ɲama-ɲamal/ instead of /ɲamal-ɲamal/ because /l/ disappears before /ɲ/ following the rule in Section 1.3.2. Reduplication can occur inside of derivational suffixes, as in the placename *Juruny-Juruny-ba* 'place of eels', derived from *juruny-juruny* 'eels'.

Reduplication of nouns usually indicates plurality and/or diminution. Reduplication seems particularly frequent when the referent is both small and plural, as in *gin* 'girl' and *gin-gin* 'little girls'; or *gajal* 'leaf' and *gajal-gajal* 'leaves'.

A substantial minority of animal and plant names involve reduplication, as in *diluny-diluny* 'rosella parrot' or *yugai-yugai* 'fern-like herb'. However, many reduplicated names are found both with and without reduplication, as in *yugu (-yugu)* 'pike' and *jin.giri (-jin.giri)* 'willie wagtail'. This suggests that the reduplication in many animal and plant names indicates plurality and/or smallness. On the other hand, some animal names so seem to be inherently reduplicated, as in *muga-muga* 'spider', *muri-muri* 'butterfly' or *biigi-biigi* 'regent bowerbird' (the regent bowerbird is named for the sun [*biigi*] because it has bright yellow feathers). All inherently reduplicated forms denote small species. Reduplication indicates diminution in the neighbouring language Duuŋidjawu, which additionally has inherently reduplicated animal names (Kite and Wurm 2004, 49).

The names of games typically are reduplications, as in *bara-bara* 'ball-ball; ball game' or *muruny-muruny* 'stick-stick; throwing sticks game', in which the base form indicates the toy used in the game. This trend is compatible with the diminutive meaning of reduplication described above, plus a metonymy extending the term for the toy to the game that involves the toy.

The colour term *gawan-gawan* 'red' is clearly derived from *gawan* 'blood', following an apparently productive pattern for colour naming.

Adjectival reduplication indicates intensity, as in (30):

(30) marumba   marumba
      good   good
      Very good
      marumba marumba (Lauterer 1895)

There is one example of a verb formed by reduplicating a noun. This is *mil-mil* 'eye-eye; have a look'.

1.5.6. Compounding

Yagara has few compounds overall. Endocentric compounds (in which one element designates the type of referent the compound denotes) with two nouns are the most frequent. These include *muru-miir* 'nose hole; nostril', *mugara-mulu* 'thunder stone; hailstone', or *nyugum-mulu* 'bucket stone'. Noun-adjective endocentric compounds are also possible, as in *bina-wali* 'ear-bad; deaf'. In all N-N and most N-Adj endocentric compounds, the final noun or adjective is the head. One N-Adj compound, *dabil-baan* 'water-salt; saltwater', seems to have the initial noun as the head. In the few V-N compounds in the data, the verb seems to be the head. This is apparent in *banman-gilin* 'pluck-fingernail; pick out as if with the fingernails' and *nyan-jina* 'go-foot; go on foot'.

There are two examples of exocentric compounds in the corpus (in which the resultant meaning is not obviously a subtype of the meaning of either element in the compound): *biigi-biribi* 'sun-little; evening'; and *muru-guji* 'nose-red', which refers to the black swan due to the bird's bright red beak.

1.5.7. Adjectives

The limited data in the text corpus does not allow us to state with confidence whether adjectives and nouns are different grammatical categories in Yagara. Many words can be used with both functions. Here, nominals are considered adjectives when they modify another nominal, as in (31), or when they occur as predicates in verbless sentences (see 1.9.1) as in (32).

(31) ngunyali   baguur   **jubui**   galga-ri
      3PL.NOM   tree   **straight** cut-PST
      They cut a straight tree;
      Wunnale bāgūr tūbuī kulkurri; (Ridley 1875)

(32) ngaja   yagar   **marumba**
      1SG.NOM   not   **good**
      I am not good;
      ŋgutta yugar murrumba; (Ridley 1875)

There is only one possible example in the texts of an NP with case that is modified by an adjective, shown in (33). In this example, if *jubui-di bibu-di* 'straight-LOC hill-LOC' is analysed as an NP in which *jubui-di* modifies *bibu-di*, then both the noun and modifying adjective bear case marking. However, *jubui-di* could also be analysed as a location word (see 1.5.9).

(33) **jubui-di**   bibu-di
      straight-LOC   hill-LOC
      straight down the hill
      tubburti bipudi (Ridley 1875)

There are no other potential examples of case-marked nouns modified by adjectives, so it cannot be determined whether case agreement on adjectives was optional or obligatory.

Based on example (34), adjectives could have a comparative meaning when used with *ngi* 'than':

(34) marumba   ngaja   **ngi**   nginda
      good   1SG.NOM   **than**   2SG.NOM
      I'm better than you.
      Marumban gaoia ngigninte. (Lauterer 1895)

Adjectives could be intensified by reduplication (see 1.5.5) or through the addition of another modifier such as *wali* 'bad, badly' as in (35) or *gurumba* 'big, greatly' as in (36).

(35) **wali**   wagara
      bad   angry
      Very angry.
      Waldee wuggera. (Hardcastle 1946–7)

(36) barany   nguun   **gurumba**   ngaja
      now   hot   **greatly**   1SG.NOM
      Very hot now, I (think)
      Birran Norn Kooroomba Nutchair (Hardcastle 1946–7)

1.5.8. Quantifiers

Quantifiers indicate the number or amount of something. These include words such as *bula* 'two, both, the two of them'; *milin* 'many'; *ngambila* 'all, everyone', and so forth.

In Yagara, quantifiers may modify a following noun. In (37), for example, *ngambila* 'all' modifies *biing-biing* 'pig'.

(37) barany **ngambila** biing-biing jubuiban nyigiran
      then   **all**   pig   quickly   run
      then all the pigs quickly run
      berren ŋamille pigpig tubbōrpun īgēren (Ridley 1875)

Quantifiers may also be used without a noun when the quantified referent is clear from context. In (38), for example, it is apparent that *ngambila* 'all' refers to 'all the information' or 'the whole story'.

(38) dagai-jin   imanuwal-ba-di   nyinyi-du
      white.man-PL   Immanuel-ABL-LOC   dwell-ATEL
      The white men staying with Immanuel
      Duggatin Immanuelpuddi ŋīnēdo

      yaa-ri   **ngambila**
      say-PST   **all**
      tell the whole story.
      Yari ŋāmbilla. (Ridley 1875)

1.5.9. Location and time words

The Yagara texts include numerous expressions that indicate time or location. These words, such as *barany* 'now, soon', may occur anywhere in a sentence, as (39)–(41) illustrate.

(39) ngaja   yaga-ri   **barany**
      1SG.NOM   do-PST   **now**
      I've finished (it) now.
      Ngutta yuggari berren. (Ridley 1875)

(40) guba-nya   nginda   ngaja   **barany**   balgal-biny
      go.on-PRES   2SG.NOM   1SG.NOM   **soon**   come-BACK
      You're going ahead, I'm coming back soon.
      Cobana-inter, utcha baro balgalpin. (Watkins and Hamilton 1887)

(41) **barany**   nguun   gurumba   ngaja
      now   hot   greatly   1SG.NOM
      Very hot now, I (think)
      Birran Norn Kooroomba Nutchair (Hardcastle 1946–7)

Location and time words such as *barany* take no suffixes. However, additional
words that describe time and place may be formed through the addition of
case endings such as -*bu*, which expresses a duration as in (42), or -*di*, which
indicates a location, as in (43).

(42) imanuwal   **ngunu-bu**   ganggir   dany-dunga
      Immanuel   **night-DUR**   dead   lie-IPFV
      That night Immanuel lay dead;
      Imanuel ŋūnūmbo kungīr daieduŋa; (Ridley 1875)

(43) barany   ngunyal   **biram-di**   nyinyi-nya
      now   3SG.NOM   **sky-LOC**   dwell-PRS
      Now he lives in the sky.
      Berren Wunnal birradi ŋinnenna. (Ridley 1875)

1.5.10. Pronouns

Yagara pronouns distinguish three 'persons': first person (*I, me* in English);
second person (*you* in English); and third person (*he, she*, etc. in English).
Two types of plurality are distinguished in the first- and second-person
paradigms. These are labelled 'dual' and 'plural' in Table 1.14 and
throughout the texts in Part 3, though it will be argued that these labels
are a simplification. Person and number will be abbreviated as '1, 2 and
3' and 'SG, DU and PL' respectively, such that 'first-person singular' is
abbreviated '1SG'.

Yagara pronouns are also divided into cases that show their grammatical role in the sentence. Pronouns may take any of the cases found on nouns (discussed in 1.5.2 and listed in Table 1.14). In addition, pronouns demonstrate a case not found on nouns in the text corpus, here called dative (abbreviated DAT). Presumably this case is possible on nouns, but simply did not occur on any nouns in the texts. The dative case mainly marks recipients as in (44), and occasionally beneficiaries as in (45).

(44) **ngari**   biribi   wujan
      1SG.DAT   little   give
      Give me a little
      Ngare perpa oodar (Lang 1846).

(45) dalbany-la   **ngari**   gimuman
      jump-OBLG   **1SG.DAT**   friend
      Jump over for me, friends
      Dulpaiila ngari kimmoman (Petrie 1904)

There is no grammatical gender in Yagara, though this is present in adjacent Yugambeh-Bandjalang (Sharpe 1998, 24). There does not seem to be a distinction between inclusive *we* (meaning 'you and I') and exclusive *we* (meaning 'us but not you'), though the dual *ngaliny* always means specifically 'you and I' in the texts. There are no instances in the texts of pronouns referring to inanimate objects. For example, *ngunyal* '3SG.NOM' occurs in contexts where it could be translated as English *he* or *she*, but never *it*.

First- and second-person singular pronouns forms are well-attested across several sources. However, not all pronouns are equally well documented. The pronoun forms in Table 1.14 are based mainly on Ridley (1875), but are informed by the other sources that included pronouns, as indicated by the original source spellings beneath each pronoun in the table.

Pronominal cases follow a so-called 'accusative' pattern, in that the subjects of transitive and intransitive sentences share one form (the nominative), whereas the objects of transitives have a different form (the accusative). The 'accusative' pattern is often contrasted with an 'ergative' one, in which the subjects of transitive sentences have ergative marking.

Table 1.14: Yagara pronouns.

	Nominative	Accusative	Dative	Possessive	Examples of other cases
1SG	**ngaja** atu (Bl); nutchair (Ha); ŋaḍa (H); atta (E); ngutta, atta (Ja); ngacia 'I', ngaoia, gaoia (L); utter, ngutter (Lg); gnatcha, ngalta, gnatja, gnatya (M); ngatta (P); yutta, ŋutta, atta (R); atta (T); atcha, utcha (W); nutchair (We); ngaja (Wu)	**ngana** mi 'me' (Bl); nanee (H); ana (Lg); nganna (M); ŋunna (R)	**ngari** ŋari (H); naree (Ha); ngrai (L); ngari (P); ŋurri (R); naree (W); nuru (We)	**ngariba** ariba (E); ŋariba, ŋariwa, ŋarijuba (H); ariba (Ja); ngaciaganowa 'my' (L); ngarebah, narebah (Lg); gnareeba, yahliebaddie (M); ngariwar (N); ŋurriba (R); nurryuba (We)	**ngaja-ba-di** (1SG-ABL-LOC) ŋuttabuddi (R)
2SG	**nginda** indo, neen (Bl); ŋintay (D); ŋintair (Ha); ŋinda (H); inta (E); ēēn (G); inta 'thou', ŋginta, inda 'you' (Ja); nginte 'thou (boy)', nginta, gninte, nginto (L); ngidna, nginter, inter (Lg); guttay, intay, inta, yinta (M); ŋinda, ŋinta, inda 'thou' (R); ngintia 'they two', inta 'thou' (T); inta, inter (W); inta, gninta (Wa); inter (We)	**ngina** inna, nanee (Ha); ine (W)	**nginu** gninoo (M); ŋinnu (R)	**nginuba** yeen, innoung (Bl); enuba (E); enuba (Ja); ngintenganowa 'thy', nguwa, ngowo (L); nenoobah, yanobah 'yours' (Lg); yinoóba, inooba (M); ŋinnuba (R)	**nginda-ba** (2SG-ABL) ŋintaba (R) **nginda-ba-di** (2SG-ABL-LOC) ŋintapuddi (R)
3SG	**ngunyal (nom.)** ullurn (Ha); wunnál (Ja); ngalam 'he' (L); gnoonyal (M); unda, wunnal (R); ungda 'he' (T) **ngunyalu (erg.)** ŋonloo (Lg); wunnalu, wunyalu, wuunyalu (R)	**ngunyana** nudna 'him' (Lg); wunnana (R)	**ngunyanu** wunnaun, wunnanu (R)	**ngunyanuba** wonanabah (Lg); wunnanūbu, wūnnanūba, wunnanuba (R)	**ngunyal-ba-di** (3SG-ABL-LOC) wunnalpuddi (R)

64

	Nominative	Accusative	Dative	Possessive	Examples of other cases
1DU	**ngaliny** *linda, nalinda, nealinda 'we or you & I' (Lg); ngadli 'we' (L); gnalleen, gnahleen (M); ŋullin 'you and I', ŋulle 'we' (R); allin 'we two' (T)*	**ngalinyana** *yalunga 'me' (Lg); ŋulleŋunna, ŋullin. ga (R)*	**ngalinyanu** *ŋulleŋunnu (R)*	–	–
1PL	**ngalba** *nulpa (Ha); alpa (M); ŋulpa (R); nhamba 'we' (T)*	**ngalbana** *ŋulpāna (R)*	**ngalbanu** *ŋulpunna (R)*	**ngalbanuba** *ngalpanganowa (L)*	–
2DU	**ngilbang** *ngilpung 'you two' (Lg); ilpūnn, ilpūn 'ye two' (R); inungei 'you two' (T)*	–	–	–	–
2PL	**ngilbula** *ngilpula 'thou (girl); (L); ŋilpūlla 'ye' (R); nuba 'ye' (T)*	**ngilbulana** *ilpūllāna, ilpullana (R)*	–	–	–
3PL	**ngunyali** *wunnale (R); layim 'they' (L)*	**ngunyalina** *wunnālina, wunnalina (R)*	–	**ngunyalinuba** *wonanewibah (Lg)*	**ngunyali-ba-nga** (3PL-ABL-ALL) *ŋulle buggā (R)*

Source: Authors' summary: sources are listed by abbreviation throughout table, see 'Abbreviations and conventions' for further details.

Despite the general accusative pattern in Yagara pronouns, Ridley (1875) five times records an ergative form *ngunyalu*, as shown in (46)–(50). In (46) and (47), *ngunyalu* marks a subject that differs from that of the previous sentence. In these examples, the pronoun *ngunyalu* is preceded or followed by the name Immanuel, to clarify who the new subject is.

(46)

yaa-ri	ngaja	nginda-ba-di	nyinyi
say-PST	1SG.NOM	2SG-ABL-LOC	dwell

He said, 'I'm staying with you.'
yari, 'ŋutta ŋintapuddi ŋinne.'

imanuwal	**ngunyalu**	yaa-ri
Immanuel	**3SG.ERG**	say-PST

Immanuel, he said, …
Immanuel wunnalu yari, … (Ridley 1875)

(47)

ngunyal	nyan-dunga	nga
3SG.NOM	travel-IPFV	and

He was travelling and
Wunnal yeatuŋa, ŋa

dagai-jin	ngambila=bu	yaa-ri	daun	gurumba
white.man-PL	all=EMPH	talk-PST	thing	great

told the white men all the great things
duggatin ŋambillabayari toŭn kurumba

ngunyalu	imanuwal	yaga-ri
3SG.ERG	Immanuel	do-PST

he, Immanuel, did.
wunnalu Immanuel yugari. (Ridley 1875)

Example (48) consists of the two concluding sentences of Ridley's Resurrection (see Section 3.4). In the second sentence, the ergative-marked subject is not new, though it is transitive instead of intransitive as in the previous sentence.

(48)

barany	ngunyal	biram-di	nyinyi-nya
now	3SG.NOM	sky-LOC	dwell-PRS

Now he lives in the sky.
berren Wunnal birradi ŋinnenna.

ngunyalu	ngalbana	nyaa-nya
3SG.ERG	1PL.ACC	see-PRS

He sees us.

Wunnalu ŋulpāna nanna. (Ridley 1875)

Ridley lists examples (49) and (50) without context (see 3.3.3), so here the ergative seems to simply emphasise the agency of the subject.

(49)   **ngunyalu**   yaraman   balga-ri
        3SG.ERG   horse   bring-PST
        He brought the horse.
        Wūnyalu yaraman bulkaiari. (Ridley 1875)

(50)   **ngunyalu**   nyaring   waya-ri
        3SG.ERG   son   send-PST
        He sent his son.
        Wunyalu nurriŋ waiari. (Ridley 1875)

The *ngunyal/ngunyalu* alternation can be compared with the alternation between bare nouns and nouns suffixed by *-du* (see section 1.5.2). The ergative forms in both alternations are rare in the texts.

In the first- and second-person paradigms, there are clearly two sets of non-singular forms. Though these are here labelled 'dual' and 'plural' for convenience, they in fact appear to distinguish a plural and a greater plural in the first person. There are fewer examples of second-person 'dual' and 'plural' pronouns than of first-person forms, so it can be concluded only that the 'dual' marks a smaller number than the 'plural' in the second person.

There are seventeen examples of the 'dual' first person across the texts, and three examples of the 'plural', all in Ridley (1875). The 'dual' *ngaliny* can refer to only a few referents, as in (51), up to the *gurumba milin milin* 'very many many' demons speaking in (52).

(51)   wi   **ngaliny**   nyan-ba   da-li-ba
        hey   **1DU.NOM**   go-SBJV   drink-SBJV
        Hey, let's go have a drink.
        Wee gnahleen yieeba jaleeba. (Meston 1986a)

(52) ngambila   magui   muyan
     all   devil   beseech
     All the demons beg,
     Ŋāmbille maguï muïan,

     wana   **ngalinyana**   waya-ba   wungga
     do.not   **1DU.ACC**   send-SBJV   hole
     'Don't send us into the pit!'
     'Wunna ŋulleŋunna waialta wunku.' (Ridley 1875)

All three instances of the first-person 'plural' refer to all of humankind everywhere, as in (53). This is consistent with an interpretation as a greater plural, along the lines of the greater plural suffix *-jangil* (see section 1.5.3).

(53) ngunyal   baluny   **ngalbanu**
     3SG.NOM   die   **1PL.DAT**
     he died for us.
     wunnal bāllūn ŋulpunna. (Ridley 1875)

The second-person forms may also designate a plural versus a greater plural, but they more obviously seem to distinguish two addressees from multiple addressees. There are four instances of the 'dual', three of which are used by God addressing Adam and Eve, as in (54). The remaining dual, (55), also specifies two people.

(54) **ngilbang**   bulabu   baluny
     2DU.NOM   both   die
     You both will die.
     Ilpūŋ budelabu balluï. (Ridley 1875)

(55) **ngilbang**   nya-ra
     2DU.NOM   go-DEST
     You two go.
     Ngilpung yera (Lang 1846)

The 'plural' second person oddly has the nominative form *ngilbula*, which appears to include the morpheme *bula* 'two'. This suggests it arose from a dual. However, it can be used for more than two referents, as when Ridley addresses a crowd of hundreds in (56).

(56) ngaja   **ngilbulana**   yaa-li
     1SG.NOM   **2PL.ACC**   say-FUT
     I'll talk to you
     ŋutta ilpūllāna yāli (Ridley 1875)

Of course, the 'duals' in (54)–(55) could be plurals that happen to involve two addressees, and the 'plural' in (56) could be a greater plural. If this were the case, then the uses of the 'dual' and 'plural' documented for the second-person paradigm would be analogous to those found for the first-person paradigm. However, it is entirely possible that both the first- and second-person paradigms included a dual or paucal, a plural, and a greater plural, and there is simply no evidence of one of these three forms in the texts. The nominal suffixes show a three-way number distinction (see 1.5.3), so a similar three-way distinction would not be unexpected in the pronoun system.

Several consultants are recorded as suggesting the additional forms *ngai* for 'I' and *ngin* for singular 'you'. These terms occur in no sentences or texts, however, and therefore seem not to have been in common usage at the time the sentences and texts were elicited. One of Holmer's consultants cites the forms *ŋai* 'I' and *ŋin* 'you' (1983, 392). Ridley also lists the forms *ŋāi, ai* and *ŋaia* for 'I', though he never includes these forms in his texts. Blackman lists both *indo* and *neen* as 'you' (1900, 60). Finally, Bannister (1986) analyses the first- and second-person nominative forms in Table 1.15 as ergative forms, and gives the nominative forms of these pronouns as *ngai* and *ngin*. In Guwar, Gabi-Gabi and Duuŋidjawu, *ngai* and *ngin* are the nominative first-person and second-person forms (Bannister 1982; Mathew 1910; Kite and Wurm 2004). Yagara speakers would have been aware of these forms due to their ubiquity in surrounding languages, but do not appear to have used the forms when speaking Yagara.

Relatively few pronouns occur in cases other than the nominative, accusative, dative and possessive. Those that appear, however, are completely regular and take the same case suffixes found on nouns. For example, the 3SG.ABL is *ngunyalba* 'from him', which is a compositional combination of the 3SG root *ngunyal* and the ablative suffix *-ba*.

However, it should be noted that the final *l* on the third-person singular base form *ngunyal* disappears before *n* and *ny*, following the general rule formulated in Section 1.3.2. As a result, the base form *ngunyal* with the possessive *-nuba* lacks an *l* (*ngunyanuba*) but *ngunyal* with the ablative *-ba* retains it (*ngunyalba*).

Based on (57) below, it seems that case marking occurs on possessive pronouns in agreement with a head noun. The only two instances of a possessed noun with case both appear in the sentence in (57), and in both, case is marked on the possessive pronoun as well as the noun.

(57)   gaa   jundal   jirban   jirban-**di**   ngariba-**di**
        that.MED woman   bone   bone-**LOC**   1SG.POSS-**LOC**
        'This woman is bone of my bone,
        'Ka jundal tjirben tjirbenti ŋurribāti,

        nga   baigal-baigal   baigal-baigal-**di**   ngariba-**di**
        and   flesh   flesh-**LOC**   1SG.POSS-**LOC**
        and flesh of my flesh:
        ŋa paigulpaigul paigulpaigulti ŋurribāti: (Ridley 1875)

1.5.11. Adnominal demonstratives

There is insufficient evidence in the texts to determine whether Yagara distinguishes two degrees of distance in its demonstrative system, as in Duuŋidjawu and Badjala (Kite and Wurm 2004, 55–56; Bell 2003, 76), or three degrees, as in Yugambeh (Sharpe 1998, 29–30). The proximal and distal are well documented both for adnominal and adverbial demonstratives. However, in both systems, there is an additional term that is less well documented, which could represent a medial or other function.

The grammar section in Ridley (1875) identifies two adnominal demonstratives, *danga* 'this' and *ngaranga* 'that'. However, the single instance of *ngaranga* in Ridley (1875) is not obviously a demonstrative, and may instead mean 'there is/was'. On the other hand, the distal demonstrative *diranga* occurs in Ridley (1875) and Meston (1986a). Another demonstrative with a less clear function, *gaa*, occurs twice in Ridley (1875).

Table 1.15 lists the adnominal demonstratives as used in the texts in Ridley (1875). These demonstratives always occur before a noun, as in *danga-na baguur-na* 'that-ACC tree-ACC'.

Table 1.15: Yagara adnominal demonstratives.

Degree of distance	Adnominal demonstrative
Proximal (near to speaker)	*diranga*
Medial or other function	*gaa*
Distal (far from speaker and hearer)	*danga*

Source: Authors' summary of Ridley (1875).

Adnominal demonstratives seem to optionally take case marking. Case marking always appears on a noun with a demonstrative, as in *diranga baguuru-na* 'this tree-ACC', and may optionally be suffixed to the demonstrative, as in *danga-na baguuru-na* 'that-ACC tree-ACC'.

A *proximal* demonstrative term generally refers to something physically close to the speaker. The adnominal *diranga* appears to be a proximal term, since in contexts such as (58) and (59) the referents introduced by *diranga* are close to the speakers. In (58), the speaker is currently located in the Country that they are referring to. And in (59), the speaker is presumably poised next to the tree they are about to cut.

(58)   garulban   ngaja   **diranga**   jar-di
      tired   1SG.NOM   **this.PROX**   Country-LOC
      I'm tired of being in this Country.
      Caroolcan gnatja teeran jargee. (Meston 1986a)

(59)   gau-Ø   ngaja   galga-li-ba   **diranga**   baguur
      stop-IMP   1SG.NOM   cut-FUT-SBJV **this.PROX**   tree
      Stop! I'm going to cut this tree.
      Kaahuu! Ngutta kulkulliba diranga bagur. (Ridley 1875)

A *distal* prototypically refers to something far from the speaker. In Ridley's version of Genesis (see 3.5), God describes to Adam and Eve the position of the Tree of Knowledge. The tree evidently is not visible to the speakers in this scene, or God would not need to explain where it is. After doing so, God makes the command in (60).

(60)   nginda   wana   **danga-na**   baguur-na da-la
      2SG.NOM   do.not **that.DIST-ACC** tree-ACC   eat-OBLG
      do not eat from that tree.
      inta wunna dungama bagurna tulla. (Ridley 1875)

Two instances of distal *danga* appear to be discourse deixis, in which *danga* refers to something previously mentioned in the conversation. In this usage, *danga* is not adnominal, but occurs without a noun. The other demonstratives are not found with this function. Both instances occur in (61).

(61) ngaja   garuba   yaa-li
     1SG.NOM   another   say-FUT
     I say to another,
     ŋutta kurruba yali,

     nginda   **danga**   yaga-li
     2SG.NOM   **that.DIST** do-FUT
     "You will do that!"
     ŋinta duŋa yuggali';

     barany   ngunyal   yaga-ri
     at.once   3SG.NOM   do-PST
     and at once he did.'
     berren wunnal yuggāri.'

     imanuwal   **danga**   bina
     Immanuel   **that.DIST** hear
     Immanuel hears that.
     Immanuel duŋa pīnaŋ. (Ridley 1875)

The texts provide only two examples of the demonstrative *gaa*, so it is difficult to determine the term's exact meaning. In both examples of *gaa*, the speaker is talking 'behind someone's back' – discussing one person while speaking to another. In both instances the exact spatial positions of the participants are unclear.

In Ridley's Genesis, when God has just created Eve and brought her to Adam, Adam speaks as in (62).

(62) **gaa**   jundal   jirban   jirban-di   ngariba-di
     that.MED woman   bone   bone-LOC   1SG.POSS-LOC
     'This woman is bone of my bone,
     'Ka jundal tjirben tjirbenti ŋurribāti, (Ridley 1875)

In (62), God is showing Eve to Adam for the first time, so God is plausibly adjacent to Eve or holding her for Adam to view. God and Adam are certainly talking about Eve as an uninvolved participant.

The relative distance between the speakers and referent is also open to interpretation in (63), in which Jesus, after speaking to the 'Commandant', apparently turns to a disciple and says the following:

(63) **gaa**   gamandan   ngana   winanga-nya
     that.MED Commandant   1SG.ACC   believe-PRS
     That Commandant believes me.'
     Kār Kommandant ŋunna wīnuŋunna.' (Ridley 1875)

It is not clear whether the disciple is nearer to the Commandant than Jesus. Again, Jesus and the disciple are speaking about someone who is present, but not an immediate participant in the exchange.

Ridley claims that the word *ngaranga* is a demonstrative on the basis of the usage in example (64). Note that *Miyanjin* 'Meeanjin; Brisbane' is used throughout Ridley (1875) as a generic word for 'city'.

(64) gabarnaum   Miyanjin   **ngaranga**   gamandan
     Capernaum   Brisbane   **there.is/was** Commandant
     Capernaum was a city. There was a Commandant,
     Kapernaŭm mīantjun; ŋuruŋa Kommandant:

Line (64) is near the beginning of the story paraphrased from Luke 7 and 8. It includes the first mention of the Commandant, who is a major character in the story that follows. It is difficult to identify the word's meaning on the basis of this single example, but it may have a role in introducing the new character.

1.5.12. Adverbial demonstratives

The adverbial demonstratives include the proximal *ngagam* and the distal *naam*. There is potentially a third adverbial demonstrative, *yugu*, which could be interpreted as a medial.

The proximal *ngagam* 'here' occurs in contexts such as (65) and (66), where it unambiguously indicates the speaker's current location. Though *ngagam* is often used to mean 'come here', as in (66), it can simply refer to the speaker's location, as in (65).

(65) nyan-ma-ba **ngagam**
go-CAUS-SBJV **here.PROX**
Let's go away from here.
Yanmerpa nahga. (Meston 1986a)

(66) **ngagam** ngaja yaa-li-ba ngina
here.PROX 1SG.NOM say-FUT-SBJV 2SG.ACC
Come here; I want to talk to you.
Gorgoy-Nutchair-Yarlivar Intair. (Hardcastle 1946–7)

In (67), the demonstrative seems to indicate a specific item or task at the speaker's location.

(67) **ngagam** nginda yaga-li-ba
here.PROX 2SG.NOM do-FUT-SBJV
Here, you do it.
Gorgoy Intair Yuggar Liviar. (Hardcastle 1946–7)

The distal demonstrative *naam,* on the other hand, unambiguously indicates a location away from the speaker, as in (68).

(68) **naam** nginda nya-ra-nya
there.DIST 2SG.NOM go-DEST-PRS
Go over there.
Nun Nair Yur-on-ner. (Hardcastle 1946–7)

In addition to the form *naam* 'there', Ridley (1875, 87) records a version with an even longer vowel, *naa–m* 'there (very far off)'. The extra-long vowel in *naa–m* metaphorically represents an extra-long distance, such as when an English speaker says *faaar away* instead of *far away*, and the length distinction is probably not lexical.

The adverbial demonstrative *yugu* occurs only once in the texts, shown in example (69).

(69) **yugu** dabingbila digi
there.MED policeman white.man
There, a policeman, a white man
jugu dabiŋbila, dege (Holmer 1983)

This sentence warns the hearer that a policeman is nearby. If the policeman is nearer to the hearer than the speaker (perhaps coming up behind them), or a medium distance from the speaker, then *yugu* may be a medial adverbial demonstrative. The adverbial demonstratives are shown in Table 1.16.

Table 1.16: Yagara adverbial demonstratives.

Degree of distance	Adverbial demonstrative
Proximal (near to speaker)	*ngagam*
Medial or other function	*yugu*
Distal (far from speaker and hearer)	*naam*

Source: Authors' summary of Ridley (1875), Hardcastle (1946–7), Holmer (1983) and Meston (1986a).

1.5.13. Interrogatives

The roots *ngan* 'who', *wanya* 'where' and *minya* 'what' occur with various case suffixes, as listed in Table 1.17, to form a variety of interrogatives. The roots *ngan, wanya* and *minya* probably are compatible with the full range of cases found on nouns listed in Table 1.12. For example, 'whose?' or 'for whom?' might be written *ngan-nuba* 'who-POSS', and 'from whom?' might be *ngan-ba* 'who-ABL'. In most interrogatives with case suffixes, the roots *wanya* 'where' and *minya* 'what' have the forms *wanyang* and *minyang*, the latter of which is identical to *minyang* 'what' in Yugambeh-Bandjalang (Sharpe 1998) and Guwar (Bannister 1982).

Table 1.17: Yagara interrogative pronouns.

English translation	Interrogative
Who? (nom.)	*ngan*
Who? (erg.)	*ngan-du* (who-ERG)
Whose? Belonging to whom?	*ngana-nuba* (who-POSS)
How?	*ngan.gu*
When?	*wanji*
Where?	*wanya*
To where?	*wanyang=gu* (where=PURP)
From where?	*wanyang-ba* (where-ABL)
What?	*minya*
What? (accusative)	*minya-na* (what-ACC)
How many?	*minyambu*

English translation	Interrogative
Why?	*minyang-di* (what-LOC)
At what? What is the matter?	*minyang=gu* (what=PURP)
Belonging to what? Of what?	*minyang-nuba* (what-POSS)

Source: Authors' summary, based on the source texts.

Interrogative pronouns generally occur at the start of a question, as in (70)–(71).

(70) **ngandu**　　ngina　　　yaa-ri
　　　who.ERG　2SG.ACC　say-PST
　　　Who told you?
　　　Ando ine yare? (Watkins and Hamilton 1887)

The ergative *ngan-du* 'who-ERG' is used for every interrogative subject of a transitive in the source texts, as in (70). However, interrogative subjects of intransitives always use the nominative form *ngan* 'who', as in (71).

(71) **ngan**　dungi-nya
　　　who　weep-PRS
　　　Who is crying?
　　　Arn Dunginna? (Hardcastle 1946–7)

The consistent use of the ergative for transitive subjects is unusual, compared with the low frequency of ergative *ngunyalu* '3SG.ERG' (see 1.5.10) or the ergative suffix *-du* on nouns (see 1.5.2). It is possible that the ergative interrogative pronoun was more frequent than other ergative pronouns or nouns.

1.6. Verbal morphology

1.6.1. Verbs

Based on the examples in the text collection, Yagara verbs have the following structure:

ROOT – (DERIVATION) – (INFLECTION) = (CLITICS)

Yagara verbs may have a series of several inflectional suffixes. These are overviewed in 1.6.2. Derivational suffixes on verbs, discussed in 1.6.3, are more straightforward. These consist only of the negation marker -*ra* and two of the suffixes that may also occur on nominals. Clitics are described in 1.8.

1.6.2. Verbal inflections

Verbal inflections are of several general types. First, there are suffixes that mark a subordinate or relative clause (here labelled 'subordination' suffixes). Next, there are suffixes that change the number of arguments that a verb requires ('valence' suffixes). Two suffixes elaborate on types of motion ('motion' suffixes); two indicate the structure of the events denoted by the verb ('aspect'); three designate tense ('tense'); and three mark mood ('mood').

The six types of inflection are summarised in Table 1.18. This section will discuss the suffixes of each type in turn.

Table 1.18: Verbal inflectional suffixes.

Type	Suffixes	Function	Position relative to other inflection in the corpus	Abbrev.
Subordination	-*ba*	T-relative/clause relativiser	Precedes Valence	-RTP
	-*dany*	NP-relative/NP relativiser	No co-occurrence	-RNP
Valence	-*li*	reflexive	After -RTP (-*ba*); precedes Tense	-REFL
	-*ma*	causative		-CAUS
Motion	-*ra*	indicates motion to a destination	Precedes Tense	-DEST
	-*biny*	indicates motion back the way one came	After -DEST (-*ra*)	-BACK
Aspect	-*du*	atelicity/unboundedness	No co-occurrence	-ATEL
	-*dunga*	imperfective		-IPFV
Tense	-*ri*	past	After -RTP (-*ba*), Motion and Valence; precedes Mood	-PST
	-*nya*	present		-PRS
	-*li*	future		-FUT
Mood	-*ba*	marks suggestions and intentions	After Tense and all other inflection	-SBJV
	-*la*	indicates obligation, 'shall'/'should'		-OBLG
	-Ø	imperative	No co-occurrence	-IMP

Source: Authors' summary, based on the source texts.

1.6.3. Subordination suffixes (-*dany* and -*ba*)

The subordination suffixes, when present, are closest to the verb stem and indicate that the verb is the head of a dependent clause. This may be either a relative clause modifying a noun within the main clause (-*dany*), or a subordinate clause with a temporal or causal relation to the main clause (-*ba*).

The relativiser -*dany* occurs on the head verb of a relative clause. In all examples in the texts, the relative clause immediately follows the main-clause noun that it modifies, as in (72)–(73). The clause could therefore be analysed as embedded in the NP, unlike in some Australian languages (Hale 1976). Relative clauses can modify nouns with any grammatical role in the main clause, and the nouns may have any grammatical role in the relative clause.

(72) dagai-jin   biing-biing   nyundal-**dany**
      white.man-PL   pig   keep.animals-**RNP**
      The pig-keeping men
      Duggatin pigpig inēlta

      nyigiran   Miyanjin-di   ngambila   yaa-ri
      run   Brisbane-LOC   all   say-PST
      run to the city; they told everything.
      igeren mientjinti; ŋambilla yari. (Ridley 1875)

(73) nyaa-nya   dagai-na   bany=gu   dany-**dany**
      see-PRS   white.man-ACC   sickness=PURP   lie-**RNP**
      He sees the man who is lying sick.
      nānna duggana paingo daīda (Ridley 1875)

There is a relativiser -*na* in the nearby language Yugambeh with a similar functional range to Yagara -*dany* (Sharpe 2020, 33).

The subordinator -*ba*, like -*dany*, occurs on the head verb of the dependent clause. A -*ba* clause precedes the main clause. The -*ba* clause may indicate simultaneity of the events in the two clauses, as in (74), or may signal that the event in the -*ba* clause immediately precedes that of the main clause, as in (75) and (76).

(74) ngunyal   jiga-**ba**-li   balga-ri
      3SG.NOM   shake-**RTP**-REFL   come-PST
      She shook as she came;
      wunnal jikkebele bulkurri; (Ridley 1875)

(75) barany   ngunyal   jirban   guda-di-ba   banman-**ba**
      then   3SG.NOM   bone   side-LOC-ABL   pluck-**RTP**
      Then, plucking a bone from the side
      Berren Wunnal tjirben kuttadiber pūnmānibēr

      junda-na   yaga-ri
      woman-ACC   make-PST
      he made woman.
      jūndāna yugāri. (Ridley 1875)

(76) ngunyal   nguru   bui
      3SG.NOM   spirit   breathe
      When he breathed spirit
      Wunnal ŋuru puï

      guri-**ba**-ma-ri   muru-di
      enter-**RTP**-CAUS-PST   nose-LOC
      into the nose,
      kurribunmurri murudi;

      barany   dagai   milbulbu-bany
      then   white.man   be.alive-INCH
      at once the white man came to life.
      berren duggai milbūlpūbun; (Ridley 1875)

Examples (74) and (76) additionally show that the suffix *-ba* precedes both of the valence-indicating suffixes, *-li* in (74) and *-ma* in (76). The relativiser *-dany* is not found in combination with any other suffixes in the text collection.

It should be noted that in *wularaba gariyagan* 'magpie goose', which literally means 'brolga that talks', the suffix *-ba* acts like a relativiser on the verb *wulara* 'talk'. This is inconsistent with the other uses of *-ba,* which marks a subordinate clause rather than a relative clause. It is possible that *wularaba gariyagan* 'magpie goose' is borrowed from, or influenced by, Badjala or another language. There is a relative subordinator suffix *-ba/-wa* in the Badjala language traditionally spoken on K'Gari (Fraser Island), though its behaviour and meaning are somewhat different than Yagara *-ba* (Bell 2003, 107).

1.6.4. Valence suffixes (*-ma* and *-li*)

Yagara has one suffix that adds a participant to an event, the causative *-ma*, and another that removes a participant, the reciprocal/reflexive *-li*.

The suffix *-ma* occurs on intransitive verbs and indicates that the process or state indicated by the verb was caused by another participant. For example, *balgal* 'rise/get up' and *milbulbu* 'be alive' are normally intransitive, but with the suffix *-ma*, they become transitive *balgal-ma* 'cause to rise' and *milbulbu-ma* 'cause to be alive' as in (77).

(77) ngunyal   ganggir   balgal-**ma**-ri
        3SG.NOM   dead   arise-**CAUS**-PST
        he made the dead rise
        Wunnal kungīr bulgunmurri,

        nga   milbulbu-**ma**-ri
        and   be.alive-**CAUS**-PST
        and made them be alive.
        ŋa milbulpumurri. (Ridley 1875)

The neighbouring languages Duuŋidjawu (Kite and Wurm 2004, 86) and Yugambeh (Sharpe 2020, 32), like many other Pama-Nyungan languages, have a causative suffix *-ma*.

When *-ma* occurs on intransitive verbs, usually those denoting self-directed motion, as in (78), it has a different meaning.

(78) yagara   ngaja   nyan-**ma**-nya
        not   1SG.NOM   go-**CAUS**-PRS
        I'm not going.
        yagara ngacia yadmanya. (Lauterer 1891)

Here, *-ma* does not add an extra argument. Instead, it seems to indicate whether the subject chooses to undertake the motion or not. Example (78) could perhaps be paraphrased as 'I won't make myself go'. In suggestions and invitations, as in (79), this sense of -*ma* often occurs with the subjunctive -*ba* (described in 1.6.2.6), which could indicate that the choice of going is offered to the addressee.

(79) nyan-**ma-ba**   ngagam
      go-**CAUS-SBJV**   here.PROX
      Let's go away from here.
      Yanmerpa nahga. (Meston 1986a)

In Gabi-Gabi and Badjala, causative -*ma* has evolved into an 'auxiliary element' (Holmer 1983, 144–45) or 'stem extension' (Bell 2003, 96) that attaches to irregular verbs before other suffixes. In Yagara, however, -*ma* as in (78) and (79) may occur word-finally, so it does not serve the function of the Gabi-Gabi and Badjala 'auxiliary element'.

The reflexive -*li* indicates that an action is done to oneself, as opposed to some other object. This can be seen in (74), repeated as (80), in which the subject is shaking herself.

(80) ngunyal   jiga-ba-**li**   balga-ri
      3SG.NOM   shake-RTP-**REFL**   come-PST
      She shook as she came;
      wunnal jikkebele bulkurri; (Ridley 1875)

Verbs that denote communal activities such as fighting, as in (81), can also take -*li*. In these contexts, the suffix could be considered a reciprocal.

(81) nyubany   baga-**li**-nya
      married.couple   fight-**REFL**-PRS
      A married couple is fighting (each other)
      ɲubaɲ bagaliɲa (Holmer 1983)

A reflexive suffix with the form -*li* is also found in Yugambeh (Sharpe 2020, 40).

Though reflexive -*li* and causative -*ma* must come after the subordinator -*ba* (as in [80]) and prior to tense-marking suffixes (see [77], [78] and [81], for example) they do not co-occur with the aspect-marking or motion suffixes in the texts.

1.6.5. Motion suffixes (-*ra* and -*biny*)

In the texts, the suffixes -*ra* and -*biny* attach only to motion verbs, and add information about the movement the verbs describe.

The semantic contribution of the suffix -*ra* is difficult to pinpoint. Verbs with -*ra* often co-occur with the naming of the destination, as in (82), in which the speaker is going to Meeanjin (Brisbane). Other examples, such as (83) and (84), also clearly imply a destination (the speaker's location in [82], and the location in which the addressee is being instructed to perform a task in [83]). The suffix -*ra* therefore is here considered to specify that motion has a clear endpoint or destination.

(82) Miganjin   ngaja   nya-**ra**-nya
      Brisbane   1SG.NOM   go-**DEST**-PRS
      I'm going to Brisbane.
      megengen ŋaja jaraŋa (Holmer 1983)

(83) ngunyal   yaa-ba-ri   ngunyana   gin   balga-**ra**
      3SG.NOM   say-RTP-PST   3SG.ACC   girl   come-**DEST**
      while saying to her, 'Girl! Come here!'
      wunnal yambari wunnana; yari; 'kin! Bulkurai!' (Ridley 1875)

(84) ngaja   ganyar   yaa   nginda   nya-**ra**
      1SG.NOM   one   say   2SG.NOM   go-**DEST**
      I say to one, 'Go there!'
      Ŋutta kunnar yā, 'ŋinta yerra'; (Ridley 1875)

In three of the four examples of -*biny* in the texts, the suffix attaches to *wira* 'return' as in (85)–(86). However, when -*biny* occurs on the verb *balgal* 'come', which does not necessarily imply 'returning', the suffix nevertheless indicates motion back towards one's origin as in (87). Lang (1846) also records the word *balgal-biny* 'come-BACK' as *bulgulpin* 'to return'.

(85) ngaliny   wira-ra-**biny**
      1DU.NOM   return-DEST-**BACK**
      We came back home.
      Gnalleen weerareppee. (Meston 1986a)

(86) nguru   wira-**biny**=bu
      spirit   return-**BACK**=EMPH
      The spirit returns!
      ŋūru wirepinebu; (Ridley 1875)

(87) guba-nya   nginda   ngaja   barany   balgal-**biny**
      go.on-PRES   2SG.NOM   1SG.NOM   soon   come-**BACK**
      You're going ahead, I'm coming back soon.
      Cobana-inter, utcha baro balgalpin. (Watkins and Hamilton 1887)

1.6.6. Aspect suffixes (-*du* and -*dunga*)

The suffix -*du* marks atelicity or unboundedness, meaning an event lacks
a clear endpoint. For example, the event in *She ran* is atelic/unbounded,
because the subject could run and then continue running. On the other
hand, the event in *She ran 10 kilometres* is telic/bounded, because the
subject could not run 10 km and then continue running 10 km. She could
run 10 more km, but could not continue running the same 10 km.

The suffix -*du* primarily occurs on verbs that denote states or activities, as
in (88)–(89), where it seems to emphasise that the event could potentially
continue indefinitely.

(88) mumbal   baan-**du**   ngalinyana
      thunder   be.angry-**ATEL**   1DU.ACC
      God is angry with us.
      Mūmbāl bāndu ŋulleŋunna. (Ridley 1875)

(89) jina-di   imanuwal-nuba   nyinyi-**du**
      foot-LOC   Immanuel-POSS   sit-**ATEL**
      he is sitting at Immanuel's feet,
      jidnendi Immanuelnūbba ŋinēdu, (Ridley 1875)

The suffix -*dunga* also has aspectual meaning and could potentially be
analysed as -*du* followed by another suffix -*nga*. However, -*nga* does not
occur without -*du* in the texts, nor does -*dunga* obviously incorporate the
meaning of -*du*. Whereas -*du* attaches to verbs that denote states or actions,
-*dunga* typically attaches to *nyan* 'go' as in (90).

(90) dagai-jin   Miyanjin-di-ba   nyan-**dunga**
      white.man-PL   Brisbane-LOC-ABL   travel-**IPFV**
      The white men in the city were going,
      Duggaitin miëntjintiber yeatuŋa, (Ridley 1875)

Other instances of -*dunga* modify stative verbs, such as *dany* 'lie' in (91). In all instances, -*dunga* appears to present as event as ongoing. In the texts, verbs with -*dunga* are often glossed using the English progressive construction *BE X-ing* as in *were going*.

(91) imanuwal ngunu-bu ganggir dany-**dunga** nga
 Immanuel night-DUR dead lie-**IPFV** and
 That night Immanuel lay dead, and ...
 Imanuel ŋūnŭmbo kungīr daieduŋa; ŋa ... (Ridley 1875)

Example (91) demonstrates that -*dunga* can be followed by the conjunction *nga*. This further indicates that the suffix -*dunga* is distinct from the conjunction *nga* and does not merely consist of the suffix -*du* followed by *nga*.

Both -*du* and -*dunga* are always the sole suffix on verbs in the texts.

1.6.7. Tense suffixes (-*ri*, -*nya* and -*li*)

The tense-marking suffixes indicate whether an event is in the past, present or future relative to the time of speaking or other reference time.

The past tense -*ri* as in (92)—(93) is frequent in the texts and occurs in Ridley (1875), Watkins and Hamilton (1887) and Hardcastle (1946–7).

(92) ngandu ngina yaa-**ri**
 who.ERG 2SG.ACC say-**PST**
 Who told you?
 Ando ine yare? (Watkins and Hamilton 1887)

(93) barany imanuwal biram-di wandi-**ri**
 then Immanuel sky-LOC rise-**PST**
 Then Immanuel rose to the sky;
 Burru Immanual birradi wundāre; (Ridley 1875)

The present tense -*nya*, as in (94)—(95), occurs in Eipper (1841a), Ridley (1875), Watkins and Hamilton (1887), Meston (1986a), Lauterer (1891), Hardcastle (1946–7) and Holmer (1983).

(94) ngan dungi-**nya**
 who weep-**PRS**
 Who is crying?
 Arn Dunginna? (Hardcastle 1946–7)

(95) yagara   ngaja   nyan-ma-**nya**
     not   1SG.NOM   go-CAUS-**PRS**
     I'm not going.
     yagara ngacia yadmanya. (Lauterer 1891)

The future tense *-li* is used in reference to future plans for oneself (96) or for others (97).

(96) ngaja   galima-**li**   ngunyalina
     1SG.NOM   punish-**FUT**   3PL.ACC
     I will punish them.'
     ŋutta kālimurri wunnālina.' (Ridley 1875)

(97) nginda   danga   yaga-**li**
     2SG.NOM   that.DIST   do-**FUT**
     'You will do that!';
     ŋinta duŋa yuggali'; (Ridley 1875)

Future *-li* also commonly occurs with the subjunctive suffix *-ba*, in which case it denotes a promise or request about a future action, as in (98)–(99).

(98) gau-Ø   ngaja   galga-**li**-ba   diranga   baguur
     stop-IMP   1SG.NOM   cut-**FUT**-SBJV   this.PROX   tree
     Stop! I'm going to cut this tree.
     Kaahuu! Ngutta kulkulliba diranga bagur. (Ridley 1875)

(99) jigan   yaa-li   imanuwal   balga-**li**-ba
     insistently say-FUT   Immanuel   come-**FUT**-SBJV
     insistently they tell Immanuel that he should come
     tiggen yali Immanuel bulkullibi (Ridley 1875)

The suffix *-li* can also indicate hypothetical future events, as in the protasis of the conditional in (100).

(100) nginda   wina   danga-na   baguur-na   da-**li**
      2SG.NOM   when   that.DIST-ACC   tree-ACC   eat-**FUT**
      If you eat from that tree,
      Ninda winna dungama bagurna tulli,

      nga   nginda   ngundu   baluny   biigi-bu
      and   2SG.NOM   surely   die   day-DUR
      on that day you will surely die.
      ŋa ŋinda ŋūndu balluia bigibu. (Ridley 1875)

1.6.8. Mood suffixes (-*la*, -*ba* and -*Ø*)

The suffix -*la* occurs in commands and other expressions of obligation, as in (101), or permission, as in (102).

(101) nya-**la**
go-**OBLG**
Go away!
Yallah! (Meston 1986a)

(102) nginda   wana   danga-na   baguur-na   da-**la**
2SG.NOM   do.not   that.DIST-ACC   tree-ACC   eat-**OBLG**
you may not eat from that tree.
inta wunna dungama bagūrna tulla. (Ridley 1875)

Like -*la*, the suffix -*ba* can occur in requests. It often occurs with the first-person dual *ngaliny*, in which case it comes across as a suggestion, as in (103) and the two instances in (104).

(103) ngaliny   juruny=gu   nyan-**ba**
1DU.NOM   eel=PURP   go-**SBJV**
Let's go to fish eels.
Gnahleen joanko yieeba. (Meston 1986a)

(104) wi   ngaliny   nyan-**ba**   da-li-**ba**
hey   1DU.NOM   go-**SBJV**   drink-**SBJV**
Hey, let's go have a drink.
Wee gnahleen yieeba jaleeba. (Meston 1986a)

The suffix -*ba* occurs in other expressions of intention, as in (105), in which the white men are going with the intention of seeing something.

(105) dagai-jin   Miyanjin-di-ba   nyan-dunga
white.man-PL   Brisbane-LOC-ABL   travel-IPFV
The white men in the city were going,
Duggaitin miëntjintiber yeatuŋa,

nyaany-**ba**   minya   yaga-ri
see-**SBJV**   what   do-PST
to see what (someone) did.
nānnibēr minna yugari. (Ridley 1875)

The suffix *-ba* occurs in expressions indicating future intentions, often in conjunction with future *-li* as in (106).

(106) gau-Ø   ngaja   galga-li-**ba**   diranga   baguur
       stop-IMP   1SG.NOM   cut-FUT-**SBJV**   this.PROX   tree
       Stop! I'm going to cut this tree.
       Kaahuu! Ngutta kulkulliba diranga bagur. (Ridley 1875)

The imperative form, as in *gau-Ø* in (106), is used in commands that lack the mood suffixes *-ba* or *-la*. The imperative form is generally identical to the uninflected stem, as is the case in Duuɲidjawu (Kite and Wurm 2004, 81). For example, *gau* 'stop' could either represent the uninflected verb *gau* or *gau-Ø* 'stop-IMP'. However, Yagara verbs roots that end in *n, ny* or *l* lose their final consonants in the imperative. This is apparent in the common greeting *wi balga* 'hey, come-IMP' in which *balgal* 'come' lacks the final lateral. The imperative of *wujan* 'give' has the form *wuja* 'give-IMP', and *gungany* 'shout' becomes *gunga* 'shout-IMP'.

1.6.9. Negation and other derivational suffixes

The only derivational suffix that occurs exclusively on verb stems is the negation suffix *-ra*. Two of the derivational suffixes that primarily appear on nominals (see 1.5.4) may also occur on verbs. These consist of *-gali* 'very X' and *-gan* 'characterised by X'. This section will discuss *-ra, -gali* and *-gan*, followed by a mention of the derivational suffixes listed in 1.5.4 that attach to nominal stems but produce verb stems.

-ra

Though not well attested, the suffix *-ra* may be used on verbs to indicate negation. The clearest instances of this process are in (107)–(109). The suffix is pronounced *-r* instead of *-ra* when the final vowel is dropped (see 1.3.1), as suggested by the brackets in Holmer's transcription *buɟiraŋ ɟabur(a)* in (108).

(107) ngaja   jugu-**ra**
       1SG.NOM   know-**NEG**
       I don't know.
       Atcha djookoora. (Watkins and Hamilton 1887)

(108) bujirang   jabu-**ra**
       boy   be.frightened-**NEG**
       Don't be frightened, boy.
       buɟiraŋ ɟabur(a) (Holmer 1983)

(109) wana   ga-**ra**
       refuse.to   give-**NEG**
       I will not give.
       Wonagra (Lang 1846)

In addition to the above example, -*ra* is documented on *wana* 'don't; forbid; refuse', resulting in *wana-ra-ra* 'no, no, don't!' collected by Lang (1846). Here, -*ra* apparently strengthens the negation meaning of *wana*. Presumably *wana-ra* 'no, don't!' with a single -*ra* suffix would be possible as well.

The usage of -*ra* to indicate negation may not be productive, since it is found on few verbs in the text collection. However, if the negation suffix -*ra* historically occurred on the verb *yaga* 'do, make', this could explain the origin of the negation marker *yagara*, which would have grammaticalised from *yaga-ra* 'do not'.

-gali

As noted in 1.5.4, the suffix -*gali* attaches to verb stems as well as nominal stems. In the texts, it usually occurs in verbless sentences such as (110). As such, it sometimes can be translated into English with a verb, as in (110). However, stems ending in -*gali* never occur in contexts where they are unambiguously verbs, whereas they may be unambiguously nouns (as in *digir-gali* 'big eater') or adjectives (as in *milin-gali* 'very many', which modifies nouns).

(110) muyan-**gali**   nginda
       ask-**VERY**   2SG.NOM
       You ask too much.
       Mooe aculle intur (Lang 1846)

-gan

The suffix -*gan* 'characterised by X' takes nominal stems as described and exemplified in 1.5.4. In Bobbiwinta's Song (Petrie 1904; see 3.3.11), the suffix appears to attach to a verb, *dalan* 'close', as in (111).

(111) dalan-**gan**-bu   ngaja   nyinyi-dunga
        close-**CHARACT**-DUR   1S.NOM   wait-IPFV
        As (the water) closed over, I was waiting
        Tallo canbu ngatta yiri duwa (Petrie 1904)

Though the derivational suffixes in 1.5.4 rarely attach to verb stems, they frequently change nominals into verbs. When a verb is created from a nominal through the addition of one of the derivational suffixes described in 1.5.4, the derivational suffixes are closer to the nominal stem than the verbal inflectional suffixes. For example, in (112) the inchoative suffix *-bany* changes the noun *nai* 'name' into the verb *nai-bany* 'to name'. (The inchoative has the form *-ba* in this example due to the following rhotic; see 1.3.2.) In (112) the derivational suffix *-bany* is closer to the nominal stem *nai* than the inflectional suffix *-ri*.

(112) nga   jara   nai-**ba**-ri   jar
        and   earth   name-**INCH**-PST   earth
        and named the earth, 'land'.
        Ŋa durrun naïburri Tār. (Ridley 1875)

1.7. Interjections

The source texts include around 25 exclamations such as *baguru* 'wow' and *yura* 'hello'. Some of these have additional functions, whereas others do not. For example, *baguru* also is a verb meaning 'be astonished', whereas *yura* 'hello' seems to be only used as an interjection.

The interjection *wi* 'hey' is particularly frequent in the texts, and is recorded in sentences by Meston (1986a), Lauterer (1891) and Gibson (1863). In the sentences, it always occurs initially, as in (113).

(113) **wi**   ngaliny   nyan-ba   da-li-ba
        hey   1DU.NOM   go-SBJV   drink-SBJV
        Hey, let's go have a drink.
        Wee gnahleen yieeba jaleeba. (Meston 1986a)

According to Lauterer (1891), *wi balga* 'hey come' was the usual Yagara greeting.

It is unclear whether *wi* 'hey' is related to the particle *wai* that occurs in songs, as in the line from the Star Song recorded by Lauterer (1891) in (114).

(114) nyawang   many   barany   **wai**
       nicely   catch   soon   **SONG**
       Catch nicely, soon, *wai!*
       Nyiewang manpawo wae (Lauterer 1891)

In the examples included in Part 3 of this volume, *wai* occurs at the end of lines in song texts. However, in two non-Yagara songs sung by Yagara speakers, transcribed by Lauterer (1891) but not included in this volume, *wai* occurs at the start of lines.

Other well-attested interjections include *yawai* 'goodbye', *gurii* 'wow' and *gau* 'hey; stop'.

1.8. Clitics

There are two apparent clitics in Yagara, the emphatic marker =*bu* and the purposive =*gu*.

The clitic =*bu* occurs following all derivation and inflection, and seems to occur on words of all grammatical categories. The clitic =*bu* indicates emphasis or absoluteness, and is particularly common on *ngambila* 'everyone; all', resulting in *ngambila=bu* 'absolutely everyone; every last one' and *yagara* 'not', producing *yagara=bu* 'never; not at all'. However, it also is found on verbs, as in *wira-nya=bu* 'return-PRS=EMPH; actually returning' in (115), where it emphasises that the return trip really occurred—as opposed to the prior attempt to return, which was delayed.

(115) barany   imanuwal   giram-di   wira-nya=**bu**
       then   Immanuel   across-LOC   return-PRS=**EMPH**
       Then Immanuel is finally returning across;
       Burru Immanuel kīrumti wirē nēbu; (Ridley 1875)

The clitic =*gu* seems to be a cognate of the purposive suffix found in many Pama-Nyungan languages, including Duuŋidjawu (Kite and Wurm 2004, 30) and Yugambeh (Sharpe 2020, 39). In the Yagara texts, =*gu* attaches to nouns, verbs or adjectives. It often indicates a purpose, such as when *ngalan* 'bream' becomes *ngalan=gu* 'to catch bream' or *dabil* becomes *dabil=gu* 'to fetch water', as in (116). However, it can also indicate a reason that is not a purpose, as in (117), in which being sick (*bany=gu*) is the reason for lying down (*da-nya*).

(116) ngalan=**gu** jar=**gu**   dabil=**gu**
   bream=**PURP** earth=**PURP** water=**PURP**
   To catch bream, to work the earth, to get water.
   Woulanco, darco, dabilco. (Eipper 1841a)

(117) ngunyanuba dagai   bany=**gu** da-nya
   3SG.POSS white.man sick=**PURP** lie-PRS
   his white man was lying sick;
   wunnanŭbu duggai paingo daina; (Ridley 1875)

1.9. Syntax

1.9.1. Simple clauses

In the text collection, the most frequent word order in Yagara is SOV (subject–object–verb), as in (118)–(119).

(118) ngaja   ngina   galgal-ba
   1SG.NOM 2SG.ACC cut-SBJV
   I'm going to cut you.
   Utcha-ine kabal-wa. (Watkins and Hamilton 1887)

(119) ngunyalu nyaring waya-ri
   3SG.ERG son   send-PST
   He sent his son.
   Wunyalu nurriŋ waiari. (Ridley 1875)

Though the subject is usually the first element in a sentence, other elements can be fronted to show topicality or emphasis. Example (120) illustrates a fronted object and (121) a fronted verb.

(120) **Miganjin** ngaja   nya-ra-nya
   Brisbane 1SG.NOM go-DEST-PRS
   I'm going to Brisbane.
   megenʃen ŋaja jaraŋa (Holmer 1983)

(121) **gindin** ngaja
   laugh 1SG.NOM
   I laughed …
   Gindan utcha … (Watkins and Hamilton 1887)

Interrogative pronouns are usually initial, as shown in (122)—(123). Example (124) is an exception.

(122) **minyanggu**   nginda   gindin
      why   2SG.NOM   laugh
      Why are you laughing?
      Minango inter gindan? (Watkins and Hamilton 1887)

(123) **wanji**   balgal   wira-biny
      when   come   return-BACK
      When are you coming back?
      Wanchee bagga weereppee. (Meston 1986a)

(124) naam   **ngandu**
      there.DIST   **who.ERG**
      Who is that?
      Naam ngandu? (Ridley 1875)

Yes/no questions may have an interrogative particle *ngi* that follows an initial predicate, as in (125)—(126), or that occurs initially, as in (127). The same particle *ngi* is occasionally found in questions that also have an interrogative pronoun, as in (128).

(125) wayara   **ngi**   nginda
      be.hungry   **Q**   2SG.NOM
      Are you hungry?
      Wuaera ngi nginte? (Lauterer 1891)

(126) bany   **ngi**   ngagam   jundal
      sick   **Q**   here.PROX   woman
      Is the woman here sick?
      Bayi ngi ngalam ds'undal 'Is she sick?' (Lauterer 1891)

(127) **ngi**   nginda   yaga
      Q   2SG.NOM   work
      Are you working?
      Uney-Intair yeaca? (Hardcastle 1946–7)

(128) wanya=gu   nya-ra-nya   **ngi**   nginda
      where=PURP   go-DEST-PRS   **Q**   2SG.NOM
      Where are you going?
      Wunyángo yadnanya ngi nginte? (Lauterer 1891)

Yagara does not have an overt copula, meaning that sentences do not always need a verb. Verbless sentences in the texts include the predicative nominal in (129) and the predicative adjective in (130).

(129) nginda **magiiba**
      2SG.NOM **friend**
      You're a friend.
      Gninda mag'ieeba. (Meston 1986a)

(130) ngambila=bu   dagai-jin   **wali**
      all=EMPH   white.man-PL   **bad**
      'All white men are bad;
      'Ŋāmbillebu duggatin waddeli; (Ridley 1875)

Yagara sentences usually have an overt subject, unless the subject is the same as in a previous clause, in which case it is frequently implicit. However, second-person subjects are omitted in directives, as in (131). Questions in the texts usually have a subject, as in (132), but do not require one, as shown by (133).

(131) ngari   balga-Ø   minyalang
      1SG.ACC   bring-IMP   thingamajig
      Bring me that whatever-it-is.
      Ngurri bulkai minyaluung? (Ridley 1875)

(132) wanya-nga   nginda
      where-ALL   2SG.NOM
      Where are you going?
      Woon-nanta-Intair? (Hardcastle 1946–7)

(133) wanji   balgal   wira-biny
      when   come   return-BACK
      When are (you) coming back?
      Wanchee bagga weereppee. (Meston 1986a)

Subjects and other arguments may be omitted when they are the same as in the previous clause, as illustrated by the five-clause sequence in (134). The subject in the first clause, *jundal* 'woman', is the same in the second clause and is therefore omitted. The next clause *guna muya danga baguur-na* 'her heart desired that fruit' has a different subject, so when the woman returns as the subject in the next clause *barany ngunyal banman* 'then, she plucked (it)', the subject must be restated as *ngunyal* 'she'. The fruit is the object in *guna muya danga baguur-na* 'her heart desired that fruit', and is also the object of the next three clauses, *barany ngunyal banman* 'then, she plucked (it)', *nga da-ri* 'and (she) ate (it)', and *nga dagai-na wujan* 'and (she) gave (it) to the white man', so the object can be omitted in all three of these clauses.

(134) jundal   ngui-ba-nya   nga   yuwan   winanga-ri
woman   believe-RTP-PRS   and   serpent   hear-PST
The woman, believing, listened to the serpent;
Jūndāl ŋuïpunāŋ yūunwīnuŋurri;

guna   muya   danga   baguur-na
heart   desire   that.DIST   tree-ACC
her heart desired that fruit.
kudna muïya dūŋa bagūrnu.

barany   ngunyal   banman
then   3SG.NOM   pluck
Then she plucked;
Burru wunnal pūnmān;

nga   da-ri   nga   dagai-na   wujan
and   eat-PST   and   white.man-ACC   give
and ate, and gave to the white man;
ŋa turri, ŋa dugganu widdan; (Ridley 1875)

1.9.2. Complex clauses

Most relative clauses are indicated by the verbal inflections *-dany* and *-ba*, which are discussed in Section 1.6.2.

The morpheme *nga* 'and' often connects clauses, as in (135).

(135) barany   ngunyal   dabil   nai-ba-ri   dabilbaan
then   3SG.NOM   water   name-INCH-PST   salt.water
Then he named the water 'sea';
Burru wunnal tabbil naïburri Tabbilbon;

nga   jara   nai-ba-ri   jar
and   earth   name-INCH-PST   earth
and named the earth, 'land'.
Ŋa durrun naïburri Tār. (Ridley 1875)

Conditional constructions are sometimes introduced by *wina* 'if/when' in the protasis (that is, the conditional clause that describes the precondition for the main clause), as in (136)–(137), which constitute two of the three examples of *wina* in the texts, all in Ridley (1875). In these constructions, the main verb in the protasis has future tense -*li* and the main verb in the apodosis (that is, the main clause) has the subjunctive -*ba*. In the source texts, the protasis *wina*-clause precedes the apodosis clause. The opposite order may be possible but not instantiated in the texts; both orders are found in Duuŋidjawu, in which the particle *wanja* has a function similar to *wina* (Kite and Wurm 2004).

(136)   nginda   **wina**   danga-na   baguur-na   da-li
       2SG.NOM   **when**   that.DIST-ACC   tree-ACC   eat-FUT
       If you eat from that tree,
       Ŋinda winna dungama bagurna tulli,

       nga   nginda   ngundu   baluny   biigi-bu
       and   2SG.NOM   surely   die   day-DUR
       on that day you will surely die.
       ŋa ŋinda ŋūndu balluia bigibu. (Ridley 1875)

(137)   nginda   yagar   baluny   barany   nginda
       2SG.NOM   not   die   then   2SG.NOM
       'You will not die. As soon as you
       Ŋinta yugar balluï. Burra ŋinta

       wina   baguur-na   ngurdi   jiladu   da-li
       when   tree-ACC   in.the.area   in.the.middle   eat-FUT
       eat from the tree in the middle,
       winna bagurna ŋurti jillerdu tulli,

       mil   nginda   yagany-ba
       eye   2SG.NOM   heal-SBJV
       your eyes will be healed;
       mil ŋinta yuggaipa; (Ridley 1875)

Verbal complement clauses and purpose clauses are discussed in Section 1.6.2 as part of the explanation of the mood suffix -*ba*.

Part 2. Dictionary

2.1. Using the dictionary

2.1.1. Pronunciation guide

As in all languages, sounds that are phonologically the same in Yagara are often pronounced differently depending on contextual factors, as discussed in Section 1.3.

Table 2.1 gives approximate pronunciations in Standard Australian English (SAE) for the sounds of Yagara as written in the dictionary. Please keep in mind that these are only rough approximations of the Yagara sounds, and the descriptions in 1.3 are a more accurate guide. Unfortunately, without native speaker consultants or fluent spoken audio recordings, the original sounds of Yagara cannot be fully reconstructed.

Table 2.1: Pronouncing Yagara words in the dictionary.

Phoneme	Context	Similar SAE sound
a	stressed syllable	under, hut
	unstressed syllable	about, naked, sedan
i	stressed syllable	peep, teak
	unstressed syllable	about, naked, sedan
u	stressed syllable	took, put
	unstressed syllable	boot, flu
aa	all	father, galah
ii	all	seed, freed
uu	all	would, sugar
ai	all	sigh, rye
ui	all	toil, enjoy

Phoneme	Context	Similar SAE sound
b	stressed syllable	**p**en, ha**pp**y
	unstressed syllable	**b**a**b**y, **b**ug
d	stressed syllable	**t**en, re**t**urn
	unstressed syllable	**d**og, i**d**ea
j	stressed syllable	ba**tch**, **ch**ild
	unstressed syllable	**j**u**dg**e
g	stressed syllable	**k**in, **c**at, tri**ck**y
	unstressed syllable	**g**et, lu**gg**ing
m	all	**m**oon, ai**m**
n	all	**n**ot, bea**n**
ny	all	ca**ny**on, bu**ny**a
ng	all	si**ng**ing, cli**ng**y
ngg	all	ju**ng**le, a**ng**ry, ha**ng-g**lider
n.g	all	u**ng**rateful, i**ng**rown
l	all	**l**ight, te**ll**ing
r	all	**r**ed, be**rr**y
w	all	**w**all, **w**ing
y	all	**y**ell, **y**awn

Source: Authors' summary, based on the source texts described in Section 1.1.4.

Short vowels and stops are different depending on whether they occur in stressed and unstressed syllables, so these contexts are differentiated in the 'Context' column in Table 2.1. Stressed syllables are usually the first syllable in a word, as described in Section 1.3.6. It is only when the second syllable in the word has a long vowel (*aa*, *ii* or *uu*) that the second syllable is stressed.

Note that *y* is always a consonant as in English *yes*, never a vowel sound as in English *fly*. The sound *ny* does not contain a vowel; *ny* is a single consonant sound even though it is written using two letters. The *ny* at the end of a word may look especially like a vowel to English speakers, as in *jaagany* 'bunyip', but this word ends in a nasal consonant, not a vowel.

2.1.2. Duplicate sources

Many of the authors of source texts copied word lists from others. A few of these copies are potentially useful, whereas most are redundant and distracting. Here, duplicate entries from the two earliest secondary sources,

Jackson (1937) and Watson (1943), are included, whereas duplicates from subsequent secondary sources, beginning with Colliver and Woolston (1975), are not.

Jackson (1937) and Watson (1943) are included in full for two reasons. Firstly, it is often difficult to distinguish when their data is copied from someone else. For example, Jackson (1937) includes duplicates of entries from Lang (1846) and others, but also lists words found nowhere else. It is impossible to say which words, if any, Jackson collected himself. Secondly, secondary sources occasionally add information not present in the original. For example, Jackson (1937) copies the entry in Ridley (1875) for *bambara* 'saw banksia', but adds the information that this tree was used for making bullroarers. Watson (1943) frequently suggests scientific names for plants and animals named by Ridley (1875) and Petrie (1904). Jackson and Watson, writing around 1940, likely had access to cultural information that is not obvious today. They may have heard Yagara spoken, or asked native speakers to repeat previously collected words, even if they did not elicit new vocabulary. These two collections therefore are more likely to contribute meaningful data than later secondary sources that are known to have had little or no contact with native speakers of Yagara.

Nonetheless, most entries from Watson and Jackson are not original and should not be considered as independent data. In particular, Watson (1943) credits Meston (1890), Petrie (1904) and Bell (1934) with much of his vocabulary. Jackson (1937) gives no information on his sources, but appears to have borrowed from Eipper (1841a), Ridley (1875), Meston (1890) and Suttor (1897).

At times, this duplication can give the impression that a word is better documented than it is. For example, *yaniri* 'want' was collected only by Ridley, but was repeated in Jackson (1937) and Watson (1943), and so has three sources listed in its entry. Words attributed to Watson and Jackson should therefore not be considered better attested than words that lack these sources.

2.1.3. Notes on definitions

Each dictionary entry includes a main definition consolidated from the various sources. Some entries also contain original definitions from the sources, which are written in quotation marks after each source's entry, in the list of sources at the end of each entry. When different sources provide similar but distinct definitions, these are normally all listed in the main definition and not repeated in the list of sources. When the definition in one source is more specific than another, such as 'sister' versus 'younger sister', the more specific definition ('younger sister') is selected for the main entry definition, unless there is evidence that the specific definition is likely to be wrong.

Definitions from the individual sources are included (in quotation marks after the original source spelling) when there are multiple conflicting definitions from a single author, such as when Lang lists *dalo* as 'fire' and *tadlo* as 'smoke', even though these clearly both belong to the entry *jalu* 'fire'. Another exception is made when a source's definition does not agree with the main definition for the entry. For example, three sources define *manganggal* as 'younger sister', so this definition is given in the main entry and not repeated below in the list of sources. However, Jackson (1937) instead defines the word as 'elder sister', so this conflicting definition is given after his transcription in the list of sources. Finally, definitions from the sources are included when they include species nomenclature that appears to be incorrect and which is therefore not adopted in the main definition. For example, Watson and Hardcastle both mention a *green leek parrot*, a term that usually referred to the superb parrot at the time of their writing. Since the superb parrot has never been found in Queensland, these words are interpreted as referring to the musk lorikeet, which is frequently confused with the superb parrot, and Watson and Hardcastle's definitions are included in the list of sources rather than the main definition.

2.2. Yagara – English Dictionary

B – b

-ba₁ *case.* ablative suffix designating motion away from a location. [bēr, ber, bā, ba, pa, bu, pu (R)]

-ba₂ *mood.* subjunctive; occurs in polite requests. [pa, va, var, viar (Ha); ba (H); pa, ba, bah (M); pa, ba, be, bi, bu, beer (R); ba (W)]

-ba₃ *subd.* occurs on the head verb of a subordinate clause. [ba, bēr, be, pu (R)]

-ba₄ *deriv.* indicates a place. [ba (Ln); ba (M); ba (W); wā (Wa)]

baabang *n.* mother's mother. [ahbong 'mother' (Bl); bar-bung (Ha); barbang 'grandmother' (Ja); bahbohn (N)]

baabun *n.* moon. [babun (H); baboon (Ja); bābūn (R); bobbin (T); bāb'ūn (Wa)] *See:* gibun; gilan².

Baabun-baabun *n.* place near Bowman's homestead south of Mt Alford township. *lit.* 'moon-moon'. [Baboon-Baboon (Ha)] *See:* baabun.

baada *v.* bite. [patter 'eat' (Bl); barter (E); barter (Ja); barter (Lg)] *See:* gaiya; gargan.

baal *excl.* get outta here!, no way! from Dharug biyal 'not, no'. [baal 'no' (Cl); baal (P); baal 'I don't know' (Su)]

Baali *n.* woman's name. [Baali (Delaney 1994)]

Baama *n.* Nudgee Waterhole Reserve. [Barmah (Bd)]

baan *adj.* nasty; hot; bitter; salty; dirty; angry. [ban (E); barn (Ha); barn, ban (Ja); ban 'hot to the touch or salt' (Lg); bandu (R); boa'rn (Wa)]

baanang *n.* jackwood. *[Cryptocarya glaucescens].* [baa nung 'jackwood' (Mac)]

baandigu *n.* excrement. *incorporates* baan 'nasty'. [bandiko (Ja); bāndiko (R)] *See:* baan; duwal; guna¹.

babimin *n.* family. [babemen (Lg)]

babiragawi *n.* pigface. *[Carpobrotus glaucescens].* *Anth:* gum from the leaves was used for insect and jellyfish stings; the fruit was eaten (FNSI). [babragowi (MMEIC)]

baga *v.* fight. [baga (H)] *See:* baji²; bagali; ganijada; ganggirma.

bagali *v.* fight each other. *lit.* baga-li 'fight reciprocally'. [pīkil (G); bagali (H); buccali 'to through [sic] the boomerang' (Lg); boongge'elee (M)] *See:* baji²; baga; -li².

bagan *n.* two-handed nulla-nulla with pick-shaped head. *Anth:* for killing by a blow to the back of the head. [bakkan 'beaked nulla' (Ja); buccan (Lg); bakkan (Ro); bâk'kan (Wa)] *See:* jabiri; mar.

bagangali *adj.* impudent. *incorporates* -gali 'very'. [bacongulle (Lg)] *See:* -gali.

bagaram₁ *n.* large bullroarer. [bugaram (Ja); bug'aram (Wa)] *See:* wabalgan.

bagaram₂ *n.* smallpox, chicken pox. [bugaram 'chicken pox' (Ja)]

bagarnuba *adj; n.* saltwater people. [bugarnuba (Wi)]

bagirang *n.* dugong. *[Dugong dugon].* [bakeerang (M)] *See:* bujumbiriba¹; guranban; gurubul; yangan¹.

baguru *excl; v.* be astonished, wow! [baggoro (Ja); bugguru (R)] *See:* =bu²; gurii.

baguuru₁ *Variant:* **baguur.** *n.* tree; wood. [boogerroo 'turpentine tree trunk/stem' (D); bagooroo (E); bagur (H); bugger-ar-o (Ha); bagooroo, bagur 'wood' (Ja); baguru (L); boggoroo (Lg); baggur (M); bāgūr (R); ba'gur (Wa)]

baguuru₂ *Variant:* **baguur.** *n.* rope or string made from tree bark. [boguru (E); baggoro (Ja); bugaroo (Kd); bagooroo, boguru (Lg); bugguru (R); woodgooroo (W); bagūru 'hair' (Wu)]

baguurugil *n.* log. *incorporates* baguuru 'tree'. [bugger-o-kil (Ha)] *See:* **baguuru**¹; **bural**; **maling**; **wambarligiri.**

Baguuruyalju *n.* man's name. *lit.* 'fast tree climber'; *incorporates* baguuru 'tree'. [Boogooroyalchew (D)] *See:* **baguuru**¹.

baibi *n.* black porpoise. [bybee (We)] *See:* **buwanggan; dalubila.**

baibun *Variant:* **baibu.** *v.* dream. [pai-abun (Ja); pai-abun (P); biboon (W); pai'abŭn (Wa)]

baigal *n.* man. from Gidabal baigal. [baigal (R)] *See:* **binigan; jaan; danbang; guri; malara; mari**².

baigal-baigal *n.* flesh, meat. [paigulpaigul (Ja); bagle-pagle 'beef' (Ln); paigulpaigul (R)]

baigan *n.* Jack jumper ant. *[Myrmecia pilosula].* [by-ee-gan (Ha)] *See:* **bigunjur**¹; **danmurin; galalang; giwarang; mugara**²; **murin.**

Baja *n.* Mt Castle; the Sleeping Assyrian. *Anth:* name of a legendary hunter, the sky god (S). [Butcha (Be); Butcha, Budjah (S)]

-bajagan *infl.* paucal suffix; designates a small number of referents. [pas'agon 'more than one' (L)]

Bajala *n.* Batjala people and language. [baʤala (H); butchalu (Lg)]

bajaragu *n.* north. [Bujarago (Be)] *See:* **dimbiny**¹; **wadi.**

baji₁ *Variant:* **baji-baji.** *adj; n.* old, old man, Elder, a long-toothed mythical old man who sends the pox when he is angry. [buggay (D); pudgere (Fi); baʤe baʤe; beʤe 'young fellow' (H); bos'ae (L); budscha (Le); budhi (Lg); puddie (Ln); begar (We); baji (Wu)] *See:* **bandar; darwan; gayabandar; gubagil; maran.gan; waliinggara.**

baji₂ *v.* strike, kill. [putni (L); bad yeba (Ln); batyee (M)] *See:* **buma.**

bajii *v.* look after someone. [bajī (Wu)]

bajiili *v.* take care of oneself, take care of each other. *lit.* bajii-li 'take care reciprocally'. [bajīli (Wu)] *See:* **bajii; -li**².

bajiram *n.* mythical ancestor, sorcerer. [bujirum (Hw); budjiram (RB)] *See:* **nan.gur.**

balan *n.* black cockatoo. *[Calyptorhynchus sp.].* [balan (H); bullum (We)] *See:* **biliyagan; biluwala; gaiyara; garara; giwang; jarbal; wiya**¹.

balbara *n.* crow's nest ash tree. *[Flindersia australis].* [bal burra (Ha)] *See:* **marugan.**

Balbula *n.* hill near Denelgin south of Mt Alford township. [Balpoola (Ha)]

balgal *Variant:* **balga.** *v.* come; bring; arise. [pal-ka (Cl); balgandy 'bring' (G); balga- (H); bulkar (Hi); pāl-ka, balkali, balkairi, balkari, bā (Ja); bulca, bulcu (Lg); bulcahee (M); bulkai, bulku, bā (R); bagajo (T); balka, bulka (W); bul'ka (Wa)] *See:* **dalbany.**

balgalbiny *v.* return. *lit.* balgal-biny 'come back'. [bulgulpin (Lg); balgalpin (W)] *See:* **balgal; -biny; wira.**

balgama *v.* grow. *lit.* balga-ma 'make rise'. [balga'nman (M); bulgunmu (R)] *See:* **balgal; duriyinma; daran**¹; **juwan**¹; **-ma; wanda.**

balim *n.* magpie-lark, peewee. *[Grallina cyanoleuca].* [bulim (S)]

Balimba *n.* Whites Hill. *lit.* balim-ba 'place of peewees'. [Bulimba (Bd); Boolimba 'Mt Cotton' (M); Bulimba (S)] *See:* **-ba**⁴; **balim.**

balimbir *n.* butterfly. [bālūmbir (Ja); balumbir, bālūmbir (R); balabiram (T); ba'limbīr (Wa)] *See:* **mari-mari**².

Balinabal *n.* Kerwin Swamp near Boonah. [Pollen-na-val (Ha)]

baling₁ *n.* money. compare with banggu 'money' in Yugambeh (Sh). [baliŋ, baliŋgam 'money' (H)] *See:* **baling**²; **balinggan.**

baling$_2$ *n.* young white man. [bolling 'young white man' (Ha)] *See:* **baling**[1]; **dagai**; **daranyjin**; **garabi**[1].

balinggan *adj.* fancy young woman, possibly an Aboriginal woman romantically involved with a white man. *lit.* baling-gan 'white man woman' or 'money woman'. [balincon 'young woman'(Fi); panlunggan 'fine (person)' (L)] *See:* **baling**[1, 2]; **-gan**[2]; **gin**; **jundal**; **mirung**; **mulagin**.

baluba *v.* put out a fire. [ballooba (Ha); palloobah (Lg)] *See:* **jalu**.

baludiriyari *v.* lose. [balloteriari (Ja); balloteriari (R); bal'loteri'ari (Wa)] *See:* **dalang**[2].

Balun.giny *n.* Coomera group. *lit.* 'river people'. [Bullongin (Allen and Lane 1914); Bullugun (Bn); Boo-long-in, Balloong-alli, Balloonjallie (M); Balun.giny (Sharpe 1998)]

baluny *Variant:* **balu.** *v.* die. [bal loinee (Ha); ballui, balupa, balluni (R); bā'lūnī, bar'lōin (Wa); baluwiyu (Wu)] *See:* **bang**; **ganggiri**.

Bamari *n.* place on Moreton Island. [Pomerree (B)]

bam-bam *n.* sexual intercourse. [pom-pom (Bl)] *See:* **burima**; **jim-jim**.

bambar *n.* path. [bumbar (J); dumbar (R)] *See:* **dumba**; **gulgan**[1].

bambara *Variant:* **bambar.** *n.* saw banksia. *[Banksia serrata]*. *Anth:* flowers were sucked for honey, bark used as dye for fishing nets (FNSI); used for making bullroarers (Ja). [bombara (B); bamberra (CW); bambara, bumbār (Ja); bambara, bumbarra (M); bumbaree (MMEIC); bumbār (R); bam'bara, bum'bar (Wa); bumbare (We)]

bambi-bambi *n.* type of fish, same type as dagadiyagubin. [pombee pombee (B)] *See:* **dagadiyagubin**.

Bamira *n.* Bummiera; Brown Lake. named by Balun.giny (Bn). *Anth:* a women's place. [Bahmeere-a (Bn); Bummel (CW); bumir, burner (H); Bumeerie, Boomirrie (M); Bamira (MMEIC)] *See:* **Balun.giny**; **bumal**; **Gambara**.

Bamiram *n.* woman's name. [Bumerum (R)]

bamirigari *n.* saltwater river, sea. [pamirrekirri (Ja); bummerycary (Lg); pāmirrikirri (R); pam'irrīkir'ri (Wa)] *See:* **burugara**; **dabilbaan**; **dagan**[1]; **yarabaan**.

-ban *deriv.* denotes a product that comes from a source. [bone (Cl); bon (M); bun (R); bin (W); bun (Wa)]

bana *Variant:* **buna.** *n.* bloodwood. *[Corymbia sp.]*. *Anth:* gum used as a red dye for staining possum rugs (Wi). [bunno (Ca); boona (D); boona (E); boona, buna (Ja); bunnah (Le); bunah (Ln); bana (H); boo-nah (Ha); bunnah (Le); boona, boonar (Lg); buna (M); būnā (Wa); bunna, buna (We)]

Banbara *n.* mountain near Cannon Creek, Ben Lomond Station. [Bun-burra, Bunburra (Ha)]

Banbunya *n.* man's name. [Panpoonyia (MB)]

banda$_1$ *n.* red-top grass. [bunda (Ha)]

banda$_2$ *adj; n.* erect, erection. [banda (H)]

Bandaanba *n.* Bundamba Creek. *lit.* bandaan-ba 'axe-stone place'. [Bundanda (S)] *See:* **-ba**[4]; **bandaan gulmang**.

bandaan gulmang *n.* stone from Beaudesert. *Anth:* good for making axes *lit.* 'axe stone' from gulmang 'axe' and Yugambeh bandahn 'stone, for tomahawk' (Sh). [Bundarn Culmung (Ha)] *See:* **gulmang**[1].

bandagambin *n.* type of tree. [būndūgumbin (R)] *See:* **-bin**.

Banda Madu *n.* Scotts Point. [Banda Mardo, Bandamardo (Bd)] *See:* **banda**[2].

Bandan.gambaba *n.* place on Stradbroke between Wallen Creek and Amity Point. [Bundngumbe Pa (Bn) named by Nunagal (Bn). *See:* **-ba**[4].

bandar *n.* honorific title, great man.
[bunda, bundŭr, bunjeru (R); bŭndŭr (Wa)]
See: **Banjur; biru; Bunda; gayabandar.**

bandara *adj.* strong, hard. [bandarra,
bandara (L); pundra (Lg); bandarra (M)]
See: **galin.**

bandibar *n.* she-oak. *[Casuarina glauca].*
[bundibar (Ja); būndĭbar (R); bun'dibār (Wa)]
See: **bila¹; wana-wanarambin.**

bandu *n.* white clay. [ban'do 'creamy white
paste of clay, gypsum or lime mixed with water'
(Bd); banda (Ja); bandu mardo (M); ban'dō
(Wa)] *See:* **mila-mila.**

bandung *n.* red-necked pademelon.
[Thylogale thetis]. [bundong (Ha)]

banduny *n.* mug. [bunduin, būnduin (R);
bun'dŭm (Wa)]

bang *adj.; n.* dead. [bong (Bl); bOŋ
(H); bory (Ja); bang 'old' (Lg); boang (T)]
See: **baluny; ganggiri; ganggirbany.**

-ba-nga *case.* indicates
accompaniment. consists of the ablative and
allative suffixes. [buggā, bukki (R)] *See:* **-ba¹;
-nga.**

ban.gaba *n.* door, entrance. *incorporates*
-gaba 'item for a purpose'. [boncabah, boncaba
(Lg)] *See:* **-gaba.**

bangalai *n.* swamp mahogany.
[Eucalyptus suaveolens]. [bang alay (Mac)]
See: **bularju; bundul; ngurbin.**

Bangamba *n.* Mud Island. *lit.* bangan-
ba 'place of mud'; named by Guwanbal
(Bn). [Bungumbah (Bn); Bungamba (CW);
Bungumba (Ln); Bungumba, Bung-umba (M);
Bungumba, Bangamba (S); Bungumba (W)]
See: **-ba⁴; bangan¹; Guwanbal.**

ban.gamba *n.* hand, fingernail.
[bangamba (H); bangoompa (M)] *See:* **mara¹;
gilan¹.**

bangan₁ *n.* mud. [baŋan (H); bagan (T)]
See: **daldari; wabum.**

Bangan₂ *n.* place name. *lit.* 'mud'.
[baŋanba (H)] *See:* **bangan¹.**

ban.gawani *v.* walk to and fro.
[ponkoane (Lg)] *See:* **nyan.**

bangga *adj.; adv.* quickly. [bānka (Ja);
bānka (R); ban'ka (Wa)] *See:* **burima; jubuiban;
mii¹; ngunbunjada.**

banggabadi *v.* call off. [pangcobade (Lg)]

banggam *n.* small basket. [bunggung,
bunggom (Ja); bunggung, bunggōm (R);
bun'gŭng bŭn'gom (Wa)] *See:* **yirimbin.**

banggany *Variant:* **bangga.** *v.* break.
[bungungdin (Ja); bongcobade 'separate cut off'
(Lg); būngūngdin 'break' (R); bun'gŭndin (Wa);
bongooi 'break' (We)] *See:* **gama.**

banggil₁ *Variant:* **banggil-banggil.** *n.*
grass. [bungil (Cl); bungill (Fi); ban (G); baŋel
(H); bungil, barygil, pungil, bon (Ja); pungil
(Lg); bungill, bungil (Ln); bungil, bunggil (M);
pungil, bungil pungil, bon, bŏn (R); bungil (Su);
bingil (W); bun', bun'gil (Wa)] *See:* **daga; dili².**

Banggil₂ *n.* pocket at Petrie. *lit.* 'grass'.
[Bungil 'near mouth of Pine River' (Bd); Bungil
(S)] *See:* **banggil¹.**

banggilgada *n.* flowers. *incorporates*
banggil 'grass'. [bungil cudda (Lg)]
See: **banggil¹.**

banggu₁ *n.* squirrel glider. *[Petaurus
norfolcensis].* [puncoo (D); panko (Ja); bong-ku
(Le); pan'ka (Wa)] *See:* **jiburu.**

banggu₂ *n.* ray (animal). [bunkoo (We)]

ban.gin *Variant:* **ban.gi.** *v.* tumble, fall.
[bunkin (R)]

Ban.ginbany *n.* Cleveland Point.
possibly lit. ban.gin-bany 'become fallen'.
[Pumpkin Bine 'Cleveland' (Bn); named by
Yagarabal (Bn)] *See:* **ban.gin; -bany; -bin;
Nyandili.**

ban.gindalinga *n.* battle, fight.
incorporates ban.gin 'fall'. [bun-gin-da-linga
(Ha)] *See:* **ban.gin; dulan.**

Ban.gu *n.* Mt Roberts. [Bunkoo (Be)]

bangui *n.* wallaby (female). [pau-i 'female little dark grey kangaroo' (Le); bongooi 'wallaby' (We)] *See:* **bugul; garil; jamban; magun; wangari; wangun.**

bangwal *n.* edible fern root; grindstone for crushing fern root. *[Blechnum cartilagineum].* *Anth:* source of native bread (FSNI); crushed using a grindstone of the same name. [bangwall (E); baŋwal, baŋol (H); bangwal 'blechnum fern' (Ja); bangwal (M); bungwall (MB); bungwal (W); bang'wal (Wa)] *See:* **danguwan.**

bani *adj.* holy. [buni (L)]

baniri *n.* gum; possibly yellowjacket. *[Eucalyptus tereticornis].* *Anth:* gum when soaked in water with its own bark makes a very lasting yellow stain (Wi). [buneri, bunēri (R)] *See:* **gargar; gilumbir.**

Banjai *n.* woman's name. [Bunjoy (Ha)]

banji *n.* male friend, brother. [banɟi (H)] *See:* **gimunggan; jimbalang; magiiba; nyungin.**

banjim *n.* quoll, native cat. *[Dasyurus viverrinus].* [bunjim (Ha); bungym (Hi); bundjim, bundsim (L)] *See:* **miburu; milgal.**

banjin₁ *n.* native bee. [bunjin (Ba)] *See:* **jalaman; gabai¹; gila²; guja¹; gunidar; mabi¹; nagi.**

Banjin₂ *n.* woman's name. *lit.* 'native bee'. [Bunjeen (Ha)] *See:* **banjin¹.**

Banjui *n.* woman's name. [Bunjoey (Be)]

Banjur *n.* skin group (male). [bandur, bandūr, Tandōr (R); Banda (RB); banda (Ro); bandur, Bandoor (W); ban'jūr (Wa)] *See:* **Barang¹; Bunda; Jarawany.**

Banjurgan₁ *n.* skin group (female). [Banjoorcan (M); bandurun, Bandagan (R); bandurun, Bandoorookun (W)] *See:* **Baranggan; Bundagan; Jarawanygan; -gan².**

Banjurgan₂ *n.* Mt French, south peak. *lit.* 'female of Banjur skin group'. [Bun-shar-gun (Ha); Bunuurgen, Bunshargun, Punchagin (S)] *See:* **Banjurgan¹; Mibaram.**

banman *Variant:* **banma.** *v.* pluck; pull; draw out. [pūnmānn (Ja); pūnmān (R); pub'man (Wa)] *See:* **banman.gilin.**

banman.gilin *Variant:* **banman.gili.** *v.* pick out. *lit.* banman-gilin 'fingernail pluck'. [pūnmāngillin 'separate' (Ja); pūnmāngillin (R); pun'man-gil'len (Wa)] *See:* **banman; gilan¹.**

banuru *n.* brigalow, spear made from brigalow. *[Acacia harpophylla].* [bonnaroo (CW); bunuro, bonooro (S)] *See:* **duriny.**

-bany *Variant:* **-ba.** *deriv.* indicates having/acquiring a property. changes a noun or adj. into a verb. [ban (L); can (M); bun, pin, punni (R); pin (W)]

bany *adj; n.* sick, sickness. [pī (G); bayi (L); paian, pie, piengo (Lg); bai, bain (R)]

Banyaraba *n.* Toowong. [Banaraba 'bend in the river, Toowong' (Bd); Banyarraba 'Milton Creek' and 'camp near Toowong station' (M)] *See:* **-ba⁴.**

banygaba *n.* medicine. *lit.* bany-gaba 'item(s) for sickness'. [piengobah, paiango-ba (Lg)] *See:* **bany; -gaba.**

banyu₁ *n.* ridge, backbone. [padnoo 'backbone' (Lg); banyo (M); ban'yō (Wa)]

Banyu₂ *n.* Banyo. *lit.* 'ridge'; possibly named by whites. [Banyo (S)] *See:* **banyu¹.**

bara₁ *n.* type of small goanna. [barra (Ja); burra, parra (Lg); burrah (M); bar'ra (Wa)] *See:* **giwa; walmuram¹; yaugira.**

bara₂ *n.* vine with yellow berries. [bara (M)]

bara₃ *n.* red fruit. [barra (Lg)]

baraabun *n.* rose-crowned fruit dove. *possibly [Ptilinopus regina].* [bra-boon 'flock or fruit pigeon' (Ha); paraabum 'cockatoo pigeon with a red crest' (Le)]

Baraami *n.* man's name. [Brummy (B)]

baraban *n.* band of vine or bark worn about head, possum twine worn across the shoulders by kippas. *lit.* bara-ban 'made from vine'. [parra-bone (Cl); brābin (G); parra bone (Ja); parrabone (M); barbun (Ro); bar'bun (Wa)] *See:* -**ban**; **bara²**; **dinggil**.

bara-bara *n.* game played with a ball. [purru 'ball' (Ja); pur'rū, pur'rū-pur'rū (Wa)]

barabil *n.* dawn. [birrabill (Be); parrabil (Lg)] *See:* **gabura¹**.

barabun *n.* fire. [paraboon (Lg)] *See:* **jalu**.

baragal *adj.* busy. [burragol (Lg)]

Baragalba *n.* Bracalba. [Bracalba (Bd)] *possibly lit.* baragal-ba 'busy place'. *See:* -**ba⁴**; **baragal**.

baragan *adj.* thin, flat, in poor condition. [burra-garn (Ha); boragan (Lg)]

baragany₁ *n.* stinging tree. *[Dendrocnide moroides].* [parragan (Cl); baran (H); burra-gun (Ha); baragun (Hi); braggain (Ja); bargan (L); burrgan (Le); barragan (M); barrakadan (R); braggan (Ro); barengun (W); brag'gain, brag'gan (Wa)] *See:* **baragany²**; **burjin**; **gimbi**.

baragany₂ *n.* returning boomerang, boomerang made from stinging tree. [bruggun (D); bargan 'woomera' (Fi); purgun, barkan (G); baran (H); barrakan, banakadan, parragan, braggan (Ja); barrabb, bargabb, barragun (M); barrakadan (R); braggan (Ro); barengun (W); baragan (Wu)] *See:* **baragany¹**; **birban**; **gawan-gawan²**; **jirabang²**; **yabun**.

baragany₃ *n.* rag made from the bark of the stinging tree for mopping up honey. [brag-gain (Wa)]

baralbin *n.* cogon grass. *[Imperata cylindrical].* [burrul 'grass' (Bn); baralbin 'blady grass' (J); boralpin 'seedy grass' (Lg)]

Baralbinbila *n.* creek on Stradbroke between Jigal-jigal and Ngara-ngaragai. *lit.* baralbin-bila 'overrun with cogon grass'; named by Nunagal (Bn). [Burrull Win Piller 'a lot of grass' (Bn)] *See:* **baralbin**; -**bila**; **Nunagal**.

Baramba *n.* Mt Peak near Peak Crossing. [Burrumpah (Be)] *See:* -**ba⁴**.

Barambin *n.* gully that passes through Victoria Park, Bowen Hills, York's Hollow. [Barrambi (Bd); Barrambin (CW)] *See:* -**bin**.

Baran *n.* Mt Samson. [Buran (Bd)]

Barang₁ *n.* skin group (male). [Barang (Bd); barrough (D); Baring (Hw); Barrang (M); Barang, Bārāng (R); barang (Ro); Barang (W)] *See:* **Banjur**; **Bunda**; **Jarawany**.

barang₂ *n.* edge of a knife. [parrang (Lg)]

barang₃ *adj.* crooked. [barang (Ba)] *See:* **bunbar**; **wandan**.

Baranggan *n.* skin group (female). [Baranga (Bd); Barranggin (M); Barangan (R); Barangun, barangan (W)] *See:* **Banjurgan¹**; **Bundagan**; **Jarawanygan**; -**gan²**.

Baranggul *n.* Flinders Peak east of Peak Crossing. [Baranggul (MMEIC)]

barany *adv.* now, soon, after, then, today, eventually. [burro (Ha); barraen (Hi); berren, burru (Ja); berehn, beren, baru (L); purren, bowya, parroo (Lg); bayan (M); berren, burra, burru, pārū (R); booren, baro (W); ber'ren, bur'ū (Wa)] *See:* **juwanin**; **yaraba**.

baranyba₁ *adj.* new. *lit.* barany-ba 'from now'. [purrenbah (Lg)] *See:* -**ba¹**; **barany**; **yingang**.

baranyba₂ *adv.* nearly. [barumpa (R); ber'renpā (Wa)] *See:* **barany**.

baranybu *adv.* immediately. *lit.* barany=bu 'really soon'. [purrenboo (Lg)] *See:* **barany**; =**bu²**.

baranygali *adj; n.* quick-tempered, quick-tempered fellow. *lit.* barany-gali 'right now'. [barengully (Hi)] *See:* **barany**; -**gali**.

bargil *adv.* for a long time. [barkil (R)] *See:* **buiyala**.

barung *n.* rufous kangaroo rat. *[Aepyprymnus rufescens]*. [burrool, moorrung (Ha); barrun 'kangaroo rat' (Ja); parrun 'kangaroo rat' (Le); parroon 'large bandicoot' (Lg)] *See:* **wugalban**.

barunyuba *n.* tree fern. *Anth:* new growth roasted and eaten, leaves used for matting (FNSI) [burunyaba, burumyaba 'tree fern' (L); broonyooba (M); bar'rūn (Wa)] *See:* **wulungga**.

barwan *adj.* wide, great. [barwan 'wide' (Ba); barwon 'great' (MMEIC)]

bayal *n.* net. [baial (Ja); baial (R); bai'al (Wa)] *See:* **durur; mandin¹; mirbang**.

Bayami *n.* God, great. from Yuin-Kuric languages. [bajami (H); Burrāni, burrai (R); Biami (Walker 1972)] *See:* **Mirir**.

Bayiba *n.* woman's name. [Baīiba (R)]

Bayimba *n.* woman's name. [Pa-im-ba (Ha)]

biba *n.* coat. word origin unknown. [beppah, bebo (Lg)]

bibaba *n.* waistcoat. *incorporates* biba 'coat'. [bebobuh (Lg)] *See:* **biba**.

Bibinira *n.* man's name. [Bippinerra (R)]

bibu *n.* hill, mountain. [vipoor (Be); beepa (Cl); bippo (Hi); beepa (Ja); beppo (Lg); bippoo, pipoo (Ln); bippo (M); bipu, bippu (R); bibba (T); beppo (W)] *See:* **dalgambar; duun**.

Bibuban *n.* North Brisbane group, speakers of Durubal. *possibly lit.* bibu-ban 'being hilly'. [Beepooban (M)] *See:* **-ban; bibu**.

Bibu-bibu *n.* ancient camping ground, site of Thomas Hardcastle's homestead in Dugandan. *lit.* 'hill-hill'. [Biboo-Biboo (Ha)] *See:* **bibu**.

bibubin *n.* mountainous country. *lit.* bibu-bin 'mountain place'. [bippoobin (Hi)] *See:* **bibu; -bin**.

Bibu Binbiyan *n.* Bippo Penbean, high land near Flying Fox Creek on Stradbroke. [Bibbo Penbean (CW); bibobenbeyan (MMEIC)] *See:* **bibu**.

Bibugan *n.* hill like a sugar loaf with a flat top. *lit.* bibu-gan 'typified by hill(s)'. [Bibādgan (G)] *See:* **bibu; -gan¹**.

bibuji *n.* hill water cataract. *incorporates* bibu 'hill'. [bippoojee (M)] *See:* **bibu; gurgundal**.

Bibu Nguyirbunya *n.* Mt Hardgrave. [Bippo Oyerpunya (CW)] *See:* **bibu**.

bidamjaran *adj.* wrong. [bidamjaran (MMEIC)] *See:* **nguniwali**.

Bidiirabul *n.* woman's name. [Biteerabul (M)]

Bidiiri *n.* woman's name. [Biteeri (W)]

bidung *adv.* near. [perduk (T)] *See:* **danyung**.

biduru *adj.* full. [bittooroo (M)] *See:* **bila²; ngumburu**.

Biga Banga Jimba *n.* Sandy Mt. [biga banga ǧimba (H)]

bigara *Variant:* **bigar**. *n.* red ironbark. *[Eucalyptus sp.]*. [pigurra (Ca); biggar (M); big'gera (Wa)] *See:* **ganaibira; jana; janduru; jum-jum; nyandala**.

bigargin *n.* big black cormorant. *[Phalacrocorax carbo]*. [bigkergin (Ha)]

bigi *n.* piccabean palm, Bangalow palm, coolamon made from palm. *[Archontophoenix cunninghamiana]*. [bicce (Ha); pikki (Ja); pik'ki (Wa)] *See:* **dagabinbigi**.

Bigil *n.* place on Stradbroke. [Bigil (MMEIC)]

bigun *n.* freshwater catfish. *[Tandanus tandanus]*. [booigoom (M); bigoon (We)] *See:* **ngamarigara; wargan**.

Bigunjin *n.* name of place and the people associated with it. *lit.* bigun-jin 'catfish people' or 'many catfish'. [Biguntine (B)] *See:* **bigun; -jin**.

bigunjur₁ *n.* ant's nest. [bigoonture (W)] *See:* **baigan; danmurin; galalang; giwarang; mugara²; murin**.

Bigunjur₂ *n.* creek on Stradbroke. *lit.* 'ant's nest'. [bigoonture (W)] *See:* **bigunjur.**

biigi *n.* sun, day. [pekey (Bl); biggery (D); beeké (E); begge (Fi); bygee (Hi); bīgi, bagee, begee, beeke (Ja); bigi (L); beegy, reeke, begee (Lg); begee, bigie, biggie 'light', begie 'day' (Ln); bi-gi (M); bīgi (R); bagee (Su); bigge (T); baga (Th); bigge (W); bī'gī (Wa); beegie (We)] *See:* **guiyar**².

biigibang *adj.* setting (of the sun). *lit.* biigi-bang 'sun dead'. [pekey-bong (Bl)] *See:* **bang; biigi.**

biigi-biigi₁ *n.* regent bowerbird. *lit.* 'sun-sun'. *[Sericulus chrysocephalus].* [beegy-beegy (Lg)]

biigi-biigi₂ *adj.* yellow. *lit.* 'sun-sun'. [beegy-beegy (Lg)]

biigibiribi *n.* evening. *lit.* biigi-biribi 'little sun'. [bīgibīrpi (Ja); bīgibīrpi (R); bī'gī-ber'pī (Wa)] *See:* **jalu-jalu; ngunu; nulbu-nulbu; yaragal.**

biigibu *adj.* sunburnt. *lit.* biigi=bu 'so much sun!'. [begeeboh (Lg)] *See:* **biigi; =bu**².

biigigaba *n.* clock. *lit.* biigi-gaba 'item for the sun'. [begee obah, beegy-oba (Lg)] *See:* **biigi; -gaba.**

biigigarany *Variant:* **biigigara.** *v.* set (of the sun). *lit.* biigi-garany 'sun fall'. [bygee gareen (Hi); begee-garan 'night' (Lg)] *See:* **biigi; garany.**

biigigurumba *n.* midday. *lit.* biigi-gurumba 'big sun'. [begee-caroomba 'noon' (Lg)] *See:* **biigi; gurumba.**

Biinbira *n.* woman's name. [Bēēnbera (G)]

biing-biing *n.* pig. from English pig. *[Sus scrofa].* [ping-ping (Ha); bīngbing (Hi); pigpig (R); ding (T)]

bijar *n.* corpse. [bitoer (N)]

bijara *n.* creek or name of a creek. [biɟara (H)] *See:* **bili; waril**¹**; yinil.**

-bila *deriv.* being affected or afflicted by a property. changes a noun or adj. into a verb. [bila (R)]

bila₁ *n.* she-oak, swamp oak. *[Casuarina glauca].* *Anth:* the timber is good firewood, nuts are burned (FNSI); balan 'black cockatoos' feed almost exclusively on the nuts of the oak trees (MMEIC). [billa (H); billair (Ha); billah (Le); bill-ai, billarr (M); bil'lai (Wa); billa (We)] *See:* **bandibar; wana-wanarambin.**

bila₂ *adj.* full. [pille (Lg)] *See:* **biduru; -bila; ngumburu.**

bila-bila *n.* crest of a cockatoo. possibly related to Yugambeh bile-bileh 'crown of head' (Sh). [billa-billa (Ja); bidla-bidla (Lg); bil'la-bil'la (Wa)]

Bilagal *n.* hill between Eagle St and the Brisbane River. [Billagal (Bd)]

bilanbin *n.* type of saltwater fish. [pillunbin (Lg)]

bilara *Variant:* **bilar.** *n.* war spear. [billar (E); billara (Ha); bilan, billar, pi-lar, pillar, peelar 'ironbark spear' (Ja); billar (Lg); pillir (Ln); bilan (R); pi-lar (Ro); pil'ar (Wa)] *See:* **bulan**¹**; ganai; jagany; jibalang.**

bilayir *n.* tree stump. [billayīr (Ja); billayīr (R)] *See:* **magul dugam; maling.**

bilba *n.* butcher bird. *[Cracticus sp.].* [pilpa (M); pil'ba (Wa)]

bili *n.* creek, gully. [pilly (M)] *See:* **bijara; waril**¹**; yinil.**

Bilijara *n.* Kedron, upper. [Pilijara (Bd)] *lit.* bili-jara 'creek land'. *See:* **bili; jara.**

bilin *n.* rainbow lorikeet. *[Trichoglossus haematodus moluccanus].* *Anth:* when lorikeets are plentiful, it's a good time for sea mullet. [billin 'parrot' (Fi); bee-linn 'blue mountain parrot' (Ha); bylen 'parrot' (Hi); pillin 'parrot' (Ja); billin 'parrot' (L); pil'en 'parrot' (Wa); billem 'parrot' (We)]

bilin-bilin *n.* king parrot. *[Alisterus scapularis].* [bilin-bilin 'parrot' (Ca); bilin bilin 'king parrot' (MMEIC)] *See:* **bilin.**

biling *n.* microbat. [beling (Ca); billing (Ja); bil'ling (Wa)]

Bilira *n.* Beveley's Spring at Mt French. [Bileera 'place' (Ha)]

Bilirba *n.* one of the Glasshouse Mountains. named by Yagarabal (Bn). [Bearlerbah 'Glasshouse Mt' (Bn)] *See:* -ba⁴.

biliyagan *n.* black cockatoo. *[Calyptorhynchus sp.].* [bil-lear-gun (Ha)] *See:* **balan**; **biluwala**; **gaiyara**; **garara**; **giwang**; **jarbal.**

bilunga₁ *n.* bullrout, freshwater stonefish. *[Notesthes robusta].* *Anth:* poisonous; do not eat (MMEIC). [billonga (We)]

Bilunga₂ *n.* woman's name. *lit.* 'bullrout'. [Billoonga (W)] *See:* **bilunga**¹.

Bilungili *n.* rock holes in Oaky Creek. [Billunkilly (Ha)]

bilurun *n.* wonga pigeon. *[Leucosarcia melanoleuca].* [billorn (Ha)] *See:* **dandali**¹; **gulun.**

biluwala *n.* cockatoo. [biluala (Ba)] *See:* **balan**; **biliyagan**; **gaiyara**; **garara**; **giwang**; **jarbal.**

bimba₁ *n.* snapper. *[Chrysophrys auratus].* [bimbah (M); bimba (M); pimba (W); bimbah (We)]

bimba₂ *v.* pierce. [bimbe (R)]

Bimbiyan₁ *n.* hill near Flying Fox Creek, north of Myora. [Pimpeyan, Penbean (S); Pimbeyan (W)]

Bimbiyan₂ *n.* man's name. [Pimbeyan (W)]

Bimi *n.* woman's name. [Beemee (W)]

Bimiraba *n.* mouth of Oxley Creek. [Beemirraba (M)]

-bin *deriv.* indicates a place; appears in plant names. [bin (Hi); bin (M)]

bina *n; v.* ear, hear, know. [pidna (Bl); bidna (Cl); pitney (E); pidner (Fi); binaŋ (H); pitney (Ja); binne (L); bidna (La); pidna, pitney (Lg); bidna, pidna (Ln); pidna, pidna (M); pinna (N); pidna, pitne, binang (R); bidna (Su); binna 'ear', binang 'know' (T); bidne (Th); pidna (W); pid'na, pinang (Wa); binnar (We)] *See:* **jugu.**

Binabira *n.* man's name. *lit.* 'beech'. [Binĕbera (G)]

binang guri *n.* person who won't listen. *lit.* 'ear person' from Yugambeh binang 'ear' and guri 'Aboriginal person' (Sh). [binung gurri (MMEIC)] *See:* **bina**; **guri.**

binanggurung₁ *n.* bearded dragon. *lit.* 'black ear' from gurung 'black' and Yugambeh binang 'ear' (Sh). *[Pogona barbata].* [pī'nang gŏr'an (Ma)] *See:* **bina**; **gurung**²; **nyara.**

Binanggurung₂ *n.* Highgate Hill. *lit.* 'bearded dragon'. [Beenung-urrung (S)] *See:* **binanggurung**¹.

binangundu *adj; n.* deaf, deaf person. *lit.* bina-ngundu 'ear-dull'. [pidnaŋūntū (R)] *See:* **bina**; **ngundu**².

binarwin *n.* blackbutt. *[Eucalyptus pilularis].* [binnarwin (D)] *See:* **girigan**; **mandili.**

binawali *adj.* crazy, deaf. *lit.* bina-wali 'ear-bad'. [binawali (H); pidna wallee (M); pidnwuddeli (R)] *See:* **bina**; **wali.**

binawanga *adj.* stubborn. *lit.* 'ear-deaf' from bina 'ear' and Yugambeh wangal/wangam 'deaf' (Sh). [binawaŋa (H)] *See:* **bina.**

Bindari *n.* lower Kedron. [Bindarri 'About Kedron Brook' (Bd)]

bindigam *n.* bottlebrush flower. *[Callistemon sp.].* [pendicup (Bd)]

Bindinba *n.* pillar box stone on Mt Alford. [Bintenbar (Be); Bin-tin-ba (Ha)] *See:* -ba⁴.

bindu-bindu *n.* type of small bird. [pindo pindo (Lg)]

bing *n.* father, father's brother. [byng (E); bing (Ha); pappen (Hi); bing, byng, ging (Ja); bing (L); byng (Lg); bing (Ln); bing (M); bing (N); bing (R); bing (T); bing (W); bing (Wa)]

bin.ga *n.* head, hat. from Yugambeh bin.ga 'hat' (Sh). [binge (H); bincare (Ha)] *See:* **bumbum; magul**[1].

bingal-bingal *n.* swallow. [pingul pingul (Lg)] *See:* **nabidi.**

bingging *n.* beetle. [bingking (L)]

bin.ging *Variant:* **bin.ging-bin.ging.** *n.* short-necked turtle. *[Emydura macquarii kreffiii].* [pin-kin (Bd); bing-ging (Ca); bingiŋ (H); binkeen (Ha); binking (Hi); pinkin, binkin (Ja); binkin (L); pinking (Le); binking binking (M); binkin (W); bin'kin (Wa)] *See:* **bubiya; dagibagam; mibaral; mujing; naguba.**

Bin.gingba *n.* New Farm. *Anth:* this name is now given to Pinkenba (P); *lit.* bin.gingba 'place of short-necked turtles'. [Pinkenbah (Bd); Binkenbar 'New Farm' (P); Binkinba 'New Farm' (S)] *See:* **-ba**[4]; **bin.ging.**

Bin.gingjuwa *n.* Spicer's Peak south of Tregony. *lit.* bin.ging-juwa 'turtle (head) lifting (above the water)'. [Binkingjoorah (Be); Binkinjoora (S)] *See:* **bin.ging; juwan.**

binigan *n.* man. [binegan (Ha)] *See:* **jaan; danbang; guri; malara; mari**[2].

binimda *n.* blood-gum. *[Corymbia sp.].* [binempta (E); binempta (Ja); binempta (Lg)]

Binin-binin *n.* place name. [pinnin pinnin (B)]

Binindiyimba *n.* Coochin-area hill near Wallace's Creek. [Bin-een-de-imba (Ha)] *See:* **-ba**[4].

binji *n.* nursery word for stomach. [bingey (Bl); bingie (Kd); binɟi (H)] *See:* **digiri.**

binjilurar *n.* stone tomahawk. [bingieelorer (Fi)] *See:* **gulmang**[1]; **mugim; nanggan; wagara**[1].

-biny *infl.* indicates motion back the way that one came. [pee (M); bi (R)]

binygar *n.* cabbage tree. *[Livistona australis].* [buikar (M); bīngpēr (R); bin'kar (Wa)] *See:* **mangargal.**

bir *n.* musk lorikeet. *[Polytelis swainsonii].* [pir 'parrot (green-leek)' (Wa)] *See:* **mirin.**

-bira *deriv.* denotes a people or their country. [perra 'tribe' (M)]

bira *n.* grog. from English beer. [bira (H); beera (Ln)] *See:* **gira**[2].

birabun *n.* table, slab. [pirraboon (Lg)]

Birali *n.* man's name. [Berali (R)]

biram *n.* sky. [birrar (Be); biram (H); birra (Ja); birra (R); biram (T); bir'ra (Wa)] *See:* **ngurun; wangan.**

biran[1] *n.* blubber. [Prin Prin Pa 'where blubbers were left by the tide' (Bn); pyrra (Lg)] *See:* **Biranba; Biran-biranba.**

biran[2] *n.* 'goorka lizard', possibly leaf-tailed gecko. [bir-run (Ha)]

Biran[3] *n.* man's name. [Bēran (G)]

Biranba *n.* spring at Petrie. *lit.* 'place of blubber'. [Ber-rimpa 'below Pine River pocket' (Bd); Berrimpa 'present place' (S)] *See:* **-ba**[4]; **biran**[1].

Biran-biranba[1] *n.* part of Amity, now underwater; between Wallen Creek and Amity Point. *lit.* 'where blubbers were left by the tide' (Bn); named by Nunagal (Bn). [Prin Prin Pa (Bn); Pirrenpirrenba (W)] *See:* **-ba**[4]; **biran**[1]; **Nunagal.**

Biran-biranba[2] *n.* man's name. [Pirrenpirrenba (W)] *See:* **biran**[1].

birban *n.* toy boomerang. [bribbun (G); bir'bun (Wa)] *See:* **baragany**[2]; **jirabang**[2]; **yabun.**

birban-birban *n.* game played with small boomerangs. [bir'bun-bir'bun (Wa)] *See:* **birban.**

biribanga *adv.* greatly, very. [birribung (R); bira-ba-nga (T)] *See:* **-gali.**

biribi *adj.* little. [brippee (Ha); birabari (Hi); parrapa (Ja); perba (Lg); berpi, birpee (M); berpi (R); pirpirbin (T); beerpa (W); ber'pī (Wa)] *See:* **jalgal; narang¹; ngambara; nala.**

Biriga *n.* Mt Toowoonan. [Ber-eager (Ha)]

birin *adv.* between. [pirren (Lg)]

Birindaliba *n.* Cemetery Creek. named by Balun.giny (Bn). [Birrindullipah (Bn)] *See:* **-ba⁴; Balun.giny.**

birinja *n.* yellow wood tree. [bare-ander (Ha); b'irrinja (M)]

biru *n.* sir. from English sir. [biro (E)] *See:* **bandar.**

Birwa *n.* Mt Beerwah. [bi'wa (H); Bileera 'place' (Ha); Birwa (M)]

biya *v.* throw. [beea (M); peea (W)] *See:* **garany.**

biyamal *Variant:* **biyama.** *v.* throw away. *incorporates* biya 'throw'. [behemal (Lg)] *See:* **biya; -ma.**

Biya Murunyba *n.* woman's name. *lit.* biya muruny-ba 'throw a stick'. [Beeamurrieba (M); Peea mareeba (W)] *See:* **-ba²; biya; muruny.**

biyara *v.* remember. [peare (Lg)]

-bu₁ *case.* durative suffix that indicates a span of time. [bu (P); bu (R)]

=bu₂ *clitic.* emphatic clitic. [poo (Lg); bu, po (R)]

buba₁ *n.* ashes. [wooppa (E); buba (H); puppar (Ha); boopah (Hi); woopa, buppa (Ja); wooppa, boopah (Lg); boopa (M); buppa (R); bup'pa (Wa)]

buba₂ *adj.; n.* white. [wooppa (E); buba (H); puppar (Ha); boopah (Hi); woopa, buppa (Ja); wooppa, boopah (Lg); boopa (M); buhpar 'white of eye' (N); buppa (R); bup'pa (Wa)] *See:* **giwara.**

buba jara *n.* white earth. *lit.* 'white earth'. [pundarah (Lg)] *See:* **buba²; jara.**

Bubal *n.* man's name. [Pub-bal (CW); Pubbal (W)]

bubalam *n.* smoke pipe. *incorporates* buba 'ashes'. [bubilam or bubulam (H)] *See:* **buba¹; jumu¹.**

bubiya *n.* sea turtle. [boobaryan (Hi); poobya (W); boonbia (We); bōw-aiyā (Wa)] *See:* **bin.ging; dagibagam; mibaral; mujing; naguba.**

bubu *Variant:* **bubu-bubu.** *n.* apple-box tree. *[Eucalyptus bridgesiana].* [pubo (Ca); boy-poy (Ha); bu-hu (M); bu'pū (Wa)] *See:* **naigura.**

budai *adj.* male. [pudhai (N)]

budara *adj.* rough. [poodra (Lg)] *See:* **mulgara-mulgara.**

buding *n.* prawn. [budiŋ (H); booting (We)]

budiri *n.* bay. [boodthere (Lg)] *See:* **bamirigari; burugara; dabilbaan; dagan¹; waril¹; yarabaan.**

budung *adj.* weak. [boodoong (Lg)] *See:* **manmal; yaran-yaran.**

buduwar₁ *n.* wedge-tailed eagle. *[Aquila audax].* [boodooar, budar (M)] *See:* **duwai; jibal; mibany; ngan-ngan.**

Buduwar₂ *n.* place in Eagle Farm. *lit.* 'eaglehawk'. [Budar (Bd)] *See:* **buduwar¹.**

buga₁ *adj.* stinky, rotten. [boogar, booga (Lg); booga (M); booghor (W)] *See:* **yila.**

buga₂ *v.* think, opine. [boggo, boogar (Lg)] *See:* **gana²; ngui; winanga.**

bugal *n.* small pine. [boocal (Lg)] *See:* **buunyi; dandardam; juunbal; gambarju.**

bugany *Variant:* **buga.** *v.* sleep. [bogan (E); bugaɲ (H); boogun (Hi); boogan, bugan, boo-gan (Ja); bogan, boogan (Lg); boogan (M); buggan, bōgan (R); booga (Su); boogun, bugan (W); bu'gan, bu'an (Wa)] *See:* **waja; yunma.**

buganyma *v.* put to sleep. *lit.* bugany-ma 'cause to sleep'. [buganmu (Ja); buganmu (R); bu'gan mŭ (Wa)] *See:* **bugany; -ma.**

bugara-bugara₁ *excl.* keep farther away. [boogara boogara (Be)]

Bugara-bugara₂ *n.* Mt Barney. *lit.* 'keep farther away'. [Boogara Boogara (Be); Bugara Bugara (Ha)] *See:* **bugara-bugara**¹.

bugawa *n.* mussel. [būkkaoa (Ja); būkkaoa (R); buk'kaōa (Wa)] *See:* **muyum**¹; **wayuung.**

bugawan *n.* Brahminy kite. *[Haliastur indus].* [bugawan 'fish hawk' (Ja); bugawan 'red-breasted sea eagle' (P)] *See:* **din.gal; miriginba**¹.

bugi *v.* swim. from Aboriginal English bogey. [bogué (E); bogue (Ja); bogue (Lg)] *See:* **yara**².

Bugu *n.* person's name. [Boko (B)]

bugui *adj; n.* subject to the in-law respect relation, an in-law subject to the respect relation. [bugo-i 'mother-in-law' (Ja)]

buguja *n.* yellow-faced whip snake. *[Demansia psammophis].* [bocudscha (Le)] *See:* **diruny.**

bugul *n.* swamp wallaby, female swamp wallaby. *[Wallabia bicolor].* [boo-gal (CW); boro (G); bug-wal (Ja); bogoll (Le); bugull (Ln); boogal (W); b-g'wal (Wa); boogool (We)] *See:* **bangui; jamban; garil; magun; wangari; wangun.**

bugur *n.* crane. [bookoor (M)] *See:* **junggi; gundurgan; muralagang.**

buguru *n.* lung. [buguru (L)] *See:* **dalu; gamang.**

bui₁ *v.* breathe. [pui (Ja); pui (R); pū'i (Wa)] *See:* **buidangal; wiya**².

bui₂ *n.* carpet python. [buiyir (R); bū'ī (Wa)] *See:* **gabul; guda**²; **juumgumulumgal; yuwan.**

buidangal *Variant:* **buidanga.** *v.* breathe. *incorporates* bui 'breathe'. [booydungal (Lg)] *See:* **bui**¹; **wiya**².

buigum *n.* mulloway. *[Argyrosomus japonicus].* [booygoon 'salt water fish' (Lg); booigoom 'dewfish' (M)] *See:* **diyala; wargan.**

buiyala *adv.* for a long time. [puïyala (R)] *See:* **bargil.**

bujal₁ *Variant:* **buja.** *v.* fart. [budʒal, budʒir (H)] *See:* **bujing.**

bujal₂ *n.* person you feel sorry for. [bujal (MMEIC)] *See:* **dagal**².

bujang *n.* mother, mother's sister. [butang (E); budʒaŋ (H); wud dung (Ha); booyarng (Hi); poojang, pujary, butang (Ja); bus'ang (L); butang, budjong (Lg); buddaan (Ln); puddang (M); buddang (N); pūjāng, būdāng (R); buddang (T); budjong (W); bud'ang, pud'ang (Wa)]

bujara *n.* morning. from Yugambeh budjarah 'morning' (Sh). [bujura (Ba)]

Bujarbin *n.* man's name. [Bood-jar-pin (CW); Boodjarpin (W)]

bujari *adj; excl.* amazing, beautiful, good. from Dharug budyari 'good, right'. [boodgeeree (Bl); budgerie (Ha); budjarang (L); boodgeree (Lg); bujura 'light' (MMEIC); budgery (P)] *See:* **galang; marumba**¹; **nyiwang.**

bujing *n.* fart. [budʒiŋ (H)] *See:* **bujal**¹.

bujingbila *excl; v.* swear word. *lit.* bujing-bila 'be afflicted with farts'. [bujin bila 'a fun swear word relating to fart' (MMEIC)] *See:* **-bila; bujing.**

bujinggin *n.* female child. [poojingking 'child' (Lg)] *See:* **bujiri; duwangjin; giba**¹; **gin; gumingguny; nyamal.**

bujiri *Variant:* **bujir.** *n.* boy. [bugēre (Fi); budʒir, budʒil, budʒal (H); budgera (Ha); boodgeree (Hi); pusiri (L); boodery, bujerï (Ln); buiyir, buiyïr (R); boojare (We)] *See:* **duwangjin; giba**¹; **gumingguny.**

Bujiriwang *n.* mountain near Mt Barney. *incorporates* bujiri 'boy'. [Budgerawong (Ha)] *See:* **bujiri.**

bujiriyagara *adj; n.* childless, childlessness. *lit.* bujiri-yagara 'no boys'. [boejer-yahgar (N)] *See:* **bujiri; yagara**¹.

Bujumbiri *n.* man's name. [Bood-joom-bir-ee (CW)]

bujumbiriba$_1$ *n.* young female dugong. [Boojumperriba (M); Boodjoombirreebar (W)] *See:* **bagirang**; **yangan**^{1}.

Bujumbiriba$_2$ *n.* woman's name. *lit.* 'young female dugong'. [Boojumperriba (M); Boodjoombirreebar (W)] *See:* **bujumbiriba**^{1}.

bujurna *adj.* open. [poodeurna (Lg)]

-bul *Variant:* **-bal; -wal.** *deriv.* designates a group or speakers of a language. [bal (H)]

bula$_1$ *quant.* two, both. [boodla (Bl); burla (E); bullair (Ha); boodela, budela, bulla, burla (Ja); bullae (L); bulla, poonlah (La); burla, boodlah (Lg); bulla (Ln); bula, boollay, boolah (M); būdela (R); bulla (Su); bullae 'two', buppur 'three' (T); budla, bulla (W); bulla (Wa)]

bula$_2$ *n.* cattle. from English bull. [buller (Fi); bula (H); bulla (Ha); bullae (L); bulla (R)]

bula$_3$ *n.* belly. [budlah (Lg)] *See:* **binji**; **digiri**.

Bula$_4$ *n.* woman's name. *lit.* 'two'. [Budla, Boodlo, Boodloo (B); Budd-la (CW); Buddla (W)] *See:* **bula**^{1}.

bulabu *quant.* both. *lit.* bula=bu 'really two'. [budelabu (R)] *See:* **=bu**^{2}; **bula**^{1}.

bula-bula *quant.* four. [boodla-boodla (Bl); bulla-bulla (Cl); burla burla (E); boodela-boodela, bulla-bulla, budela-budela (Ja); burl burla (Lg); bulla-bulla (Ln); bula-bula (M); budela budela (R); bulla-bulla (Su); boodla boodla (W); bud'ela-bud'ela, bulla-bulla (Wa)] *See:* **bula**^{1}; **gagara**^{2}.

bulagaba *adv.* of two. *lit.* bula-gaba 'item(s) for two'. [boodlunggobah (Lg)] *See:* **bula**^{1}; **-gaba**.

bulagan *n.* cohabitation. *lit.* bula-gan 'being a couple'. [budla-gan (Ba)] *See:* **bula**^{1}; **-gan**^{1}; **mibanja**.

bulaganyara *quant.* three. [burla ganar (E); cun nara bull air (Ha); burldganin (Ja); bullae-kanyara (L); burla ganar (Lg); boodla kunara (W)] *See:* **bula**^{1}; **majan**; **ganyara**^{1}.

bulagi *n.* Sydney blue gum. *[Eucalyptus saligna]*. [bool lugi (Ha)] *See:* **durambai**; **manggara**.

Bulagu *n.* Boggo region. *possibly lit.* bula=gu 'for the purpose of the two (trees)'; possibly named for two trees formerly at the top of present-day Wilkins St E (Dawson 2011). [Bolgo, Boggo (McClurg 1975); Bloggo, Boggo (MacKenzie 1992)] *See:* **bula**^{1}; **=gu**.

Bulalbul *n.* man's name. [Bul-al-pul (Ha)]

bulan$_1$ *adj; n.* regulation spear for ritualised battle, spear-shaped. [pullen (Kd); pollon 'narrow' (Lg)] *See:* **bilara**; **ganai**; **jagany**; **jibalang**.

Bulan$_2$ *Variant:* **Bulan-Bulan.** *n.* Amity Point. *lit.* 'regulation spear'; named by Nunagal (Bn). [Bullum (Bn); Pulan (CW); balin (H); Brempa (M); Bullon (Ln); Budlan, Pulan Pulan 'long point' (MMEIC); Bulan, Ballan, Pulan, Bullon (S); Ballan (W)] *See:* **bulan**^{1}; **Nunagal**.

Bulan$_3$ *n.* woman's name. [Poodlin (B); Puddlin (W)]

bulan-bulan$_1$ *n.* ritualised battle with regulation spears. [pullen-pullen (Kd); pullen pullen 'general fight' (MB)]

Bulan-bulan$_2$ *n.* Pullen Pullen Creek. *lit.* 'ritualised battle with regulation spears'. [Bullen Bullen (Bd)] *See:* **bulan-bulan**^{1}.

bularam$_1$ *quant.* second, another. [bubiran, boolieram (M)] *See:* **bula**^{1}; **garuba**.

Bularam$_2$ *n.* alternate name for Kaboora (Blue Lake). *Anth:* the preferred name for Blue Lake is Kaboora *lit.* 'the other one'; named by Nunagal (Bn). [bularam (H)] *See:* **bularam**^{1}; **Gabura**^{2}; **Nunagal**.

bularju *n.* swamp mahogany. *[Lophostemon suaveolens]*. [blurtchu (Ja); bull ortu 'gum with foliaceous bark' (Le); bulartchu (M); bulōrtum (R); bulurtchu (Ro); bul'urchū (Wa)] *See:* **bangalai**; **bundul**; **ngurbin**.

Bulban *n.* site of Coochin Coochin Homestead in Boonah. [Bulbon (Ha)]

buliman *n.* policeman. from English policeman. [buliman (H)] *See:* **dabingbila; gamadan; mug-mug.**

bulimari *v.* bend. [poolemurry (Lg)]

Bulina Bilina *n.* woman's name. [Polleena Berleena (Ha)]

bulirbin *n.* large grass-tree. *[Xanthorrhoea sp.].* [boolirrpan (M)] *See:* **-bin; dagabin[1]; garguru; ngilarun[1].**

bulu *n.* scrotum. [bulu, buru 'penis' (H); bul 'scrotum' (N)] *See:* **dugai; gumbawala; gumi; mujin.**

bululum *n.* common fly. [poolooloom (W)] *See:* **dudambara; wagun[2].**

bulumbir *n.* type of bean. [boodloomber (B)] *See:* **giji; magarabal; yugam.**

bulun *n.* flesh, fat. [boodloon 'fat' (Lg); bullum 'skin', budelum, būdelum 'flesh and blood' (R)] *See:* **dinggal[1]; mii[2]; mugan[1]; yun-yun.**

bulurjambin[1] *n.* turpentine tree. [Bool'oorchambin (M); Bulurjambin (S)] *See:* **gilawara.**

Bulurjambin[2] *n.* Enoggera; its traditional caretakers. *lit.* 'turpentine tree'. [Bool'oorchambin (M); Bulurjambin (S)]

buluwalung *n.* pelican. *[Pelecanus conspicillatus].* [bulualum (Ja); boalloong (M); bulualum (R); bul'ūalŭm (Wa)] *See:* **gulugan[1]; junggara.**

bulwalam *n.* nose piercing, nose ornament made of bone. [buluwalam (Ja); bullewalam (R); bul'ūalŭm (Wa)]

bulwar *n.* parrot fish. [bulwar (Ba)]

buma *v.* strike, smite. [poodmare 'lift up' (Lg); bumma (R); bomar (W)] *See:* **baji[2].**

bumagarla *v.* kill. *incorporates* buma 'strike'. [boomgarla (Ln)] *See:* **buma; ganijada; ganggirma.**

bumal *n.* wood. [bummal (W)]

bumangbin *n.* scrub fruit. [bomangpin (Lg)] *See:* **-bin.**

bumbal[1] *n.* fruit used as chewing gum. [bumbal (H)]

bumbal[2] *n.* back of a knife. [poombul (Lg)]

bumbaru *n.* clothing. [bombāro 'skins or clothes' (G)] *See:* **garang-garang.**

bum-bum *n.* head. [bum bum (H); kom (Ja); kom (R); boompum (We)] *See:* **bin.ga; magul[1].**

Buna *n.* Red Hill. *lit.* 'bloodwood tree'. *Anth:* present-day Boonah was named by whites (Ha; S) [Boonah (S)] *See:* **bana.**

bunba *n.* tailor fish. *[Pomatomus saltatrix].* [poonba (B); poonbah (M); pun'ba (Wa); poonbah (We)]

bunbar *adj.* crooked. [poonpur (Lg)] *See:* **barang[3]; wandan.**

bunbi *n.* dilly bag. [bunbi (H); boonby (Ha); bunbay (Ln)] *See:* **dili[1]; gulai.**

Bunbinbin *n.* woman's name. [Boonbinpin (W)]

bun-bun *n.* pheasant coucal. *[Centropus phasianinus].* [boon boon (Ca); bun bun (H); boon-boon (We)]

Bunda *n.* skin group (male). [Poonta (Bd); Puntah (D); bunda (Hw); Bunda (M); bundar (R); Bunta (W)] *See:* **Banjur; Barang[1]; Jarawany.**

Bundagan *n.* skin group (female). [Poontaran (Bd); Bundagun (Hw); Buntaygan (M); bundargun (R); Buntagun (W)] *See:* **Banjurgan[1]; Baranggan; Jarawanygan; -gan[2].**

bundai *n.* blackberry. *[Rubus fruticosus].* [bundai (R)]

bundal[1] *n.* cunjevoi. *[Alocasia brisbanensis].* *Anth:* poisonous; used to treat stinging nettles (FNSI). [bundel (H); bundal (M); bun'dal (Wa)]

bundal[2] *n.* hair. [bundel (MMEIC)] *See:* **gabui; nadang.**

Bundal₃ *n.* Boondall. *lit.* 'cunjevoi'; possibly named by whites. [Bundall 'crooked creek' (Ca); Bundal (S)] *See:* **bundal**¹.

Bunduba *n.* woman's name. [Boon-doo-ba (CW); Boondooba (W)]

bundul *n.* type of mahogany. *[Eucalyptus sp.].* [boondool (MMEIC; Aunty Margaret Iselin)] *See:* **bangalai; bularju; ngurbin**.

bundur *n.* plant with leaves used to make an ointment, the ointment. [poondoor, pboondoorr (B); boondoor (Lg)]

Bundurbira *n.* North Pine River- and/or Mt Samson-area group. *lit.* bundurbira 'people of the ointment plant'. [Pundan purra, Boondoorburra (Lg); Boondoorperra (M)] *See:* **bundur; -bira**.

bunggara *Variant:* **bunggar.** *n.* leaf, foliage. [boonggir 'turpentine tree foliage' (D); boong-gera (Ha)] *See:* **gajal**.

Bunurajali *n.* Albert River group. [Boonoorajallie (M)]

bunuru₁ *n.* rosewood tree. *[Dysoxylum fraserianum].* [boonarung (Lg); bunuro (M)] *See:* **wajari**.

Bunuru₂ *n.* Rosewood. *lit.* 'rosewood'. [Boonooroo, bunuro (S)] *See:* **bunuru**¹.

Buraadangal *n.* John Hooper's homestead, 10 Church St in Boonah. [Bra-tangal (Ha)]

burabi₁ *n.* type of tree. [burabi (R)]

Burabi₂ *n.* Bribie Island. possibly named by whites. [Boorabee (Redland City Council 2023a)] *See:* **burabi**¹.

bural *n.* log. [burāl (Ja); bural, burāl (R); bur'al (Wa)] *See:* **baguurugil; bana; maling; wambarligiri**.

burambigara *n.* type of shark. [boorambickara (Hi)] *See:* **buwai; gayanggan; gura-guragan; nirang**.

buran *n.* south wind. [borru (E); boor-run (Ha); boran 'wind', borru 'west wind' (Ja); buran (L); borru, booran 'west wind' (Lg); booran (Ln); buran, boorun (M); barin 'south'; burran 'west'; buran 'wind' (T); boran (Th); booran (W)] *See:* **gubi**²; **yanggar; wiral**.

buranda *n.* forest oak. *[Allocasuarina torulosa].* [biangre (Lg); buranda (M)] *See:* **buruda; gundiba; ganjil; yarara**.

burang *n.* whiting. *[Sillago sp.].* [boygun (E); buroŋ (H); boygun (Ja); pooran, booren, boygun (Lg); boor'enn, boorenn (M); boorong (We)]

Burangba *n.* Luggage Point. *lit.* burang-ba 'place of whiting'. [Boorennba (S)] *See:* **-ba**⁴; **burang**.

burara *n.* sedge, possibly tall club-sedge. *[Bolboschoenus fluviatilis].* *Anth:* seeds ground to make flour (FNSI). [burara (Ba)]

burganbalam *n.* yellow fungus, dye made from fungus. *[Leucocoprinus birnbaumii].* [pur'ganpal-lam 'yellow ochre' (Bd); pŭrgan-pal'lam (Wa)]

burgin banbil-banbil *n.* type of small bird. [poorgin pumbel pumbel (Lg)]

burging *n.* east wind. [burging (L); boorgin (Lg); burgin (M); bŭr'gin (Wa)] *See:* **dun.gai; gubi**²; **nyaban; winjia**.

burgun *n.* widower. [burguhn (N); boorgoon (W)] *See:* **buwa; buwadiya; ganibagu**.

burgunda *v.* carry. [boorcoonda (M)]

buridan *n.* bread. from English bread. [buredn (L)]

Buriimbam *n.* lagoon in Dugandan. [Breambum (Ha)]

burima *adj; adv; excl.* quick, quickly, exclamation of appreciation during intercourse. [burrima (E); borĕēma (G); burima (H); burrima (Ja); burrima, pootena (Lg)] *See:* **bangga; jubuiban; gumuwara; jim-jim; mii**¹; **ngunbunjada**.

burin *n.* wasp; small hornet. [boorin, burin (L)]

burjin *n.* stinging tree. *[Dendrocnide moroides]*. [burjeen (Ha)] *See:* **baragany**[1]; **gimbi**.

buruda *n.* black oak. *[Allocasuarina littoralis]*. [boruda (E); bor-ror-yer (Ha); boruda 'forest oak', burutha 'myrtle' (Ja); burrndah (Le); boruda (Lg); buruda, burnda (M); burutha (R); bur'ūda (Wa)]

Burudabin *n.* Booroodabin. *lit.* buruda-bin 'place of black oaks'. [Burudabin 'place of oaks' (Bd); Burudabin (S)] *See:* **buruda**; **-bin**.

burugara *n.* sea, river. [burugara 'sea' (L); borugera 'river' (Fi)] *See:* **bamirigari**; **dabilbaan**; **dagan**[1]; **waril**[1]; **yarabaan**.

burugari *n.* cypress pine. *[Callitris sp.]*. *Anth:* green bark was used by women to carry coals; women did not make fire using fire sticks (MMEIC). [burogari, booroggerie (M)] *See:* **waran**[1].

Burugingmiri *n.* Moreton Bay confederacy of Ngugi, Nunagal and Guwanbal peoples. [Buruginmiri (J); Booroogeenmeerie (M); Boo.ging, Boo.ging.mil, Boo.ging.mill 'seaside people' (J)] *See:* **burging**; **burugara**; **Guwanbal**; **Ngugi**; **Nunagal**.

Buruguwa *n.* Brisbane River, lower part. possibly burugara ''river'. [Brogoa (Le)] *See:* **burugara**; **Jirwamban**; **Maiwar**.

burul[1] *n.* bora ring, site of the man-making ceremony, the man-making ceremony. [bool (E); bool (Ha); boongeelinah (Hi); bul (Ja); būl, burūl (Wa)] *See:* **giba**[1].

Burul[2] *n.* place name. *lit.* 'bora ring'. [Booral (Ln)] *See:* **burul**[1].

Burul[3] *n.* man's name. [Būrrul (R)]

burumbigan *adj.* employed. [borombigun (Lg)]

burumbin *n.* flower spike of the garguru 'grass-tree'. *Anth:* flower spikes were soaked until water was saturated with honey, which was drunk fresh or fermented (MMEIC). [broombin-talo-yucka (G); broomby (Haworth 2011)] *See:* **-bin**; **burumbin jalu yaga**; **garguru**.

burumbin jalu yaga *n.* fire starter made from burumbin 'flower spike'. *lit.* 'burumbin (that) makes fire'. [broombin-talo-yucka (G); broombni-talo-yucka (Hw)] *See:* **burumbin**; **jalu**; **garguru**; **yaga**.

burunda *n.* swan. [burunda (MMEIC)] *See:* **muruguji**; **nyuring**.

buruuwal *adj.* long, tall. [broe-al (Hp); [buel (L)]; booyal (M); puiyala (R); Hp contests M's version] *See:* **milindu**; **murul**.

buun *n.* knee. [poon (Cl); bone (Fi); bun (H); poon, bon (Ja); bunn (L); puhn (N); bon, bōn, bun (R); puhn (T); bōn (Wa)] *See:* **walar**.

buunyi *Variant:* **buunyi-buunyi**. *n.* bunya. *[Araucaria bidwillii]*. [baɲa, baɲal 'pine tree' (H); bon-yee (M); bonyi (P); bŭn'yī (Wa)] *See:* **bugal**; **dandardam**; **juunbal**; **gambarju**.

buwa *v.* marry. [boo-un-na (Ha); booa (M)] *See:* **ganinjibuwari**; **wiyari**.

buwadiya *n.* bachelor. *incorporates* buwa 'marry'. [budier (N)] *See:* **buwa**.

buwal *n.* whirlwind. [booarl (Be)] *See:* **buran**; **burging**; **dimbiny**[1]; **dun.gai**; **gubi**[2]; **junggai**[1]; **nyaban**; **winjia**.

buwalgan *n.* bush stone-curlew. *[Burhinus grallarius]*. [bualgan, bujulgan, biulgan (H); brolgun (Ln); bohin (M); buelgun (We)] *See:* **garal**; **gariyagan**; **guwir**.

buwanggan *n.* porpoise. [poobegan (B); weedon paregun (W); booangun (We)] *See:* **dalubila**; **-gan**[1].

buwarawa *v.* run. [buaraoa (Ja); buaraoa (R); bua-raōa (Wa)] *See:* **nyigiran**.

buwargari *n.* other side. [boargery (Lg)]

buwai *n.* shark. [pow-why, poai (Ja); poai (R); põ'ai (Wa)] *See:* **burambigara; gayanggan; gura-guragan; nirang.**

buwaiya *v.* dive. [bouwaia (E); bouwaia 'dive', bo-wai-ya 'turtle' (Ja); bouwaia (Lg)]

Buwubira *n.* caretakers of Long Pocket in Indooroopilly. [Buwubira, Bohobbera, Bu-obbera (M)] *See:* **Duuwung²; -bira.**

buyu *n.* lower leg. [pyyoo, puyso (Cl); puyso, puïyo, pyyoo (Ja); booyoo 'leg' (Lg); buyu (M); puïyo, boyu 'leg', boga, boa 'shin' (R); booyoo (W); bū'yū, pūi'yō (Wa)] *See:* **darany; mangara; wulu.**

Buyuba *n.* Newmarket, Enoggera saleyards, Enoggera Creek crossing near Bancroft Park. *lit.* buyu-ba 'of the lower leg'. [Buyuba (Bd); Booy'ooba (M)] *See:* **-ba⁴; buyu.**

D – d

Daan *n.* Mt Mitchell. [Taan (Ga)]

daaran *n.* forearm. [tāron (Ja); tāron (R)] *See:* **wayaba.**

daba *adj; adv.* far. [tappa (Lg)] *See:* **yangbang.**

Dabai *n.* Bulimba Creek. [Doboy (S)]

dabal *n.* type of berry that grows on the beach. [dubbul (Ja)]

dabara-dabara *adj.* quick. [tabbra tabbra (Lg)] *See:* **bangga; mii¹.**

dabaragan *n.* type of tree. [tabracan (Lg)]

dabarama *v.* hurry up. *lit.* dabara-ma 'make quick'. [tubbrama (Lg)] *See:* **dabara-dabara; -ma.**

dabi *n.* end. [tabe (Lg)]

dabil *n.* water. [tabbul (Bu); darbil (Ca); yabbil (D); dabil (E); tabbill (Fi); dabil (H); tabbil (Ha); darbil (Hi); tabbil, dabil, tah-bil (Ja); dabil (L); dabil (Lg); tabill, dabil (Ln); tabbil (M); tabbil (R); tah-bil (Su); tabbil (W); tab'bil (Wa); dubbeel (We); dabil (Wu)] *See:* **gabing; ngarawin.**

dabilbaan *n.* salt water. *lit.* dabil-baan 'salt water'. [ban tabil (Bd); dabil-ban (E); tabbilbon, tah-bil ban, dabil ban, tabbil-bōny 'dead water' (Ja); dabil ban, tabil ban (Lg); tabbilbōn (R); tab'il-ban (Wa)] *See:* **baan; dabil; bamirigari; burugara; yarabaan.**

dabilbala *n.* Brisbane box tree. *Anth:* gum is used in a medicine to reduce swelling (DF); *incorporates* dabil 'water'. *[Lophostemon confertus].* [tabilpalla (B); dabilbello (E); dabilbello, tabilpulla 'myrtle' (Ja); tabil-palla 'worm eucalypt' (Le); dabilnala (H); dabilbello (Lg); tabbil-pala (M); tabilpulla (R); tab'bilpūr'ra, tab'bilpal'la (Wa); dobil nulla (We)] *See:* **dabil; ngarang.**

dabilgan *n.* oar. *lit.* dabil-gan 'thing typified by water'. [dabalgan (P)] *See:* **dabil; -gan¹.**

dabilyanmana *n.* running water. *lit.* dabil-yanmana 'water run'. [tabbil-yanmunna (Bd)] *See:* **dabil; yanmana.**

dabingbila *n.* policeman. word origin unknown; *possibly incorporates* -bila 'afflicted by'. [dabiŋbila (H)] *See:* **-bila; buliman; gamadan; mug-mug.**

dabir *n.* shoulder scarification marks. [tappere (Lg)]

dabira *Variant:* **dabir.** *n.* shield. [dabira (E); tabbīr 'club, shield', tan (Ja); dabira (Lg); tabbīr (R); dabberi 'club' (T)] *See:* **gundan².**

Dabirim *n.* site of former Teviot State School in Croftby. [Tub-berim (Ha)]

dadam *n.* taro. *Anth:* not good to eat raw, it must be cooked (MMEIC). *[Colocasia esculenta].* [dadab (MMEIC)] *See:* **dam¹; diya-diya; guba³; madara.**

daga *n.* long grass. [tūkkā (R); dak'kā (Wa)] *See:* **banggil¹; wagarbin.**

dagabin₁ *n.* swamp grass-tree, firestick from this tree. *[Xanthorrhoea sp.].* *Anth:* resin used to strengthen canoes, tools and weapons; spear used as firestick (FNSI). [dakkabin (Ja); dakkabin, tucabbin 'firestick (Stradbroke)', chucabbil 'firestick (Brisbane)' (M); dakkibin (P); tuckabin (W)] *See:* **-bin; bulirbin; garguru; jaludiya; ngilarun¹.**

Dagabin₂ *n.* possibly Canaipa Point on Russell Island. *lit.* 'grass-tree'. [Dakabin (S)] *See:* -bin; dagabin¹.

Dagabin₃ *n.* Dakabin railway station. *lit.* 'grass-tree'; possibly named by whites. [Dakabin (Q)] *See:* -bin; dagabin¹.

dagabinbigi *n.* piccabean palm, bangalow palm. *lit.* dagabin-bigi 'grass-tree-piccabean palm'. *[Archontophoenix cunninghamiana].* [dak ka bin pikki (CW)] *See:* bigi; dagabin¹.

dagadiyagubin *n.* type of fish, same type as bambi-bambi. [dugatiyagobin (B)] *See:* bambi-bambi.

dagai *Variant:* **dagai-dagai; digi.** *n.* white man, flayed corpse, ghost. [dagai, dege dege (H); dargun (Ha); duggai (Ja); doegehr, doeger (L); duggai (Ln); duggai (R); degga (W); dŭgai, dhŭgai (Wa)] *See:* magarang; majari.

dagai jaan *n.* man with a white beard. *lit.* 'ghost man'. [dege chin (MMEIC)] *See:* dagai; jaan.

dagairu *n.* stranger, wandering white man, jackeroo. *possibly incorporates* dagai 'white man'; possible source of English jackeroo (Wa). [dhuggai-ee-roo, dhugai-lu 'white people' (Bd); tockeroo 'strange black' (MB); dŭgai-īū, dhūgai-īū 'wandering white man' (Wa)] *See:* dagai.

dagal₁ *n.* heart. [dugui, dugul (L); dugul (N); tugul, dogul (R)] *See:* guna².

dagal₂ *Variant:* **daga.** *v.* pity. [tūgūl (Ja); tūgūl (R)] *See:* bujal².

Dagalaba *n.* River at Bulimba. *lit.* dagal-ba 'heart place'. [Tuguluwa 'shape of crescent moon' (Bd); tugulawa (M); dugula-ba (N); Tugulawa (S); tug'ūlawā (Wa)] *See:* -ba⁴; dagal¹.

Dagalandin *n.* man's name. [Dugalantin (R)]

dagan₁ *n.* sea waves. [tu-gun (M); tug'ŭn (Wa)] *See:* bamirigari; burugara; dabilbaan; yarabaan.

dagan₂ *n.* mist. from Guwar dagam. [dagan (Ba)]

dagaru₁ *n.* beach tamarind. *[Cupaniopsis anacardiodes].* *Anth:* edible yellow fruits (FNSI); used for medicine (MMEIC). [tuc ker roo (CW); dagaro (Lg)]

Dagaru₂ *n.* man's name. *lit.* 'beach tamarind'. [Tukeru (B)] *See:* dagaru¹.

Dagawamba *n.* Samsonvale. [Takawompa (Bd)] *See:* -ba⁴.

dagi₁ *n.* sugar. from English sugar. [toki (Bl)]

dagi₂ *n.* toothache. from English sugar. [taggee (Lg)]

dagibagam *n.* hawksbill turtle. *[Eretmochelys imbricata].* [tuckabin (W); dukiebugum (We)] *See:* bin.ging; bubiya; mibaral; mujing; naguba.

daginy *n.* quartz crystal, rainbow spirit that puts quartz crystals in streams. *Anth:* each nan.gur possessed a crystal for healing and magic; crystals gave the ability to fly (Hw). [dakki (Ja); dakki, dākki (R); tag'gan, tārgan; dak'ki 'quartz splinter, used as a knife' (Wa)] *See:* bajiram; gaya; gayabandar; gundir; maamba; nan.gur; yilal.

dagung *adj.* round. [tacoong (Lg)]

Dagura *n.* man's name. [Takoora, Takoorra (B)]

Daguwi *n.* Birch's camp at Amity Point. [Tāgkuoe (B)]

daigam *n.* lawyer vine. *[Smilax australis].* [taigam (M); tai'gan (Wa)] *See:* ngabu.

daigil *n.* white cedar tree. *[Melia azedarach].* [day gil (Ha)] *See:* mamin; wuji.

Daiguriba *n.* place name. [Dairkooreeba (W)] *See:* -ba⁴.

dal₁ *Variant:* **da** *v.* eat, drink. [tultoo (Cl); dalto (E); tultoo, dalto (Ja); dalto, talto, tadlivah (Lg); jaleeba (M); toelli 'taste' (N); tulle, tulli, turri (R); danan 'drink' (T); tudleba (W); dŭr'ri (Wa)]

dal₂ *n.* branch, stick. [tullong 'stick' (Cl); taull 'turpentine tree branches' (D); tullong 'stick' (Ja); tal 'branch' (Lg)] *See:* **diniri; muruny; nguruwa; yirul**¹.

dala *n.* temples of forehead. [dula; dullah (N)]

dalabila *n.* outlaw. [tallabilla (M); tal'labil'la (Wa)] *See:* **-bila.**

dalaga *n.* myall, acacia scrub. *[Acacia sp.]*. [dulaga (Ba)] *See:* **din-din; gabany.**

dalagan *adj; adv.* together. [tallacan (Lg)] *See:* **ganyardi.**

Dalaibi *n.* man's name. [Dalaipi (S)]

dalajalumbi *n.* type of bird. [dalajalumbi (MMEIC)]

dalam *n.* grey creek kangaroo (female). [tallum (Le)] *See:* **giriwan.**

dalan₁ *Variant:* **dala.** *v.* stopper, close. [düllünguntumurri (Ja); toodlah (Lg); tallo (P); dullun (R); dül'lüngün, tüm'merrī (Wa)]

dalan₂ *Variant:* **dala.** *v.* stay. [dullan (R)] *See:* **nyundal.**

dalandala₁ *n.* geebung tree and fruit. *[Persoonia sp.]*. [dulandella (Ja); dulandella (M); dulandella (P); dul'endel'la (Wa)] *See:* **gumbara.**

Dalandala₂ *n.* Geebung. *lit.* 'geebung tree(s)'. [Dul-endel-la (Bd)]

Dalandalayinil *n.* Zillmere Water Holes in Geebung. *Anth:* formerly five creeks; now one remains; *lit.* dalandala-yinil 'geebung creek(s)'. [Dul-endel-la Yinnell (Bd)] *See:* **dalandala**¹; **yinil.**

dalang₁ *n.* pipe clay, wet clay, mud. [düllāng (Ja); düllāng (R)] *See:* **mila-mila.**

dalang₂ *adj.* lost. [tullang, tullung (Lg)] *See:* **baludiriyari.**

dalangjili₁ *n.* black rock, sandstone. [duruŋ ɟili, duluŋɟili, duliŋɟili (H)] *See:* **dalang**¹; **gurung**².

Dalangjili₂ *n.* Tuleenderly Creek on Stradbroke. *lit.* 'black rock'; named by Balun.giny (Bn). [Dullun Gilly (Bn); duruŋ ɟili, dulunɟili, dulinɟili (H); durungjili (MMEIC)] *See:* **Balun.giny; dalangjili**¹; **gurung**².

Dalangmul *n.* man's name. [Tullongmool (Hp)]

dalany *n.* throat. [daluɲ, d'alaɲ 'tongue' (H); dalan 'tongue' (La); talli 'neck' (Lg); thelann, dalan, dunung 'throat' (N); thelann 'throat'; tallain 'tongue' (T); dalan 'tongue' (Th); dun'ūng 'throat' (Wa)] *See:* **jugung.**

Dalawala *n.* Spring Hill forested area. [Tallawalla (Bd)]

Dalawana *n.* man's name. [Dulluwunna (R)]

dalbany *Variant:* **dalba.** *v.* jump, sit up, arise. [toolpon (Cl); toolpon (Ja); dalbain (R)] *See:* **balgal.**

dalbara *n.* type of lizard, possibly marbled gecko. *[Christinus marmoratus]*. [talburra (M)]

daldari *n.* mud. [dulturee (We)] *See:* **bangan**¹; **wabum.**

daldu *v.* chew. *lit.* dal-du 'eat in an ongoing way'. [tultoo (Su)] *See:* **dal**¹; **-du**²; **jambil.**

dalgaba *n.* food. *lit.* dal-gaba 'item(s) for eating'. [dalleaba (Ha); talkuba (R)] *See:* **dal**¹; **dubaru; -gaba; jin-jin manjari; mungin.**

dalgai *n.* dead, dry tree. [dulgai (Ja); dulgai (R); dūl'gai (Wa)] *See:* **dawajangar; wang.**

dalgal *n.* dirt, crumb. [dulgul 'small piece' (Lg); dülgül 'dirt' (Wa)] *See:* **jara.**

Dalgamban *n.* Mt Lindesay. [Tulcambun (Be); Gual-gum-bun (Ha)] *See:* **dalgambar.**

dalgambar *n.* very large mountain. [talgumbur (Ln)] *See:* **bibu; Dalgamban.**

dalgi *n.* lightning bug, firefly. [talgi (Ca)]

Dalgibira *n.* Nerang group. [Talgiburra (M)] *See:* **-bira.**

daliba *excl; v.* let's eat/drink! *lit.* da-li-ba 'let's eat/drink together'. [tadlivah (Lg); jaleeba (M); jadliyaba (MMEIC); tudieba, tudleba (W)] *See:* -ba²; dal¹.

daligamana *v.* love. [talecamanna (Lg)] *See:* gawan²; -ma; -nya.

dalin *n.* light. [dudlen (W)] *See:* gidibila; jalungai.

Dalipi *n.* man's name. [Dulipi (Kd)]

Dalmar *n.* possibly Ipswich. [Tulmur (Bd)]

dalu *n.* lung. [dullo (R)] *See:* buguru; gamang.

dalubila *n.* porpoise. [tabobilla (CW); tharloobilare 'a whale' (Hi); talobilla 'porpoise', dālūbilla 'whale' (Ja); tallubilla, tālūbilla 'whales' (R); tal'ōbilla 'porpoise' (Wa)] *See:* -bila; buwanggan.

Dalu Diyamariba *n.* man's name. [Thudlo Teamariba (B)]

dalwalbin₁ *n.* cotton tree. *[Hibiscus tiliaceus].* *Anth:* used for light fish spears (FNSI); used for making shields [dalgarbin (H); talwalpin (Ja); talwalpiin (W); dulburpin (We)] *See:* -bin; gurwa.

Dalwalbin₂ *n.* Redland Bay, Point Talburpin. *lit.* 'cotton tree'; named by Yagarabal (Bn). [Dullburrerpin 'beach cotton trees' (Bn); Talwalpin (Ln); Talwalpin (S)] *See:* dalwalbin¹; Yagarabal.

dam₁ *n.* yam. from English yam and/or Yugambeh dam. *[Dioscorea transversa].* [dum (Bd); tam, tarm (Ja); tamm (Le); darm (M); tārm (Wa)] *See:* dadam; diya-diya; guba³; madara.

dam₂ *n.* creeper herb. [dām (R)]

dama *n.* large fishing net. [tummar 'crayfish net' (Ja); tumma (R)] *See:* bayal; durur; mandin¹; mirbang.

Damala *n.* Norman Creek. [Tumulla (Bd)]

Damaman *n.* Petrie Bight and Customs House site. [Tumamun (Bd)]

Damamarin *n.* Murphy's Creek. *lit.* 'where the fishing nets were burned in a grass fire'. [Tamamareen (S)]

damanya *v.* be eating. *lit.* dal-ma-nya 'be eating (because you want to)'. [tanmanna (T); janmanya (Wu)] *See:* dal¹; -ma; -nya.

Damba *n.* alternate name for Goompi (Dunwich). [Dumba (CW); Dumba (S)] *See:* -ba⁴; Guumbi².

Dambaal *n.* pathway between the bora rings in Petrie. *Anth:* the larger bora ring was at Nyinduru-Nyinyidu, and the smaller around Peter Curtin Park (Bd). [Dumpaal (Bd)] *See:* Nyindurunyinyidu.

dambil *adj; n.* blunt-edged, blunt spear. [tam'bil (Wa)] *See:* ngundu².

dambil-dambil *n.* game played with blunt spears. *lit.* 'blunt-blunt'. [tam'bil-tam'bil (Wa)] *See:* dambil.

dambiri *n.* type of grey gum. *[Eucalyptus sp.].* [dambirri 'short-barked gum' (Le)]

Dambirin *n.* Mt Tambourine. *lit.* 'yam cliff' from Yugambeh dam 'yam' and birin 'cliff', or 'lime' from Yugambeh jamburihm 'lime' (Sh). [Dumbirin (M)] *See:* dam¹.

damburu₁ *Variant:* **dambur.** *n.* lip, mouth. [tambora (Cl); dambur, dambul (H); damberoo (Ha); tambora, tamburu (Ja); toomburu, toemburu (L); tambroo (Lg); tambaroo, tambore (Ln); tambur, tambooroo (M); tāmburū, dambro, dambur (R); tambur (T); tam'būr (Wa); doombooree (We)] *See:* nyanda¹.

damburu₂ *adv.* more. [tambroo (Lg)] *See:* -gali; milin; manyal.

damburubila *adj.* full to the mouth. *lit.* damburu-bila 'mouth-full'. [tambroo pille (Lg)] *See:* -bila; damburu¹.

Damgaiba *n.* Boggy Creek camp; Eagle Farm. [Tumbalburr (Bd); Tumkaiburr (CW)] *See:* -ba⁴.

damil *n.* skin, hide. [tummil (Ln); dumil (N); dam (R)] *See:* **gali²; yun-yun.**

damin *n.* type of black fruit. [tummin (Lg)]

dana *n.* dogwood tree. *[Jacksonia scoparia].* *Anth:* gum and resin used as adhesive (FNSI). [denna (Ja); denna (M); den'na (Wa)]

danagany *n.* lightning. [tangan (Cl); tudnagain, tunggain, tangan (Ja); jongang (Ln); changan (M); tunggain, tudnagain (R); tangan (Su); tun'gain, tud'nagain (Wa)] *See:* **jalubiram; jil; maral.**

danbal *adj.* forbidden. [tunbul (R)]

danbang *n.* man. [dun'bang (Wa)] *See:* **binigan; jaan; guri; malara; mari².**

danbar *n.* maggot. [tunbur (Ja); tunbur (M); tun'bŭr (Wa)]

Danburi *n.* man's name. [Danbury (B)]

dandali₁ *n.* wonga pigeon. *[Leucosarcia melanoleuca].* [dun'dall'i (Wa)] *See:* **bilurun; gulun.**

Dandali₂ *n.* man's name. *lit.* 'wonga pigeon'. [Dundahli (M)] *See:* **dandali¹.**

dan-dan *adj.* cold. [tan-tan (Cl); danton (E); ɟanɟan (H); danton, tan-tan (Ja); danton, tantan (Lg); tantan (T); tantan (W)] *See:* **yigil.**

dandara *Variant:* **dandar.** *n.* chest; ribs. [dandar (H); tundera (Ja); dandarra, dandara 'breast' (L); taendoer (N); tundera, dundolīn (R); dandara (T); tun'derā (Wa); dundarra (We)]

dandardam *n.* pine tree. [dundardum (Ba)] *See:* **bugal; buunyi; juunbal; gambarju.**

dandibin *n.* water plant or shrub. [duntibbin (R)] *See:* **-bin.**

dandiiri *v.* meet. [dandiyri (Ja); dāndīiri (R); dan'di-i'ri (Wa)] *See:* **ngadan; -ri.**

dandildila *v.* kiss. [dāndildelaiina (Ja)] *See:* **-nya; nyubi.**

dandurir *n.* black wallaroo. *[Macropus bernardus].* [dandurer (Ha)]

danga *demonstrative.* that (distal). [ding-a, dinga (Lg); duŋa, dūŋa (R)] *See:* **gaa; naam.**

dan.gabing *adj.* soft. [tuncabbing (Lg)]

dangan *n.* native orange. *[Citrus australis].* [dungan 'native orange' (Ha); tungin 'wild guava' (Lg)]

Dangarbin *n.* Teviot caves and district. [Dungarbin (Ha)] *See:* **-bin.**

Dan.gardu *n.* person's name. [Dunkartu (B)]

dang-dang *adj.* lightweight. [tangtang (Lg)] *See:* **wirui.**

danggal₁ *n.* red or black banksia with yellow flowers; its fruit. *[Banksia sp.].* *Anth:* the bark of the red honeysuckle was used in tanning [daŋgal (H); tangul (Lg)]

danggal₂ *n.* eyeball. [toengoel (N)] *See:* **mil.**

danggan *n.* bowels. [tungan (M); tunggin (R)] *See:* **magurabal.**

Danggari *n.* Green Island. [Tangar (CW); Tanggeera (M); Tanggeera, Tangaree, Doongerri (S); Tangaree (W)] *See:* **Milwaba.**

Danggu *n.* woman's name. [Danggu (MMEIC)]

danggul *n.* water pepper, arse smart. *[Persicaria hydropiper].* *Anth:* used to stupefy fish [tang-gul (M); tang'gŭl (Wa)] *See:* **nuralgir.**

Danggulba *n.* Hay's Inlet. *lit.* danggul-ba 'water pepper place'. [Dungulba (S)] *See:* **-ba⁴; danggul.**

Dan.gum₁ *n.* hole near Cossart's first mill site in Dugandan. [Dun-goom (Ha)]

Dan.gum₂ *n.* man's name. [Dun-goom (Ha)]

danguwan *n.* edible fern root. *[Blechnum indicum].* *Anth:* source of native bread (FSNI). [dangum (E); tangwann (Le); dingowa (MMEIC)] *See:* **bangwal.**

danmurin *n.* anthill. *incorporates* murin 'green-headed ant'. [tānmurrin (Ja); tānmurrin (R); dabbun 'ant' (T); tan'mŭrrin (Wa)] *See:* **baigan; bigunjur¹; dany; galalang; giwarang; mugara²; murin.**

-dany *subd.* occurs on the head verb of a relative clause. [ta, dai, deni, du (R)]

dany *Variant:* **da.** *v.* lie, rest. [daïn, dai-emurri (R)]

Dany-dany *n.* rocky pass in Oaky Creek. *lit.* 'lots of resting'. [Dane-Dane (Ha)] *See:* **dany.**

danyung *adj; adv.* near. [tanneung (Lg)] *See:* **bidung; jigandi.**

daragan *n.* bird's nest fern. *[Asplenium sp.].* *Anth:* fronds were used for matting (FNSI). [tong (Ha); deregen (L)]

daran₁ *Variant:* **dara.** *v.* grow. [durun, duruthūnga (Ja); durun, duruthūnga (R); dur'un (Wa)] *See:* **balgama.**

Daran₂ *n.* lagoon in Fortitude Valley. *Anth:* 'the Valley Baths area' (Bd). [Tarun (Bd)]

Daranggari *n.* Terangeri, Stradbroke Island, Point Lookout on Stradbroke Island. possibly from darau 'loose stones'. [terangeri (CW); deraŋeri (H); Terangery 'Stradbroke Island' (Ln); Cherangeree, Taramgaree Cabalchoo, Tarangeree-Cabalchoo (M); Terangeree (S); Terangeree 'Point Lookout' (W)] *See:* **darau.**

Daranggari Gabalju *n.* Stradbroke group. [terangeri (CW); deraŋeri (H); Cherangeree, Taramgaree Cabalchoo, Tarangeree-Cabalchoo (M)] *See:* **Daranggari.**

darany *n.* thigh, upper leg, branch. [turra (Cl); ɟiraŋ (H); durra, tarra (Ja); tarang, tderra 'thigh', terra 'small branch of tree' (Lg); thurra 'leg'; tarrang-gni, jarra (M); t-hoera (N); durra, darrang (R); derang 'leg or branch' (S); tarra 'leg' (T); tar'rang, dher'ang (Wa)] *See:* **buyu.**

daranygaba *n.* trousers. *lit.* darany-gaba 'item(s) for thighs'. [taranggoba, tarang-aba (Lg); derrangūba (R)] *See:* **darany; jiruda; -gaba.**

daranyjin *n.* white men. *lit.* darany-jin 'thigh-people' possibly in reference to white men's covered legs. [taratchin (Lg)] *See:* **dagai; darany; -jin; garabi¹.**

darau *n.* loose stones. [tarau (Wa)] *See:* **gindal; mulu¹; nalanggira.**

daraubang *n.* hailstone, hail. [tharoobarng (Hi); teraba (L); teraba (R)] *See:* **darau; mugaramulu.**

darawa-darawa *adv.* as much, as much. [darawa-darawa (L)]

darganbin *n.* cane. [darkanbean (E); darkanbean (Ja); darkanbean (Lg)] *See:* **-bin.**

darigany *n.* bone. [darigany (Wu)] *See:* **ding; garal-garal; jirban.**

Dariganygali *n.* bush pub at Carney's Creek. *lit.* darigany-gali 'lots of bones'. [Tarri-gun-gully (Ha)]

Daringga *n.* Taringa. possibly from darau 'loose stones'; possibly named by whites. [Taringa 'stones' (S)] *See:* **darau.**

darum *n.* type of guava, brushwood. [darum 'brushwood' (Ja); tarroom 'wild guava' (Lg); dārūm 'brushwood' (R); dār'ūm 'brushwood' (Wa)] *See:* **dila; guji-gujin.gal.**

Darumba *n.* Tarampa. *lit.* darum-ba 'place of guava'. [Tarampa 'place of wild lime' (S)] *See:* **-ba⁴; darum**

darun *n.* handle. [taroon (Lg)]

darung *n.* sea vine, goat's foot vine. *Anth:* leaves used to ease headaches and stonefish stings (FNSI). *[Ipomoea pes-caprae subsp. brasiliensis].* [tharook (FNSI; MMEIC)]

darwan *n.* Elder, great man. [turwan (Kd); turrwan (M)] *See:* **baji¹; bandar; gayabandar.**

daun *n.* creature, thing. [daoun (R)] *See:* **minyalang; nanajin.**

daunbin *n.* bird. *possibly incorporates* daun 'creature'. [daounpin (Ja); dowanpin (Lg); daoŭnpin (R)] *See:* **daun**; **jibi**.

dawajangar *adj.* withered. [dau'wadhŭngūr 'like a withered tree' (Wa)] *See:* **dalgai**; **wang**.

-di *case.* locative suffix indicating location at, on or inside a place. [ti 'ablative' (Cu); de 'at' (Lg); gee (M); di, ti (R)]

dibing₁ *n.* mosquito. [deebing (Bl); mibing (Ca); tibing (Ja); tibbin (Lg); debing, dibbing (Ln); tibbin (M); tībing (R); dibbing (W); dib'bin (Wa)]

Dibing₂ *n.* Deebing Creek. *lit.* 'mosquito'. [Deebing (Q)] *See:* **dibing**¹.

diga *n.* root of native yam. [dikka (Le)]

Digaga *n.* man's name. [Tikukka (W)]

Digam *n.* Cabbage Tree Creek. [Tighgum (Bd)]

digan *adj; adv.* earnest, earnestly. [tiggen (R)]

digi *v.* live. [tikki (T)] *See:* **ngun**.

digirgali *adj; n.* big eater, eats a lot. *lit.* digiri-gali 'plenty of belly'. [digirgali (H)] *See:* **digiri**; **-gali**.

digiri *Variant:* **digir**. *n.* belly, stomach. [diggery (Cl); diggery 'body' (Fi); digir (H); diggery 'abdomen', tīggeri 'belly, stomach' (Ja); diggere, deggere (Lg); tigeree (Ln); diggaree (M); digerah (N); tiggeri, dickery (R); diggery (Su); dungur (T); diggori (W); tig'gerā (Wa)] *See:* **binji**; **bula**³.

digiribila *v.* have a full belly. *lit.* digiri-bila 'stomach-full'. [tiggere pille (Lg)] *See:* **-bila**; **digiri**.

digiri wayara *v.* have an empty belly. *lit.* 'stomach is empty'. [tiggere wairoo (Lg)] *See:* **digiri**; **wayara**.

dila *n.* brushwood. [dila (Ja); dillār (R)] *See:* **darum**.

dilgam *n.* fantail mullet. *[Paramugil georgii]*. [tigum (Lg); dilgum (We)] *See:* **juruny**¹; **gang-gang**²; **ngandagal**¹.

Dilgan *n.* man's name. [Dilguhn (N)]

dili₁ *n.* woman's bag made of grass or hair. origin of English dilly 'dilly bag'; a freshwater Yagara word (P). [dilli (M); dili (P); dil'la (Wa)] *See:* **bunbi**; **banggil**¹; **gulai**.

dili₂ *n.* spiny-head mat-rush, any grass or hair used for making dilly bags. *[Lomandra longifolia]*. [dilli 'xerotes longifolia' (Ja); dilli (M); dili (P); dil'la (Wa)] *See:* **bunbi**; **banggil**¹; **gulai**.

diluny-diluny *n.* rosella parrot. *[Platycercus sp.]*. [dilion-dilion (Ha)]

Dimali *n.* woman's name. [Timallee (B)]

dimanggali *n.* sacred, taboo. *incorporates* either -gali 'very' or gali 'skin removed from a corpse'. [dim'ingl'li (Bd); dimmanggali 'sacred to the dead' (Ja); dimanggali (Ro); dim'mingal'li (Wa)] *See:* **-gali**; **gali**².

dimany *n.* camp. [deemain (D)] *See:* **jalubaluba**; **giba**²; **ngagamwaga**.

Dimbal *n.* woman's name. [Dimbal (W)]

dimbiny₁ *n.* north wind. [whinpin 'strong wind' (Be); dimbiɲ 'star' (H); tin bin (Ln); tinbin, timbin (W)] *See:* **gubi**²; **wadi**.

Dimbiny₂ *n.* woman's name. *lit.* 'north wind'. [Timbin (W)] *See:* **dimbiny**¹.

Dimbuuna *n.* woman's name. [Dimboona (S)]

Dimbuunaba *n.* Wail Rock at Point Lookout. *lit.* Dimbuuna-ba 'place of Dimbuuna'. [Dimboona-ba (QYAC sign)] *See:* **-ba**⁴; **Dimbuuna**.

dim-dim *n.* type of small bird. [tim tim (Lg)]

Dimgil *n.* man's name. [Timgil, Timgill (B); Tim-gil (CW); Timgil (W)]

Dinalgin *n.* Denelgin, the Bowman homestead south of Mt Alford township. *lit.* 'camp of animals'; probably named by whites. [Denelgin (Ha)]

dinari *adj.* few. [tinnare (Lg)]

dinbir *n.* locust, cicada. *[Cyclochila australasiae]*. [dinpir (Ja); dinpere (Lg); dinpīr (R); din'pīr (Wa)]

Dindaba *n.* Tindappah; Garden Island. *Anth:* a lookout place to watch for the incoming sea mullet in season (Sh). [Tindappah (Redland City Council 2023a)] *See:* -ba⁴.

dindili *n.* dracaena. *[Dracaena sp.]*. [dindilli (Le)]

din-din *n.* scrub, jungle. [tin-tin (G)] *See:* dalaga; gabany.

ding *n.* bone. [ding (Ja); ding (T); ding (Wa)] *See:* darigany; jirban; garal-garal.

din.gal *n.* sea eagle. *[Haliaeetus leucogaster]*. *Anth:* sea eagles would signal the location of schools of fish. [tin-gal (M)] *See:* bugawan; miriginba¹.

dingga *n.* canoe. from English dinghy. [dinka (CW)] *See:* gundul²; yaribu.

dinggal₁ *adj; n.* fat. [dingal (E); dingal (Ja); tinggal (L); dingal (Lg); tingal (M); dingal (T); dingal (W); tin'gal (Wa)] *See:* mii²; mugan¹; yun-yun.

dinggal₂ *n.* type of small shell. [diŋgal (H)] *See:* gara¹; guumbi¹; magul²; walamgan.

Dinggalba *n.* Tingalpa. *lit.* dinggal-ba 'place of shells' or possibly 'place of fat'. [diŋgalba (H); Tingalpa (L); dhingu-ba 'place of throwing' (S); tingalpa (W)] *See:* -ba⁴; dinggal².

dinggil *n.* ornamental band worn around the forehead. [tanggil (Ja); ting'gil (Wa)] *See:* baraban.

dinibau *n.* body hair. [tinebow (Lg)]

dinin.giri *n.* forest kingfisher. *[Todiramphus macleayii]*. [tinninkerree (B)]

diniri *Variant:* **dinir.** *n.* firewood, sticks. [dinir (H); dinnarie (Ha)] *See:* dal²; jalu.

dirambila *n.* yellowtail kingfish. *[Seriola lalandi]*. [deeambilla (M); deerumbilla (We)]

diranga *demonstrative.* this (proximal). [dedum 'here' (Lg); teeran (M); dirangum (R)] *See:* ngagam¹.

Diraranbal *n.* Beaudesert. [Derraranbull (Be)]

dirbang *n.* type of shrub. [dīrbāng (R)]

diriiri *n.* seagull. [teereerie (M)]

Dirim *n.* Curtis' Crossing at Carney's Creek. [Tirim (Ha)]

diruny *n.* yellow-faced whip snake. *[Demansia psammophis]*. [deerooyn (W)] *See:* buguja; bui²; guda²; yuwan.

dirwa *n.* type of fruit. [deerwah (Lg)]

diya *n.* tooth. [deea (E); teaa (Fi); diaŋ, ɟiraŋ (H); de-air (Ha); tier, deer (Ja); tiya, deer (La); deea, dea (Lg); tear (Ln); tiar, tear, deea (M); tih-a (N); tiër, dīa, dangal, danga (R); deer (Su); tigia (T); deea (W); tī'ār (Wa); deer (We)]

diyabula *n.* back teeth. *lit.* diya-bula 'tooth-two'. [tih-a-bulla (N)] *See:* bula¹; diya; diyaganyara.

diya-diya *n.* yam. *lit.* 'tooth-tooth'. *[Dioscorea transversa]*. [de-ah de-ah (D)] *See:* dadam; dam¹; guba³; madara.

diyaganyara *n.* front teeth. *lit.* diya-ganyara 'tooth-one'. [tih-a-koena (N)] *See:* diya; diyabula; ganyara¹.

diyagarany *n.* gums (of mouth). *lit.* diya-garany 'teeth descend'. [tih-akoerin (N)] *See:* garany; diya.

diyala *n.* mulloway. *[Argyrosomos japonicus]*. [dthiela 'do saltwater' (Lg)] *See:* buigum; wargan.

Diyali *n.* man's name. [Tiallee (B)]

diyi *n.* type of stringybark. *[Eucalyptus sp.]*. *Anth:* bark used for wrapping a corpse (Wi). [tī, diura (Ja); dei e (Le); tī (R); diūra (Wa)] *See:* gundul¹; jilgan; jura.

diyiin *adv.* today. [dirai (T); diyīn (Wu)]

-du₁ *case.* ergative case. *Anth:* used only on unexpected subjects of transitive verbs. [du (Cu); u (Ha); do (Lg); du (R); do (W)]

-du₂ *asp.* marks atelicity/ unboundedness; indicates that an event is ongoing or lacks a clear endpoint. [tu (P); tu, du, dū (R)]

dubaru *n.* sugar cane. *[Saccharum officinarum].* [tubero 'food' (B); toobroo 'sugar cane' (Lg)] *See:* **dalgaba; jin-jin manjari; mungin.**

Dubawa *n.* Raby Bay. possibly named by whites. [Doobawah ((Redland City Council 2023a)]

duburugang *n.* boil. [toobroocung (Lg)]

dudambara *n.* fly. [dudambara (H); doodunburra (Ja); ts'unbara (L); toonbar (Lg); juenburra, dudunburra (Ln); dūdunburra (R); du'denbŭrra (Wa)] *See:* **bululum; wagun².**

dudambarajuwal *n.* small scrub frequented by flies. *incorporates* dudambara 'fly'. [juenburrajuel (Ln)] *See:* **dudambara.**

Dudari *n.* man's name. [Doodaree (W)]

dugai *n.* penis, tail. [doogi, toogi (Cl); doogai (E); duge (H); doogi, toogi 'penis', doogai 'tail' (Ja); dooegai 'penis', dugee (Lg); dugi; tugai 'male cauda' (N)] *See:* **bulu; gumbawala; gumi; mujin; wanggin.**

dugal *n.* back of body. [toocel (Fi); toggul (Ja); dogoon (Lg); toggul (R); tog'gel (Wa)] *See:* **mabara.**

Dugandan *n.* Mt Dugandan. *possibly lit.* 'up' from Yugambeh dugun 'above' (Sh). [du-gondon (Ha)]

duguu *n.* saltwater cod. [toogoo (D); duggoo (Ha); dogo (Le); duku: (Ti); tō'kō (Wa)] *See:* **gujung.**

duilgal *n.* flycatcher. *[Myiagra inquieta].* [twilcul 'large wagtail with white throat' (B)]

duiwai *n.* scorpion. [dooyway (Lg)] *See:* **gandarba.**

dujin *Variant:* **duji.** *v.* enjoy. [dujin (R)]

dulan *n.* battle. [tulen (Ja); doolung (Lg); tul'an (Wa)] *See:* **ban.gindalinga.**

Dulangbari *n.* Bribie Island group. [Toolongburry (Lg)]

dulbang *n.* diamond fish. *[Monodactylus argenteus].* [dulpung (We)]

dulbi-dulbi *n.* yellowtail scad. *[Trachurus novazelandiae].* [doolbee doolbee (M)]

Dulmur *n.* flat area on the Brisbane side of Oxley Creek. [Doolmoor (M)]

dulu *adj.* half full. [toodloo (Lg)]

dulugamari *adj.* empty. *incorporates* dulu 'half full'. [tooloogamare (Lg)] *See:* **dulu; wayara.**

dulul *n.* loud noise; bang. [dool-ol-pil (Ha); dooloolpin (Ln)] *See:* **dululbin.**

dululbin₁ *n.* gun. *lit.* dulul-bin 'noise-plant'. [dool-ol-pil (Ha); dooloolpin (Ln)] *See:* **-bin; dulul; ganaral.**

Dululbin₂ *n.* woman's name. *lit.* 'gun'. [Tudloalbun (W)] *See:* **dululbin¹.**

Dumali *n.* man's name. [Doo-mal-lee (CW); Doomallee (W)]

dumba *n.* road. [toomba (M); tumbar (R)] *See:* **bambar; gulgan¹.**

Dumbani *n.* man's name. [Toompanee (B); Toom-pan-ee (CW); Toompanee (W)]

Dumbar *n.* man's name. [Toonbar (S)]

dumbiribi *n.* koala. *[Phascolarctos cinereus].* [dumbripi (Ja); tumperpy 'native dog' (Ln); toomirrpie (M); dum'pribī (Wa); dombearpee (We)] *See:* **gula²; marangbi.**

dunbam₁ *n.* staghorn fern. *[Platycerium superbum].* [doon bum (Ha); dumbam (L)]

Dunbam₂ *n.* Pinkenba. *Anth:* this name is now given to the Doomben Racecourse in Ascot (P); *lit.* 'staghorn fern'. [Dumben, Doomben, Dunbain (P); Doomben 'Pinkenba' (S)] *See:* **dunbam¹.**

Dunbiyan *n.* man or boy's name. [Doon-be-an (Ha)]

dundim *n.* shipworm; cobra grub. *[Teredo navalis].* [doon-dim (Ha)] *See:* **ganyi**; **gambu**.

dundu *n.* point of land. [toondoo (Lg)]

-dunga *asp.* imperfective; signals that an event is ongoing or uncompleted. [dunga 'constantly' (Ba); dua, tunga, lunga (Lg); duwa (P); duŋa, tuŋa, thūŋa (R)]

dun.gai *n.* east wind. [doongul 'north wind'; dunkay (E); dunkay (Ja); dunkay (Lg); tun'gipin (Wa)] *See:* **burging**; **gubi²**; **nyaban**; **winjia**.

dungala *adj; adv.* inside. [toongulla (Lg)] *See:* **ganul¹**; **gurin**.

dun.gala *n.* black bream. *[Acanthopagrus sp.].* [tungala, tingala (B); dan.gilan (H); dungalla, dang-alla (M); dungellar (We)] *See:* **ginbun**; **man.gal**; **ngalan¹**.

Dungaluma *n.* Tangalooma on Moreton Island. [daŋaluma (H); doongalooma (We)]

dungi *v.* weep. [doongeem (Bl); toongeenya (M); dunggih 'tear of eye' (N); dūŋinnā, dūŋidū (R); dungana (T)]

dungura *n.* bed. [toongoora (Ln)] *See:* **wura²**.

dunguru *n.* menstrual period. [toongoorroe (B)]

durambai *n.* Sydney blue gum. *[Eucalyptus saligna].* [thurambai (Mac)] *See:* **bulagi**; **manggara**.

duran *Variant:* **dura**. *v.* hang something. [duadinare (Lg); duran (R)]

Durandur *n.* Woodford. *lit.* 'tree grub'. [Doorandoor (Bd)]

durar *n.* channel-bill cuckoo. *[Scythrops novaehollandiae].* [doorrare (Ha)]

durbin₁ *n.* bracken fern. *[Pteridium esculentum].* *Anth:* inside of stems used to treat stings; fronds used for matting (FNSI). [turbin (B); jur-pin (CW); dūrvin (Ja); durvin, dūrvin (R)]

Durbin₂ *n.* place on Moreton Island. *lit.* 'bracken fern'. [turbin (B); durbin (Ba); durvin, dūrvin (R)] *See:* **durbin¹**.

Durbin₃ *n.* man's name. *lit.* 'bracken fern'. [Trepin (B)] *See:* **durbin¹**.

dur-dur *n.* nape of neck. [durdur (E); durdun (Ja); durdur (Lg)] *See:* **giling**; **ngaran¹**.

duribang₁ *n.* type of owl. [doorebung (We)] *See:* **gingga**; **gum-gum**; **nyinggal**; **wumanggan²**.

Duribang₂ *n.* woman's name. *lit.* 'owl'. [doorebung (We)] *See:* **duribang¹**.

during *n.* needle. [dooring (Lg)]

duringgaliba *v.* sew. *lit.* during-galiba 'needle sew'. [dooring galeba (Lg)] *See:* **during**; **galiba**.

duriny *n.* brigalow. *[Acacia harpophylla].* [doo-rine (Ha); darri (Le); dūrrī 'kind of shrub' (R)] *See:* **banuru**.

duriyinma *v.* lift. *incorporates* -ma 'causative'. [duriyinma (MMEIC)] *See:* **balgama**; **daran¹**; **juwan**; **-ma**; **wandi**.

Duru *n.* man's name. [Dūrū (R)]

Durubal₁ *n.* Turrbul people and their language. *possibly lit.* darau-bal 'people of loose stones'. [Toorbal (E); darabal, darabul (H); Taraubul, Turr'ubūl (Wa)] *See:* **-bul**; **darau**.

Durubal₂ *n.* Toorbul Point. [durbul (MMEIC)]

durur *n.* net. [dourour (E); dourour (Ja); dourour (Lg)] *See:* **bayal**; **mandin¹**; **mirbang**.

duun *n.* hill. [tōōn (G)] *See:* **bibu**.

Duunburu *n.* name of several different hills. *lit.* 'hill of the kangaroos'. [Tōōnboro (Wa)] *See:* **bugul**; **duun**.

duurjagum *adj.* sour. [doorsaccum (Lg)] *See:* **duurwali**; **jugung**.

duurwali *adj.* too sour. *incorporates* wali 'bad'. [doourwadli (Lg)] *See:* **duurjagum**; **jugung**; **wali**.

duuwung₁ *n.* eastern koel. *[Eudynamys orientalis].* [tuwong (M); tū-o'ng (Wa)]

Duuwung$_2$ *n.* Long Pocket in Indooroopilly. *Anth:* home of the Buwubira people (M); *lit.* 'eastern koel'. [Dow-oon (M); Tuwong (S)] *See:* **Buwubira; duuwung**^{1}.

duwai *n.* wedge-tailed eagle. *[Aquila audax]*. [dew-air (Ha); tu-wai (M); tū'wai (Wa)] *See:* **buduwar**^{1}; **jibal; mibany; ngan-ngan**.

duwal *n.* dog excrement. [dual (Ja); dunggul, dūal (R)] *See:* **baandigu; guna**.

duwanggal *Variant:* **duwang.** *n.* younger brother. [djuang (G); duaŋgal (H); jew ang (Ha); duangal (Ja); dewing (Ln); tuwoeng (N); duangal (R); doang 'brother' (T); duong (W); du'angal (Wa)] *See:* **ngabang**.

duwangjin *n.* youths, boys. *lit.* duwang-jin 'younger brothers'. [juanchin 'girl' (N); dūandin 'boy' (R)] *See:* **bujiri; duwanggal; -jin; giba**^{1}; **gumingguny**.

duwir *n.* quail bird. [du-wir (Ja); dū'wīr (Wa)]

Duwunan *n.* land on the banks of Burnett's Creek. origin of English name Mt Toowoonan. [Toowoonan 'Lightbody's' (Ha)]

G – g

ga *v.* give, bring. [care, gra 'not give' (Lg); ga 'bring' (Wa)] *See:* **-ra**^{1}; **wujan**.

gaa *demonstrative.* that (medial). [kār, ka (R)] *See:* **danga; yugu**^{1}.

Gaandin *n.* woman's name. [Carndin (Ha)]

-gaba *deriv.* indicates item(s) for dealing with the referent of the stem. [gobah, -aba (Lg); gūba (R)]

gababanguru *n.* nankeen kestrel. *[Falco cenchroides]*. [kapapangooroo, capapāngoor (B)]

gabagabal *Variant:* **gabagabalbaguuru.** *n.* message stick. *incorporates* baguuru 'wood' [cabūgabul (G); Kabugabul-bageru (Hw)] *See:* **baguuru**^{1}.

gabagiri *Variant:* **gabagir.** *n.* brother-in-law. [koerwahkihr 'brother in law, son in law' (N); kabakerie (W)]

gabai$_1$ *adj; n.* smallest native bee, its white honey, sweet, sugar. *[Tetragonula carbonaria]*. [cobbi (Bl); kabboy (Cl); cubbay (D); cabbear (Ha); karbi (Hk); kabbai (Ja); kobae, kawae (L); cobboi (Lg); ka'vai (M); kubba (W); kab'bai (Wa)] *See:* **banjin**^{1}; **jalaman; gila**^{2}; **guja**^{1}; **gunidar**^{1}; **mabi**^{1}; **nagi**.

Gabai$_2$ *n.* moiety. *Anth:* named for the gabai native bee (McConvell 2018). [Cubba (Clark 1916)] *See:* **gabai**^{1}; **Gamil**.

gabala$_1$ *n.* bobuck, scrub possum. *[Trichosurus cunninghami]*. [carpala (Hi); kappolla (Ja); copalla 'a large opossum darker than the common one' (Le); kuppola (Ln); kapolla 'scrub possum … larger than the forest one, and also much darker' (P); kap'pella (Wa)] *See:* **gubi**^{1}.

Gabala$_2$ *n.* Cubberla Creek at Kenmore. *lit.* 'scrub possum'. [Cubberla (Bd); kabarla (S)] *See:* **gabala**^{1}.

Gabalaba$_1$ *n.* Capalaba. *lit.* gabala-ba 'place of the scrub possum'. [Kapallaba (Redland City Council 2023a)] *See:* **-ba**^{4}; **gabala**^{1}.

Gabalaba$_2$ *n.* woman's name. [Cabalba (M)]

gabany *n.* scrub. [kabin (Ca); cubbon (D); cubbun (Ha); cabun (Hi); kabban (Ja); cobawer 'large scrub' (Ln); cappan (M); kab'ban (Wa); gabuny (Wu)]

gabi *adj; n.* black, dark, night. from Guwar gabi. [cuppee (Ha); cappee (Lg)] *See:* **gujun; gurung**^{2}; **ngunu**.

gabim *n.* moss, mossy ground. [gabem (H)] *See:* **murung**.

gabing *n.* water. [kapping (Cl); gabiŋ (H); kuddum, kapping (Ja); caping (Ln); capemm (M); kapping (Su)] *See:* **dabil; ngarawin**.

Gabingba *n.* Capemba; Big Hill
on Stradbroke. *lit.* gabing-ba 'place of
water'; named by Balun.giny (Bn). [Capunba
(B); Capembah 'Big Hill; water there' (Bn);
Capeembah (CW); gabemba 'the big hill at
Myora' (H); Campemba 'spring running water'
(Ln); Capemba 'place of water' (S); kapemba
(W)] *See:* -ba⁴; gabing¹.

gabiny *adj.* hungry. [gabiɲ (H)]
See: wayara.

gabui *n.* hair of the head. [kabboey (Cl);
kapui (E); cobue (Fi); cab-boy (Ha); kabui,
kapui (Ja); kabui (L); kapui, cubboue (Lg);
cabooee, kaboüi (Ln); cabooi (M); kahboi (N);
kabui (R); cubboa eu (Th); kā'būī, kar'bung
(Wa)] *See:* bundal²; nadang.

gabujan *n.* meal made of mullet.
[caption (B)]

gabul₁ *n.* carpet python. *[Morelia spilota].*
[cobbil (Ca); cobbull (D); gabul (H); cabbul
(Ha); garbool (Hi); kabul (Ja); kobbel (Le);
cobbool (Lg); cobbull, kabul (Ln); kābool,
cabbool (M); kābul (R); kabool (W); kāb'ul
(Wa)]

Gabul₂ *n.* Kobble Creek. *lit.* 'carpet
python'. [Cobble (S) *See:* gabul¹.

Gabuljar *n.* Caboolture; its traditional
caretakers. *Anth:* a python raised by children
grew huge, ate its benefactors, disappeared into
Gabura and reappeared in Gabuljar (Bn); *lit.*
gabul-jar 'carpet snake country'. [gabul-dar (Ba);
Gabullther (Bn); Ka-boltur (E); gabulɟa, gabul
ɟa' (H); Cabulteur (Lg)] *See:* gabul¹; jaagany;
jara.

gabun *adj.* great. possibly borrowed from
Dharug. [gabon (Lg)] *See:* gurumba.

gabura₁ *n.* dawn. [gabura (H)] *See:* barabil.

Gabura₂ *n.* Kaboora, Blue Lake. *Anth:*
a man-eating carpet snake (Bn) or bunyip lived
here; *lit.* 'carpet snake'; named by Nunagal (Bn).
[Karboora (Bn); Kaboora (CW); gabura (H);
Karboora (S)] *See:* Bularam²; gabul¹; jaagany;
Nunagal; -ra¹.

gadara *n.* five corners fruit. *[Styphelia
viridis].* *Anth:* fruit eaten raw (FNSI); these
bushes have been burnt out by bushfires
(MMEIC). [gutta-rulla (CW); gadara (H)]
See: jibang.

Gadaraba *n.* place name. *lit.* gadara-ba
'place of five corners fruit'. [gadaraba (H)]
See: -ba⁴; gadara¹.

gadigal *n.* forest. [kūdigul (R)]

gaga *n.* ceremonial platform on which
initiation rites were conducted. [kakka
'wonderful' (Ja); kak'ka (Wa) *See:* burul¹; giba¹.

gagal *n.* softwood tree with hard red
berry. [gug-gul (Ha)]

gagalum *Variant:* gagalu. *v.* stop. [kagalōm
(Ja); kagalōm (R); kāg'olom (Wa)] *See:* gau.

gagara₁ *Variant:* gagar. *n.* echidna.
[Tachyglossus aculeatus]. [gargarra (Hi); kaggarr
(Ja); kokkerah (Le); coggara (Lg); cockoora (Ln);
caggara (M); kag'gar (Wa)]

gagara₂ *quant.* four. [cogara (Lg)]
See: bula-bula.

Gagaramalbil *n.* Mt Gravatt. *incorporates*
gagara 'echidna'. [Cahgarm'ahlbil (M); Kaggar-
mabul, Caggara-mahbill (S)] *See:* gagara¹.

gagargal *n.* black wattle tree. *[Acacia
concurrens].* *Anth:* pods and leaves used as soap,
timber used for weapons, seeds used for flour
and chewing (FNSI). [gagargin (H); cug-ger-cul,
kagarkal, kuggerkul (Ha); kagarkal (Ja); kakrakall
(Le); kagarkal (M); kag'arkal (Wa); gugarkill
(We)]

Gaguniba *n.* place name. [Gagoonipa
(B)] *See:* -ba⁴.

gaguwan *n.* kookaburra. *[Dacelo
novaeguineae].* [gaguan (H); kar-gerum (Ha);
kakoowan, kakowan (Ja); cowoong (M);
kakōwan (R); kakoom (W); kak'ōwan (Wa)]
See: ganggun-gun.

gaiban *n.* sloe bush, blackthorn. *[Carissa
spinarum].* [ky-ee-bun (Ha)]

gaiya *v.* bite. [gaiya (Ba)] *See:* baada; gargan.

gaiyang *n.* vein. [kaiyung (Ja); kaiyung (R)]

gaiyara *Variant:* **gaiyar.** *n.* sulphur-crested cockatoo. *[Cacatua galerita].* [kera 'cockatoo' (Ca); kiara (Ha); kyyarra (Hi); kaiyar, kai-yar (Ja); geyera (L); kirra 'cockatoo' (Lg); kaiyar (Ln); kanjar (M); kaiyar (R); keara (W); kai'yar (Wa)] *See:* **balan; biliyagan; biluwala; garara; giwang; jarbal.**

gaiyarbin *n.* headband made of yellow reeds. *incorporates* gaiyara 'sulphur-crested cockatoo'. [kaiirbin (Ja)] *See:* **-bin; gaiyara.**

gajal *Variant:* **gajal-gajal.** *n.* leaf. [kadgal-kadgal (Cl); kadgal kadgal (Ja); cuddal (Lg); kajal (W)] *See:* **bunggara.**

gaji₁ *v.* blacken one's face with grease and charcoal. *Anth:* charcoal for gaji was made from powdered bloodwood bark (Ja) [kuttee (E); kuttee (Ja); kuttee (Lg)]

gaji₂ *n.* vulva. [gaɟi (H)] *See:* **jindur; junu; jurung; nyaral.**

Gajira-gajira *n.* Grampian Hills, Deebing Heights. *possibly lit.* 'drip drip'. [Gudgera-Gudgera (Ha)] *See:* **gajiru.**

gajiru *v.* drip. [cudgeroo (Ha)]

gajur *n.* coral. [gutture (We)]

galabi *v.* leave behind unintentionally. [gullabi (Lg)] *See:* **ngura.**

galalang *n.* ant. [gulalung (L)] *See:* **baigan; bigunjur¹; danmurin; giwarang; mugara²; murin.**

Galali *n.* name of language in western QLD. [galali (H)]

galamang *n.* blue quandong, blue fig tree. *[Elaeocarpus grandis].* [cullamung (Ha)] *See:* **jambal; ganin; ganin.gar; gurai; murabal; nguwanga; nyada.**

galambin *n.* pallid cuckoo. *[Cacomantis pallidus].* [ker-lum-bin 'grasshopper hawk' (Ha)]

galan *n.* cloud. [coah (Cl); calen (Ln); kalen (W); garlen (We)] *See:* **marun; guwaa.**

galang *adj.* good. from Wakka Wakka galang 'good'. [kalongore (Bl); kalangŏŏr (G); gallon (Lg); kal-lang-ur (M); galang (T)] *See:* **bujari; marumba¹; nyiwang.**

galan-galan₁ *adj.* short. [culluncullun (Lg)]

Galan-galan₂ *n.* Wellington Point. *possibly lit.* 'cloudy'. [Cullen Cullen (M)] *See:* **galan.**

Galangga *n.* common woman's name. [Kalangga (L)]

Galanggaba *n.* common man's name. [Kalanggaba (L)]

Galbin *n.* woman's name. [Gulpin (Kd); Gulpin (S)]

galbuny *n.* lyrebird. *[Menura sp.].* [caboon (Ca); galbunya (J)]

galga *n.* small amount, drop (of liquid). possibly one's share or 'cut' of food or drink. [culga 'drop' (Lg)] *See:* **galgal.**

galgal *Variant:* **galga.** *v.* cut. [kaii, kabari, kulkurri (Ja); culca 'cut', culga 'drop' (Lg); kulku (R); kapa, kabal (W); kābarī, kai'ī, kul'kūrrī (Wa)]

Galgali *n.* woman's name. *lit.* galga-li 'cuts herself'. [Colcolly (G)] *See:* **galgal; -li².**

galgaribin *n.* grass-bugle reeds, necklace made from grass-bugle reed seeds. [kalgree-pin (Cl); kulgrīppin (G); kalgree pin, kulgaripin (Ja); calgarpin (Lg); kaiirbin (R); kulgaripin (Ro); kai'-ir-bin, kalgurpin (Wa)] *See:* **-bin.**

galgaribin ganai *n.* reed spear. *lit.* 'reed spear'. [cullgery pim cansi (Ln)] *See:* **bilara; -bin; bulan¹; galgaribin; ganai; jagany; jibalang.**

galgulang *n.* noisy friarbird. *[Philemon corniculatus].* [calcoollang (B); galgulaŋ (H); c'alcool'ang (M); gulcoolung (We)]

galguru *Variant:* **galgur.** *n.* yam-stick. [kalgur (Ja); kalgooro (W); kal'gŭr (Wa)]

-gali *deriv.* very, plenty, typified by.
[gul, kully (Ha); cully (Hi); kolle, kulle (R); kŭllē (Wa)]

gali₁ *v.* dance. *lit.* ga-li 'dance ourselves'.
[kallee (Cl); kallee (Ja)] *See:* -li².

gali₂ *n.* skin removed from corpse. [gali (Ba)] *See:* damil; yun-yun.

galiba *v.* sew. [galepa (Lg)]

Galigural *n.* possibly Breakfast Creek.
[Kulligral (Bd)] *See:* Yuwargara.

galil *n.* finger, toe. [gallil (Lg)]

galimal *Variant:* **galima.** *v.* punish.
[kalimul (R); kalliamarra 'fear' (T)]

Galimbin₁ *n.* man's name. [Cullimpine (Ha)]

Galimbin₂ *n.* Wild Horse Mt.
[Kullimpin (Be); Cullimpine (Ha)] *See:* -bin.

galin *adj.* sharp, strong. [cullan 'sharp' (Lg); galine 'strong' (M)] *See:* bandara.

galinda *n.* small-eyed snake. *[Cryptophis nigrescens].* [kallinda 'black snake ... with slaty-coloured abdomen ... very poisonous' (Le)]

Galindabin *n.* Ashgrove. *lit.* galinda-bin 'place of small-eyed snake'. [Kallindarbin (Bd)] *See:* -bin; galinda.

Galinggral *n.* waterhole in Fortitude Valley. *Anth:* 'Fortitude Valley Station area' (Bd). [Kullingral (Bd)]

galubal *Variant:* **galuba.** *v.* cough.
[coolooghal (B); callopel (Le); calloopal (Lg)]

galuma *adv.* long ago. [kaloma (Ja); kaloma (M); kalōma (R); kal'ōma (Wa)]

gama *v.* break. [gumma (Bn); cumma (M); kama (R)] *See:* banggany.

gamadan *n.* policeman. possibly from English 'Commandant'. [gamadan (H)] *See:* buliman; dabingbila; mug-mug.

gamagu *excl.* here it is! [comago (Lg)] *See:* =gu; ngaranga.

gamalgalam *n.* willie wagtail. *[Rhipidura leucophrys].* [gumulkulum (Be)] *See:* jin.giri; jin. gilinggan.

gamang *n.* lungs. [cummong (Lg)] *See:* buguru; dalu.

Gambal *n.* Condamine River group.
[Cumbal (Lg)] *See:* -bul.

Gambalgari *n.* name of language at Amity Point. [gambalgari (H)]

gambangga *n.* scarification pattern of the Amity Point people. [cambongcare (Lg)]

Gambara *n.* alternate name for Bummiera (Brown Lake). *Anth:* the preferred name for Brown Lake is Bummiera. [gambara (H); Canyabra (M)] *See:* Bamira.

gambarju *n.* hoop pine. *[Araucaria cunninghamii].* [gumbarto (E); gambarto (Ja); gambarto (Lg); kumbartcho (M); kum'bardhū (Wa)] *See:* bugal; buunyi; dandardam; juunbal.

Gambarjubin *n.* Pine Mt. *lit.* gambarju-bin 'place of hoop pines'. [Kambratchabin (S)] *See:* -bin; gambarju.

gambu *n.* shipworm; cobra grub.
Anth: edible 'grub', actually a bivalve mollusc *[Teredo navalis].* [combo (Hp); kam'bo (Wa)] *See:* dundim; ganyi.

gambugi *n.* slender yabby. *[Cherax dispar].* [cumbookie 'freshwater crayfish' (M)]

Gambugiba *n.* Vulture St 'near the Dry Dock' in Brisbane. *lit.* gambugi-ba 'place of yabbies'; named by whites. [Cumbooquepa (M)] *See:* -ba⁴; gambugi.

Gambula *n.* man's name. [Compulla (MMEIC)]

gamdung *adj.* soft, wet. [camdoong (Lg)]

Gamgagulum *n.* Chinatown.
[Gomcag'ooloom 'where chinks are' (M)]

Gamil *n.* moiety. [Kamil (Clark 1916)] *See:* Gabai².

gaming *n.* mother's brother. *Anth:* Gaming 'Uncle' is a term of respect for a male Elder. [car-ming 'uncle' (Ha); garnill (Hi); cumming (Lg); koeming (N); kame (W)]

gaminggan *n.* father's mother. [gar-ming-jin 'father's mother' (Ha); ganilcan 'grandmother, aunt' (Lg); kŭm'ingŭn (Wa)] *See:* -gan².

Gamu *n.* woman's name. [Cummo (B); Cummou (W)]

Gamunyari *n.* person's name. [Camoonyeree, Caimmooneree, Cammooneree (B)]

-gan₁ *deriv.* denotes an animal, state, or time span characterised by a property. [cun (Hi); kan (L); gur (La)]

-gan₂ *Variant:* **-gin.** *deriv.* feminine suffix. [gan (H); gan (Hi); gun (R); kun (W); gŭn (Wa)]

gana₁ *adj.* thirsty. [kunna (Ha); cadna (Lg); cadna (M); kudna (W)]

gana₂ *v.* hear, think, understand. [gana (MMEIC)] *See:* winanga.

ganai *n.* war spear, reed spear, fishing spear. [cunnayr (D); cunna (Fi); canna (G); genare (Hi); kannai 'scrub sapling spear; fishing spear' (Ja); connoi (Lg); canay (M); gunnai (R); ganai (Ro); kana (T); kuni (W); kân'nai (Wa)] *See:* bilara; bulan¹; jagany; jibalang.

Ganaiba *n.* Canaipa on Russell Island. *Anth:* the farmers here shot many Aboriginal people, whose spears were left on the ground (MMEIC, Aunty Margaret Iselin); *lit.* ganai-ba 'place of spears'. [ganaba (H); caneipa, kunipa (W)] *See:* -ba⁴; ganai.

ganaibira *n.* type of ironbark. *[Eucalyptus sp.].* *incorporates* ganai 'war spear'. [kanei perah (Le)] *See:* bigara; ganai; jana; janduru; jum-jum; nyandala.

ganajara *n.* drought. *lit.* gana-jara 'thirsty-earth'. [kunjarra (Bd)] *See:* gana¹; jara.

ganal *n.* brushtail possum (female). [gunnal (Le)] *See:* gubi¹; widiging.

Ganalbin *n.* Canalpin on Stradbroke. probably named after white contact. [Canalpin (Fison 1889)] *See:* -bin.

ganangur *adv.* like this, thusly, in this manner. [kan-nang-ur (M)]

Ganara *n.* hill on Moreton Island. [Ganara (CW)]

ganaral *n.* rifle. [ganaral (H)] word origin unknown. *See:* dululbin¹.

ganarin *n.* rushes. [gunurren (Bn)]

Ganarinbin *n.* place on Stradbroke between Tuleenderly Creek and Wallen Wallen Creek, north of Wurangbila. *lit.* ganarin-bin 'place of rushes'; named by Balun.giny (Bn). [Gunurren Pin (Bn)] *See:* Balun.giny; -bin; ganarin.

Ganarumba *n.* man's name. [Kunaroombar (W)]

gandandi *adj.; adv.* slow, slowly. [gandanti (E); gandanti (Ja); gandanti (Lg)] *See:* yan.gua.

gandarba *n.* scorpion. [cun-dar-ba (Ha)] *See:* duiwai.

gangga *n.* eastern osprey. *[Pandion haliaetus cristatus].* [kunka (M)]

gang-gang₁ *n.* egg. from English egg. [goŋ goŋ (goŋgoŋ) (H); gung gung (Ha); congon (Ln); kunggung (M); kongkong (W); kong'-kong (Wa)]

gang-gang₂ *n.* mullet (male). [cong cong (Lg)] *See:* dilgam; ngandagal¹.

ganggirbany *Variant:* **ganggirba.** *v.* die. *lit.* ganggiri-bany 'become dead'. [kungirpun (R)] *See:* baluny; -bany; bang; ganggiri.

ganggiri *Variant:* **ganggir.** *adj.; n.* dead. [kunglary (Ln); cangeerie, gangeerie, gang-geerie (M); kungir (R); kangere, kungera (W)] *See:* baluny; bang.

ganggirma *v.* kill. *lit.* ganggiri-ma 'make dead'. [angirma (Lg); kungirmu (R)] *See:* bumagarla; ganijada; ganggiri; -ma.

ganggun-gun *n.* kookaburra. *[Dacelo novaeguineae].* [googargun (Hi); cangoongoon (Ln); kang-goon-goon (M); kang'gangan (Wa); gookgogun (We)] *See:* gaguwan.

Ganginyangin *n.* Moreton Island.
[Cungen-Yungen, Cung-an-yung-an (M)]
See: **Murgambin.**

Gangula *n.* possibly D'Aguilar.
[Kongoola (Bd)]

gani₁ *n.* skull, head. [gudnee 'cobbera' (Lg)]

gani₂ *v.* tie. [gani (Ba)] *See:* **nany.**

ganibagu *n.* widower. [gani-ba-gu (Ba)]
See: **burgun.**

ganibawininigan *n.* widow. [gani-ba-winingin; wihninaikoen (Ba)] *See:* **-gan².**

ganijada *v.* kill. [ganijata (MMEIC)]
See: **bumagarla; ganggirma.**

ganin *n.* small fig. *[Ficus sp.].* *Anth:* tasty edible figs (FNSI). [ganin (H); kunnin (Ja); kunnin (R); gunnin (We)] *See:* **galamang; ganin.gar; gurai; jambal; murabal; nguwanga; nyada.**

Ganinbinbila *n.* Breakfast Creek Point. *lit.* ganin-bin-bila 'having places with figs'. [Ganan-binbilla (CW)] *See:* **-bila; -bin; ganin.**

ganin.gar *n.* small fig. *[Ficus sp.].*
[cunnincre 'small fig tree' (Lg)] *See:* **galamang; ganin; gurai; jambal; murabal; nguwanga; nyada.**

ganingira gidar *n.* native hop bush.
[Dodonaea triquetra]. [kaningira kidtar (B)]
See: **gin-ginga.**

ganinjibuwari *n.* marriage. *incorporates* buwa 'marry'. [canindboary (Ln); caneenjee booarrie (M)] *See:* **buwa.**

ganjabai *n.* wild arrowroot. *[Canna indica].* *Anth:* young tubers are edible.
[cungeboy (Yerrilee 1921)]

ganjiil *n.* corroboree. [cunjeel (CW)]
See: **gawabiri; ngari²; yiyara; yuwar.**

ganjil *n.* forest oak. *[Allocasuarina torulosa].*
[gunjil (Ba)] *See:* **buranda; gundiba; yarara.**

Ganju *n.* man's name. [Kunjo (W)]

ganul₁ *adj; adv.* indoors, inside. [gonool (Lg)]

Ganul₂ *n.* Dividing Range. *lit.* 'inside'.
[Gunool (Be)] *See:* **ganul¹.**

ganya *n.* tent-like structure built for one person. [gunyah (Bl); gaɲa, gaɲi (H); goannar (T)] *See:* **ngumbi¹.**

ganyagu *v.* go home. *lit.* ganya=gu 'seek one's tent'. [gaɲigu (H)] *See:* **ganya; =gu.**

ganyara₁ *Variant:* **ganyar.** *quant.* one, someone, alone. [canyahra, kamarah (Cl); ganar (E); cun nara (Ha); kunnar, kamarah, ganar (Ja); kanyara (L); kamarah, karawo (La); ganar, cannara (Lg); cunnergh (Ln); goonahra, canyahra (M); kunnar (R); kamarah (Su); kalim (T); kunara (W); kun'nar, gan'ar (Wa)] *See:* **yaja.**

ganyara₂ *n.* crocodile. *[Crocodylus sp.].*
lit. 'one'. [kunyurra (Ca); canyahra 'From Townsville to Cooktown' (M)]

ganyardi *adj; adv.* to one mass or heap, together. *lit.* ganyar-di 'to one location'.
[ganar-di (Ba)] *See:* **dalagan; -di; ganyara¹.**

ganyi *n.* shipworm; cobra grub. *[Teredo navalis].* [kan-yi (Ja); kan'yī (Wa)] *See:* **dundim; gambu.**

gara₁ *n.* shell. [gara (H)] *See:* **dinggal²; guumbi¹; magul²; walamgan.**

gara₂ *n.* grey kangaroo (female).
[Macropus giganteus]. [carar, bara (L)]
See: **dalam; giriwan; guruuman; mari¹; yima.**

garabi₁ *n.* white working man. from English croppie 'convict labourer'. [croppe (Fi); karapi (L)] *See:* **dagai; daranyjin.**

Garabi₂ *n.* creek in Fortitude Valley.
Anth: running from Bridge St along the N side of Wickham St to Galinggral (Bd). [Kurrabi (Bd)] *See:* **Galinggral; garabi¹.**

Gara-gara *n.* Karragarra Island. *lit.*
'many shells'. [Karrag'-a-ra (We)] *See:* **gara¹.**

Gara-garanganbili *n.* Bartley's Hill.
[Karakara Onbili 'Swan and Bartley's Hill'; Karakaranpinbilli 'Newstead' (Bd)] *See:* **bili; gara².**

Garaji *n.* Currigee on South Stradbroke Island. [Currigee (CW); garaɟi (H)]

garal *n.* beach stone-curlew. *[Esacus magnirostris].* [garal (H); gurrell (We)] *See:* buwalgan; gariyagan; guwir.

garal-garal *n.* bone. [geralgeral (Ja); gir'al-gir'al (We)] *See:* darigany; ding; jirban.

garamgalgal *n.* tulip satinwood. *[Rhodosphaera rhodanthema].* [curumgulgal 'satin wood' (Ca)]

garan₁ *Variant:* **garan-garan.** *n.* Moreton Bay ash. *[Corymbia tessellaris]. Anth:* burns without smoke (Wi). [curran curran (B); gorrum (Ha); gurran (Le); kuran (M); kuran' (Wa)]

garan₂ *n.* ropy coastal vine called 'sea charlie'. *Anth:* horizontal vines used for lacing a camp. [garran (M)]

garanba *v.* bathe. [carunpa (Lg)]

Garanbang *n.* large waterhole (Fletcher's). *lit.* garan-bang 'dead ash tree'. *Anth:* White Swamp, N.S.W. [Curranbong (Ha)]

Garanbin *n.* woman's name. [Garanpin (M); Kuranpin (W)]

Garanbinbila *n.* the point in Newstead Park. *lit.* garan-bin-bila 'having places with vines'. [Garanbiribilla (M); Garranbinbilla, Karakaran-pinbilli (S)] *See:* -bila; -bin; garan².

garangam *n.* gentleman. possibly related to garang-garang 'clothing'; cognate with Yugambeh kamaran 'head man' (Sh). [krung num, kurr nung (Ha); garrnarron (Hi); goeranam (L)] *See:* garang-garang; garangamgan.

garangamgan *n.* gentlewoman. *lit.* garangam-gan 'gentleman-woman'. [garrnarroncun (Hi)] *See:* -gan²; garang-garang; garangam.

Garangan *n.* long expanse of pools and fens. [Karrŭngun (G)]

garang-garang *n.* cloak, clothes, blanket. [grang-grang (Bl); granggran (Fi); greng greng 'skins or clothes' (G); karanggaran (Ln); garang-garang 'skins' (MB); geranggerang (R)] *See:* bumbaru; gubi garang-garang.

garany *Variant:* **gara.** *v.* throw, fall, go down, set (of the sun). [kurrai (Ja); carreen 'through', carreen 'fall down' (Lg); carran (M); kurrai (R); kar'rai (Wa)] *See:* biya.

garara *Variant:* **garar.** *n.* black cockatoo. *[Calyptorhynchus sp.].* [karara, karēr (Ja); karara, karēr (R); kar'ara, kar'er (Wa)] *See:* balan; biliyagan; biluwala; gaiyara; giwang; jarbal.

Garbanban *n.* Canoe Creek group. [Corbonpan (Lg)] *See:* -ban.

gargan *Variant:* **garga.** *v.* bite. [gār'gan (We)] *See:* baada; gaiya.

gar-gar *n.* type of gum. *[Eucalyptus sp.].* [gargar (E); gargar (Ja); gorr gorr (Le); gargar (Lg)] *See:* baniri; gilumbir.

gargun *n.* large kingfisher. [cargoon (Ca); kargon (M)]

garguru *n.* grass tree. *[Xanthorrhoea sp.].* [kurgaroo (G); kalgoro, kolgoro (Le); cargoora (M)] *See:* bulirbin; dagabin¹; ngilarun¹; winbulin¹.

Gari *n.* common man's name. *Anth:* especially common on K'Gari (Fraser Island); possible loan from English 'Curry'. [Colly (B); gari (H)]

gariiba *n.* tide. [greeba (E); greeba (Ja); greeba, garebah (Lg)] *See:* jargariiba¹; yunggariiba.

gariing *n.* maiden's blush. *[Sloanea australis].* [kareeing (Mac)]

garil *n.* wallaby (female). [carril (Ha); garrill (Hi); garil (L); körril 'female paddimelon' (Le)] *See:* bugul; bangui; jamban; magun; wangari; wangun.

Gariwariba *n.* man's name. [Curreewurryba (W)]

gariyagan *n.* brolga. *[Antigone rubicunda]*.
[gariagan (H); gurigan 'beach stone-curlew'
(MMEIC); gurreeargan (We)] *See:* **junggi**; **gilil-
gilil**[1]; **gundurgan**.

garuba *n.* another. [garba (E); carrobba
(Ha); kurruba 'another', kurruga 'second'
(Ja); garba (Lg); kurruga (R); kur'rugā (Wa)]
See: **bularam**[1].

garubabany *Variant:* **garubaba**. *v.* crowd,
throng. *lit.* garuba-bany 'one becomes
another'. [kūrūkaba (R)]

garuda *n.* red-bark tree. [garuda (Ba)]

garulban *adj.* tired. [garu:lban, caroolpan,
caroolcan (M)] *See:* **gawanwalunbina**.

garumbin *n.* type of plant. possibly
from Yugambeh karambin 'pine', the origin of
Currumbin place name (Sh). [caroombin (Lg)]
See: **-bin**.

garwaligu *adv.* time past, yesterday.
possibly from English 'good while ago' (Ja).
[garwaliko (E); garwaliko (Ja); garwaiko (Lg)]
See: **ngunuwara**.

Garwang *n.* crossing near Minto Crag.
[Kurr-wong (Ha)]

gau *excl.* hey, stop, wait! [cao 'an
expression of surprise', cahoo 'wait' (Lg); kahu!
'stop!' (R)] *See:* **gagalum**.

Gaubanbi *n.* Rosewood. *lit.* 'scrub place'.
[Cowbanpy (S)] *See:* **-bin**.

gaura-gaura *adj.* too cold. [cowra-cowra
(Lg)] *See:* **dan-dan**; **yigil**.

gawabiri *n.* corroboree. from English
'corroboree' borrowed from Dharug. [caubiree
(Lg)] *See:* **ganjiil**; **ngari**[2]; **yiyara**; **yuwar**.

gawal *n.* scrub turkey. *[Alectura lathami]*.
[gumbul (Ha); kao-al (Ja); kao-al 'cock-of-wood'
(R)] *See:* **wagun**[1].

gawan[1] *n.* blood. [gawan gawan (H); kaoun,
giwor, kaoin (Ja); ganden, gaudn (L); kaoun
(Ln); cow-woon (M); kaoün, giwūr (R); kakke
(T); kowan, kowan (W); gīwūr, kā'ōūn (Wa)]
See: **guji**[2].

gawan[2] *Variant:* **gawa**. *v.* love. [gawan (Ba)]
See: **daligamana**.

gawanduwanbin *n.* red-leafed shrub.
incorporates gawan 'red'. [gurantuanpin (R)]
See: **-bin**; **gawan**[1].

gawan-gawan[1] *adj.* red. *lit.* 'blood-blood'.
[gawa gawa (H); kaoinkaoin (Ja); cowoon-
cowoon (Lg); kau-ni kau-ni, cowan (M);
kaoïnkaoïn (R); kuttingae 'red' (T); gowen-
gowen (We)] *See:* **gawan**[1].

gawan-gawan[2] *n.* orange mangrove;
red mangrove. *Lit.* 'red'. *[Bruguiera
gymnorhiza or Rhizophora stylosa]*. Anth:
roots were used to make boomerangs (FNSI)
[cowwoyn 'gum' (D); gawa gawa (H); kau-ni
kau-ni, cowan (M); kaoïnkaoïn (R); gowen-
gowen (We)] *See:* **baragany**[2]; **birban**; **gawan**[1];
jirabang[1]; **yabun**.

Gawan-gawan[3] *n.* the red part of
Redcliffe, also the name of Cowan
Cowan on Moreton Island. [Kau-in-
kau-in 'the red part of Redcliffe' (Bd)] *lit.* 'red'.
See: **gawan-gawan**[1].

gawanwalunbina *adj.* tired, lazy.
possibly lit. gawan wali-bila 'having bad blood'.
[cowen wollunbine (Lg)] *See:* **-bila**; **garulban**;
gawan[1]; **wali**.

gawany *Variant:* **gawa**. *v.* drive, chase,
follow. [kawane (R)]

gawibiba *adj.* ready. [cohipeppa,
cobebeppu (Lg)]

gaya *n.* power. [kaia (R)] *See:* **gayabandar**.

gayabandar *n.* person of power. *lit.*
gaya-bandar 'great man (of) power'. [kaiabunda,
kaiabundu (R)] *See:* **bandar**; **gaya**; **nan.gur**.

gaya guriliyidal *n.* hibiscus, kurrajong.
[kaya kurrilii-i-dall 'Hibiscus (Coorjaong)' (Le)]

gayanggan *n.* shark. [gay-ang-gan (CW)]
See: **burambigara**; **buwai**; **gura-guragan**;
nirang.

gayawur *n.* rainbow. *incorporates* gaya
'power'. [kai-ao-ur (Ja); kai-ao-ur, kai-ao-ŭr (R);
kai'aōŭr (Wa)] *See:* **gaya**.

gi *n.* nail. [gi (H)]

giba₁ *n.* initiated male youth. [kipper (B); kipper (Bl); kipper (Cl); kipperah (D); kipper (E); kipure (Fi); gibar (H); kippa (Ha); kippa (Ja); kipper (Lg); kipper, kippar (Ln); kippa (M); kipper (MB); kiper (N); kippa (R); gibber 'chief' (T); kipper (W); kip'pa (Wa)] *See:* bujiri; duwangjin; gumingguny.

giba₂ *v.* camp. [gibba 'camp here tonight' (Ln)] *See:* dimany; jalubaluba; ngagamwaga.

Gibamandin *n.* inlet between Mathieson Park and Sweeney Reserve. *Anth:* excellent fishing site (Bd); *lit.* giba-mandin 'fishing net of initiated youth(s)'. [Givermandin (Bd)] *See:* giba¹; mandin¹.

Gibara *n.* Keperra. *lit.* 'place of initiated youths' (S). [Keperra (S)] *See:* giba¹.

Gibarum *n.* hole near Bruckner's sawmill on Bruckner Hill Rd in Dugandan. [Gib-bearum (Ha)]

Gibiba *n.* creek on Stradbroke between Tuleenderly Creek and Wallen Wallen Creek, north of Ganarin-bin. [Geebeebah (Bn)] *See:* -ba⁴.

gibing-gibing *n.* oystercatcher. *[Haematopus sp.].* [kgibbiring (B); kibbing kibbing (M)]

gibiri *n.* pretty-face wallaby, whip-tail wallaby. *[Macropus parryi].* [que berie (Ha)] *See:* bugul; bangui; jamban; garil; magun; wangari; wangun.

gibun *n.* moon. [kibbom (Ja); kibbun (Ln)] *See:* baabun; gilan².

gidibila *n.* light. [gidibila (H); kittibilla (Ja); kittibilla (M); kittibilla (R); kitte (T); kit'tabil'la (Wa)] *See:* dalin; jalungai.

Gidilbin *n.* man's name. [Giddeel Bean (Ha)]

giga *n.* shoulder. [kika, kicka (Ja); kiker (N); kikka, gikka (R); kik'ka (Wa); gityure (We)]

Gigabira *n.* Durundur (Woodford)-area group. *lit.* 'shoulder people'. [Keecooyburra (Lg); Giggaburra (M)] *See:* -bira; giga.

gigirilbin *n.* herb. [kēgirelpin (R)] *See:* -bin.

gijaambalgin *n.* frigate bird. *[Fregata ariel].* [ketchambulgan (M)]

giji *Variant:* **giji-giji.** *n.* crab's eye, precatory bean. *[Abrus precatorius].* *Anth:* poisonous; medicinal use for unwanted pregnancy; seeds used for decoration (FNSI). [giddee giddee (CW); gidgee (FNSI)] *See:* bulumbir; magarabal; yugam.

gijigagari *n.* clam. [gidîgagari (H)] *See:* yugari.

Gijiri *n.* woman's name. [Kidgeree (B)]

gijubal *Variant:* **gijuba.** *v.* spit. [kezupal (Lg)] *See:* mali.

gijur *adj.* short. [gijur (Ba)] *See:* biribi; jalgal; narang¹; ngambara; nala.

gil *Variant:* **gi.** *v.* urinate. [gil (H); keel 'to piss' (Lg); geel (M)] *See:* jalang; nya.

gila₁ *n.* dingo's tail ornament worn on headband. [killar (Fi); killā (G); gilla (Ja); gilla (Ro); gil'la (Wa)] *See:* dinggil.

gila₂ *n.* large dark bee; its high-quality honey. *possibly [Apus mellifera].* [gila (H); kīlla (Ma)] *See:* banjin¹; jalaman; gabai¹; guja¹; gunidar; mabi¹; nagi.

Gilajin *n.* Mt Alford and its caretakers. *lit.* gilan-jin 'crescent moon people'. [Gillaydan (Be); Gailladin, Gillaydan (S)] *See:* gilan²; -jin.

gilalan *n.* little girl. [killalān (Ja); killalan, killalān (R)] *See:* gin; gingali; nyaramgan.

gilan₁ *Variant:* **gilin.** *n.* fingernail. [gillin (Cl); killin (Fi); killin 'fingers', gillin 'nails' (Ja); gillen (M); kilinn (N); killin, gillin (R); gillin (We)] *See:* magara.

gilan₂ *Variant:* **gilin.** *n.* crescent moon.
[gillaydan (Be); gillan (Cl); kibbom (E); gillan (Fi); gilan, gilen, ɟalan, ɟalal (H); geelen (Hi); killen, gillen (Ja); gilen (L); killin (Lg); gillan, keelen (Ln); kilen, gillenn 'the new moon' (M); killen (R); gillen (Su); gallan (Th); gilen (W); kil'len (Wa); gelen (We); gilin (Wu)] *See:* **baabun**; **gibun**.

gilangan *Variant:* **gilanga.** *v.* turn.
[gillūŋin (R)]

gilan-gilan₁ *n.* fishhook. *lit.* 'moon-moon'. [killin killin (Lg) *See:* **gilan**².

gilan-gilan₂ *v.* fish. [gillen-gillen (Bl); gilenkilen (Ha)]

gilawara *n.* turpentine tree. [killa wara (Mac)] *See:* **bulurjambin**¹.

Gilba *n.* boy's name. [Gilpa (B)]

gilbumba₁ *adj.* acceptable skin group for marriage; 'straight' marriage.
[gilbumpa, gilboompa (CW)] *See:* **gilgamari**.

Gilbumba₂ *n.* Hill at Bowen Bridge Road. *lit.* 'acceptable skin group for marriage'. [gilbumpa, gilboompa 'location of Garrick's house' (CW)] *See:* **gilbumba**¹.

gilgamari *Variant:* **dal gilgamari.** *adj.* acceptable skin group for marriage; 'straight' marriage. [gilgamari (H); dal gilgamari 'Aboriginal marriage system' (MMEIC)] *See:* **gilbumba**¹.

gilil-gilil₁ *n.* black-necked stork, jabiru. from Mibiny gilin-gilin. *[Ephippiorhynchus asiaticus].* [kilil kilil (M); killil-killil (Wa)] *See:* **junggi**; **gariyagan**; **gundurgan**.

Gilil-gilil₂ *n.* man's name. *lit.* 'black-necked stork'. [Killil Killil (B); Killil-killil (W)] *See:* **gilil-gilil**¹.

giling *n.* neck. [gileŋ (H); jul-line (Ha); gilleng (We)] *See:* **dur-dur**; **ngaran**¹.

gilumbir *n.* type of gum. *[Eucalyptus sp.].* [gillumbir (R)] *See:* **baniri**; **gar-gar**.

Gilwanba *n.* Nundah racecourse. [Gilwunpa (CW)] *See:* **-ba**⁴.

gima *n.* type of bandicoot. [kimi 'marsupial rat found amongst rocks in scrubby areas' (Le); kibmah 'a kind of bandicoot' (Lg)]

gimbi *n.* stinging tree. *[Dendrocnide moroides].* *Anth:* dangerous plant; do not touch (MMEIC). [gimbi (H); gimpa (M)] *See:* **baragany**¹; **burjin**.

Gimbujil *n.* man or boy's name. [Gim pudgil (Ha)]

gimunggan *n.* friend. appears to incorporate the feminine suffix -gan. [geemoong-gan (M); woentiminggoen (N); kimmoman (P) *See:* **banji**; **-gan**²; **magiiba**; **nyungin**.

gin *n.* girl. [gin (B); gin (H); ginn, kin (Ha); kīn (Ja); gin (L); keen (Ln); kehn 'virgin' (N); kin, kīn (R); gin, kin (Wa); gin (We)] *See:* **jundal**; **nyaramgan**.

gina *v.* grind a knife. [gidna (Lg)]

ginabulum *n.* type of tree. [kidnabullum (R)]

ginairanda *n.* frilled lizard. [ginairrunda (Bd)] *See:* **binanggurung**¹; **nyara**.

ginbin *n.* Eurasian coot. *[Fulica atra].* [ginbin (M)]

Ginbul *n.* man's name. [Kynpool (B)]

ginbun *n.* bream. *[Acanthopagrus sp.].* [kinburn (B) *See:* **dun.gala**; **man.gal**; **ngalan**¹.

Ginda *n.* man's name. [Kinta (W)]

gindal *n.* stone. [gindall (Fi)] *See:* **darau**; **mulu**¹; **nalanggira**.

Gindara₁ *n.* hill on Moreton Island. [Kindara, Gindara (CW); kindara (W)]

Gindara₂ *n.* woman's name. [Kindara, Gindara (CW); kindara (W)]

Gindariba *n.* man's name. [Gindareeba (W)]

gindigan *n.* joking around. *lit.* gindin-gan 'laughing time'. [gindiɟaŋ (H)] *See:* **-gan**¹; **gindin**.

gindin *Variant:* **gindi.** *v.* laugh, joke. [gindi (Cl); kindänné (E); gindi (H); gindi, kindanne (Ja); kindlinn'I, kinda (Lg); gindi (Su); kindei (T); gindan (W)]

gingali *n.* little girl. *lit.* gin-gali 'very much a girl'. [gingali (H)] *See:* -**gali**; **gin**; **gilalan**.

gingga *n.* night owl. [kinka (M)] *See:* **duribang**[1]; **gum-gum**; **nyinggal**; **wumanggan**[2].

ginggal munyi biriba[1] *n.* honey bulrush, its smell. *[Typha sp.].* [kinggalmoonyeerpirriba (M); kingal moonji pimba (W)]

Ginggal Munyi Biriba[2] *Variant:* **Ginggal.** *n.* woman's name. *lit.* 'honey bulrush'. [Kinggalmoonyeerpirriba (M); Kingal moonji pimba (W)] *See:* **ginggal munyi biriba**[1].

ging-ging *n.* itch, prickly heat. [giggle-giggle 'itchy, prickly heat' (Bl); gingging (J); kingking 'prickly heat or itch' (Lg)]

Gin.gibin *n.* woman's name. [Keen.gibbin (Ha)]

gin-gin[1] *n.* children, little girls. [kinkin 'a girl' (Lg); kin-kin (W)] *See:* **jajam**; **mulam**; **nyaramgan**; **nyamal**.

gin-gin[2] *n.* scarlet robin. *[Petroica boodang].* [gengin (H); ghen ghen (We)]

gin-ginga *n.* native hop bush. *[Dodonaea triquetra].* *Anth:* leaves and hops soaked to make mead; when the hop bush flowers, oysters are at their best (FNSI). [kin gin ga (CW)] *See:* **ganingira gidar**.

ginin *n.* sandfly, mosquito. [kinnen (M); kin'nen (Wa)]

ginyinggara *n.* oyster. [giɲigir, giɲiger, ɟinɟirga, ɟinɟirgar (H); kin-yingga (Ja); kingingera (Ln); keenyingurra (M); ginyingarra, kinyingarra (W); kin'yungā (Wa)] *See:* **guumbi**[1]; **ningi-ningi**[1].

gira[1] *n.* dry earth, sand, country, north. [gira (H); gira (Ja); kirri, geera (M); girar (R); goyarra (T); kir'ra, gir'ar (Wa)] *See:* **jagun**[1]; **jara**; **yarang**[1].

gira[2] *n.* rum. from Gabi-Gabi gira 'fire' (Bell 1994). [gira (H); geera (Ha)] *See:* **bira**.

Gira[3] *n.* man's name. *lit.* 'north' or 'country'. [Gee-ra (CW); Geera (W)] *See:* **gira**[1].

giraaman *n.* flying fox. [grammon (Bl); ciraumun (D); giraman (H); graymon (Ha); gramman (Ja); kiddemmon (Le); kraamon (Lg); kieraman (W); girra'man (Wa); gurranum (We)]

giram *adv; n.* across. [kireum (Lg); kīrgūm, kīrumt (R)] *See:* **ngulumari**.

giran *n.* scrub tick. [geerrun (Ha)]

girawali[1] *adj.* split, broken. *lit.* gira-wali 'bad place'. [kerwalli (Ja); ker'wallī (Wa)]

Girawali[2] *n.* high part of Shorncliffe. *lit.* 'broken'. [Ker Walli (Bd)] *See:* **gira**[1]; **girawali**[1]; **wali**.

girba *adj.* small. [cerpa (Ln)] *See:* **biribi**; **jalgal**; **narang**[1]; **ngambar**; **nala**.

girgal *n.* fibula. [geergul (Lg)] *See:* **jirban**.

Girgamban *n.* South Brisbane group. [Kircumpan (Lg)] *See:* -**ban**; **giram**.

girigan *n.* blackbutt. *[Eucalyptus pilularis].* *Anth:* bark used for covering huts (DF) and making buckets sealed with wax (Wi); when the blackbutt is in flower, it means that parrot fish are in the bay. [girigan (H); gira (T); geregun (We)] *See:* **binarwin**; **mandili**.

Girila *n.* woman's name. [Kerella (G)]

giriman *n.* body. [kereman (T)]

giriwan *n.* grey creek kangaroo (male). [guttamon 'male swamp wallaby' (Ha); giriwon 'small kangaroo' (L); kiddibon, kiddewamm 'male little dark grey kangaroo' (Le)] *See:* **dalam**; **gara**[2]; **guruuman**; **mari**[1]; **yima**.

giwa *Variant:* **giwa-giwa.** *n.* lace monitor. *[Varanus varius].* [gu-air (Ha); gi-wer (Ja); kju-e (Le); guea (Lg); gewah gewah 'goanna in Moonjine' (M); gīw'er (Wa)] *See:* **bara**[1]; **walmuram**[1]; **yaugira**.

Giwabin *n.* the high part of Harper's Hill in the Cascade Gardens in Surfer's Paradise; Goanna Hill. *lit.* giwa-bin 'place of lace monitors'. [Gu-air bin (Ha)] *See:* -bin; giwa.

giwang *n.* white cockatoo. [kehwong (M)] *See:* balan; biliyagan; biluwala; gaiyara; garara; jarbal.

giwara *adj.* white. [currarn (Ha); giwere (L)] *See:* buba².

giwarang *n.* white ant, termite. related to giwara 'white'. [giwerong (L)] *See:* baigan; bigunjur¹; danmurin; galalang; giwara; mugara²; murin.

giya *v.* sing, call. [kiana, gie (Lg); kia (M)]

giyagara *adj.* lazy. [kiagara (Lg)] *See:* gawanwalunbina.

giyagarabany *adj.* unable. *lit.* giyagara-bany 'become lazy'. [kiagarapan (Lg)] *See:* -bany; giyagara.

giyali *v.* sing together, accompany singing. *lit.* giya-li 'sing ourselves'. [kiale (Lg); kialli (M)] *See:* giya; -li².

Giyambi *n.* old station hut on Fyffe's Plains near Coochin. [Ke-amby (Ha)]

giyi *adj.* lustful. [kiyi (Bl)]

=gu *clitic.* purposive clitic that indicates a goal. [co (E); gu (H); ga (Ha); go, gu (M); gu (R); go (W)]

guba₁ *v.* go on. [goovare (Hi); cobana (W)] *See:* -nya; nyan.

guba₂ *excl.* goodbye. *lit.* 'go on'; or, from English 'go away' (L). [go wa (L)] *See:* yawai².

guba₃ *n.* large white yam. [coobah (Bd)] *See:* dadam; dam¹; diya-diya; madara.

gubagil *adj.* old. [gubagil (J); coobaggil (Lg)] *See:* baji¹.

gubalbin *n.* curlew sandpiper. *[Calidrus ferruginea]*. [goobalbin (M)]

gubama *v.* lead. *lit.* guba-ma 'make go on'. [coobamana 'to lead' (Lg)] *See:* guba¹; -ma; -nya.

gubang *n.* frog. [guboŋ, gobaŋ (H)] *See:* jaraagil; naji; wagal.

gubargan *n.* blue-tongued lizard. *[Tiliqua scincoides]*. [cubbargin (Ha); goobargan (Hi); goragan (Le); coobahgan (M)]

gubi₁ *n.* brushtail possum. *[Trichosurus vulpecula]*. [kopee (Cl); coopee (D); gabi (H); guppee 'forest possum' (Ha); goopy (Hi); ku-pi 'forest possum' (Ja); kupi (L); kuppi (Le); coopee (Lg); coopee, coope (Ln); kubbee (M); ku-pi (P); kubbi (R); goopee (W); kūp'ī 'grey forest opossum' (Wa); gubi (Wu)] *See:* gabala¹; ganal; widiging.

gubi₂ *Variant:* **gubi-gubi**. *n.* wind. [gubi (H); kubbee-kubbee (W); goobie (We)] *See:* buran; burging; dimbiny¹; dun.gai; junggai¹; nyaban; winjia.

Gubi₃ *n.* woman's name. *lit.* 'brushtail possum'. [Goo-bee (CW); Goobee (W)] *See:* gubi¹.

Gubidabin *n.* Samford. *incorporates* -bin 'place' and possibly gubi 'possum'. [Kupidabin (Bd)] *See:* -bin; gubi¹.

gubi garang-garang *n.* possum cloak. *lit.* 'brushtail possum cloak'. [coopy grang grang (D)] *See:* garang-garang; gubi¹.

gubilban *Variant:* **gubilba**. *v.* set up. [coobilpun (Lg)]

gubu-guburan *n.* native raspberry. *Anth:* edible (FNSI). [cooboorgooyri (B); kūbbūkubbūran (R)] *See:* malgam; yalabin.

Guburabil₁ *n.* Fred Johnstone's homestead at Carney's Creek. [Cobrabil (Ha)]

Guburabil₂ *n.* man's name. [Cobrabil (Ha)]

Gubuuru *n.* Coopooroo. *probably a corruption of Gulbuurum*. ['Coor-poo-roo, with accent on the poo' (M)] *See:* Gulbuurum.

Gubuuru-Jagin *n.* South Brisbane group. [Coopooroo-jaggin (M)] *See:* Gubuuru; Gulbuurum.

guda₁ *n.* side of body, area to the side. [kutta (Ja); guta 'rib' (L); kutar (N); kutta (R); koota (W); kut'ta (Wa)]

guda₂ *n.* snake. [guttar (Ha); cootah (Hi)] *See:* **bui²**; **juumgu**; **mulumgal**; **yuwan**.

Guda₃ *n.* person's name. *lit.* 'side'. [guda (Ba); guta (L); kutar (N); kutta (R); koota (W); kut'ta (Wa)]

Gudagiri *n.* man's name. [Kuttageeri (W)]

gudajirban *n.* rib. *lit.* guda-jirban 'side bone'. [kutahr-chirben (N)] *See:* **guda¹**; **jirban**.

gudal *n.* bushes. [kuddal (Ja); kuddal (R); kud'der (Wa)]

Gudanu *n.* man's name. [Gootenoo (W)]

gugi *n.* egg. from English egg. [gugi (H)] *See:* **gang-gang¹**.

Gugin.gambal *n.* Dugandan railway station, hills and lagoons. [Coo-gen-cumbel (Ha)]

Gugingbul *n.* woman's name. [Kukingboel (W)]

guibila magul *adj.* grey headed. *incorporates* magul 'head'. [kui pille moggool] *See:* **magul¹**; **magul buba bundal**.

guiyar₁ *n.* type of trevally, generic term for fish. [gurjar, gurar, guria, gurian (H); kuīyur (Ja); kuiyur, kooyar 'generic word for fish' (M); kuīyur (R)] *See:* **janbilbin**; **gulbural**.

guiyar₂ *n.* sun, day. [kuiyar (Ja); kuiyar (R)] *See:* **biigi**.

guiying *n.* red clay. [guiying (Ja)] *See:* **guji¹**.

guja₁ *n.* small black native bee, its dark honey. *[Austroplebeia australis]*. [kgoodua (B); koonee-da (Cl); coochaw (D); guʃa (H); cootcha (Hi); kootchar (Hk); ku-ta (Ja); kootsia, kuts'æ (L); coota (Lg); coocha (Ln); ku-lā (M); kū'ta (Wa)] *See:* **banjin¹**; **jalaman**; **gabai¹**; **gila²**; **gunidar**; **mabi**; **nagi**.

Guja₂ *n.* Mt Coot-tha. *lit.* 'small native bee'. [Gootcha (M); Kuta, Gootcha (S)] *See:* **guja¹**.

Gujabila *n.* Grandchester. *lit.* guja-bila 'having honey'. [Goojabila (S)] *See:* **-bila**; **guja¹**.

gujal *n.* gammon, nonsense, lie. [guʃal, guʃa (H)] *See:* **nyalang**.

gujalgan *n.* mischief, lying. *lit.* gujal-gan 'gammon time'. [guʃalgan (H)] *See:* **-gan¹**; **gujal**.

gujam *n.* flame, fire. [guʃam (H); kuddum, kuiyum, goyum (Ja); kuddum, kuïyim (R)] *See:* **jalu**.

gujan *Variant:* **guja**. *v.* dare. [coojon (Ln)]

guji₁ *adj.* red clay used as paint. [coochie (Be); guʃi (H); kootchin, godjeen (Ha); kutchi (Ja); kutchi (M); guiying (R); kutchin, kūt'chi, gui'dhing (Wa)] *See:* **guiying**.

guji₂ *adj.* red, the shade of red clay or red stone. [coochie (Be); guʃi (H); kootchin, godjeen (Ha); kutchi (Ja); kutchi (M); guiying (R); kutchin, kūt'chi, gui'dhing (Wa)] *See:* **gawan¹**.

guji₃ *n.* castor oil plant. *[Ricinus communis]*. *lit.* 'red'; *Anth:* introduced plant. [kudgee (FNSI)]

Guji-gujiba *n.* Cuchiemudlo Island. *Anth:* red paint was obtained here for corroborees (Bn); *lit.* guji-guji-ba 'red-red place'. [Goochee Goochee Pah (Bn); Goojinggoojingpa (M)] *See:* **-ba⁴**; **guji¹**; **Gujimulu**.

guji-gujin.gal *n.* native guava. *[Eupomatia laurina]*. [kuide kuidencul 'small guava' (Lg)] *See:* **darum**.

Gujimulu *n.* Cuchiemudlo Island. *lit.* 'red stone'. [Cootchie Moodlo (B); Coochie Mudlow (Ln); Coodgee Mudlow (S); coodgee mudlow (W)] *See:* **guji²**; **Guji-gujiba**; **mulu¹**.

Gujin-gujin *n.* Coochin Station, red ridge near Wallace's Creek. *lit.* 'red-red'; Thomas Alford defined Coochin Coochin as 'many black swans'. [Coochin Coochin (Be); Kootchin Kootchin (Ha); Coochin Coochin (S)] *See:* **guji²**.

Gujira *n.* Ipswich. [Coodjirar (Be)]

gujiwang *n.* flea. [gujiwang (Ba)]

gujun *n.* dark, night. [guɟun (H); koodgoom (W); goojoon (We)] *See:* **ngunu; gurung-gurung.**

gujundabu *adv.* tomorrow, morning. [goojandabboo (M); koodgoondaboo (W); goojoonchebba (We)] *See:* **mulagu¹; ngunugaba; ngunuwara.**

gujung *n.* rock cod. *[Lotella rhacina].* [coodjoong (B); coojung (M); goojung (We)] *See:* **duguu.**

gula₁ *n.* grass seed ground into flour. [goolah (Ga)]

gula₂ *n.* koala. from English koala borrowed from Dharug. *[Phascolarctos cinereus].* [gula (H)] *See:* **dumbiribi; marangbi.**

gula₃ *adj.* angry, displeased. [coola (Bl); koola (E); koold, koola (Ja); koola (Lg)] *See:* **wagara².**

gulai *n.* woman's bag, dilly. a saltwater Yagara word (P). [kulai (P); goolay (W)] *See:* **bunbi; dili¹.**

gulambarun *n.* pied currawong. *[Strepera graculina].* [qul-lamberoon (Ha); coolamberoon 'small whistling dove' (Le); caloomba (M)] *See:* **jarwang; mirum.**

gulbural *n.* fish like a trevally without scales and with poisonous fins. [cullburral 'trevally' (Bn); gu'l, gulbul (H)] *See:* **janbilbin; guiyar¹.**

gulburbin *n.* sea grass, dugong food. [cool-bool boorpin (CW); gulburbin (MMEIC)] *See:* **-bin.**

Gulbuurum *n.* Norman Creek; Annerley. *Anth:* probable source of English 'Coopooroo' (M); popular camping and fishing area (Bd). [Kulpurum 'vicinity of Cornwall and Juliette Streets' (Bd); Kulpurum 'Norman Creek' (S)]

guldan *n.* bottle tree. *[Brachychiton rupestris].* [coolton (D)] *See:* **jinbigari.**

gulgal *n.* potato. *[Solanum tuberosum].* [goolgul (Lg)]

gulgan₁ *n.* road, path. [gulgan 'camp' (J); coolgwan (Lg); gulwun, kulgun (R); kul'gun (Wa)] *See:* **bambar; dumba.**

Gulgan₂ *n.* route across Teviot Range. *lit.* 'path'. [Kulgun (S)] *See:* **gulgan¹.**

gulgilun.gin *Variant:* **gulgilun.gi.** *v.* go round about. [coolgilloon gin (Lg)]

gulimbi *n.* type of bluish-coloured pademelon (male). [koolembe (Le)] *See:* **gumang.**

gulmang₁ *n.* stone axe. [culmung, goolman (Ha); gul'man (Wa)] *See:* **binjilurar; mugim; nanggan; wagara¹.**

Gulmang₂ *n.* Mt Gulman. lit 'axe'. [Goolman (S)] *See:* **gulmang¹.**

gulugan₁ *n.* pelican. *[Pelecanus conspicillatus].* [cooloocan (Ln); cooloocan, kulukan (M)] *See:* **buluwalung; junggara.**

Gulugan₂ *n.* possibly Murrumba Downs. *lit.* 'pelican'. [Kulukan (Bd); Kulukan, Gooloogan (S)] *See:* **gulugan¹.**

Gulum *n.* woman's name. [Coolloom (B); Kooloom (W)]

gulun *n.* wonga pigeon. *[Leucosarcia melanoleuca].* [kuloin (Be); gooloon 'wild pigeon' (Ca); coollwen (D); coolun 'Vanga Vanga pigeon' (Le); gooloon, coodloon (Lg); gooloon (M)] *See:* **bilurun; dandali¹.**

gulurur *n.* brown hawk. *[Falco berigora].* [koolooroor (M)]

Guluwin *n.* Wooloowin/Lutwyche. *lit.* 'place of a certain type of pigeon' (Bd); gulun-bin 'place of wonga pigeons'. [Kuluwin 'Thoroldtown & O'Conneltown' (Bd)] *See:* **gulun¹.**

gulwal *n.* noise. [goolwal (Lg)]

gumabila *n.* water spring. [goomabilla (M)] *See:* **-bila.**

gumang *n.* type of bluish-coloured pademelon (female). [ku-mang (Ja); gumang (Le); coomang (M); kum'ang (Wa)] *See:* **gulimbi.**

Gumbaban *n.* Taylor's Ridge group. [Coompabun (Lg)]

gumbal₁ *adj; adv.* only, merely, mere. [kūmbal (R)] *See:* **ngundu**¹.

gumbal₂ *n.* tasty treat found inside mullet. [gumbal (MMEIC)]

gumbara *Variant:* **gumbar.** *n.* geebung tree and fruit. a saltwater Yagara word. *[Persoonia virgata]. Anth:* the flowers were sucked for honey, and the fruit eaten (FNSI). [koombarra (CW); gumbar (H)] *See:* **dalandala**¹.

gumbawala *n.* penis. [gumbawala (H)] *See:* **bulu; dugai; gumi.**

Gumbiliba *n.* man's name. [Goombilleba (W)]

Gumbumba *n.* woman's name. [Koempoembah (N)]

gum-gum *n.* boobook, mopoke. *[Ninox boobook]*. [coom-com (D); gum gum (H); coom-coom (Lg)] *See:* **duribang**¹; **gingga**¹; **nyinggal; wumanggan**².

gumi *n.* glans of penis. [gumi (H)] *See:* **bulu; dugai; gumbawala.**

gumingguny *n.* uninitiated boy. [goominguin (W)] *See:* **bujiri; duwangjin; giba**¹.

gumuwara *v.* be intimate. [gumuwara (H)] *See:* **bam-bam; burima; jim-jim.**

guna₁ *n.* excrement, vine with stinky yellow flowers. *[Hibbertia scandens]*. [guna (H); kudena (Ja); goodna (Ln); gudna (M); kudena, gunang 'ox's dung' (R); koodna (W); gūd'nadung (Wa)] *See:* **baandigu; duwal.**

guna₂ *n.* heart, liver. [goedna (L); kudna (R); kud'der (Wa)] *See:* **dagal**¹.

Guna₃ *n.* Goodna. *lit.* 'excrement'; probably named by whites. [Goodna 'dung' (S)] *See:* **guna**¹.

gunabila *v.* lose bowel control. *lit.* guna-bila 'be afflicted with excrement'. [gunang bila 'unexpected loss of bowel control' (MMEIC)] *See:* **-bila; guna**¹.

gunaim *n.* hoop pine. *[Araucaria cunninghamii]*. from Waga-Waga gunem. [coonname (D)] *See:* **bugal; buunyi; dandardam; juunbal; gambarju.**

gunamali *v.* excrete. *lit.* guna-ma-li 'make excrement'. [gunamali (H)] *See:* **guna**¹; **-li**²; **-ma.**

gunambarang *n.* John Dory. *[Zeus faber]*. [gunambarag (We)]

Gunanjigirara *n.* Laidley Creek. *lit.* 'going down creek'. [Goonanjee-gerrara (S)]

gunbing *n.* banded wobbegong. *[Orectolobus ornatus]*. [gunbing (We)]

Gunburiyan *n.* Mt Coonowrin. *lit.* 'crooked neck'. [gunburijan, gunuran (H)]

gunda *n.* type of fish. [coonta (B)]

gundan₁ *n.* corkwood tree. *[Endiandra sieberi]*. [coontun, coonton (D); gundin, gunden (H); gun-tarn 'scrub kurrajong tree' (Ha); coontarn (Hi); kuntan, goon (Ja); coontan (Ln); guntan, goontan (M); kuntan (R); kuntan (Ro); koontaw, kontan (W); kun'tan (Wa)]

gundan₂ *n.* shield made from corkwood tree. [coontun, coonton (D); gundin, gunden (H); gun-tarn 'scrub kurrajong tree' (Ha); coontarn (Hi); kuntan, goon (Ja); coontan (Ln); guntan, goontan (M); contar (MB); kuntan (R); kuntan (Ro); koontaw, kontan (W); kun'tan (Wa)] *See:* **dabira.**

gundi *n.* elbow, lower arm. [O'pee (Cl); g'pee (Ja); gutnti 'elbow' (L); kundah (N); gundi 'elbow' (R); goontie (W)]

gundiba *n.* forest oak. *[Allocasuarina torulosa]*. [koon deeba (CW); kūndībar (R)] *See:* **buranda; ganjil; yarara.**

gundir *n.* quartz crystal. *Anth:* each nan.gur owned a crystal for healing and magic; crystals gave the ability to fly (Hw). ['magic crystal' (Ja); gundal (H); kun'dri (Wa); guundir (Wi)] *See:* daginy; gaya; gayabandar; maamba; nan.gur; yilal.

gundul₁ *n.* stringybark tree, tree bark. *[Eucalyptus sp.].* [gondola (Cl); coondall 'turpentine tree bark' (D); gondol (E); gundull 'bark' (Fi); condōle (G); gundu (H); goondool (Hi); gondol, kundul, koondu, gondole, condole (Ja); goondool (L); gondol (Lg); koondoo (M); kūndu (R); kundul (Ro); gondol, kundo (T); koondool, goondool (W); kūn'dū (Wa)] *See:* diyi; jura.

gundul₂ *n.* bark canoe. [gondola (Cl); condōle (G); gundu (H); goondool (Hi); gondol, kundul, koondu, gondole, condole (Ja); goondool (L); gondol (Lg); coondul 'canal' (Ln); koondoo (M); condole (MB); kūndu (R); kundul (Ro); gondol, kundo (T); koondool, goondool (W); kūn'dū (Wa)] *See:* dingga; yaribu.

gundurgan *n.* brolga; native companion. *[Grus rubicunda].* [coondaroocan (Lg); koondoorgia, kundurkan (M); kundūr'kan (Wa)] *See:* bugur; junggi; gariyagan; gilil-gilil¹; muralagang.

Gunduwali *n.* woman's name. [Koondoowallee, Koondoorwallee, Coondoowalle (B)]

gung *n.* water, whiskey, alcoholic drink. from Badjala gung 'water' (Bell 2003). [coong (Bl); guŋ (H); kong (Ha); goonko 'sea' (Ja); goong (M); kung (T); kong, kung (Wa)]

gungany *Variant:* **gunga.** *v.* shout, cry, sing (of birds). [koorgun (Ha); koongarro (Ja); kungain (R); koongarra (TK)]

gunganya *n.* birdsong. [cungunna (Ha)] *See:* gungany; -nya.

gunggal₁ *n.* shade. [guŋgal (H); goongul (We)]

gunggal₂ *Variant:* **gungga.** *v.* cover something. [kūnka (Ja); kūnka (R)]

gunggama *v.* make something cover something. *lit.* gunggal-ma 'make cover'. [kūnkamu (Ja); kūnkamu (R); kan'ka-mū (Wa)] *See:* gunggal²; -ma.

gun-gunwan *n.* emerald dove. *[Chalcophaps longirostris].* [goon-goon-wonn (Ha)]

guni *n.* hip. [koenih (Ba)]

gunidar *n.* bee fly. [koonee-da 'bee fly' (Ja); coonedar 'bee' (Lg); coonegara 'bee' (Ln)] *See:* banjin¹; jalaman; gabai¹; gila²; guja¹.

gunigal *n.* plain, flat country. [kongil (Cl); koondgil 'land' (Ja); goonigul, coodnegul (Lg)]

Gunimba *n.* Cape Moreton. [Gunemba (CW)] *See:* -ba⁴.

gunin-gunin *excl; n.* poor thing, someone you feel sorry for. [gunin gunin (MMEIC)] *See:* gunman; ngari ngaram.

gunman *excl.* compassionate interjection, 'poor thing!', 'poor love!'. [kunmān (Ja); kunmān (R); kun'man (Wa)] *See:* gunin-gunin; ngari ngaram.

Gunul Gabalju *n.* St Helena Aboriginal group. [Coonool-Cabalchoo (M)]

gura₁ *n.* red bottlebrush tree. *[Callistemon sp.].* [gorra (Ha)]

Gura₂ *n.* woman's name. [Coora (W)]

gurabi *adv; v.* behind, be behind. [coorape (Lg); gūrpiŋga, gūrpinje (R)]

Guragubi *n.* location of Bowen's Bridge in Canning Downs. [Gooragooby (Hall 1928)]

guraguda *n.* boat deck. [kurragutta (R)]

gura-guragan *n.* shark. [gurragurragan (We)] *See:* burambigara; buwai; gayanggan; nirang.

gurai *n.* large fig. *[Ficus macrophylla].* [gurai (Ja); gurai (R); gura'i (Wa)] *See:* galamang; ganin; ganin.gar; jambal; murabal; nguwanga; nyada.

guralbang₁ *n.* brown snake. [coorril (Fi); coralbong (Ha); gooraltung (Hi); kuralbang (Ja); guralbang (L); coor'albong, coorahlbang (M)]

Guralbang₂ *n.* Kooralbyn. [Kooralbyn (S)] *See:* **guralbang**¹.

guranban *n.* intestines and skirt of dugong. *Anth:* made into sausages and considered a delicacy (MMEIC). [cooran-pah, gurrunpun (CW); gurunbin, guramban (H); gurna (R)] *See:* **bagirang**; **gurubul**; **yangan**¹.

Gurawi *n.* woman's name. [Coorahwee (M)]

gurawin *Variant:* **gurawi.** *v.* roll. [coorowen (Lg)]

gurbi-gurbi *adj; adv.* properly. [coorpee coorpee (Lg)]

gurbingai *n.* initiation ceremony. [kur'bingai (Wa)]

gurdir *n.* spotted gum. *[Corymbia sp.]*. [coorder (Lg)] *See:* **ngurgurga**; **yara**¹.

gurgundal *n.* water cataract. [g'oorcoond'al (M)] *See:* **bibuji**.

guri *adj; n.* Aboriginal, Aboriginal person. from Yugambeh guri (Sh). [goeranam 'black man' (L); goori, goorie (MMEIC)] *See:* **gin**; **jaan**; **malara**; **mari**².

gurii *excl; v.* be astonished, an expression of astonishment. [cooree (Lg); goorai (Kd); kurī (R); Ku-ré! (Ro); korē (Wa)] *See:* **baguru**.

Gurijaba *n.* Koureyabba Creek on Stradbroke. named by Balun.giny (Bn). [Koori Jubba (Bn); guridaba, guridabu (H)] *See:* **Balun.giny**.

guril *n.* rakali, water rat, melomys. *[Hydromys chrysogaster; Melomys cervinipes]*. [corril (Ha); gooril (Hi); kureel (Ja); kurril (Le); coorill (M); guril (T); kooril (W); kur'il (Wa); gurrall (We)]

Gurilba *n.* West End, Milton bend. *lit.* guril-ba 'place of water rats'. [Kurilpa, Kureelpa, Cooreelpa (M); Kurilpa (S)] *See:* **-ba**⁴; **guril**.

gurin *Variant:* **guri.** *v.* enter. [kurrin (R)] *See:* **dungala**; **ganul**¹.

gurindin *n.* red scrub fruit. [cooreenden (Lg)]

Guru *n.* woman's name. [Kooroo (W)]

gurubul *n.* part of the dugong that tastes like bacon. [gurrupul (MMEIC)] *See:* **bagirang**; **guranban**; **yangan**¹.

guru-guru *n.* type of saltwater fish. [cooroo cooroo (Lg)]

gurumba *adj; adv.* big, great, greatly, plenty, long. [koorombah (Cl); cooroombah (D); korumba (E); gurumba (H); kooroomba (Ha); kuroomba, koorombah (Ja); korumba, caroomba (Lg); kurumba (M); kurūmba (R); cooroomba (W); kurūm'ba (Wa)] *See:* **buruuwal**; **murul**.

gurumba garaba *n.* many. *lit.* 'plenty another'. [goombaggarapo (M)] *See:* **garuba**; **gurumba**; **milin**; **manyal**.

gurung₁ *adj.* charcoal. [gorun (E); koorun (Fi); guruŋ, guroŋ, duruŋ (H); gouroun, kurun, kūroin, kurrun (Ja); gurun (L); gorun, corooen (Lg); gooroon (M); kūroïn, kurun, kūrun (R); kuruim (T); kur'un, kur'oin (Wa)]

gurung₂ *adj.* black. [gorun (E); koorun (Fi); guruŋ, guroŋ, duruŋ (H); goorum, currarn 'white' (Ha); gouroun, kurun, kūroin, kurrun (Ja); gurun (L); gorun, corooen (Lg); coonanghm 'dark' (Ln); gooroon (M); kūroïn, kurun, kūrun (R); kuruim (T); kur'un, kur'oin (Wa)] *See:* **gabi**; **gujun**; **gurung-gurung**.

gurung-gurung *n.* darkness. *lit.* 'black-black'. [guruŋ guruŋba (H); koorunkoorun, kūrun (Ja); kōrunkōrun (R)] *See:* **gujun**; **gurung**.

Gurung-gurungba *n.* creek near Myora. *Anth:* this creek was caused by soakage and once had an islet covered with bladdy grass (Bn); *lit.* gurung-gurung-ba 'place of darkness'; named by Balun.giny (Bn). [gurun-gurun (Ba); Cooroon Cooroon Pa (Bn); guruŋ guruŋba (H); kōrunkōrun (R)] *See:* **-ba**⁴; **Balun.giny**; **gurung-gurung**.

guruuman *n.* old man kangaroo, grey kangaroo. *[Macropus giganteus].* [goorooman (Bl); karoman (Ca); groo-man (Cl); carroomen (D); guruman (H); kruman (Ha); gooroomon (Hi); kurooman, grooman, kuruman, groman (Ja); guruman, guranam (L); coodomen 'wallaby' (Lg); grumaan (Ln); kurūman, gurūman (R); grooman (Su); gurō'man, kur'ūman (Wa)] *See:* gara²; giriwan; jamban; mari¹; yima.

gurwa *n.* cotton tree. *Anth:* 'similar to cotton ... Acrid unfit for food till prepared. Blossom red' (Le); *possibly [Bombax ceiba].* [gurrwah (Le)] *See:* dalwalbin¹.

guumbi₁ *n.* pearl oyster; its shell. *Anth:* a totem of one of the groups on Stradbroke island (MMEIC). [coompee (B); goenbi, guambi, gumbi (H); goompee (M); coompee (W); coompie (We)] *See:* dinggal²; gara¹; ginyinggara; magul²; walamgan.

Guumbi₂ *n.* Goompi, Dunwich. *lit.* 'pearl oyster'; named by Balun.giny (Bn). [coompee (B); guambi (Ba); Goompee (Bn); coom-pee, goompie (CW); goenbi, guambi, gumbi (H); goompee (M); coompee (W); coompie (We)] *See:* Balun.giny; guumbi¹.

guwaa *n.* cloud, rain. [goa (Fi); goowar (Hi); kaoh (Ja); guwah 'cloud', guma 'rain' (L); coah (Lg); gual (Ln); gua (R); koah (Su)] *See:* galan; marun.

Guwaangumbi *n.* Humpy Flat near Grantham. *lit.* guwaa-ngumbi 'rain humpy'. [Goanumby 'green bark' (S)] *See:* guwaa; ngumbi.

Guwaawiniwa *n.* Goat Island. *incorporates* guwaa 'cloud; rain'. [Goa-Wennewar (CW); Goa Wennewar (S); Goa wennewar (W)] *See:* guwaa.

Guwalbiyan *n.* woman's name. [Quelbeean (W)]

Guwanbal *n.* Gowanbal people of southern and central Stradbroke Island, speakers of Jandai. *Anth:* a clan of the Nunagal (H); caretakers of St Helena and Mud Island (Bn). [Goobempull (Hn); Goenbal (H); Coobennpil (M); Gowenbal (MMEIC); Geonpul (W)] *See:* -bul.

Guwar *n.* Moorgumpin (Moreton Island) language, language of the Ngugi people. [Guwar (Ba); Go (M); Goowar, Gooar (W); Gowar (Ti)] *See:* Ngugi.

guwaramduwanbin *n.* tulipwood. *[Harpullia pendula].* [guarrimtenberra, guarrim-tenberra (M); guran tuanpin (R)] *See:* -bin.

guwir *n.* beach stone-curlew. *[Esacus magnirostris].* [kū'wīr 'stone plover' (Wa)] *See:* buwalgan; garal.

Guwirmandadu *n.* Hemmant. *incorporates* guwir 'bush stone-curlew'. [Kuwirmandadu (S)] *See:* guwir.

J – j

jaagany *n.* bunyip that lives in sacred waters. *Anth:* usually takes the form of a giant carpet snake. [jāgaɲ (H); targon, taggan (S)] *See:* Gabura²; Gabuljar; warajam.

jaagul *n.* cheek. [taggal (Cl); taggal (Ja); jahgul (M); jargool (We)] *See:* wanggal.

jaan *Variant:* **jaan-jaan**. *n.* Aboriginal man. [ɟan (H); tyan, dan-tyan (Ja); daan (Ln); tyān, dān, dan (R); dan (T); dan, dhan (Wa)] *See:* guri; malara; mari².

jaanmalara *n.* Aboriginal man. *lit.* jaan-malara 'Aboriginal man'. [dam-muliery (Ln)] *See:* jaan; malara.

jabam *n.* witchetty grub. *[Endoxyla leucomochla].* *Anth:* when the witchetty grubs were on the move, the mullet would soon come (Delaney 1994). [ɟabam, ɟabum (H); jubbum (M)] *See:* jubar.

Jabaninba *n.* place near Amity Point. [Jaboninpah (B)] *See:* -ba⁴.

jabiri *Variant:* **jabir.** *n.* nulla-nulla for hunting and fighting. [jubbay 'padjmelon stick' (D); jabbeerree 'wadj' (Fi); jaberry bangooba (G); ɟabir (H); taberee (Ha); jabbree (Hi); taberi, tabri (Ja); chalberrie (M); taberi, tabbīr (R); tabri (Ro); tab'eri, dha'beri (Wa)] *See:* **bagan; mar.**

jabu *v.* be frightened. [ɟabu, ɟabur(a), ɟabul (H)]

Jabubira *n.* Nerang group. [Chabbooburra (M)] *See:* **-bira.**

jagan *n.* eel, flathead. [tāgin (B); dagan (E); dagan (H); dargun (Ha); tāgu (Ja); tayan (Le); dagan, dagun, taggin, taagun (Lg); duggin, chagine (M); tāgun (R); dāgŭn, tāgūn (Wa); duggen (We)] *See:* **juruny¹.**

jagany *n.* spear. [jugany (Wu)] *See:* **bilara; bulan¹; ganai.**

jagi *n.* mysterious light, jack o'lantern, tribal spirit. from Guwar jargee 'mysterious light' (MMEIC). [ɟagi (H)]

jagin-jagin *n.* silky oak. *[Grevillea sp.].* [tungun (Ca); jagine-jagine (M)] *See:* **ngarabin.**

Jagiri *n.* Bruckner's Mt or Scubby Mt. *Anth:* near Boonah. [Juggerie (Ha)]

jagu *adv; excl.* altogether, completely, enough! [tāgo (Ja); taggoom (Lg); jāgo, tāgo (R); jāg'ō, dhā'go, tāg'ō (Wa)]

jagun₁ *n.* earth, country, place. from Gabi-Gabi dhagun 'home' (J). [tagun (T); dhāgŭn (Wa)] *See:* **gira¹; jara.**

jagun₂ *n.* devil. [tāgin (B); ɟa'gun, dagun (H); tāgun (R); dāgŭn, tāgūn (Wa)] *See:* **magui.**

jajam *n.* baby. [ɟaɟam (H); cher-chum (Hp); johannin (Ja)] *See:* **mulam; nyaramgan; nyamal.**

jajari *n.* sister, single girl. [ɟaɟari (H); dāddi 'sister' (R); dad'di (Wa)] *See:* **jajing; gin; manganggal.**

jajing *n.* elder sister. [tading (E); ɟaɟiɳ (H); dadjeen (Ha); jasing (Hi); dadi 'younger sister', tading 'sister' (Ja); tshasin, ds'as'in 'sister' (L); tading, tadding 'sister' (Lg); tadding 'sister' (Ln); tahding 'sister' (N); dadi (R); kandan 'sister' (T); tchudden (W); dad'di (Wa)] *See:* **jajari; manganggal.**

jalagada *adj; adv.* beyond. [dialagatte (Lg)]

jalaman *n.* carpenter bee. *[Xylocopa sp.].* [ɟalaman (H); tsalumban 'black bee' (L)] *See:* **banjin¹; gabai¹; gila²; guja¹; gunidar; mabi¹; nagi.**

jalang *n.* urination (of women). [ɟalaɳ (H)] *See:* **gil; nya.**

Jalba *n.* woman's name. [Tjlulba (B)]

jalbang *n.* cockspur briar tree. *[Maclura cochinchinensis].* [julbung (Ha)]

jalgal *adj.* small, short. [cialgal, ts'algal (L); chalgal (M)] *See:* **biribi; gijur; narang¹; ngambara; nala.**

jalgara *n.* vitae tree. *[Vitex trifolia var. trifolia].* [jull-gurra (Ha)]

jaliny *n.* nautilus, oval breast ornament made of nautilus. [doli (B); ɟulin (H); dullin 'large mussel' (Ja); dūllin (R); tulin (Ro); chuleen (S); chuleen (W); dul'in (Wa); juleen (We)]

jalu *n.* fire. possibly incorporates ergative suffix -lu (H). [darlow (Bu); dahlo, tahlo (Cl); dalo (E); tallu (Fi); ɟalu, ɟal (H); darlo (Ha); jarloo (Hi); tahlo, dahlo, dalo, darlo, tālu (Ja); tsalo, ds'alo (L); dalo, daloh 'fire', tadlo 'smoke' (Lg); charlu, jalo, darlo (Ln); tālu (R); tahloo (Su); dalo (T); darloo (Th); darlo (W); dār'lō (Wa); jarlow (We)] *See:* **baluba; gujam.**

jalubaluba *n.* camping place. *lit.* jalu-baluba 'put out fire'. [darlobolpal (M); dār'lō-bol'pa' (Wa)] *See:* **baluba; dimany; jalu; giba²; ngagamwaga.**

jalubiram *n.* lightning. *lit.* jalu-biram 'fire sky'. [bala-biram (T)] *See:* **biram; danagany; jalu; jil; maral.**

145

jaludiya *n.* firestick. *lit.* jalu-diya 'fire tooth'. [jireabbin (M); jarlowdeer (We)] *See:* diya; jalu.

jalu-jalu *n.* evening, fire time. *lit.* 'fire-fire'. [dallo dallo 'evening' (Lg)] *See:* jalu.

jalu mali *v.* smoke (tobacco). *lit.* 'spit fire'. [tadloo mulli (Lg)] *See:* jalu; mali.

jalungai *n.* light created by humans. *incorporates* jalu 'fire'. [julnair (Ha); tsalngae, dsalngnae (L); telgna (R); tel'ngai (Wa)] *See:* jalu.

jalwang *n.* long knife. [jalwang (M); Hp rejects this word]

jam *n.* meat, food. from Waga-Waga djam. [ɟam (H)] *See:* dalgaba; murang; yuri¹.

jaman *n.* white stone implements. [jum-mon (Ha)]

jambal *n.* big-leafed fig. *[Ficus sp.]*. [djumbul (J)] *See:* galamang; ganin; ganin.gar; gurai; murabal; nguwanga; nyada.

jamban *n.* black-striped wallaby. *[Notamacropus dorsalis]*. [dscham-pan (Le)] *See:* bangui; jamban; gara²; garil; giriwan; guruuman; magun; mari¹; wangari; wangun; yima.

jambil *Variant:* **jambi**. *v.* chew, suck. [jumbil (Bn)] *See:* daldu.

Jambinbin *n.* Jumpinpin Channel. from Yugambeh jambinbin 'root sucker of the pandanus tree' (Sh); possibly related to jambil 'chewing; sucking' (Bn); *Anth:* site of the original isthmus between the islands, broken through by explosives from a shipwreck, followed by a cyclone (MMEIC). [ɟambinbin, ɟambanban (H); Jumpin Pin (Bn)]

Jambuwa *n.* man's name. [Jambour (Ha)]

jamgam *n.* dusky moorhen. *[Gallinula tenebrosa]*. [jomn-gum (Ha)]

Jamgambal *n.* name of language. [ɟamgambal (H)] *See:* -bal; jamgam.

jam-jam *n.* bellbird. *[Manorina melanophrys]*. [jum-jum (Be)]

jan₁ *adj.* wet. [jun (Ha); tun (Lg)]

jan₂ *adj.* greedy. [tan (Lg)]

jana *n.* grey ironbark. *[Eucalyptus siderophloia]*. [shadna (Fi); judnen (Ln); dhū (Wa)] *See:* bigara; janduru; jum-jum; ganaibira; nyandala.

janbilbin *n.* trevally. [junbillpin (We)] *See:* gulbural; guiyar¹.

jandai₁ *neg.* no, not. used only in Jandai. [jandeer, jannderr (M); jandai (W)] *See:* munjan¹; yagara¹.

Jandai₂ *n.* South and central Stradbroke Island language, language of the Guwanbal people. [Jandeer, Janderr (M); tchandi, jandi (W)] *See:* Guwanbal.

Jandaiwal *n.* Jandai speaker(s). [jenderwal (MMEIC)] *See:* -bul; Jandai².

jandigung *n.* New South Wales sassafras. *[Doryphora sassafras]*. [tdjeundegong (Mac)]

janduru *Variant:* **jandur**. *n.* narrow-leafed ironbark. *[Eucalyptus crebra]*. *Anth:* (swellings) provide water, more drinkable than Angophora (DF); burns without smoke; the ash is applied to mothers after childbirth (Wi); wood used for waddies and spears (P). [tandur (Ca); choonnoo (D); danduru (E); ɟandur (H); jun-nor (Ha); dandura, tandur (Ja); tandurr (Le); danduru, tantaroo, choodenoo (Lg); tandur, janderoo (M); tandur (Ro); tan'dur (Wa); jundoor (We)] *See:* bigara; jana; jum-jum; ganaibira; nyandala.

jan.gali₁ *adj; n.* greedy fellow, very greedy. *lit.* jan-gali 'very greedy'. [juncully (Hi)] *See:* jan²; -gali.

Jan.gali₂ *n.* man's name. *lit.* 'greedy fellow'. [Dunkely (E)] *See:* jan²; jan.gali¹.

jan.gan *n.* wet season. *lit.* jan-gan 'wet time'. [din'gan (Bd)] *See:* -gan¹; jan².

Janggilbin *n.* Mt Cotton. [Jungalbin (Bn)] *See:* -bin.

-jangil *infl.* greater plural suffix; indicates a surprisingly large number of referents. [dziangil, djsiangil 'over five' (L)] *See:* **-jin**.

jangil junggu *excl.* that way! [tchdangil choong-gu (CW)]

jang-jang *n.* marrow. [tchung tchung (Lg)]

jan-jan *n.* gold. [junchun (We)]

janjari *n.* little trickster people who used to live in the area. cognate with Yugambeh janjari 'spirit' (Sh). [janjari (F); ʤanʤari (H)]

janji *n.* white mangrove. *[Avicennia marina]*. [tintchi (Ja); tintchi (M); tin'chī (Wa); junchee (We)] *See:* **gawan-gawan²**; **yabun**.

jara *Variant:* **jar.** *n.* earth, country. [dar (E); gera (Fi); ʤa (H); tār, durran, dār, darra, dar (Ja); ts'arra (L); dar, tdarra (Lg); tār, dār, durrun (R); ta 'land' (T); djara (W); dār, jā, dha (Wa); jara (Wu)] *See:* **jagun¹**; **gira¹**.

jaraagil *n.* type of frog. *Anth:* found in swamps, small, green and yellow (MMEIC, Uncle Pat Iselin). [jer-ar-gil (Ha); taroggin (Lg); char'ahgill (M); jaragill (We)] *See:* **gubang**; **naji**; **wagal**.

jarabadi *quant; n.* about three miles. *incorporates* jara 'country'. [tarpade (Lg)] *See:* **-ba⁴**; **-di**; **jara**.

Jaragawan-gawan *n.* woman's name. *lit.* jara-gawan-gawan 'country red'. [Jahracowan cowan (M); Djarcowancowan (W)] *See:* **jara**; **gawan-gawan¹**.

Jarajil *n.* Kangaroo Mt, Wallace's Creek. [Ja-rachel (Ha)]

jarajina *n.* footprint, foot track. *lit.* jara-jina 'earth foot'. [tya'-din'na (Wa)] *See:* **jara**; **jina**; **ngaran²**.

jarangbina *adj.* drunk. *incorporates* bina 'ear'. [dare-ung pinna (Ha)] *See:* **bina**.

Jarawany *n.* skin group (male). [Terwine (Bd); Charwine (D); Therwain (Hw); Turwhine (M); Derwain (R); Deroain (RB); de-ro-ain (Ro); Darawan, darawang (W); tŭr'wan (Wa)] *See:* **Banjur**; **Barang¹**; **Bunda**.

Jarawanygan *n.* skin group (female). [Terwine-gan (Bd); Therwain-wurumi (Hw); derwaingun (R); Deroingan (RB); Darawangun (W)] *See:* **Banjurgan¹**; **Baranggan**; **Bundagan**; **-gan²**.

jarbal *n.* black cockatoo. *[Calyptorhynchus sp.]*. [churbull (D)] *See:* **balan**; **biliyagan**; **biluwala**; **gaiyara**; **garara**; **giwang**.

jarbany *n.* island. *lit.* jara-bany 'turn into earth'. [turbum (Lg)] *See:* **-bany**; **jara**.

jargariiba₁ *n.* ebb tide. *lit.* jara-gariiba 'land tide'. [jar-gariba (Ba)] *See:* **gariiba**; **jara**; **yunggariiba**.

Jargariiba₂ *n.* Peel Island. *lit.* 'ebb tide'; or 'place of many shells' (MMEIC); named by Nunagal (Bn). [Tjacoorba (B); Jailcooroobah (Bn); Chercrooba (M); Dairkooreeba, Chercrooba, Turkroor (S)] *See:* **-ba⁴**; **jargariiba¹**.

Jargiran *n.* woman's name. [Djurrgeerun (W)]

jari *n.* brown tree snake. *[Boiga irregularis]*. [jarree 'red tree snake' (Ha)]

Jarjidanariba *n.* man's name. [Tcharcheedunareeba (W)]

Jarlamban.gan *n.* woman's name. [Tsarlumbankan (L)]

jarwang *n.* magpie. cognate with Wiradjuri durrawan 'currawong', the source of English currawong. [ʤaragan (H); joounpyn (Hi); jalwang (Hp); jawang (MMEIC); churwung (We)] *See:* **gulambarun**; **mirum**.

Jayam *n.* woman's name. [Djaium (W)]

jibal *n.* wedge-tailed eagle. *[Aquila audax]*. [ʤibal (H); dibbil (Ja); dibbil (R); dib'bil (Wa)] *See:* **buduwar¹**; **duwai**; **ngan-ngan**.

jibalang *n.* fish spear. [ʤibalaŋ (H)] *See:* **bilara**; **bulan¹**; **ganai**; **jagany**.

jibang *n.* five corners plant with green star-shaped fruit, its fruit. *[Styphelia viridis]*. *Anth:* fleshy green five-cornered fruit similar to a gooseberry, fruit eaten raw (FNSI). [ɟibaŋ (H)] *See:* **gadara.**

Jibara *n.* Logan River-area confederacy of Yagara and Mibiny speakers. [Chepara (Hw); Djibara (J)]

jibi *n.* bird. [jippi 'feathers' (Bd); dhip'pi, jip'pi (Wa)] *See:* **daunbin.**

Jibiba *n.* place name. named by Balun.giny (Bn). [Geebeebah (Bn)] *See:* **-ba**⁴; **Balun.giny.**

jiburu *Variant:* **jibur.** *n.* sugar glider. *[Petaurus breviceps]*. [yeer-ar-roo (Ha); jiborer (Hi); chibur 'small gray flying squirrel' (Ja); dscheberu 'little grey squirrel' (Le); jeeboor (M); chi'bur (Wa)] *See:* **banggu**¹.

Jiburubili *n.* Jeebropilly. *lit.* jiburu-bili 'sugar glider creek'. [Jeebroopilly (M); Jeebropilly (S)] *See:* **bili; jiburu.**

Jiburugargan *n.* Mt Tibrogargan. *lit.* jiburu-gargan 'sugar glider bites'. [Tib'ro-wuc'cum 'flying squirrel hungry' (Bd)] *See:* **gargan; jiburu.**

Jiduugun *n.* woman's name. [Jeeto'ogoon (M)]

jiga *v.* shake. [jikke (R)]

jigagara *n.* coral eel. [ɟigagara (H); geegargera (We)]

jigal-jigal₁ *n.* type of tree. [ɟigal ɟigal (H)]

Jigal-jigal₂ *n.* Chiggil Chiggil Creek, south of Wallum Creek. *lit.* 'type of tree'; named by Nunagal (Bn). *Anth:* has high-quality oysters (H). [tjigil tjigil, Tigil Tigil (B); Chigell Chigell (Bn); ɟigal ɟigal (H)] *See:* **jigal-jigal**¹.

jigan *adv.* often, insistently. [tjigen (R)]

jigandi *adv.* almost, near. [tjigenti (R)] *See:* **bidung; danyung; -di; jigan.**

jil *n.* lightning. [tjil (Ja); tjil (R)] *See:* **danagany; jalubiram; maral.**

jila *n.* sand eel. [ɟila (H); jillar (We)]

jiladu *adj; adv.* central, in the middle. [jillērdu, jillerdu (R)]

jilai *v.* stand up. [jil-lila 'stand' (Ja); delaiena 'stand up' (Lg)]

Jilba *n.* man's name. [Tjilpa (B); Tchilper (W)]

Jilbangbin *n.* woman's name. [Jeelbungbin (Ha)]

jilgan *n.* stringybark. *[Eucalyptus globoidea]*. [jilgan (Ba) *See:* **diyi; gundul**¹.

Jilmari *n.* woman's name. [Chilmerrie (M); Djilmorr (W)]

jiman-jiman *n.* flaky-barked tea tree. *[Leptospermum trinervium]*. *Anth:* yellow wood; branches used for making brooms (FNSI); small white sweet fruits like berries. [ɟiman ɟiman, ɟima ɟima (H); cheeminchamin (M)] *See:* **nambur**²; **ngujuru.**

jimbalang *n.* owner, possessor, friend. from Yugambeh jimbalang (Sh). [jimbillung (Hi); jimbalungga 'male/poor fellow' (MMEIC)] *See:* **banji; gimunggan; magiiba.**

jimbaljin *n.* female owner or female friend. possibly from Yugambeh jimbalang 'owner' (Sh). [ɟimbalɟin, ɟimbalɟen 'mother' (H)] *See:* **gin; jimbalang.**

jimbum *n.* sheep. *[Ovis aries]*. potentially related to English jumbuck 'sheep' or Bandjalang ɗimbaŋ 'sheep'. [jimboom (Ha)] *See:* **manggi.**

jim-jim *n.* sexual intercourse. [ɟim ɟim (H)] *See:* **bam-bam; burima; gumuwara; wiruwira.**

-jin *infl.* plural suffix; designates many referents. [jin (H); dzin '3 to 5' (L); tin (R); tin, tchin (W)] *See:* **-bajagan; -jangil.**

jina *n.* foot, footprint. [chidna (Cl); sidney (E); gidna (Fi); ɟina (H); gin-nair (Ha); tinda, dīnda, tīnda, sidney, chidna (Ja); citne, tsitne (L); chidna, tenang (La); chidna, tidna (Ln); sidney, tchidna (Lg); tidna (Ln); tchidna, chidna (M); tidna (R); chidna (Su); tchidna (W); din'ang, tid'na, dinna (Wa); jinna (We)]

jinagaba *n.* boot, shoe. *lit.* jina-gaba 'item(s) for feet'. [chindnnagobah (Lg); dinnanguba, dinnangūba (R); din'ang-gu'ba (Wa)] *See:* **jina**; **-gaba**.

jinbigari *n.* scrub bottle tree. *[Brachychiton discolor].* [jin biggen, jin biggarie (Ha); dschinbikri (Le)] *See:* **guldan**.

jinbura *n.* roots of the freshwater reed called yigibin. *Anth:* celery-like roots were roasted and eaten (M). [jinboora (M)] *See:* **nambur**¹; **yari**; **yigibin**¹; **yigilu**

jindabang *n.* flintstone. [jindabarng (Hi)]

jindan *n.* stone chisel. [jinden (Ha)]

jindur *n.* female genitalia. [chindur (N)] *See:* **gaji**²; **junu**; **jurung**; **nyaral**.

jinduru-jinduru *n.* eyelashes. [chindroo chindroo (Lg)] *See:* **jindur**.

jingam *n.* ground orchids. *[Spathoglottis sp.].* [chingum (M)]

jinggalgal *n.* waterlily, spider lily. *[Crinum pedunculatum].* *Anth:* sap had medicinal purposes (FNSI). [dzienkalkal, ds'enkalkal (L); dongall kall (Le)] *See:* **muyu**.

Jin.gilingbin *n.* Bulimba ferry (west). *lit.* 'willie wagtail's place'. [Chinkeelimbin (M)] *See:* **-bin**; **jin.gilinggan**.

jin.gilinggan *n.* willie wagtail. *[Rhipidura leucophrys].* [ɟiniliŋan (H)] *See:* **jin.giri**; **gamalgalam**.

jin.giri *Variant:* **jin.giri-jin.giri.** *n.* willie wagtail. *[Rhipidura leucophrys].* [jimgire, jimgari (H); jingeria jingeria (We)] *See:* **jin.gilinggan**; **gamalgalam**.

Jin.gumirja *n.* Macleay Island. [Jencoomerchar (M); Jencoomerha (S)] *See:* **jara**.

Jiniba *n.* woman's name. [Tjineba (B)]

Jinji-Jinji *n.* name of language. [ɟinɟi ɟinɟi (H)]

jin-jin *n.* food. [jinjan (MMEIC); tchindgen (W)] *See:* **dalgaba**; **dubaru**; **manjari**; **mungin**.

Jin-jinba *n.* Little Peak, next to Mt Peak. *lit.* 'place of food'. [Jinjinpah (Be)] *See:* **-ba**⁴; **jin-jin**.

jiraba bugany *Variant:* **jiraba buga.** *v.* go to sleep. *incorporates* bugany 'sleep'. [dieraper boogon (Lg)] *See:* **-ba**; **bugany**.

jirabang₁ *n.* prickly stem tree used for boomerangs. [jeerabung (M)] *See:* **baragany**¹; **birban**; **gawan-gawan**²; **yabun**.

jirabang₂ *n.* boomerang. [jeerabung (M)] *See:* **baragany**²; **birbun**; **gawan-gawan**²; **yabun**.

jirai *n.* edible gum from the wattle tree. [cheray (Lg)] *See:* **jiraigar**; **nguwuny**.

jiraigar *n.* wattle tree. *[Acacia sp.].* *Anth:* when the wattle had a lot of flowers, it would be a good year for tailor fish (Delaney 1994). [cheraycre (Lg)] *See:* **gagargal**; **jirai**.

Jiraman *n.* Wilson's peak. *lit.* 'man's knee'. [Jirramin (Be); Jiramon (Ha); Jirraman (S)] *See:* **buun**.

jiran *n.* white woman. word origin unknown. [tjerran (R)] *See:* **waimirigan**.

Jiraruba *n.* place name. *lit.* 'full of shells'. [Jereruba (Ln)] *See:* **-ba**⁴.

jirban *n.* bone. [tjirben (Ja); ciribetn, tsiribetn (L); chilben (Ln); chirben (N); tīrben, tjīrben (R); tcheerben, toheeben (W); tyir'ben (Wa)] *See:* **darigany**; **ding**; **garal-garal**.

Jirigai *n.* man's name. [ɟirigai (H)]

Jiriran *n.* man's name. [Tjirieran (B)]

jiruda *n.* trousers. from English trousers. [tseruse (L)] *See:* **daranygaba**.

Jirwamban *n.* Brisbane River, lower part. [Dscherwampon (Le)] *See:* **-ban**; **Buruguwa**; **Maiwar**.

jubar *n.* witchetty grub. *[Endoxyla leucomochla].* from Bandjalang djubar. [ɟubar (H)] *See:* **jabam**.

Jububajur *n.* man's name. [Djurpoorbudjur (W)]

jubui *adj.* straight. [choobooi (M); tūbuī (R)] *See:* **nganiyiba**; **yilung**.

jubuiban *adv.* quickly. *lit.* jubui-ban 'result of going straight'. [tubborpun (R)] *See:* -ban; bangga; burima; jubui; mii¹; ngunbunjada.

Juga *n.* man's name. [Tjukka (B)]

jugaali *v.* drink. [jugaali (Wu)]

jugu *v.* know, understand. [djookoo (W)] *See:* bina.

jugung *n.* tongue. [ɟugen (H); choorogong (Ja); ts'urugung (L); thurgoom (Ln); choorgoong (M); turgoeng (N); choorogong (Su); djurgoom (W); jurgan (We)] *See:* dalany.

Jujimayali *n.* people on Stradbroke. [choochibbmehally (W)]

jumar *n.* buttocks. [doomur (Lg)] *See:* mabi²; naral.

jumirugurumjin *n.* saw banksia. *[Banksia serrata]*. [junchum, janjalcan, choomeroogooroomchin (M)]

jum-jum *n.* black ironbark. *[Eucalyptus sideroxylon]*. [choom choom (D)] *See:* bigara; jana; janduru; ganaibira; nyandala.

jumu₁ *Variant:* **jum.** *n.* smoke. [jumoor 'smoke signal' (Be); jumoo (Fi); joomoo (Hi); duun, toomo (Ja); tsiuma, ts'umo (L); dooloo (Ln); dūūn (R); tchummoo (W); dū-ūn (Wa); jumu (Wu)] *See:* bubalam; jalu.

jumu₂ *n.* tobacco. [dooloo (Ln)] *See:* bubalam; jalu.

Junabin *n.* woman's name. [Tjunnbin, Tjunobin, Tjunnbin (B); Djoonabin (W)]

jundal *Variant:* **junda** *n.* woman. [choondall (D); jundall (Fi); ɟundal (H); jūndāl (Ja); ds'undal (L); tooral (Lg); jundal, goondal 'a black woman' (Ln); gundal, joohdahna (M); thundahl (N); jūndāl (R); dundalja (T); junda, tchundal, jundab (W); jun'gal (Wa); jundool (We); jundal (Wu)] *See:* gin.

jundalgin *n.* Aboriginal woman. *lit.* jundal-gin 'Aboriginal woman'. [doondulgin 'a black gin' (Lg)] *See:* gin; jundal.

Jundubari *n.* Maryborough and Fraser Island language (H), Brisbane River to Tin Can Bay higher order social organisation (J). [ɟundabara, ɟundabari (H); Djundubari, Joondoobarrie, Joondooburrey (J)]

Jundubira *n.* possibly Bribie Island. [Joon-do-burra (Bd)]

jungga *v.* to fish. [jungga (MMEIC)]

junggai₁ *n.* west wind. [ɟuŋgai (H); jungay (Ln); tchoongie, tchoongee (W)] *See:* gubi²; wiyan¹; yabarin.

Junggai₂ *n.* man's name. *lit.* 'west wind'. [Jungai (Delaney 1994)]

junggara *n.* pelican, native companion. from Guwar djungara. [junn-gurra (Ha); tchoongarra (W)] *See:* buluwalung; gulugan¹.

junggi *n.* brolga, native companion. *[Grus rubicunda]*. [toongie (Ln); toongie, tunggi (M); tchoongie, tchoongee (W); tun'gī (Wa)] *See:* bugur; gariyagan; gilil-gilil¹; gundurgan; muralagang.

junggul *n.* pandanus, bread-fruit tree, coastal screw-pine. *[Pandanus tectorius]*. *Anth:* the ripe fruit were eaten (FNSI); root suckers were soaked in a honey mixture and chewed (Sh). [tiunggul (Ja); tiungul, tiunggūl (R); tī'ungal (Wa)] *See:* winam¹.

junguru *Variant:* **jungur.** *n.* knife. [choonarroo (D); ɟuŋur (H); choong-er-roo (Hp); tang-ur 'stone knife'; tungaroo (Lg); tan'gūr (Wa); junguru (Wu)] *See:* jalwang.

junu *n.* womb. [junu 'vulva' (H); djunoo (MMEIC; Uncle Denis Moreton)] *See:* gaji²; jindur; jurung; nyaral.

Jununggan *n.* woman's name. [Joonoonggan (M)]

jura *Variant:* **jura-jura.** *n.* type of stringybark. *[Eucalyptus sp.]*. [turra turra (Le); diura (M); diura (Ro)]

jurbil *n.* totem-centre. *Anth:* a location where increase rites for a totem were performed (RB). [djurbil (RB)] *See:* yuri².

Juriyandaju *n.* North Ipswich convent. *lit.* 'diamond snake'. [Jooriandadjo (S)]

jurum-jurum *n.* rain. [jorum-joorum (Cl); turumturum (E); tchurm-tchurm (G); joorum, jurrum, turumturun (Ja); turumturum (Lg); joorum-joorum (Su); turrumturrum (T)] *See:* **nyurung.**

jurung *n.* vulva. [ɖuroŋ (H)] *See:* **gaji²; jindur; nyaral.**

juruny₁ *Variant:* **juruny-juruny.** *n.* silver eel, short-finned eel. [*Anguilla australis*]. coorooin coorooin (B); ɖuru 'mullet' (H); jooroon 'eel' (Hi); choorooin 'silver eel' (M)] *See:* **dilgam; jagan; gang-gang²; ngandagal¹.**

Juruny₂ *n.* woman's name. *lit.* 'silver eel'. [Coorrooyn (B) *See:* **juruny¹.**

Juruny-jurunyba *n.* Flying Fox Creek, north of Myora. *lit.* 'place of eels'. [Coorooin Coorooinpah (B); Cooroign-Cooroign-Pa 'place of silver eel' (S)] *See:* **-ba⁴; juruny¹.**

juumgu *n.* red-bellied black snake. [*Pseudechis porphyriacus*]. [toom-go (Cl); jo-um-goo (Ha); joombgoong (Hi); toom-go, tumgu (Ja); jongo (Le); choomgool (W); tūmga (Wa)] *See:* **bui²; guda²; mulumgal; yuwan.**

juunbal *n.* hoop pine. [*Araucaria cunninghamii*]. [june bul (Ha); joonbal oompy 'pine house' (Hi); ts'unbul (L)] *See:* **bugal; buunyi; dandardam; gambarju; gunaim.**

juunburu *n.* eastern sea garfish. [*Hyporhamphus australis*]. [coolbooroo (B); joonboroo (M)]

Juwai-juwai *n.* area in Toowong. [Jo-ai Jo-ai (Bd)]

Juwalga *n.* Teviot Falls. [Duelcare (Ha)]

juwan₁ *Variant:* **juwa.** *v.* lift, raise. [joorah (Be); jooanma (M)] *See:* **balgama; duriyinma; daran¹; wanda.**

juwan₂ *n.* fish. [towan (Lg); tow-wan, jowan (Ln); joan, to-wan (M); dun (MMEIC); toon, joon (W)]

Juwanbin *n.* the low part of Harper's Hill in the Cascade Gardens in Surfer's Paradise. *lit.* juwan-bin 'raised place'. [Ju-am-bin (Ha) *See:* **-bin; juwan¹.**

juwanin *adv.* eventually. [johanin 'by and by' (Cl)] *See:* **barany; yaraba.**

juwum *n.* native melon. [*Cucumis trigonus*]. [choowoom (Bd)]

L – l

-la *mood.* indicates physical or social obligation; occurs in commands. [la (Ha); lah (M); la (P); la (R)]

labiya-labiya *adv.* quickly. [labbia labbia (Lg)]

-li₁ *tns.* future tense suffix. [li (Ha); lie (M); li (R)]

-li₂ *valn.* reflexive or reciprocal suffix. [le, li (R)]

M – m

-ma *valn.* causative suffix. [ma (E); mi, mu (Ha); ma (L); mah, mer, mee (M); mu (R); ma (W)]

maamba *n.* supernatural being. *Anth.* lives in the sky; source of sacred quartz crystals (Hw). [Maamba (Hw) *See:* **daginy; gundir; nan.gur.**

mabalbana *v.* smile. [ma-bul-punna (Ha)]

mabara *Variant:* **mabar.** *n.* back of body. [mobarah (Cl); mobarah (Ja); muhbar (N)] *See:* **dugal.**

mabi₁ *n.* little native black bee, its honey, wax. [mappi (Ja); mabi (H); map'pi (Wa)] *See:* **banjin¹; jalaman; gabai¹; gila²; guja¹; gunidar; nagi.**

mabi₂ *n.* anus, posterior. [mabi (H)] *See:* **jumar; naral.**

mabi₃ *n.* tree kangaroo. [muppee (M)] *See:* **gara²; giriwin; guruuman; jamban; mari¹; yima.**

Mabi$_4$ *n.* Mt Coot-tha. *lit.* 'native bee'. [Mappee (S)] *See:* **mabi**^{1}.

Mabi-mabiba *n.* One Mile, north of Dunwich. *lit.* mabi-mabi-ba 'place of many native bees' or 'place of posteriors'; Bn recorded Rosy Campbell's response to the name as 'the answer matters pertaining to it', possibly as a warning about the interpretation 'place of posteriors' (Bn); named by Balun.giny (Bn). [Muppee Muppee Bah (Bn); Moopi Moopi Pa 'creek at One Mile Swamp' (CW)] *See:* **-ba**^{4}; **Balun.giny**; **mabi**^{1}.

Mabinbila *n.* Bird Island. *Anth:* 'two languages here used' (Bn); *lit.* 'stone' from Yugambeh-Bandjalang mabinbila 'stone' (Sh); *lit.* 'place where people evacuated' (Bn); named by Balun.giny (Bn). [Moppee milla (B); Muppinbillowah (Bn); Moopanbilla (CW); Muppanbilla, Moppanbilla (M); Moppanbilla (S); Moopee Millar (W)] *See:* **-bila**; **mabi**^{1}.

mabiri *n.* navel. [moberee 'umbilicus' (Cl); moberee 'naval' (Ja); moball (M)] *See:* **nimbir**.

mada *v.* be sticky. [mudhe (S)]

Madabili *n.* Mutdapilly. *lit.* mada-bili 'sticky creek'. [Mutdapilly (S)] *See:* **bili**; **mada**.

madar *n.* ghost. [mudhar (R)] *See:* **dagai**; **magarang**; **magui**; **marau**.

madara *n.* yam. *[Dioscorea transversa]*. [mud-dara (Ha)] *See:* **dadam**; **dam**^{1}; **diya-diya**; **guba**^{3}

Madari *n.* Murrarrie. *lit.* mada-ri 'was sticky'. [Mudherri (S)] *See:* **mada**; **-ri**.

maga *v.* eat. [moggo (Lg)] *See:* **dal**^{1}.

magamba *n.* possum girdle, belt for carrying implements. [mocamba (Cl); mocamba, makamba (Ja); mocamba (M); mak'ambā (Wa)]

magara *n.* fingernail. [mūkkūra (Ja); mūkkūra (R); muk'karā (Wa)] *See:* **gilan**^{1}.

magarabal *n.* Leichhardt bean tree. *[Cassia brewsteri]*. [muggerapul (Ha)] *See:* **bulumbir**; **giji**; **yugam**.

magarang *n.* ghost, white man. [makoron (Ja); makoron, makūrrang (R)] *See:* **dagai**; **magui**; **majari**; **marau**.

magiiba *n.* friend. [mag'ieeba (M)] *See:* **banji**; **gimunggan**; **jimbalang**; **nyungin**.

magil$_1$ *n.* water dragon. *[Intellagama lesueurii lesueurii]*. [magil, muggil (Ha); magil (Ja); maggil (Le); moggil, muggil (M); mag'gil, mog'gil (Wa)]

Magil$_2$ *n.* Moggill Creek. *lit.* 'water dragon'. [Moggill (S)] *See:* **magil**^{1}.

Magil-magil *n.* possibly Kenmore area. *lit.* 'water dragons'. [Maggil Maggil (Bd)] *See:* **magil**^{1}.

magin *n.* type of male relative. [magin 'uncle's father' (Ba)]

magui *n.* ghost, devil, white man. [muggowie (D); magui, mog-wi; mogwi 'outlaw' (Ja); moggowe 'soul, spirit' (Lg); mahgoi (N); māguī, maowi, maiyi (R); mŭtyī, māō'wi, mog'wī (Wa)] *See:* **dagai**; **madar**; **magarang**; **marau**; **yuwanji**.

maguijan *n.* spirit land, fairy tale. *incorporates* magui 'devil, ghost'. [mog-wi-dan 'story' (Ja); mog'widhan 'spirit land' (Wa)] *See:* **jara**; **magui**.

magul$_1$ *n.* head. [maggol (Cl); magul (E); magul (H); mug-il (Ha); magool, mūgūl, maggol, magul (Ja); magul (L); moggool, mawgool, magul (Lg); magool (Ln); mag-ul (M); mahgul (N); māgūl (R); maggol (Su); magul (T); magool (W); māg'il (Wa); māgul (Wu)] *See:* **bin.ga**; **bum-bum**.

magul$_2$ *n.* razorback shell. [magul (H)] *See:* **dinggal**^{2}; **gara**^{1}; **guumbi**^{1}; **walamgan**.

Magul$_3$ *n.* steep rocky hill with pine trees in the summit. *lit.* 'head'. [Mogool (G)] *See:* **magul**^{1}.

magul buba bundal *n.* white hair. *lit.* 'white-hair head'. [mugul buba bundel (H); mugool boopa bundal (We)] *See:* **buba**^{2}; **bundal**^{2}; **guibila magul**.

magul dugam *n.* tree stump. *incorporates* magul 'head'. [moggool toogum (Lg)] *See:* **bilayir**; **maling**.

magulgaba *n.* hat. *lit.* magul-gaba 'item for the head'. [moggoolaba, mawgool-aba (Lg); magul kuba (Ln); magulkuba (R); magil-ku'ba (Wa)] *See:* **magul¹**; **-gaba**.

magul gawan-gawan *n.* red hair. *lit.* 'red head'. [mugool gowen gowen (We)] *See:* **gawan-gawan¹**; **magul**.

magul gurung *n.* black hair. *lit.* 'black head'. [mugool gurong (We)] *See:* **gurung²**; **magul**.

magulugul *n.* skull. *incorporates* magul 'head'. [magulloogul (Lg)]

magun *n.* brush-tailed rock wallaby. *[Petrogale penicillata].* [muc-koon (Ha)] *See:* **bugul**; **bangui**; **garil**; **jamban**; **wangari**; **wangun**.

magurabal *n.* guts, bowels. [mogoorapul (Lg)] *See:* **danggan**.

mai *n.* Moreton Bay chestnut. *[Castanospermum australe].* [mai (Ja); maai (Le); mai (M); mei (Wa)]

maidamari *n.* wing. [made murry (Lg)]

Maiwar *n.* Brisbane River, upper part, platypus breeding area near Mt Stanley. *lit.* 'platypus' from Duuŋidjawu mairwar (S), me:war (K). [Mairwar, Mairwah, Mairrwarrh (S); Mairwar (Wi)] *See:* **Buruguwa**; **Jirwamban**.

maja *n.* full man. [mutta (Ja); mutta (R)] *See:* **malara**.

majan *quant.* three. [madan (H); muddan, mujan (Ja); mujan, madan (La); majan, mahjan (M); muddān (R); mujan (Su); mud'den (Wa)] *See:* **bulaganyar**.

Majanbili *n.* Tent Hill group. *lit.* majan-bili 'three creeks'. [Muttong billy (Lg)] *See:* **bili**; **majan**.

majanbula *quant.* five. *lit.* majan-bula 'three-two'. [mudden budela (Ja); bullae nga bullae kanyara (L); muddanbudela (R); mud'den bud'ela (Wa)] *See:* **bula¹**; **majan**.

majan.gundanbin *n.* creeping vine or herb. *lit.* majan-gundan-bin 'three shield plant'. [muttanguntunbin (R)] *See:* **-bin**; **gundan²**; **majan**.

majan-majan *quant.* six. *lit.* 'three-three'. [muddan-muddan (R)] *See:* **majan**.

majari *n.* evil white man, liar, murderer, evil spirit. [muggery, muggowie (D); mudhar (Ja); mujeri (R); mud'har (Wa)] *See:* **dagai**; **magarang**; **magui**.

maji *v.* join. [muttee (Lg)]

majira *n.* infant's excrement. *cognate* with Yugambeh madhir 'infants' shit' (Sh). [mudgera (Ca)] *See:* **baandigu**; **duwal**; **guna¹**.

maladiri *adv.* all gone. [mulladere (Lg)]

malara *Variant:* **malar**. *n.* black man. [mullar (Cl); mullerrah (D); malar (E); mullera (Fi); mallara, mullera (Ha); mullar, malar (Ja); mullera 'black fellow' (Lg); mullera, muliery, muliergh (Ln); mallara (M); muhlah 'boy' (N); mullar (Su); malar (W); mal'lara (Wa); mullar (We)] *See:* **binigan**; **danbang**; **jaan**; **guri**; **mari²**.

malaragaba *n.* black man's possessions. *lit.* 'item(s) for a man'. [mullaragobah, mullera-g-aba (Lg)] *See:* **malara**; **-gaba**.

malbaribu *v.* bring back. [mulpurriboo (Lg)] *See:* **-bu**.

malgam *n.* native gooseberry; wild raspberry. [mulgum (J)] *See:* **gubu-guburan**; **yalabin**.

Malgaram *n.* person's name. [Mulkcrum (Kd)]

mali *n; v.* spit. [muhlih (N)] *See:* **gijubal**.

maling *n.* log, tree stump. [mulloom (Fi); moo lum (Ha); mulling (Ja); mulling (R); mul'ling (Wa)] *See:* **baguurugil**; **bilayir**; **bural**; **magul dugam**; **wambarligiri**.

malunda *n.* headache. [molloondah (Lg)]

mama *v.* press. [mumma (R)]

mamba *n.* wharf. [mumpa (R)]

mambarabany *Variant:* **mambaraba.** *v.* become emaciated. *incorporates* -bany 'become'. [mumbarrapun (Lg)] *See:* -bany.

Mambayiba *n.* woman's name. [Mumb-yee-ba (CW); Mumbyeeba (W)]

mamgal *Variant:* **mamga.** *v.* punch (with fist). [momkoll 'kill' (Bl); mumkul 'fist' (L); muncull 'punish' (MB)]

mamin *Variant:* **mamin.gir.** *n.* red cedar. *[Toona ciliata].* [mominkir (D); mam-in (M); mumin (Mac); mam'in (Wa)] *See:* **daigil; wuji.**

mamugal *n.* wompoo fruit-dove. *[Ptilinopus magnificus].* [mommoogol (Lg)]

mamugamugan *n.* type of seabird. [momucommoocan (Lg)]

mamun *n.* wrist. [mommoon 'arm' (Lg); mamuhn 'wrist' (N)]

mamura mana *v.* reduce to powder. [momoora munnu (Lg)]

mamuum *n.* south. [mumoorm (Be)] *See:* **yanggar.**

Mananjali *n.* Mununjali, a Yugambeh language traditionally spoken in the Beaudesert area. [manangfali (H)]

mandany *n.* native plum. *[Davidsonia johnsonii].* [mun-tine (Ha); muntine 'red fruit' (Lg)]

mandili *n.* blackbutt. *[Eucalyptus pilularis].* [mundeli (Le)] *See:* **binarwin; girigan.**

mandin₁ *n.* fish net. [mundin 'crayfish net', 'fish net' (Ja); mandin, muntong 'pademelon net' (M); mundin (R); man'din, mun'tung (Wa)] *See:* **bayal; dama; durur; mirbang.**

Mandin₂ *n.* North Pine. *lit.* 'fish net'. [Mandin (S)] *See:* **mandin¹.**

man.gal *n.* bream. *[Acanthopagrus sp.].* [mun-gal (CW)] *See:* **dun.gala; ginbun; ngalan¹.**

manganggal *n.* younger sister. [manangal (H); muhgungkul 'elder sister' (Ja); mungungkul 'sister' (R); mungunkul (W); mun'gŭnkŭl (Wa)] *See:* **jajari.**

mangara *n.* leg, calf. [mungurra (Ha)] *See:* **buyu; darany; wulu.**

mangargal *n.* cabbage tree. [mung-arcal 'cedar' (M); mungur kall (We)] *[Livistona australis].* *See:* **binygar.**

manggara *Variant:* **manggar.** *n.* blue gum. *[Eucalyptus tereticornis].* [mungara 'blue gum', mungari 'spotted gum' (Ca); mangar, mungarra, mungurra (Ha); mungarra 'blue gum' (Ja); mangorr, mongorra '(gum) with smooth shining bark' (Le); mungra 'blue gum' (Lg); mungarra (Ln); mungar, munggarra (M); munggar (R); mŭn'gar (Wa); mungure, mungere (We)] *See:* **bulagi; durambai.**

manggi *Variant:* **manggi-manggi.** *n.* sheep. *[Ovis aries].* [monkey (L); munkimunki (R)] *See:* **jimbum.**

mangin *Variant:* **mangi.** *v.* be ashamed. [mūnin (R)]

mangun *adj.* comfortable. [mongoon (Lg)]

manjari *n.* food. possibly 'food taboo to minors' based on Gabi-Gabi cognate mundja (Bell 1994). [manjari (MMEIC)] *See:* **dalgaba; dubaru; jin-jin; mungin.**

manmal *adj.* weak, bad. [manmal (L); manmmul (R)] *See:* **budung; yaran-yaran.**

many *Variant:* **ma.** *v.* take, catch, get, carry. [mănim (G); mahe (Lg); mani (R)] *See:* **mara¹.**

manyal *n.* plenty. [munyal (W)] *See:* **gurumba garaba; milin.**

mar *n.* heavy nulla-nulla for fighting. [mur (Ja); mur (Ro); mūr (Wa)] *See:* **bagan; jabiri.**

mara$_1$ *n.* hand. [murrah (Cl); marra (E); marra (Fi); mara (H); mar-rar (Ha); murrah, marra, murra (Ja); mara (L); murrah (La); marra (Lg); murra, munagh (Ln); marra (M); moera 'hand, knuckle' (N); murra, marra (R); murrah (Su); morrah (Th); murra (W); mŭr'ra (Wa); murra (We)] *See:* **ban.gamba.**

mara$_2$ *v.* steal, catch, get, tell (a lie). [mari (H); mar, marra (Lg); mahra (M)]

maral *n.* lightning. [marlo (Ha); marahl, maral (L); mooral (Lg)] *See:* **danagany; jalubiram; jil.**

maran *n.* father's sister. *Anth:* Maran 'Aunty' is a term of respect for a female Elder. [maran (H); moering (N); maran (W)]

maran.gan *n.* old woman; female Elder. *lit.* maran-gan 'aunt woman'. [marintin 'woman' (Cl); maragun 'old woman' (H); marintin 'woman' (Su)] *See:* **baji; maran; waliinggara.**

marangbi *n.* koala. *[Phascolarctos cinereus].* [murrumpi (Be); murrungpie (D); mar-raphie, mur-rumphie (Ha); marungpy (Hi); merrang-pi (Le)] *See:* **dumbiribi; gula**^{2}.

maranjal *n.* octopus. [maranʃal (H)]

maran-maran *n.* Pleiades. *lit.* '(father's) sisters'. [maran-maran (Ba)] *See:* **maran.**

marau *n.* ghost, spirit. [marrow (Ln)] *See:* **dagai; magarang; magui; nguru**^{1}.

marbana *n.* finger lime. *[Citrus australasica].* [murpono (Lg)]

mari$_1$ *n.* grey kangaroo. *[Macropus giganteus].* [murree (Fi); mari (H); murree (Ha); murri (Ja); maree, murrey, murry (Ln); munnee (M); murri (R); murray (W); mŭr'ri, māri (Wa); murry (We)] *See:* **gara**^{2}; **giriwan; guruuman; yima.**

mari$_2$ *adj; n.* Aboriginal, Aboriginal man. from NSW languages. [mari (H); murrie (M)] *See:* **jaan; guri; malara.**

maril$_1$ *n.* stepmother. [mahreel (M)]

Maril$_2$ *n.* Spring Hill. *lit.* 'stepmother'; this was an older name for Spring Hill (M). [Mahreel (S)] *See:* **maril**^{1}.

mari-mari$_1$ *n.* game in which boys throw spears at a rolling round of bark as practice for kangaroo hunting. *lit.* 'kangaroo-kangaroo'. [murri murri (CW)] *See:* **mari**^{1}.

mari-mari$_2$ *n.* butterfly. [murrie-murrie (M)] *See:* **balimbir.**

Mariyagara *n.* place between Redland Bay and Logan River. 'kangaroo, where he lies down' (Bn); *incorporates* mari 'grey kangaroo'; *possibly lit.* mari yagara 'no kangaroos here'. [Murrayjaygre (Bn)] *See:* **mari**^{1}; **yagara.**

marugan *n.* crow's nest ash tree. *[Flindersia australis].* [murrogun 'teakwood' (Mac)] *See:* **balbara.**

marumba$_1$ *adj; adv.* good, sweet, well, lovely. [murroonbah (Cl); marumba (E); marumba (H); marroomba (Ha); maroomba (Hi); murroomba, marumba, murrūmba, murroonbah (Ja); marumba, maroombah (Lg); marrumba, murrumba (Ln); murroomba (M); murrūmba (R); murroonbah (Su); maroomba (W); mur'rumba (Wa)] *See:* **bujari; galang; nyiwang.**

Marumba$_2$ *n.* Murrumba. *lit.* 'good'. [Murrumba (P)] *See:* **marumba**^{1}.

marumbadi *adv.* well paid. *lit.* marumba-di 'in a good place'. [marooboodee 'pay well' (Lg)] *See:* **-di; marumba**^{1}.

marun *n.* cloud. [mar-roon (Ha); muttan (Lg)] *See:* **galan; guwaa.**

marura *n.* hornet. [moroora (Lg)]

maun.ga *v.* want. [mowunca (Lg)] *See:* **naruida; wangal; yaniri.**

Mawung *n.* Flinders Peak group. [Mawoong (Lg)]

mayabiya *n.* composer of songs. [meyerbeer (L)]

155

mayal *n.* Aboriginal person living in a traditional way. from English myall. [myall (Bl)]

mayalba *v.* wake. [mayalba (MMEIC)]

mibanja *n.* cohabitation. [mibanja (Ba)] *See:* bulagan.

mibany *n.* wedge-tailed eagle. *[Aquila audax].* [mebon (M)] *See:* buduwar¹; duwai; jibal; ngan-ngan.

mibaral *n.* turtle. [mibaral (H)] *See:* bin. ging; bubiya; dagibagam; mujing; naguba.

Mibaram *n.* Mt French, north peak. [Meeborrum (Ha)] *See:* Banjurgan².

Mibiran *n. Variant:* **Mibu.** woman's name. [Mibu, Miberran (Delaney 1994)]

miburu *Variant:* **mibur.** *n.* small red possum, possibly ringtail possum. *[Pseudocheirus peregrinus].* [mibroo 'small species of opossum' (D); mi-ber-or 'scrub possum' (Ha); mibur 'native cat' (Ja); meberu 'like a squirrel, no lateral expansions, tail 5/4' long' (Le); mebroo 'red opossum' (Lg); mī'būr 'native cat' (Wa)] *See:* banjim; milgal.

midildin *n.* eyebrow. [mithiltin (Ja); midiltih (N); mithiltin (R)] *See:* mil.

migan₁ *n.* spike, thorn. [mīgan (Wa)]

Migan₂ *n.* spikey part of Knapp's peak. *lit.* 'spike'. [Mie gun (Ha); Mie-gun, Miggun (S)] *See:* migan¹.

Miganaba *n.* Broadwater. *incorporates* migan 'spike' and -ba 'place'. [Megunnubber 'separate part of Stradbroke ... Broad Water' (Bn)] *See:* -ba⁴; migan¹.

migim *n.* perch. [me'gim (Bd)]

mii₁ *adj.* quick. [meei (M)] *See:* bangga; burima; jubuiban; ngunbunjada.

mii₂ *adj; n.* fat, body. [mee 'fat' (H); mi 'bread' (Lg)] *See:* dinggal¹; mugan¹; yun-yun.

miir *n.* hole. [mīr (Ja); meare (Lg); mihr (N); mīr (R); mīr (Wa)] *See:* wangga.

miir-miir *adj.* full of holes. *lit.* 'hole-hole'. [mirre mirri (Lg)]

Miji *n.* woman's name. [Midjee (M)]

mijim *n.* midyimberry. *Anth:* edible sweet spotted white berry. *[Austromyrtus dulcis].* [midgun, midgin (B); miɟam (H); mijim (Ja); mijim (M); mijim (P)]

mijiri *n.* forehead. [migeerree 'head' (Fi); midgeree (Ha)] *See:* yilim.

mil *n.* eye. [mee (Bl): mill (Bu); mil (Cl); mill (E); mil (Fi); mil (H); mil (Ha); mia, mil (Ja); mil (L); mel, mill (La); mill, mil (Lg); mil (Ln); meel (M); mil (N); mil, mīa (R); mill (Su); millo (T); mill (Th); mil (W); mil (Wa); mill (We)] *See:* danggal².

mila-mila *n.* pipe clay, white ochre. [milla milla (M)] *See:* dalang¹.

milbang *adj.* blind. *lit.* mil-bang 'eye-dead'. [milbong (Bl); mil-bung (H)] *See:* bang; mil; milngundu; milwali; walibajin.

milbanya *v.* be awake. *incorporates* mil 'eye'. [mealpanye (W)] *See:* mil; -nya.

milbi *n.* eyelash. *incorporates* mil 'eye'. [milpih (N)] *See:* mil.

milbul *adj.* alive, active. *incorporates* mil 'eye'. [milbool (M)] *See:* mil.

milbulbu *v.* be alive, be active. *incorporates* milbul 'active'. [milbulpu (Ja); milbulpu (R); mil bul'pū (Wa)] *See:* =bu²; mil; milbul.

milgal *n.* European cat. *[Felis catus].* *possibly lit.* mil-gali 'intense eyes'. [milgall (Fi)] *See:* miburu; banjim.

Milgaro *n.* Laidley. [Milgero (Be)]

milgiri *n.* sweetheart. *Anth:* eyes are associated with romance; *possibly incorporates* mil 'eye'. [milgari (H); mileree (Ln); milkirrie (M); milkere (We)] *See:* mil.

milin *quant.* many. [millen (Ha); millen (Ja); millen (Lg); millen (M); millen, mulla (R); mil'lin (Wa); milindi 'plenty' (Wu)] *See:* gurumba garaba; manyal.

milindu *adj.* long (time). [millendu (R)] *See:* buruuwal; murul.

milin.gali *adj.* very many. *lit.* milin-gali 'very many'. [millenculle 'five' (Lg); millen kully (Ha); millenkulle (Ja); millenkolle, millenkulle (R); milling-kalla 'four' (T); mil'len kŭllē (Wa)] *See:* -gali; milin.

Milinggiri *n.* woman's name. [Mill-ingirr (CW); Milinggeree (M); Millingirr (W)]

Milin Yimban *n.* North Pine lagoon. [Mil'lin Yimbun (Bd)] *lit.* 'many bulrushes'. *See:* milin; yimban[1].

miliri *adj.* clean. [mellery (Lg)]

mil-mil *v.* look, see. *lit.* 'eye-eye'. [mil-mil (Bl); mill mill (E); mil-mil (Ja)] *See:* mil; ngulagu; nimgiba; nyaany.

milngundu *adj.* blind. *lit.* mil-ngundu 'dull eyes'. [mil-ngunju (Ma)] *See:* milwali; walibajin.

Milwaba *n.* Green Island. [milwaba (H)] *See:* Danggari.

milwali *adj.* blind. *lit.* mil-wali 'bad eyes'. [milwala, milwali (H); milwaddeli (Ja); milwaddeli, milwāddeli (R); mil wad'li (Wa)] *See:* mil; milbang; milngundu; wali; walibajin.

mi-mi *n.* juniper, myoporum. *[Myoporum acuminatum].* [mee mee (CW)]

mindi *n.* banksia. *[Banksia sp.].* [mintee (M); minti (P); min'ti (Wa)]

minggal-minggal *n.* collared sparrowhawk. *[Accipiter cirrocephalus].* [miŋgal miŋgal (H); mingel mingel (We)]

Mini-mini *n.* person's name. [Menemene (Kd)]

Minjiriba *n.* Minjerribah, Stradbroke, southern end of Stradbroke. *possibly lit.* 'place of mosquitoes' from Yugambeh munyjur 'mosquito' (Sh) and -ba 'place of'. [Moondarawa 'southern point of Stradbroke' (Bd); Minjerriba (CW); minǰiriba (H); Moonjerabah 'southern end of Stradbroke Island' (Hn)] *See:* -ba[4].

minya *Variant:* **minyang.** *interrog.* what? [menäh (E); miɲaŋ (H); minyar (Ha); menah, minna (Ja); menah, minya (Lg); minta, (M); minya, minna (R)]

minyalang *n.* thingamajig, whatever-it-is, substitute for swearword. [miɲalaŋ, miɲulaŋ (H); meenyalla (M); minyaluung (R)] *See:* minya.

minyambu *interrog.* how many?, how long? [minyambo (CW); menyembu (L); winyanpa (M)] *See:* -bu; minya.

minyana *interrog.* what? (accusative). [minyana (Lg)] *See:* minya; -na.

minyangdi *interrog.* why? *lit.* minyang-di 'at what'. [meniänti (E); menianti (Ja); menianti, minyanta 'where' (Lg)]

minyanggu *interrog.* why?, what is the matter? *lit.* minyang=gu 'for what purpose'. [menango (E); miɲaŋgu (H); menango, minyungo, minyango, minyangobah 'what is that for' (Lg); minago 'What do you want' (Ln); minyanggo (M)] *See:* =gu; minya.

minyangnuba *interrog.* belonging to what?, of what? [minyangoboh (Lg)] *See:* minyan; ngananuba; -nuba.

Mirabuga *n.* Southern Cross; a mythical hero. [Mirrabooka (MMEIC)]

Mirabul *n.* man's name. [Mirapool (S)]

Mirbaba *n.* Indooroopilly, site of railway bridge. [Mirbapa (CW)] *See:* -ba[4].

mirbang *n.* kangaroo net. [merbung (Ja); mirbong (M); merbung, mērbung (R); mir'bang (Wa)] *See:* bayal; durur; mandin[1].

miri *Variant:* **mir.** *n.* tame dog, camp dingo. *[Canis familiaris].* [mirri (Fi); miri (H); meerie (Hi); mehee (Hi); mirri (Ja); meyi (L); mee (Lg); milree (Ln); mēyē, mirri (R); mehee (Su); miga (T); mee (W); mē'yē, mir'ri (Wa); miri (Wu)] *See:* ngagam[2]; ngal-ngal; yuragin.

mirigin *n.* star. [meeregan (Fi); mirigan (H); merrigen (Hi); mirregin, mirrigin (Ja); mirigin (L); mirregan (Lg); mirrigan, meragin (Ln); mirrigin (M); mirregin (R); mirrigin (Su); miriyan (T); mirigen (W); mir'ragin (Wa); mirrigen (We)] *See:* dimbiny[1].

miriginba₁ *n.* sea eagle. *[Haliaeetus leucogaster].* [miriginba (MMEIC)] *See:* -ba⁴; bugawan; din.gal; mirigin.

Miriginba₂ *n.* Meriginpa; Hill at Amity. *lit.* 'place of stars'; possibly the source of miriginba 'sea eagle'. [Meriginpa (S)] *See:* -ba⁴; mirigin; miriginba¹.

mirimbal *n.* hand signs. *Anth:* used in hunting. [mir'rimbŭl (Wa)] *See:* mara¹.

mirin *n.* musk lorikeet. *[Polytelis swainsonii].* [mee-rinn 'green leek parrot' (Ha)] *See:* bir.

Mirir *n.* God. [mirīr, mirir (R)] *See:* Bayami.

mirum *n.* magpie. *[Gymnorhina tibicen].* [mirrum 'bird' (Ja); meroom 'bird' (Lg); mir'rin (Wa)] *See:* gulambarun; jarwang.

mirung *n.* young woman. [mirru 'wife' (Ja); merum (N); mirrūng, mirru (R); mir'rang, mi'rrū (Wa)] *See:* balinggan; jundal; gin; mulagin.

Miwa *n.* person's name. [Meewa (B)]

miwil *n.* hoar frost. [mewil (Lg)] *See:* wala; yiran.

Miyanda *n.* spike of land below Hamilton. [Meandah (CW)] *See:* migan¹.

Miyanjin *Variant:* **Miganjin; Miginjin.** *n.* Meeanjin, Brisbane, Gardens Point and its caretakers. *lit.* migan-jin 'point people'; also means 'city' in Ridley (1855). [Miganchan 'from Migan Chagum' (Bd); Miguntyun (Be); Mia-njin, Mi-an jin, Me-an-jin (CW); megenɉen (H); Megandsin (Le); Maginchin (Bay), Meeannjin (south) (M); Meeyantin, Megantchin (W); mīganchan' (Wa)] *See:* -jin; migan¹.

mubar *n.* rat. [moobor (Bd)]

muburum₁ *n.* storm. [muburum (H)]

Muburum₂ *n.* man's name. *lit.* 'storm'. [Muburum (MMEIC)] *See:* muburum¹.

muga-muga *n.* spider. [moogga-moogga (Ha); moggowe moggowe (Lg)]

mugan₁ *adj; n.* fat. [mărōm (G); muggarn (Ha); mugan (L); moogan (Lg); mogwan (Ln); moyen 'skin' (W)] *See:* dinggal¹; mii²; yun-yun.

Mugan₂ *n.* man's name. [Mokon (Borey and Laurer 1984); Mugan (H)]

mugara₁ *Variant:* **mugar.** *n.* thunder, thunderstorm. [mogara (E); mugar (H); moograh (Hi); mugara, mogarra, mogara (Ja); mugara (L); mogara, moogara (Lg); moozra, muggara, moogerah (Ln); mugara, moogarra (M); mugara (R); muganra (T); moo-gara (W); mūg'ara (Wa); moogar (We)] *See:* mumbal.

mugara₂ *n.* bulldog ant. [moogerah (Ha)] *See:* baigan; bigunjur¹; danmurin; galalang; giwarang; murin.

Mugara₃ *n.* Mt Greville, country between Mt Greville and Cunnigham's Gap. *Anth:* known for thunderstorms; *lit.* 'thunderstorm'. [Moogerah (Be); Moogerah (Ha); Moogerah (S)] *See:* mugara¹.

mugaramulu *n.* hailstone. *lit.* mugara-mulu 'thunder stone'. [moogerah mullor (Ha)] *See:* daraubang; mugara¹; mulu¹.

mugim *Variant:* **muyim.** *n.* stone axe. cognate with Waga-Waga muyim 'stone axe' (K). [mogim (G); mujim (H)] *See:* binjilurar; gulmang¹; nanggan; wagara¹.

mug-mug *n.* policeman. [mug mug (H)] *See:* buliman; dabingbila; gamadan.

mugul *n.* thumb. [mugul (H); mukool (We)]

Mugulngura *n.* woman's name. [Moogoolgnoora (M)]

mujin *n.* testes, tail. [muɟin (H); moochee 'tail' (M)] *See:* bulu; dugai; wanggin.

mujing *n.* eastern snake-necked turtle. *[Chelodina longicollis].* [muɟeŋ (H)] *See:* bin. ging; bubiya; dagibagam; mibaral; naguba.

mujiru-mujiru *n.* type of fruit. [modtheroo moodtheroo (Lg)]

Mula *Variant:* **Mulabin.** *n.* Oxley Creek. [Moola, Moolabbin (M)]

mulagin *n.* young woman, maid. *incorporates* gin 'woman'. [mulagin; muloengeh (Ba)] *See:* **balinggan; gin; jundal; mirung; mulagu²; mulam; nyaramgan.**

mulagu₁ *adv; n.* the next day, tomorrow. [mullago (E); mullago 'tomorrow' (Ja); mullago, moodlago 'to morrow', moolagha 'day' (Lg); mudelago (R)] *See:* **gujundabu; ngunugaba; ngunuwara.**

mulagu₂ *n.* young man. [mulagu (Ba)] *See:* **mulam; mulagin.**

mulam *n.* baby boy. [molum 'infant' (Fi); mooalam 'baby', mualam 'boy' (Ja); mulam (L); mōalam, mualum (R); mōlŭm 'young boy' (Wa)] *See:* **jajam; nyaramgan; nyamal.**

Mulbaju *n.* man's name. [Moolpajo (Be)]

mulgara *Variant:* **mulwara.** *n.* ritual scarification. [mulgarrah, mulwarra 'tribal marks' (Ja); moolgara (Lg); moolgarra (M); mulwarra (R); mulwarra or mulgarra (S); mulgarrah (Su)]

mulgara-mulgara *adj.* rough. *lit.* 'scar-scar'. [mulgra mulgra (Lg)] *See:* **budara; mulgara.**

mulu₁ *n.* stone. [moodlo (Bl); mullu (Bn); moodlow (D); mulu (H); mudlo, mullor (Ha); mooloo (Hi); moola (Ja); mullon 'big stone' (Ln); moola (Su); mullo (T); mudlo (W); mud'lō (Wa); mudlo (We)] *See:* **darau; gindal; nalanggira.**

Mulu₂ *n.* Moodlu railway station. *Anth:* probably the name of a rocky hill, now quarried for road metal (Q); *lit.* stone. [Moodlu (Q)] *See:* **mulu¹.**

mulula *n.* sand. *incorporates* mulu 'stone'. [mulula (H)] *See:* **mulu¹; yarang¹.**

Mulumba₁ *n.* Mooloomba, Point Lookout, also high part of Knapp's peak. *lit.* mulu-ba 'place of stone'. [Moodloomba 'Point Lookout' (B); mudlu-ba 'stony place' (Ba); Mullumbah 'Point Lookout; stones there' (Bn); Mooloomba 'north end' (CW); Maloomba 'Knapp's peak' (Ha); Mulumba (Ln); Moodloomba 'Rocky Point west of Point Lookout' (S)] *See:* **-ba⁴; mulu¹.**

Mulumba₂ *n.* man's name, name of the Sky Hero. [Mudlumba (MMEIC)] *See:* **-ba; mulu¹.**

mulumgal *n.* death adder. *[Acanthophis antarcticus]*. [nun-nuncal (Ha); mulunkun (Ja); mundulkun (L); monolkung (Le); moonalcoom (Ln); mooloomkul (W)] *See:* **bui²; guda; juumgu; yuwan.**

Mulu-mulu *n.* hill near Petrie's Pocket. *lit.* 'stones'. [Mudlo-Mudlo (S)] *See:* **mulu¹.**

Mulurubin *n.* man's name. [Molrooben, Mulroober (MB); Molrubin (Kd); Molrubin (S)]

mumbal *n.* heavy thunder, God. [mumbal (H); mumbul (Ha); moonbal, mūmbāl (Ja); mūmbāl (R); mum'bal (Wa)] *See:* **mugara¹.**

mundara *n.* weapon. [moondra (Lg)]

mun.ga *n.* rushes for making dilly bags, baskets or nets. [moon.ga (CW); muŋge, nunge (H)] *See:* **yunggiri.**

Mun.galba *n.* Moongalba, Mission at Myora. *Anth:* visitors to the area were allowed to camp and fish here; *lit.* 'sitting down place'; 'dragging (a net)' (Bn). [mungalba (H); Moongalba (Bn)] *See:* **-ba⁴.**

mungin *n.* food. [moongeen (M)] *See:* **dalgba; dubaru; jin-jin manjari.**

Munipi *n.* person's name. [Munipi (Kd)]

munjan₁ *neg.* no. used only in Munjan. [moonjine (G); moonjine (M); moonjan, moondjan (W)] *See:* **jandai¹; yagara¹.**

Munjan₂ *n.* Moondjan, language of the Nunagal people of northern Stradbroke. [moonjine (M); moondjan (S); moonjan, moondjan (W)] *See:* **munjan¹; Nunagal.**

munura *n.* white wood. [moonoora (Lg)]

munyal *excl.* won't listen. [munyal (MMEIC)]

Mura *n.* Shorncliffe. [Moora 'on the cliff' (Bd); Moora 'Sandgate' (M)]

murabal *n.* fig. *[Ficus sp.]*. [moorapul (Lg)] *See:* **galamang; ganin; ganin.gar; gurai; jambal; nguwanga; nyada.**

muralagang *n.* brolga. [mooralucung (Lg)]
See: **bugur**; **junggi**; **gundurgan**.

Muralu *n.* man's name. [Murallo
(MMEIC)]

murang *n.* meat. [muraŋ (H)] *See:* **dalgaba**;
jam; **yuri**[1].

Murgambin *n.* Moorgumpin,
Moreton Island. [Mulgumpin (Bn);
Moorgumpin (CW); mulganbin (H);
Moaraganpin (Ln); Gnoorgannpin (M);
Murgambin (MMEIC); Moorgumpin (W)]
See: **-bin**; **Ganginyangin**.

Murigan *n.* Myora Mission. [murgin-
muthin rtap-dha (CW); murigan (H)]

murin *n.* green-headed ant.
[Rhytidoponera metallica]. [moorn (Ha)]
See: **baigan**; **bigunjur**[1]; **danmurin**; **galalang**;
giwarang; **mugara**[2].

murjanggari *n.* sun. [mrjungary (Ln)]

muru *n.* nose. [muroo (Be); moorro (Bl);
murro (Cl); mulroo (E); mooru (Fi); muru
(H); mur-ror (Ha); mooro, murro, mulroo (Ja);
murra, murru (L); mulroo, moroo (Lg); murroo,
mooroo (Ln); muru, mooroo (M); moerru (N);
mūro (R); murro (Su); murro (T); moral (Th);
mooroo (W); mu'rū (Wa); murrow 'nostril'
(We); mūru (Wu)] *See:* **nunbulga**.

muruguji *Variant:* **muruji**. *n.* black
swan. *lit.* muru-guji 'red nose'. *[Cygnus
atratus].* [muroorcoochie (Be); maragin,
murugilɟi (H); murroo kutchin, murru-kootchin
(Ha); mooroocoochie (Hi); marutchi (Ja);
mooroochil (Ln); mooroochie, mooroocoochie
(M); maroochie (W); mu'rū-guji, mu'rū-ū'tchī
(Wa); murroogilchi (We)] *See:* **burunda**; **guji**[2];
muru; **nyuring**.

murul *adj.* long. [murul (Ba)]
See: **buruuwal**; **milindu**.

murumiir *n.* nostril. *lit.* muru-miir 'nose
hole'. [moerru-mihr (N); murudi, marrunala
(R)] *See:* **miir**; **muru**.

murumurul *n.* ibis. *[Threskiornis molucca].*
lit. muru-murul 'long nose'; extrapolated
from Yugambeh muru kurahr 'long nose; ibis'
(Sh) and the place name Muru-murul-bin.
[Mooroomoor'oolbin (M); Mooroo-mooroolbin
(S)] *See:* **muru**; **murul**; **Murumurulbin**.

Murumurulbin *n.* Sandbank below
Hamilton suburb. *lit.* muru-murul-bin
'long nose place'; possibly 'place of the ibis'.
[Mooroomoor'oolbin (M); Mooroo-mooroolbin
(S)] *See:* **-bin**; **muru**; **murul**; **murumurul**.

murung *n.* moss. [moorong (CW)]
See: **gabim**.

muruny *n.* small throwing stick.
[mu'rŭn (Wa)] *See:* **dal**[2]; **diniri**; **nguruwa**;
yirul[1].

Murunydu *n.* Mooroondu Point,
Thorneside. *lit.* muruny-du 'throwing stick
(does something)'. [Mooroondu (Redland City
Council 2023b)] *See:* **-du**; **muruny**.

muruny-muruny *n.* game played with
throwing sticks. [mu'rŭn-mu'rŭn (Wa)]
See: **muruny**.

Muum *n.* Mt Moon (Walkabout Mt).
[Moorm (Be); Moorm (Ha)]

Muumgara *n.* Mt Clunie. [Mormgurra
(Ha)]

muyan *Variant:* **muya**. *v.* desire, ask for.
[mooe 'ask' (Lg); moyum (R)]

muyu *n.* waterlily root. *[Nymphaea
gigantea].* *Anth:* the bulb is edible. [mooyoo
(M)] *See:* **jinggalgal**.

muyum[1] *n.* mussel. [moyum (E);
mooyoom, mooyum, mooyung 'a muscel, also
a book' (Lg); moyumko (R)] *See:* **bugawa**;
wayuung.

muyum[2] *n.* book, paper. [moyum (E);
mooyoom, mooyum, mooyung 'a muscel, also a
book' (Lg); moyumko (R)]

N – n

-na *case.* accusative case used on some objects of transitive verbs. [na (Cu); na (R)]

naam *demonstrative.* there (distal). [nām (Ja); nām, nam (R); nam, n'am (Wa)] *See:* danga; yugu¹.

naara *Variants:* **naar, naara-naara.** *n.* Pacific black duck. *[Anas superciliosa].* [nār (H); nar-orr (Ha); nar (Ja); marrar, narah, (M); nar (R); nār (Wa); nara (We)] *See:* ngalgal; ngau.

Naarda *s.* Nudgee. from naara 'black duck'. [Nar-dha (S)] *See:* naara; naji.

nabidi *v.* swallow. [nubede (Lg)] *See:* bingal-bingal.

nadang *n.* hair. [nadaŋ (H)] *See:* bundal²; gabui.

naga *n.* watershed. [nukku (Ca)]

nagi *n.* English bee. *[Apis mellifera].* word origin unknown. [nuki (Ln)] *See:* banjin¹; gabai¹; gila²; guja¹; gunidar; jalaman; mabi¹.

Nagin *n.* man's name. [Nuggin, Nuggyn (B); Nogun, Nug-gin, Nogin (CW); Nuggin (W)]

naguba *n.* humpback turtle. [nargobar (We)] *See:* bin.ging; bubiya; dagibagam; mibaral; mujing.

nagum-nagum *n.* candle. word origin unknown. [nogoom nogoom (Lg)]

nai *v.* name. [nay (Ha); nai-i (Ja); nai-i (R); nai' (Wa)] *See:* nari.

naigura *n.* apple box tree. *[Eucalyptus bridgesiana].* [naycora (Ha)] *See:* bubu.

Naimany *n.* man's name. [Naimany (E)]

najang *n.* mother's father. [naɖaŋ, nadaŋ (H)]

naji *n.* type of frog, possibly Australian green tree frog. *Anth:* naji were dug up from dried mud and pressed to obtain water (Bd); possibly the origin of the suburb name Nudgee. *possibly [Litoria caerulea]* [nudgee (Bd)] *See:* gubang; jaraagil; wagal.

najigam *n.* native Tibouchina. *[Melastoma affine].* [najigam (MMEIC)]

nala *adj.* small. [nulu (M); nūl'a (Wa)] *See:* biribi; jalgal; narang¹; ngambara.

nalanggira *n.* stone. [nullungirra, nullinggirra (Ja); nullunggira (R)] *See:* darau; gindal; mulu¹.

naluru *n.* crab. [nalloor (CW); nalaroo (MMEIC)] *See:* winyam; yirin.

nambany *Variant:* **namba.** *v.* appear, show, shine. [nūmbāni, numbai (Ja); nūmbāni, numbai (R); num'bai (Wa)]

nambur₁ *n.* water weed, herb. [nambūr (R)] *See:* jinbura; yari; yigilu.

nambur₂ *n.* tea tree bark. [nambour (M)] *See:* jiman-jiman; ngujuru.

Namgaran *n.* hill near Bulimba. [Numcahran (M)]

Namirala *n.* possibly Fortitude Valley. [Numeralla (Bd)]

namui *n.* acacia. *[Acacia sp.].* [namui (Ba)]

nanajin *n.* things. *incorporates* plural -jin. [nunantjin (Ja); nunantjin (R); nun'antgin (Wa)] *See:* daun; -jin.

nangal *n.* sweat. [nangul (Ha)]

nangalbanga *adj.* polite. [nangalpunga (Lg)]

nanggan *n.* stone tomahawk. [nunggarm (Ha); nungan (Hi); nungun (Lg)] *See:* binjilurar; gulmang¹; mugim; wagara¹.

Nanggu *n.* man's name. [Nunko (W)]

nangiba *v.* show. [nangevah (Lg)] *See:* -ba².

nan.gur *n.* sorcerer. [ngan.gur 'spirit' (R); narngur (Wi)] *See:* bajiram; daginy; gayabandar; gundir.

nanjara *adv.* not yet. [nanjara (Lg)]

Nanjili *n.* woman's name. [Nundgily (W)]

nany *Variant:* **na.** *v.* tie, fasten. [nuone (Lg); nunni (R)] *See:* gani².

nanyam *n.* burny vine bark, used as string. *incorporates* nany 'tie'. *[Alchornea scandens]*. [nannam (M); nannam (Ro); nan'nam (Wa)] *See:* **nany.**

naral *n.* buttocks. [narral 'nates' (Cl); narral (Ja)] *See:* **jumar; mabi².**

narang₁ *adj.* little. [nerang (Bl); nerang (Ca); narang (Lg)] *See:* **biribi; jalgal; ngambara; nala.**

Narang₂ *n.* swampy area near Eagle St. *lit.* 'small'. [Narong (Bd)] *See:* **narang¹.**

Narangba *n.* Narangba. *lit.* narang-ba 'little place'. [narang-ba (Ba); narang (Lg); Narangba (S)] *See:* **-ba⁴; narang¹.**

nari *n.* name. [nurri (Ja); nurri (R); nŭr'ri (Wa)] *See:* **nai.**

naruida *v.* want. [naruita (Lg)] *See:* **maun. ga; muyan; wangal; yaniri.**

narung *n.* seaweed. [naroong (We)]

Nidurwal *n.* person's name. [Niturwall (B)]

nigar *n.* periwinkle sea snail. *[Bembicium auratum]*. [niggar (Ja); nig'gar (Wa)]

nigi-nigi *n.* masturbation. [nicky-nicky (Bl)]

nijigum *n.* black-mouth bush. *[Melastoma malabathricum]*. *Anth:* the sweet fruit stains the mouth blue-purple (FNSI). [nujigum, nijigum (FNSI)]

nilga-nilga *n.* cow's horn. [nilga-nilga (Ha)] *See:* **bula².**

nimbir *n.* navel. [nembir (R)] *See:* **mabiri.**

nimgiba *v.* see. [neemgeeba (W)] *See:* **-ba²; mil-mil; ngulagu; nyaany.**

ninba *v.* take. [ninpa (Lg)] *See:* **-ba²; many; mara¹.**

ningi-ningi₁ *n.* oyster. [ninge ninge (Ca); ningi-ningi (M)] *See:* **ginyinggara; guumbi¹.**

Ningi-Ningi₂ *n.* group on Bribie Island. *lit.* 'oyster'. [niɲi niɲi (H)] *See:* **ningi-ningi¹.**

Niral *n.* man's name. [Ner-ral (Hp)]

nirang *n.* shovel-nosed shark. *Anth:* a species of ray. *[Aptychotrema rostrata]*. [neerang (M)] *See:* **burambigara; buwai; gayanggan; gura-guragan.**

-nuba *case.* possessive suffix. [nganowa (L); ngoboh, weupa (Lg); nŭbba, nubba (R)]

nubal *adj.* annoyed. [nooval (Lg)]

Nugimba *n.* man's name. [Nookembar (W)]

Nugun *n.* St Helena Island. [Nuggin, Nuggyn (B); Noogun (Bn); Nogun, Nug-gin, Nogin (CW); Nugoon (Ln); Noogoon (M); Noogoon, Nogun (S); Nuggin (W)]

nugunja *n.* sole fish. [noogoonchar (We)]

nulbu-nulbu *n.* evening. [nulbu nulbu (H); nooboogooboo (W); noolpoo-noolpoo (We)] *See:* **biigibiribi; jalu-jalu; ngunu; yaragal.**

nulu *adv.* always. [noodloo (Lg)]

Nunagal *n.* Noonuccal, northern Stradbroke people, speakers of Munjan. [nunagal (H); Noonuccal (M); Noonukul (W); Noonuckle (We)]

nunbulga *n.* nose. [nunbulga (H)] *See:* **muru.**

Nunilbira *n.* Ipswich people. [Nundilpara 'Limestone tribe' (Lg); Noonillburra (M)] *See:* **-bira.**

Nuninya *n.* woman's name. [Nooninya (Borey and Laurer 1984)]

Nunungga *n.* man's name. [Nunungga (N)]

nuralgir *n.* type of scrub wood. *Anth:* the glutinous milky sap is used to stun fish. [nuralkir (D)] *See:* **danggul.**

nuram *Variant:* **nuram-nuram.** *n.* wart, pockmark. [nuram-nuram (Ja); nuram (M); nŭr'am (Wa)]

Nuranyum *n.* man's name. [Nur-an-eun (CW); Nuraneum (W)]

nurung *n.* cockle. [murang (T); nurong (We)]

nuun.gali *v.* sneeze. *possibly incorporates* -gali 'very'. [nuoonculle (Lg)] *See:* -**gali**.

Nuwaju *n.* man's name. [nuaɟu (H)]

nuwinbil *n.* small bird. from Yugambeh nuɲanybil 'bird' (Sh). [newinbill (M)]

NG – ng

-nga *case.* allative suffix designating motion towards a location. [nta (Ha); nga, ŋga, ŋu (R)]

nga *conj.* and. [nga (L); nga (R); nga (Wa)]

ngabang *n.* elder brother. [awang (E); ner bung (Ha); ngubbunga (Ja); awang (Lg); mubbung (Ln); ngabong (N); ngubbunga, ābāng (R); nabang (W); ngub'bing (Wa)] *See:* **duwanggal**.

ngabu *n.* lawyer cane. *[Calamus australis].* [ngaboo (B)] *See:* **daigam**.

ngadaliba *adj.* last. [nguddaliba (Lg)]

ngadan *Variant:* **ngada**. *v.* meet, touch. [ngadun, ngadūn, ŋādün (R)] *See:* **dandiiri**.

ngadang *n.* pelvis. [nguttang (Lg)]

ngagali *adv.* too much. *lit.* nga-gali 'and plenty'. [aculle (Lg)] *See:* -**gali**; **nga**.

ngagam₁ *demonstrative.* here (proximal). [nahga (Ha); goggum (Ja); ngalam 'he' (L); ngaga 'that' (Lg); ngāgām (M); goggum (R); gog'gŭm (Wa)] *See:* **diranga**.

ngagam₂ *n.* dingo, tame dog. from Yugambeh ngagam (Sh). *[Canis familiaris].* [nangum (Ca); ŋagam (H); nargun (Ln)] *See:* **miri**; **ngal-ngal**; **yuragin**.

ngagam-ngagam *excl.* come here! *lit.* 'here, here'. [gēēba (G); gogo-gogoe (Lg)] *See:* **ngagam**¹.

ngagamwaga *v.* camp. *incorporates* ngagam 'here'. [kakum waga 'camp here tonight' (Ln)] *See:* **dimany**; **giba**²; **jalubaluba**; **ngagam**¹.

Ngaijiraba *n.* Sugar Loaf Mt. [N-oi zer-a-ba (Ha)] *See:* -**ba**⁴.

ngaja *pron.* I, 1SG.NOM. [atu (Bl); nutchair (Ha); ŋaḍa (H); atta (E); ngutta, atta (Ja); ngats'a, ngacia, ngaoia, gaoia (L); utter, ngutter (Lg); gnatcha, ngalta, gnatja, gnatya (M); yutta, ŋutta, atta, ŋāi, ai, ŋaia (R); atta (T); tcha, utcha (W); ngai, ngai'ta (Wa); nutchair (We); ngaja (Wu)]

ngajagarara₁ *n.* lobster. [gnatchgarahra (M)]

Ngajagarara₂ *n.* hill on Moreton Island. *lit.* 'lobster'. [Uttakharrarrha (B); Atta Carrara (W)] *See:* **ngajagarara**¹.

Ngajagarara₃ *n.* woman's name. *lit.* 'lobster'. [Uttakharrarrha (B); ngajagarara (Ba); gnatchgarahra (M); Atta Carrara (W)] *See:* **ngajagarara**¹.

ngalan₁ *n.* bony bream. *[Nematalosa erebi].* [woulan (E); malaŋ (H); woulan, ngullum (Ja); woulan, oolan 'female mullet' (Lg); walan, wulan, gnoolan, gnollan (M); ngullun (R); ngul'lŭn (Wa); mulung (We)] *See:* **dun.gala**; **ginbun**; **man.gal**.

Ngalan₂ *n.* site of Royal Brisbane Hospital. *lit.* 'bony bream'. [Walan (S)] *See:* **ngalan**¹.

ngalba *pron.* we, 1PL.NOM. [nulpa (Ha); alpa (M); ŋulpa (R); nhamba (T)]

ngalbana *pron.* us, 1PL.ACC. [ŋulpunna, ŋulpāna (R)]

ngalbanu *pron.* us, 1PL.DAT. [ŋulpunna (R)]

ngalbanuba *pron.* our, 1PL.POSS. [ngalpanganowa (L)]

Ngalda *n.* hill on Moreton Island. [Alta, Ul-ta (CW)]

ngalgal *n.* wood duck. *[Chenonetta jubata].* [ngulgul (R)] *See:* **naara**; **ngau**.

ngaliny *pron.* we (you and I), 1DU. NOM. [linda, nalinda, nealinda 'we or you & I' (Lg); ngadli 'we' (L); gnalleen, gnahleen (M); ŋullin 'you and I', ŋulle 'we' (R); allin 'we two', nhamba 'we' (T)]

ngalinyana *pron.* us (you and me),
1DU.ACC. [yalunga 'me' (Lg); ŋulleŋunna,
ŋulleŋunnu, ŋullin.ga (R)]

ngalinyanu *pron.* us (you and me),
1DU.DAT. [ŋulleŋunnu (R)]

ngal-ngal *n.* wild dingo. *[Canis
familiaris]*. [ŋaI ŋaI (H); nulgul (Ha); uigull
(Hi); ngulngul (Ja); ngalgal (L); allgull (Le);
ngulgul (R); ungal (W)] *See:* **gila**¹; **miri**;
ngagam².

Ngalungbin *n.* Lytton. [Alongpin (Ln);
Gnaloongpin (M)] *See:* **-bin**.

ngama *excl.* hey!, come look! [umma 'an
ejaculation calling attention' (G)] *See:* **wi**.

ngamarigara *n.* freshwater catfish.
[Tandanus tandanus]. [ngāmerikurra (Ja);
ngāmerikurra (R); ngam'errīkŭrra (Wa)]
See: **bigun**; **wargan**.

ngamba₁ *conj.* like, similar to. [ngāmba
(Ja); ngāmba (R); ngam'ba (Wa)]

Ngamba₂ *n.* man's name. [Umpha (Ha)]

ngambara *adj.* small. [ngambar, nambara
(MMEIC)] *See:* **biribi**; **jalgal**; **narang**¹; **nala**.

ngambila *n.* all, everyone. [ngābille (Ja);
ngambilla, ngambille (R)]

Ngamingba *n.* woman's name.
[Gnahminba (M); Ngamingba (W)]

ngamu *n.* breast, milk. [narmoung (Bl);
hammo (Cl); ammoo (E); ammoo 'milk',
hammo 'nipples' (Ja); ngominoo (Lg); mummoo
(Ln); ommuli, ahmoo (M); ngammu, ngammur
(R); ummoo (W); ngung'gŭr, omŭlli (Wa)]

ngamuban *n.* milk. *lit.* ngamu-ban 'breast
product'. [ummoobin (W)] *See:* **-ban**; **ngamu**;
nyamany-nyamany.

ngan *interrog.* who? (nominative). [ngan
(L); ngan'du (Wa)]

ngana *pron.* me, 1SG.ACC. [mi 'me'
(Bl); nanee (H); ana (Lg); nganna (M); ŋunna
(R)]

nganan *adj.* heavy. [nannun (Lg); gnanin
(M)]

ngananuba *interrog.* whose?,
belonging to whom? [nganaweupa (Lg)]
See: **minyangnuba**; **-nuba**.

nganbadagu *v.* consent. [anbedaggo (Lg)]

nganbil *Variant:* **nganbi**. *v.* yawn, gape.
[anbil (Lg)]

ngandagal₁ *n.* mullet. [ngandi'kul (Bd);
undall (D); andeikal (E); anduccul (Fi); jindilgal
(H); un-dair-cul (Ha); undecal (Hi); ngandakul,
andeikal, andakal (Ja); andäkal (Le); andeikal,
undekul 'male mullet' (Lg); guandaccal, andaccal
(M); ngandakul (R); andekal, nundarill, andaccal
(W); nundarill (We)] *See:* **dilgam**; **gang-gang**².

Ngandagal₂ *n.* Fisherman Island. *lit.*
'mullet'. [Andaccah (S)] *See:* **ngandagal**¹.

ngandu *interrog.* who? (ergative).
[ngandir (Ja); ando (Lg); ngan'du (Wa)]

ngan.gu *adv; interrog.* how, like this.
[ngangpo (L)] *See:* **=gu**; **ngan**.

nganiyiba *adj.* straight. [nganiyiba
(MMEIC)] *See:* **jubui**; **yilung**.

ngangaba *v.* seek. [ngangabah (Lg)]
See: **ngananuba**.

ngangabum *adv.* time past. [langaboom
(Lg)] *See:* **ngangabum dadi**.

ngangabum dadi *adv.* short time
since. *incorporates* ngangabum 'time past'.
[langaboom tadde (Lg)]

ngangalinga *n.* face. [ngangulinga (Lg)]
See: **nguwar**; **yibaru**.

ngangan *n.* king parrot. *[Alisterus
scapularis]*. [uongan, nongan (Fi)] *See:* **bilin-
bilin**.

ngan-ngan *n.* wedge-tailed eagle.
[Aquila audax]. [an-an, guan guan (M); an'an
(Wa)] *See:* **buduwar**¹; **duwai**; **jibal**; **mibany**.

ngaraan *adv; n.* fine weather. [orōn (Lg)]

ngaraang-ngaraang *n.* mantis. [orōng
orōng (Lg)]

ngarabin *n.* silky oak. *[Grevillea sp.]*.
[ŋarabin (H)] *See:* **-bin**; **jagin-jagin**.

ngaragan *adj; n.* pregnant, pregnant person. [ngargarran (M); urumkun (W)] *See:* -gan²; nyamalbila.

Ngaraiyu *n.* person's name. [ngaraio (B)]

Ngaraju *n.* man's name. [Gnurradju (W)]

ngaran₁ *n.* neck. [nolun (Fi); gunuran (H); yurrun (Ja); muhluhn (N); ngarran (R); ngur'rŭn (Wa)] *See:* dur-dur; giling.

ngaran₂ *n.* footprint, track. [ngaran (Ba)] *See:* jarajina.

ngarang *n.* gum-top box tree. *[Eucalyptus moluccana].* *Anth:* bark for covering huts; bee excrement at the base is a sign of honey (DF); can be burnt to purify a place (Fensham 2021). [nurran 'gum tree' (Fi); nā-run (Ha); gnarran (Le); ngeureung 'stringybark' (Mac)] *See:* dabilbala.

ngaranga *v.* there is/was, there are/ were. [ŋuruŋa (R)] *See:* gamagu; naam; yugu¹.

ngara-ngaragai₁ *Variant:* **ngara-ngarawai.** *n.* wild heather. *Anth:* the flowers were used for decorative purposes (FNSI). [ngarrawarrawai (B); ŋara ŋarawai, ŋara ŋaragai (H)]

Ngara-ngaragai₂ *Variant:* **Ngara-ngarawai.** *n.* long, winding creek at One Mile near Dunwich. *lit.* 'sound made by person retching' (Bn); or possibly 'wild heather'; named by Balun.giny (Bn). [ngarrawarrawai (B); Nurrow Nurrow Guy (Bn); ŋara ŋarawai, ŋara ŋaragai (H)] *See:* Balun.giny; ngara-ngaragai¹.

Ngara-ngarawariba *n.* person's name. [ŋara ŋarawariba 'a "surname"' (H)]

ngararar₁ *n.* red-stemmed gum. [urarrar (Be); urar (P)]

Ngararar₂ *n.* Bremer River. *lit.* 'red-stemmed gum'. [Urarrar (Be)] *See:* ngararar¹.

ngarawin *n.* water. [ngaraoin (Ja); ngaraoïn (R)] *See:* dabil; gabing.

ngari₁ *pron.* me, 1SG.DAT. [ɲari (H); naree (Ha); ngrai (L); ngari (P); ŋurri (R); naree (W); nuru (We)]

ngari₂ *v.* celebrate. [gara, gera, ngari (CW); karli (Ha)] *See:* ganjiil; yiyara; yuwar.

ngariba *pron.* my, 1SG.POSS. [ariba (E); ŋariba, ŋariwa, ŋarijuba (H); ariba (Ja); ngaciaganowa 'my' (L); ngarebah, narebah (Lg); gnareeba, yahliebaddie (M); ngariwar (N); ŋurribā, ŋurriba (R); nurryuba (We)]

Ngariigambila *n.* place near Mt Alford, now the Scenic Rim Brewery. [Recum-pilla 'Ander's store, Mt Alford' (Ha)] *See:* -bila.

ngaring *n.* chin. [ngering (N)] *See:* waul.

ngari ngaram *excl.* compassionate interjection. *possibly lit.* 'my baby!'. [aree-a-rarm (Bl)] *See:* gunin-gunin; gunman; ngari²; nyaramgan.

ngaruwing *n.* coachwood. *[Ceratopetalum apetalum].* [ngnaa rewing 'coach wood' (Mac)]

ngau *n.* Australian wood duck. *[Chenonetta jubata].* [gnowo, now-woo 'duck' (Cl); ngua-u, uya (Ja); ngouwoo (Lg); hau (Ln); ngoro-oo 'black duck' (M); nga (R); ngou 'black duck' (S); ngou (W); ngau'-ū (Wa)] *See:* naara; ngalgal.

ngawundanman *n.* eldest. [ngaroudenmun (Ja); ngawundenmun (R); ngaw'id'inmum (Wa)] *See:* jajing; ngabang.

ngawur *adj; n.* female. [ngawur (N)]

ngi *interrog.* question marker; 'than' in comparatives. [ngi (L)]

ngilarun₁ *n.* forest grass tree. *[Xanthorrhoea sp.].* *Anth:* 'skirt' of tree was processed to produce a strong resin (FSNI). [ilaroon (W)] *See:* bulirbin; dagabin¹; garguru.

Ngilarun₂ *n.* man's name. *lit.* 'forest grass tree'. [Yillaroon (W)] *See:* ngilarun¹.

ngilbang *pron.* you two, youse two, 2DU.NOM. [ngilpung 'you two' (Lg); ilpūnŋ, ilpūŋ 'ye two' (R); inungei (T)]

ngilbula *pron.* you all, youse, 2PL.
NOM. [ngilpula (L); ŋilpūllā 'ye' (R); inungei
'you two', nuba 'ye' (T)]

ngilbulana *pron.* you all, youse, 2PL.
ACC. [ilpūllāna, ilpullana (R)]

ngimbun *n.* blue flax lily. *[Dianella
caerulea]*. *Anth:* the blue berries were not eaten
(FNSI). [imboon (W)]

Ngimiba *n.* person's name. [Immieva (B)]

ngina *pron.* you, 2SG.ACC. [inna, nanee
(Ha); ine (W)]

nginda *pron.* you, 2SG.NOM. [indo,
neen (Bl); gintay (D); intair (Ha); ŋinda, ɲinda
(H); inta (E); ēēn (G); inta 'thou', nginta, inda
'you' (Ja); nginte 'thou', nginta, gninte, nginto
(L); ngidna, nginter, inter (Lg); intay, inta,
yinta, gnintay, intay (M); ŋinda, ŋinta, inta,
inda 'thou', ŋinta, inta (R); ngintia 'they two',
inta 'thou' (T); inta, inter (W); inter (We); inta,
gninta (Wa)]

nginggaran *n.* Aboriginal woman.
[yeran (Ja); īnggurun, ingaran (R); in gurin
(Wa)] *See:* **gin**; **guri**.

nginjuru *n.* worm. [nginjuru (Ba)]

nginu *pron.* you, 2SG.DAT. [gninoo
(M); ŋinnu (R)]

nginuba *pron.* your, 2SG.POSS.
[yeen, innoung (Bl); enuba (E); enuba (Ja);
ngintenganowa 'thy', nguwa, ngowo (L);
nenoobah, yanobah 'yours' (Lg); inooba, yinoóba
(M); ŋinnuba (R)]

Ngiri *n.* man's name. [Eeree (W)]

Ngirubin *n.* place name. [ŋerobin (H)]
See: **-bin**.

Ngugi *n.* caretakers of Moorgumpin
(Moreton Island), speakers of Guwar.
[Nagur, Nigger (B); Nooghies (Bn); ŋugi (H);
Gnoogee (M)] *See:* **Guwar**.

ngugul *n.* type of fish. [oogool (Lg)]

ngui *v.* believe. [noy (Ha); ngui (R)]
See: **gana²**; **winanga**.

nguibina *n.* truth. *lit.* ngui-bina 'ear
believes'. [noy-pinung (Ha)] *See:* **bina**; **ngui**.

ngujubugu *v.* sell. [oodiopoggo (Lg)]

Ngujurba *n.* alternate name for
Bummiera (Brown Lake). *lit.* ngujuru-ba
'place of tea trees'; *Anth:* the preferred name for
Brown Lake is Bummiera. [Gnoojoorpa (M)]
See: **-ba⁴**; **Bamira**; **ngujuru**.

ngujuru₁ *n.* broad-leafed tea tree.
[Melaleuca quinquenervia]. *Anth:* bark used
for bandages, keeping food clean, and ganya
construction; when the tea trees are in full
bloom, there will be an abundance of honey
(MMEIC). [ngudur (Ja); ɲuɟur (H); rguduru
(Ro); oodgee (W); ngū'dŭr (Wa); noojoor (We)]
See: **jiman-jiman**; **nambur²**.

Ngujuru₂ *n.* Ngudjuru, Lamb Island.
lit. ngujuru 'tea tree'. [Ngudooroo (Redland City
Council 2023a)] *See:* **ngujuru¹**.

ngul *Variant:* **ngul-ngul**. *n.* louse. [oongool
(B)]

ngulagu *v.* look. [ngoodlago (Lg)] *See:* **=gu**;
mil-mil; **nyaany**; **nimgiba**.

Ngulawara *n.* Kangaroo Point.
incorporates wara 'open water'. [Oodlawirra,
Oodlawurra (Bd)]

ngulumari *adv.* across. [uulumery (Lg)]
See: **giram**.

ngumar *n.* flood. [oomar (Be)]
See: **yanmana**.

ngumbi *n.* house, humpy. origin of
English humpy 'traditional Aboriginal dwelling'.
[oompee (B); umpee (Cl); umpie (E); umphie
(Ha); umpie, umpee, ngudur (Ja); humpy (L);
umpie, umpe, oomi (Lg); humpy (Ln); humpy
(MB); umpi (R); oompi (W)] *See:* **ganya**.

Ngumbi Bang *n.* Humpybong, area
at the Brisbane River estuary and its
caretakers. *lit.* 'dead house'. [Humpybong (B);
Umpie Boang (E); ŋumb i boŋ (H); Oomim-
bun 'Humpybong group' (Lg); Humpybong
(W)] *See:* **bang**; **ngumbi**.

Ngumbi Dagai *n.* Nundah, the German mission at Nundah. *lit.* 'houses of white men'. [Umpie Daggur (S)] *See:* **dagai**; **ngumbi.**

Ngumbi Gurumba *n.* Brisbane. *lit.* 'many houses'. [Umpie Korumba (S)] *See:* **gurumba**; **ngumbi.**

ngumburu *adj.* full. [oombroo (Lg)] *See:* **biduru**; **bila²**.

Ngumgaru *n.* man's name. [Ngoom-gar-roo (CW); Ngoomgarroo (W)]

ngun *Variant:* **ngu.** *v.* live. [oon, oonle (Lg)] *See:* **digi.**

nguna *interrog.* which? [oona (Lg)]

Ngunabi *n.* woman's name. [Gnoonappee (W)]

ngunadada *n.* mallee scrub. [oodnadatta (Bd)]

nguna-ngunan *adj; n.* spiral shape. [ngoona ngoonan (Lg)]

ngunbunjada *adv.* quickly. [ngunbunjada (MMEIC)] *See:* **bangga**; **burima**; **jubuiban**; **mii¹.**

ngundana *v.* go together. [ngoontanna (Lg)] *See:* **dalagan**; **ganyardi**; **nyan.**

ngundu₁ *adv.* only, surely, lest, but. [ŋūndū, ŋūndu (R)] *See:* **gumbal¹.**

ngundu₂ *adj.* blunt, not sharp. [ngoontoo (Lg)] *See:* **dambil.**

Ngundu₃ *n.* woman's name. *lit.* 'only, surely'. [hoontoo, oontoo (B); Oonto (W)] *See:* **ngundu¹.**

ngunguma *v.* burn. *possibly incorporates* -ma 'causative'. [ngunguma (Wu)] *See:* **-ma.**

nguniwali *adj.* wrong. *incorporates* wali 'bad'. [gnooniewullie (M)] *See:* **bidamjaran**; **wali.**

ngunu *Variant:* **ngunu-ngunu.** *n.* evening, night. [oonar (Be); woolgooloo 'sunset' (Ca); ŋunu (H); oon, nunga-nunka (Ha); ngoonnoo, yunnu, ngnnu (Ja); nguno (L); danoo 'night' (Ln); ngoonoo (Lg); ngūnnū (R); muno 'darkness' (T)] *See:* **biigi-biribi**; **jalu-jalu**; **nulbu-nulbu**; **yaragal.**

Ngunubi *n.* man's name. [Gnoonoopi (W)]

ngunubu *adv.* for the night, overnight. *lit.* ngunu-bu 'for the duration of the night'. [ngūnnunubbū (R); nooboogooboo (W); nŭn'nŭnŭb'bū (Wa)] *See:* **-bu**; **ngunu.**

ngunugaba *adv.* tomorrow, morning. *lit.* ngunu-gaba 'belonging to the night'. [unungaba (E); nun-dab-boor (Ha); unungabo (Ja); ngubuga (L); unungabo, woonoongaboo 'to morrow', woonoogara 'yesterday' (Lg); ngoobo'oga, ngubuga-la-bu (M); nooboogooboo (W)] *See:* **-gaba**; **gujundabu**; **mulagu¹**; **ngunu**; **ngunuwara.**

Ngunuranbin *n.* woman's name. [Gnoonooranpin (M)]

ngunuwara *adv.* tomorrow. *incorporates* ngunu 'night'. [oonoowarra (Hi); ngundara, ugunúara 'yesterday' (L); ngoonoowar 'yesterday' (Lg); ngunuwara (Wu)] *See:* **gujundabu**; **mulagu¹**; **ngunu**; **ngunugaba.**

ngunyal *pron.* he/she/they, 3SG. NOM. [ullurn (Ha); wunnāl (Ja); ngalam 'he, she' (L); gnoonyal (M); unda, wunnal (R); ungda 'he' (T)]

ngunyali *pron.* they, 3PL.NOM. [wunnale (R); layim 'they' (L)]

ngunyalina *pron.* them, 3PL.ACC. [wunnālina, wunnalina (R)]

ngunyalinuba *pron.* their, 3PL.POSS. [wonanemibah (Lg)]

ngunyalu *pron.* he/she/they, 3SG. ERG. [ngoonloo (Lg); wunnalu, wunyalu, wuunyalu (R)]

ngunyana *pron.* him/her/them, 3SG. ACC. [nudna 'him' (Lg); wunnana (R)]

ngunyanu *pron.* him/her/them, 3SG. DAT. [wunnaun, wunnanu (R)]

ngunyanuba *pron.* his/her/their, 3SG. POSS. [wonanabah (Lg); wunnanūbu, wūnnanūba, wunnanuba (R)]

ngura *v.* leave behind, not take. [oora, oorapa (Lg)] *See:* **galabi**.

ngurbin *n.* brown mahogany. *[Eucalyptus robusta]*. [gnorpin (CW)] *See:* **-bin; bangalai; bularju; bundul**.

ngurdi *adv.* in the area. *lit.* nguru-di 'in the shape'. [ngurti (R)] *See:* **-di; nguru²**.

ngurgurga *n.* spotted gum. *[Corymbia sp.]*. [urgorka (Le); oorcouraca (Lg)] *See:* **gurdir; yara¹**.

ngurgurgaban *n.* settler's flax. *[Gymnostachys anceps]*. [urgorkapan (Le)]

ngurin-ngurin *n.* dragonfly, gadfly. [gnoorin gnoorin (M)]

nguru₁ *Variant:* **ngur.** *n.* breath, spirit, shadow. [nguru (Ja); ngūrul (R); nguru (Ro); ngū'rū (Wa)] *See:* **marau**.

nguru₂ *Variant:* **ngur.** *n.* shape, area. [ngōr (Ja); ngōr (R); nōr (Wa)]

Ngurujung *n.* Milton. [Uruthuck (Bd)]

nguruman *Variant:* **nguruma.** *v.* hide oneself. [nguruman (R)]

ngurun *n.* sky. from Yugambeh ngurun 'sky' (Sh). [nurroon (Fi); ooroon (Hi)] *See:* **biram; wangan**.

ngurun.gali *n.* robber. *possibly lit.* nguru-gali 'very shady'. [ooruncully (Hi)] *See:* **-gali; nguru²**.

nguruny *n.* emu. *[Dromaius novaehollandiae]*. [morun (Fi); morrion (Ha); oorun (Hi); nguyi, ngui (Ja); moorum (Ln); narooing, gnoorooin (M); nguyi (R); moorun (W); ngur'ūin, ngu'yi (Wa)]

nguruwa *adj; n.* small branches, made of small branches. [oorooe (Lg)] *See:* **dal²; yirul¹**.

nguun *adj.* hot. from Yugambeh nguun 'hot'. [norn (Ha)]

nguwai *adv.* in two or three days. [ngoowai (Lg)]

nguwanga *n.* sandpaper fig, large brush fig with oblong leaves, heart-shaped at the base, its densely haired, edible fruit. *[Ficus coronata]*. [ngoa-nga, ngōangā (Ja); gnau wan (Le); ngwange (Lg); ngoa-nga (M); ngōangā (R); ngōa-nga (Wa)] *See:* **galamang; ganin; ganin.gar; gurai; jambal; murabal; nyada**.

nguwan.gingan *n.* son's wife, husband's mother. [nguwoenkingen (N)] *See:* **-gan²; gin**.

nguwar *n.* face. [ngoh-ar (N)] *See:* **ngangalinga; yibaru**.

Nguwararu *n.* person's name. [Ngwararo (B)]

nguwinginin *Variant:* **nguwingini.** *v.* read. [ngwengenen (Lg)]

nguwuny *n.* gum from the spotted gum. [ngowoon (Lg)] *See:* **jirai**.

NY – ny

-nya *tns.* present tense suffix. [na (E); ner, na, nya (Ha); nya (L); na, nya (M); nā, na, ne (R); nye, nya (W); nyah (We)] *See:* **nyan**.

nya *v.* urinate. [ɲā (H)] *See:* **gil; jalang; nyan**.

nyaany *Variant:* **nyaa.** *v.* see. [nanni (Ja); nan, nanabajoo (Lg); nha (M); nanni, nāni (R); nganka (T); neem (W); nya'nī (Wa)] *See:* **mil-mil; ngulagu; nimgiba**.

nyaban *n.* east wind. [yiaban (Ba)] *See:* **burging; dun.gai; gubi²; winjia**.

nyada *n.* small fig. *[Ficus coronata]*. *Anth:* the rough leaves were used to smooth boomerangs, spear shafts and axe handles (FNSI). [nuta (L); nurra (Lg); nyuta (M); nyūt'a (Wa)] *See:* **galamang; ganin; ganin.gar; gurai; jambal; murabal; nguwanga**.

nyala *excl; v.* go!, be gone! *lit.* nya-la '(you) must go!'. [yellah 'be gone' (Cl); yellah 'be gone' (Ja); yallah (M)]

nyalang *Variants:* **nyala, nyalang-nyalang.** *v.* tell lie(s). [nalaŋ nalaŋgin (H); nullungmurri (R)] *See:* **gujal; nyalanggali.**

nyalanggali *adj; n.* liar, lying. *lit.* nyalang-gali 'lies plenty'. [un-un-gully (Ha); ooruncully (Hi); nullancalle 'lie' (Lg); nallau-galli (M)] *See:* **-gali; gujal; nyalang.**

nyalanggan *n.* telling lies. *lit.* 'time of lying'. [nyalangken (W)] *See:* **-gan; gujal; nyalang.**

nyama *n.* upper arm. [yamma (E); yabner 'arms' (Fi); jama (H); yum-mar (Ha); yumma (Ja); yabma (L); yamma, yabmah 'shoulder' (Lg); yamma (M); yoemah (N); yumma, yamma (R); yamma (T); yŭm'ma (Wa); nyama (Wu)]

nyamal *Variant:* **nyama-nyamal.** *n.* child, baby, young animal. [narral (Cl); nummorl (D); ɲamal (H); nammul (Ha); nãmmūl (Ja); nammul (Lg); nam-ul (M); nãmmūl (R); numil-numil (W); nyam'ŭl (Wa)] *See:* **gin-gin[1]; jajam; mulam; nyaramgan; nyamal.**

nyamalbila *adj.* pregnant. *lit.* nyamal-bila 'child-having'. [nammulpille (Lg)] *See:* **-bila; ngaragan; nyamal.**

nyamalmilin *n.* the children in a family. *lit.* nyamal-milin 'many children'. [ngarul-milan (Ba)] *See:* **milin; nyamal.**

nyamany-nyamany *n.* nursery word for milk. [nyammyn nyammyn (B)] *See:* **ngamu.**

Nyaminba *n.* woman's name. [Ahminba (M)]

nyan *Variant:* **nya.** *excl; v.* go, travel, walk. [yan (Bl); yarreto 'walk' (Cl); yarto (E); jara (H); yur-on-ner, yenee 'bring' (Ha); yarto, yādeni, yennan, yarreto (Ja); yarto, ya (Lg); yarra (M); yā, ye, yea (R); yanna (T); yie (W); yan'man (Wa)] *See:* **ban.gawani; guba[1]; nya; -nya.**

Nyanbabari *n.* man's name. [Anbaybury (E)]

nyanda[1] *n.* mouth, river mouth, waterhole, lagoon, swamp. [nundare (Hi); nundah 'lagoon'; nundah 'mouth' (M); nyan'da (Wa)] *See:* **damburu[1]; wira-wira.**

Nyanda[2] *n.* Nundah. *lit.* 'waterhole'. [Nanda (S)] *See:* **nyanda[1].**

Nyandaba *n.* South Pine River mouth. [Andurba (Bd)] *lit.* nyanda-ba 'river mouth place'. *See:* **-ba[4]; nyanda[1].**

nyandala *n.* silver-leafed ironbark. *[Eucalyptus melanophloia].* [undalla (D); undallah (Ha); undala (Lg)] *See:* **bigara; jana; janduru; jum-jum; ganaibira.**

Nyandili *n.* Cleveland. [Nandeebie (M); Nindilly (S); Nindilly (W)] *See:* **Ban.ginbany.**

nyangga *adj; n.* hot, heat. [nyunka (Be); nangka (E); nunker, nunka, norn (Ha); nungcar (Hi); nangka (Ja); nanka, nangka (L); nunka, nangka (Lg); urun (T); nunka, numka (W)] *See:* **yawani.**

nyanggagan *n.* summer. *lit.* 'hot time'. [noen'gagan (L)] *See:* **-gan; nyangga.**

nyanjina *v.* go on foot. *lit.* nyan-jina 'go foot'. [yan din'na (Wa)] *See:* **jina; nyan.**

nya nya *excl.* get out of the way! *lit.* 'go, go'. [yah-yah (Ha)] *See:* **nyan.**

nyara *n.* bearded dragon. *[Pogona barbata].* [nair-ar (Ha); narah (Hi); nera (Le); nurrah 'jew lizard' (Lg); nharangapee 'jew lizard' (M)] *See:* **binanggurung[1].**

nyaral *n.* vagina. [ɲaral, ɲaro (H); noerroel (N)] *See:* **gaji[2]; jindur; jurung; yunu.**

nyaramgan *n.* baby girl, young girl. [eurumpcon (Fi); yur-un-cul 'sister' (Ha); yarumkun (Ja); yuramkan (L); yurumkun (R); urumkun, yu'umkin (Wa)] *See:* **-gan[2]; mulam; nyamal.**

nyaring *n.* son. [narring (Hi); nurring, nurridmun, narring (Ja); narring (M); naring 'nephew' (N); nurring (R); ngarring 'boy' (T); naring (W); nãrring (Wa)]

nyaringgan *n.* daughter. *lit.* nyaring-gan 'female son'. [ɲaragagan, ɲarigigaɲ (H); narringan (Hi); nurringun (Ja); naringgoea 'daughter; niece' (N); nuringun (R); nŭr'ingŭn, nar'ringgŭn (Wa)] *See:* -gan²; nyaring.

nyigiran *Variant:* **nyigira.** *v.* run. [īgerē (Ja); yeegeera (M); īgerē, īgēren (R); nyigi (Wu)] *See:* buwarawa.

nyinduru *Variant:* **nyindur.** *n.* scrub leech. [ninduro (Lg); nindur, indooroo (M); nin'dur, nyin'dur, nyin'dur (Wa)]

Nyindurubili *n.* Indooropilly. *lit.* nyinduru-bili 'leech creek'; possibly named by whites. [Yinduru-pilli (CW); Indooroopilly (M); Yinduru-pilli (S)] *See:* bili; nyinduru.

Nyindurunyinyidu *n.* Sweeney Reserve bora site in Petrie. *lit.* nyinduru-nyinyi-du 'leech is sitting' (Bd). [Nindur-ngined-do (Bd)] *See:* -du; nyinduru; nyinyi.

nyinggal *n.* powerful owl. *[Ninox strenua].* [ingull 'hoot owl' (D)] *See:* duribang¹; gingga; gum-gum; wumanggan².

nyinyi *v.* sit, dwell, exist. [nginnen, ginnila (Ja); nginna, ngeneggella (Lg); gneenih (M); inen (P); ɲinne, ɲinē (R); yin (W)]

nyinyili *v.* sit down. *lit.* nyinyi-li 'seat oneself'. [gin-nila (Cl); jiɲili- (H); gin-nila (Su); yinila, ninila (W)] *See:* -li²; nyinyi.

nyiwang *adj.; adv.* nice, nicely, beautiful. *Anth:* not used to describe humans. [njewang, niewang, niua (L)] *See:* bujari; galang; marumba¹.

nyubany *n.* married couple. [ɲubaɲ (H)]

nyubanyjal *n.* husband. *incorporates* nyubany 'married couple'. [noobunchal (Hi)] *See:* nyubany; nyugunbing.

nyubanyjalgan *n.* wife. *lit.* nyubanyjal-gan 'husband woman'. [noobuuchalgun (Hi)] *See:* -gan²; nyubany; nyubanyjal; nyugunbinggan.

nyubi *v.* kiss. [nyubi (H); yoobee (M); yubee (We)] *See:* dandildila.

nyugum *n.* bucket, coolamon, bailer shell. *[Melo diadema].* [newcane (Cl); nokum (E); nugum (Ha); niugam, newcane, nokum (Ja); nokum, nogoom 'conch shell' (Lg); niugam (Ro); niū'gam (Wa); nugum (We)] *See:* bigi; wundal; yabar².

nyugum mulu *n.* stone used for rubbing bark to make it water-tight for buckets. *lit.* 'bucket stone'. [nugum mullor (Ha)] *See:* mulu¹; nyugum.

nyugunbing *n.* husband. *incorporates* bing 'father'. [noogoonping (W)] *See:* bing; nyubanyjal.

nyugunbinggan *n.* wife. *lit.* 'husband woman'. [naginggoen (N); noogoonpingun (W)] *See:* bing; -gan²; nyubanyjalgan.

nyundal *Variant:* **nyunda.** *v.* wait, look after animals, keep animals. [undal, ūndal, inēl (R)] *See:* dalan²; gau.

nyunggiya *n.* soft twigrush. *[Cladium procerum].* *Anth:* common reed, used for weaving and prawn fishing (FNSI). [ungaire, nyungair (FNSI)]

nyungin *n.* comrade, friend. [ɛwang 'brother', uingun 'friend' (Ja); uïngun (R); yūingin (Wa)] *See:* banji; gimunggan; jimbalang; magiiba.

nyuring *n.* black swan. *[Cygnus atratus].* [newring (M)] *See:* burunda; muruguji.

nyurung *n.* rain. [uror (Be); uto (G); yerro (Ha); euro (Lg); yurong, yeerong (M); yurru (T); yurong (Wa); yurrow (We)] *See:* jurum-jurum.

Nyurungbili *n.* Yeerongpilly. *lit.* nyuring-bili 'rain creek'. [yurun-bi-la (Ba); Yurong-pilli (Bd); yurong-pilli, Yeerongpilly (M); Yurong-pilly 'rain coming' (P)] *See:* -bili; nyurung.

Q – q

Quandamooka *n.* Pacific Ocean, Moreton Bay. probably a Yugambeh-Bandjalang word. [Quandamouk 'Pacific Ocean' (Ga)]

R – r

-ra₁ *asp.* indicates motion to a destination. [ru (E); ra (H); ree, r-o (Ha); re (Lg); re (M); rā, rai (R); ra (W)]
-ra₂ *deriv.* indicates negation on a verb. [ra (H); ra (Lg); ra (W)]
-ri *tns.* past tense suffix. [ir (Ha); re (M); ri, rai (R); re (W)]

W – w

-wa *mood.* verbal suffix designating intention or future prediction. [wa (P); ia; ïa (R); wa (W)]

waa-waa *n.* warning sound of crow, crow, human lookout, 'row, row!' said in a boat. *[Corvus orru].* [wāwā (H); wau-wau (Ha); wowul, wowa (Ja); warah (M); wowul, wowa (R); Wa Wa 'row row' (S)] *See:* wabayin; wagam; waryum.

Waba *n.* Bunya group. [whapah 'neighbouring Aboriginal group' (D); Wappa 'Archers Bunya tribe' (Lg)]

wabalgan *n.* small bullroarer tethered to a whip. [wabulkan (G); wabulkan (Hw); wobbalkan (Ja); wab'balkan (Wa)] *See:* bagaram¹.

wabayin *n.* crow. *[Corvus orru].* [wabayen (MMEIC)] *See:* waa-waa; wagam; waryum.

wabum *n.* mud, yellow. [wobum (Ja); wabum (Lg); wobum, wōbum (R); wōbŭn (Wa)] *See:* bangan¹; daldari.

Wabuunariba *n.* woman's name. [Wapurnareeba (W)]

wadi *n.* north wind. [wadi (Ba)] *See:* dimbiny¹.

wagal *n.* bullfrog. [wogull (We)] *See:* gubang; jaraagil; naji.

wagam *n.* crow. *[Corvus orru].* [wāgam (H); wā-gun (Ha); wankan, waagun (Ln); wagum 'fowl' (T); wokun (W); warcum (We)] *See:* waa-waa; wabayin; waryum.

wagara₁ *Variant:* **wagar.** *n.* stone tomahawk. [woggera (Ha); wahgarra (Hi); waggarr (Ja); wogara (Lg); wogara (Ln); waggara, wahgarra (M); waggar (W); wâg'gar, wâggarī (Wa)] *See:* binjilurar; gulmang¹; mugim; nanggan.

wagara₂ *adj.* angry. [wugara (Ba)] *See:* gula¹.

wagarbin *n.* long grass. [wugarpin (R); wug'arpin (Wa)] *See:* banggil¹; -bin; daga; wagara¹.

wagi-wagi *n.* Australasian Swamphen. *[Porphyrio melanotus].* [wahgi-wahgi 'redbill' (M)]

wagun₁ *n.* scrub turkey. *[Alectura lathami].* [woggon (Bl); wargon (Ca); wahgoon (D); waggan (Fi); woggan (Ha); wahgoon, wahwoon (Ja); woggoon (Ln); wahgoon, wargon (M); war'gūn (Wa)] *See:* gawal.

wagun₂ *n.* fly, insect. [āgārn (Ja); wahgoon (M)] *See:* bululum; dudambara.

Wagun₃ *n.* man's name. *lit.* 'scrub turkey'. [Wag-gun (CW); Wogan (E); Waggun (W)]

wai *excl.* particle used in songs. [wae (L)]

Waimba *n.* person's name. [waimba (H)]

waimirigan *Variant:* **mirigan.** *n.* white woman. from English 'white Mary' and feminine suffix -gan. [muragan, waɲmiri (H); wy-mary-gin (Ha); whymerigan (L)] *See:* -gan²; jiran.

waja *v.* sleep. [wodieh (Lg)] *See:* bugany; yunma.

Wajabau *n.* young man's name. [Wujbour (B)]

wajari *n.* rosewood tree. *[Dysoxylum fraserianum]*. [woggerree (D); wudgerie (Ha)] *See:* **bunuru**[1].

wajin *n.* platypus. *[Ornithorhynchus anatinus]*. [wadjeen (M)]

wala *n.* frost. [wulla (Ha)] *See:* **miwil; yiran.**

walamgan *n.* shell. [wolumgan (E); wolumgar (Ja); wolumgan (Lg)] *See:* **dinggal**[2]; **gara**[1]; **guumbi**[1]; **magul**[2].

Walan[1] *n.* glade with lagoons, south of Barambin. [Walan (Bd)]

Walan[2] *n.* Wallen Creek. [Wallon (Creek) (Bn)] named by Nunagal (Bn).

walangan *n.* blade made of bone. [wolangan 'blade bone' (Lg)]

walangara *n.* long water. [wallangarra (M)]

Walan-walan *n.* Wallen Wallen Creek. named by Balun.giny (Bn). [Wullun Wullun (Bn)] *See:* **Balun.giny.**

walar *n.* kneecap. [wollar (Lg)] *See:* **buun.**

Walbaligu *n.* man's name. [Walbaligo (G)]

Walbul *n.* man's name. [Walpaul (Ha)]

wali *adj.* bad. [wadle, wadly (Cl); wodley (D); warlee (E); wattāry 'lying', wallī 'cold' (G); wullie 'talkative' (Ha); wadlee, warlee, waddeli (Ja); warlee (Lg); wadli, wallee (M); waddeli (R); wadlee (Su); wadley (W); wad'eli, wad'li (Wa)] *See:* **warang.**

waliba *adj.* boiling. [uollebah (Lg)] *See:* **-ba; wali.**

walibajin *n.* blind people. *lit.* wali-ba-jin 'people who've become bad'. [wadli-ba-din (Ba)] *See:* **-ban; -jin; milbang; milngundu; milwali; wali.**

walibina *excl.* sorry to hear that. *lit.* wali-bina 'bad to hear'. [walibina 'that bad' (Lg); 'garang' (Wa)] *See:* **wali-waligarang.**

waliinggara *Variant:* **waliinggar.** *n.* old woman. [wilingere (Fi); walinga (H); werlinga (Ha); walingara, wallinggara (L); wallingar (Lg); walingera, wallingargh (Ln); wulingger (N); wollingar (W); wullingoor (We); walinggara (Wu)] *See:* **baji**[1]; **maran.gan.**

walima *v.* make mischief. *lit.* wali-ma 'make bad (things)'. [waddy murry (Lg)] *See:* **-ma; wali.**

Walin *n.* woman's name. [Wahlin (M)]

wali-waligarang[1] *n.* long coarse grass. *lit.* wali-wali-garang 'unpleasant blanket'. [walliwallinggarān (R); wal'liwal'lin garang (Wa)] *See:* **daga; garang-garang; wali; wagarbin.**

Wali-waligarang[2] *n.* creek on Stradbroke. *lit.* 'long coarse grass'. [walin-walin-garang (Ba); walliwallinggarān (R); wal'liwal'lin]

walmuram[1] *n.* sand goanna. *[Varanus gouldii]*. [wahlmoorum (Ha)] *See:* **bara**[1]; **giwa; yaugira.**

Walmuram[2] *n.* Mt Ballow. *lit.* 'sand goanna'; this name was mistakenly assigned to Mt Maroon and is the source of the English name Maroon (Ha). [Almoorum 'Mt Maroon' (Be); Wahlmoorum (Ha); Wahlmoorum (S)] *See:* **walmuram**[1].

Wamam *n.* Mt Edward. [Wummum (Be)]

wamba *v.* wear. [wumba (R)]

wambany *adj; n.* venereal disease, having venereal disease. *incorporates* bany 'disease'. [womboyne (Bl)] *See:* **bany.**

wambarligiri *n.* log. [wombarleygeerree (Fi)] *See:* **baguurugil; bural; maling.**

wana *excl; v.* don't, forbid, refuse to. [wonnah (Cl); wonnah (Ja); wona (Lg); wunna (R)]

Wanagin *n.* Mount Pleasant, Hamilton. [Wunnuckin (Bd)]

Wanaigubung *n.* waterhole at Milbong. *lit.* 'one hole'; incorporates Yugambeh gubuŋ 'hole' (Sh). [Wunai gubung (S)]

wana mada *excl.* an exclamation. from Gabi-Gabi wana madja 'don't (do that) there' (Bell 1994). [wanamada (H)] *See:* **wana.**

Wanangga *n.* man's name. [Wudnangga (R)]

wanangin *Variant:* **wanangi.** *v.* drown. [wunungin (R)]

wanarara *excl.* no, no, don't! *lit.* wana-ra-ra 'don't-not-not'. [wunnarara 'no' (Lg)] *See:* **-ra²; wana.**

wana-wanarambin *n.* she-oak, swamp oak. *[Casuarina glauca].* [wunn wunna rumpin (CW)] *See:* **bandibar; bila¹; -bin.**

wanda *v.* go up. [wunda (R)] *See:* **nyan; wangan.**

wandal *adv.* around. [wundal (Ba)]

wandan *adj.* crooked. [wandan (M)] *See:* **barang³; bunbar.**

Wandaru *n.* man's name. [Wandaroo (MMEIC)]

wandi *v.* rise, lift. [wanti (M); wundā (R); wan'ti (Wa)] *See:* **balgama; duriyinma; daran¹; juwan¹.**

wandima *v.* climb. *lit.* wandi-ma 'make rise'. [wantima (Bd)] *See:* **-ma; wandi.**

wang *n.* withered leaf, dry leaf. [wung (Ja); wung (R); wur'ŭng, wŭng (Wa)] *See:* **dalgai; dawajangar.**

wanga *n.* no-good girl. [waŋa (H)]

wangal *Variants:* **wanga, wangal-wangal.** *v.* want. possibly from English 'wangle' (MMEIC). [wangal (MMEIC); wangle-wangle (W)] *See:* **maun.ga; naruida; yaniri.**

wangalban *adj.* striped. [wong-alpun (Lg)]

wangan *n; v.* sky, heaven, above, place above. [waŋ, waŋan (H); wangan (Lg); wungun (R)] *See:* **biram; ngurun; wanda.**

wanganba *n.* vest-like garment for the arms and waist, made of skin. *incorporates* wangan 'above'. [wungīnpa (G)] *See:* **wangan**

wangandi *adv.* above. *lit.* wangan-di 'at above'. [wongunty (Be); wungunti (R)]

Wangandi Biradi *n.* Heaven. *lit.* wangan-di biram-di 'located above the sky'. [Wongunty Birarchi (Be)] *See:* **biram; -di; wangan.**

wangan-wangan *adj; adv.* way up high. *lit.* 'above-above'. [wangan wangan 'top of a tree' (Lg)]

wangari *n.* swamp wallaby. *[Wallabia bicolor].* [wangari (J)] *See:* **bugul; bangui; jamban; garil; magun; wangun.**

wangga *adj; n.* hole, mouth, deep. [wongah (Cl); wongah (Ja); wunggō, wunko (R); wongah (Su); wungaw (W)] *See:* **miir.**

wanggal *n.* cheek. [wongall (Fi); wungal (Lg); woengoel (N)] *See:* **jaagul.**

wanggaljirban *n.* jawbone. *lit.* wanggal-jirban 'cheek bone'. [woenggoel-chirben (N)] *See:* **jirban; wanggal.**

wangga ngarabin₁ *n.* silky oak. *lit.* 'hole silky oak'; may indicate a silky oak tree with a hole in it. *[Grevillea sp.].* [wunkermany (E); unnagurgunpin, unngurgunpin (We)] *See:* **ngarabin; wangga.**

Wangga Ngarabin₂ *n.* man's name. *lit.* 'silky oak'. [Wunkermany (E)]

wanggin *n.* tail. [wonggin (Ro)] *See:* **dugai; mujin.**

wangun *n.* old man wallaby, male wallaby. [wongoon 'male paddimelon' (Le); wangun (Ln)] *See:* **bugul; bangui; jamban; garil; guruuman; magun; wangari.**

Wanigani *n.* man's name. [Wunny-cunny (CW); Wunnycunny (W)]

waninga *n.* rain-making ceremony. [waninga (Bd)]

wanji *interrog.* when? [ngatte (Lg); winchei, wanchee (M)]

wanya *interrog.* where? *Gram:* temp/condit subordinator in Waga-Waga (wanja/wanya) and Badjala (wanya); Yagara seems to have 'wina' for this function. [winya (Bl); wunna (E); wanɟa, waɲa, wana (H); wunna (Ja); wunja, wunya (L); wunna, wuntya, nganga (Lg); wanya (M); wuniya, wanya, wunnia (W); wunya (Wu)]

wanyadi *interrog.* where at? *lit.* wanya-di 'where at'. [wunyanta 'where' (Lg)]

wanyagu *interrog.* where to? *lit.* wanya=gu 'where to'. [wunyángo (L); winyanpa (M)] *See:* **yinjagu.**

wara₁ *n.* open water or river. [wāra (M)] *See:* **waril¹.**

Wara₂ *n.* Sandgate. *lit.* 'open water'. [Warra 'Sandgate' (Bd); Warra (CW); wāra (M); Waar-rar 'Brisbane River' (P)] *See:* **wara¹.**

Waraba *n.* bora site near present-day Mater Hospital. *lit.* wara-ba 'open water place'. [Waraba (Bd)] *See:* **-ba⁴; wara¹.**

warabana *n.* bushfire. [warrahbanar (Be)] *See:* **jalu.**

warabari *n.* smoke. [warrahbarey (Be)] *See:* **jumu¹.**

warajam *n.* bunyip, bugbear. *Anth:* each person has one of these spirits, which they can talk to in a waterhole; the spirit is invisible and inaudible to others. [warrajum (Hi); worridziam, worrid's'am (L)] *See:* **jagany; wara¹.**

waram₁ *adj.* left-handed. [warrām (G)]

Waram₂ *n.* Redcliffe point. [Warum (Bd)]

warambul *n.* watercourse. *incorporates* wara 'open water'. [warrumbool (M)] *See:* **-bul; wara¹.**

waran₁ *Variant:* **waran-waran.** *n.* tree root. [warrun (Bn); pullan (Lg); warran-warran 'cypress pine tree roots' (M)] *See:* **burugari.**

waran₂ *n.* type of weapon. [warran (Lg)]

warang *adj.* bad, cold. [worang (Bl); warrūng (G); waraŋ (H); warang (J); wurring (Ln)] *See:* **wali.**

Waran Gamari *n.* wetlands between Tuleenderly Creek and Wallen Wallen Creek. *lit.* waran gama-ri 'the roots broke'; 'Here trees fall over because the roots are undermined by the fresh water underneath' (Bn); named by Balun.giny (Bn). [Warrun Gummare (Bn)] *See:* **Balun.giny; gama; -ri; waran¹.**

Wara-wara *n.* Victoria Point. *lit.* 'lots of open water'. [Warrer Warrer (Bn)] *See:* **wara¹.**

Warbai *n.* Ipswich-area group. [Warpai (Bd)]

wargan *n.* catfish, mulloway. [wagguine 'eels' (D); wargan, dagan (H); woggun (Ha); dugan (Ja); wakan 'jewfish' (Le); wargun (We)] *See:* **bigun; buigum; diyala; ngamarigara.**

waril₁ *n.* freshwater river, creek. [wooril (Fi); warril (Ha); warrill (Hi); warril (Ja); waril (L); warril (Lg); warrill (Ln); warril (M); waar-rai (P); warril (R); war'ril (Wa)] *See:* **bili; bijara; wara¹; yinil; yuma.**

Waril₂ *n.* Warrill Creek. *lit.* 'river'. [Warill (S)] *See:* **waril¹.**

Waringari *n.* Oaky Creek area. [Warren currie, Warren-kurrie 'George Johnson's' (Ha)]

waru *Variant:* **waru-waru.** *n.* fence. *Anth:* the word may come from the name of a weir for fishing, which is made the same way as a brush fence (G). [warra-warra (G); war'rū (Wa)]

warunggul *adj.* mighty. [warunggul (MMEIC)]

waru-waru *n.* game with string, cat's cradle. *lit.* 'fence-fence'. [wurra-wurro (Ha); war'rū-war'rū (Wa)] *See:* **waru.**

waryum *n.* crow. *[Corvus orru].* [wareum (We)] *See:* **waa-waa; wabayin; wagam.**

waul *n.* chin. [woul (Fi); wowul (L); woul (Lg); wawyal (Ln); wowl (M); waooroo (We)] *See:* **ngaring.**

wawan *n.* fowl. from Duuɲidjawu wawun 'scrub turkey' (K). [wawan 'fowl' (H)]

waya₁ *v.* send. [waia (Ja); wyal (Lg); waia (R); wia (W); wī'a (Wa)]

waya₂ *n.* corner. [weia (Lg)]

wayaba *n.* forearm. [waiyaba (Ba)]
See: **daaran.**

wayara *v.* be hungry, be empty. [wyaroo (Bl); waiaroo (E); wāirou (G); waira (H); waiara, waiaroo (Ja); waiaroo, wyrah (Lg); wiyarra (M); waiara (R); waara (W); wai'ara (Wa)]
See: **gabiny.**

wayarabang *adj.* starving to death. *lit.* wayara-bang 'hungry-dead'. [wāirou-bong (G)]
See: **bang; wayara; wayaragali.**

wayaragali *adj; n.* starving, starving person. *lit.* wayara-gali 'very hungry'.
[wyraculle (Lg)] *See:* **-gali; wayarabang.**

wayuung *n.* mussel. [wyoong (We)]
See: **bugawa; muyum**¹.

wi *excl.* hey, oi! *Anth:* usually to get attention before saying something. [wēē (G); we (L); wee (M)] *See:* **ngama; yura.**

wi balga *excl.* hello, welcome. *lit.* 'hey come!'. [we balka (L)] *See:* **yura.**

wibara *n.* fire. from Yugambeh waybar (Sh). [weybra (Ca); wy burra (M)] *See:* **jalu.**

widan *n.* forested country. [widden (Ha)]

widiging *n.* brushtail possum (male). [widdiging (Le)] *See:* **gubi**¹**; ganal.**

wigaliba *adj; adv.* downhill. [wiculliba (Lg)]

wigu *interrog.* interrogative marker on a tag question, similar to English 'eh?' or 'right?'. [wiga (P); ēko (R)]

wiilbara *n.* cart. from English wheelbarrow. [wielbara 'dray' (Lg)]

wijaban *n.* dog. [wijaben (Ln)] *See:* **gila**¹**; miri; ngagam**²**; ngal-ngal.**

Wijambarigun *n.* woman's name. [Weejamperrigin (M); Weedjumparegun (W)]

Wiji-wijibin *n.* Swan Bay. *possibly lit.* wuji-wuji-bin 'place of red cedars'. [Wiggy Wiggy Pin (Bn); Wiji-Wiji-Pi (CW)] *See:* **-bin; wuji.**

Wilangga *n.* woman's name. [Weelangah (N)]

Wilgunariba *n.* woman's name. [Wilcoonereeba (W)]

Wilwinba *n.* Observatory Hill in Spring Hill. [Wilwinpa (CW)] *See:* **-ba**⁴**.**

wina *conj.* then, when. [wina (Ba)]

winam₁ *n.* pandanus, bread-fruit tree, coastal screw pine. *[Pandanus tectorius]*. *Anth:* ripe fruit were eaten (FNSI); root suckers were soaked in a honey mixture and chewed (Sh). [winnum (B); winam (H); winnam (Ja); winnam (M); wynnum (W); win'nam (Wa); wynnum (We)] *See:* **junggul.**

Winam₂ *n.* Wynnum. *lit.* winam 'pandanus' or winyam 'soldier crab'. [winnum (B); winam (Ba); wynnum (CW); winam (H); winnam (M); wynnum (W); win'nam (Wa); wynnum (We)] *See:* **winam**¹**; winyam.**

winanga *v.* hear, believe, know. [winnanga, winnange (Lg); weenangee (M); wininga (N); winungu (R); winanga (T)] *See:* **gana**²**; ngui.**

winbulin₁ *n.* grass tree. *[Xanthorrhoea sp.]*. [whinpullin (Be)] *See:* **bulirbin; dagabin**¹**; garguru; ngilarun**¹**.**

Winbulin₂ *n.* Minto Crag. *lit.* 'grass trees'. [Whinpullin (Be); Whinpullin (S)]

winil *n.* water hole. [wennell (Hi)]

winjia *n.* east wind. [wincey (Ln); winchia (W)] *See:* **burging; dun.gai; gubi**²**; nyaban.**

win-win *adj.* bare. [winwin (Lg)]

winyam *n.* soldier crab. *[Mictyris longicarpus]*. [winam (H); winyam, weenhum, weenyam (M); waynum (We)] *See:* **naluru; yirin.**

winyiba₁ *n.* little bittern. *[Ixobrychus dubius]*. [wiɲiba, winiba (H)]

Winyiba₂ *Variant:* **Winy.** *n.* woman's name. *lit.* 'bittern'. [Wynuiba, Win (B); Weeneeba (CW); Weeneeba (W)] *See:* **winyiba**¹**.**

wira *v.* return, go home. [virenna 'arrive', wirepi 'come back' (Ja); werra, werara (Lg); wīrē (R); wir'e (Wa)] *See:* -ra[1].

wiral *n.* south wind. [wyral (Lg)] *See:* buran.

wira-wira *n.* lagoon, place where there is water. [wira wira (H)] *See:* nyanda[1].

wirui *adj.* lightweight. [wiroi (M)] *See:* dang-dang.

wiruwira *n.* sexual intercourse, sexually active man. [wiruwira, wiruwara (H)] *See:* bam-bam; burima; gumuwara; jim-jim.

wiya[1] *n.* black cockatoo. *[Calyptorhynchus sp.]*. [weah (M)] *See:* balan; biliyagan; biluwala; gaiyara; garara; giwang; jarbal.

wiya[2] *v.* breathe. [wiar (T)] *See:* bui[1]; buidangal.

wiya[3] *v.* let go, hold out, extend. [wia 'hold out or extend'; wia 'let go' (W)]

wiyan[1] *n.* west. [wian (M)] *See:* junggai[1]; yabarin.

Wiyan[2] *n.* woman's name. [Wy-an (CW); wianmal (M); Wyan (W)]

Wiyanba *n.* Bald Hills. *lit.* wiyan-ba 'west place'. [wian (Ba); Wyampa (CW)] *See:* -ba[4]; wiyan[1].

wiyari *v.* marry. [wiare (Lg)] *See:* buwa.

wugalban *n.* rufous bettong, kangaroo rat. *[Aepyprymnus rufescens]*. [woogelpun (We)] *See:* barung.

wugalibila *adv; n.* daylight, daytime. [hoogalibbila (Lg)] *See:* -bila.

wugaru[1] *n.* whirlpool. [woogaroo (S)]

Wugaru[2] *n.* Woogaroo. *lit.* 'whirlpool'. [Woogaroo (S)] *See:* wugaru[1].

wugulumba *n.* toad. [wookoolumbah (We)]

wujan *Variant:* **wuja.** *v.* give, bring. [woo-die-ger (Ha); oodan, oodar (Lg); wooja (M); wuddā (R); wud'da (Wa)] *See:* ga.

wuji *n.* red cedar. from Yugambeh wudheh (Sh). *[Toona ciliate]*. [wood-dair (B); woodgee (Ca); woodjee (M)] *See:* daigil; mamin.

wula *n.* word. [woolla (Bl); wulla (Lg)]

wulara *v.* talk. [wullera (Ha); wullara (Lg); wooller (MB); wulara (Wu)] *See:* wula; yaa.

wularaba gariyagan *n.* magpie goose. *lit.* wulara-ba gariyagan 'brolga that talks'. *[Anseranas semipalmata]*. [woolar-paugarragan (M)] *See:* -ba[3]; gariyagan; wulara.

wularagali *adj; n.* talkative, big talker. *lit.* wulara-gali 'talks a lot'. [wullera kully (Ha)] *See:* -gali; wulara.

wularama *v.* talk. *lit.* wulara-ma 'make talk, let yourself talk'. [wularama (Wu)] *See:* -ma; wulara.

wulu *n.* ankle. [olu (Fi); woodloo 'heel' (Lg); wuhluh (N)] *See:* buyu; darany.

wulun *Variant:* **wulu.** *v.* whirl around. [woolloon (M)]

Wulun.gaba *n.* Woolloongabba. *lit.* wulun-gabing 'whirling water' (M); also suggested 'fight-talk place' (Clark 1916) and wulungga-ba 'place of tree ferns' (L). [woolloongabba (L); Woollongabba (M)] *See:* -ba[4]; gabing; wulun; wulungga.

wulungga *n.* tree fern. [woolloonga (L)] *See:* barunyuba.

wumang *n.* wife's father, daughter's husband. [wumang (Ba); wuhmenn (N)]

wumanggan[1] *n.* wife's mother. [wumang-gin (Ba)] *See:* -gan[2]; wumang.

wumanggan[2] *n.* owlet-nightjar. *[Aegotheles cristatus]*. [wamankan 'owl' (Ja); wom'ankan 'night hawk' (Wa)] *See:* duribang[1]; gingga; gum-gum; nyinggal.

wumanggari *n.* cross-cousin (male). [woo-muggerie (Ha); warrmogree (Hi); womugiri 'brother' (L)] *See:* wumang

wumanggarigan *n.* cross-cousin (female). [wamugari-gin (Ba)] *See:* -gan[2]; wumang; wumanggari.

Wumbunggaru₁ *n.* Spring Hill. *Anth:* this newer term for Spring Hill was a man's name (M). [Woomboonggoroo (M)]

Wumbunggaru₂ *n.* man's name. [Woomboonggoroo (M)]

Wumunyguru *n.* Taringa. [Woomooonygoroo (CW)]

Wunarajimi *n.* Helidon spring. *lit.* 'where the clouds fell down'. [Woonarrajimmi (S)]

Wunaring *n.* swamp near Bowman's dwelling at Mt Brisbane by Lake Wivenhoe. [Woonaring (Ha)]

wundal *n.* bucket. from Yugambeh wundal 'bowl' (Sh). [wondul (Ha)] *See:* **nyugum**; **yabar²**.

wunyi *v.* hear. [wūnyi (Wu)] *See:* **winanga**.

wura₁ *v.* put, lay down. [woora (E); woora (Ja); woora (Lg); wune (R)] *See:* **yibiri¹**.

wura₂ *n.* bed. [woora (E); woo-a-oll (Ha); woora (Lg)] *See:* **dungura**.

Wurabinda *n.* camp in Spring Hill. *Anth:* 'at the waterhole' near York's Hollow (Bd). [Woorabinda (Bd)]

Wurangbila *n.* swampy place north of Mt Alford, also the name of a Stradbroke location between Tuleenderly Creek and Wallen Wallen Creek slightly north of Waran Gamari. Stradbroke location named by Balun.giny (Bn). [Woorong Piller (Bn); Woorang-pilla (Ha)] *See:* **Balun.giny**; **-bila**.

wurar *adv.* distant. [wurrar (T)]

wurungali *adj; n.* wicked. *incorporates* -gali 'very'. [woorooncullia (Lg)]

Y – y

yaa *v.* talk, say. [yarleem (Bl); ya (Ja); ya, ea, eu (Lg); ya, yā (R); yā (Wa)] *See:* **wulara**.

yabar₁ *n.* kurrajong. [yepper (D); uppar (Le); yabarba (S)]

yabar₂ *n.* bucket, vessel. [yuppar (R); yŭp'par 'Bucket. (a coined word.)' (Wa)] *See:* **nyugum**; **wundal**.

Yabarba *n.* Helidon. *lit.* yabar-ba 'kurrajong place'. [Yabarba (M); Yabarba 'kurrajong' (S)] *See:* **-ba⁴**; **yabar¹**.

yabarin *n.* west. [Yarbarine (Be)] *See:* **junggai¹**; **wiyan¹**.

yabun *n.* milky mangrove. *[Excoecaria agallocha]*. *Anth:* roots very strong and used for boomerang making; milky sap causes temporary blindness (MMEIC). [yubboon (We)] *See:* **baragany¹**; **birban**; **gawan-gawan²**; **janji**; **jirabang¹**.

yaga *v.* do, make, work. origin of English yakka 'work'. [yacker (Bl); yuggi, yuggar, yeaca (Ha); yakka (Ja); yaga, yacca (Lg); yugā, yakka (R); yak'ka, yang'ga (Wa)]

yagany *v.* *Variant:* **yaga.** heal. [yuggān, yuggai, yugai (R)]

yagara₁ *Variant:* **yagar.** used only in freshwater Yagara. *neg.* no, not. [yagar (E); jagara (H); yuggera (Ha); yugar, yagar (Ja); yagara (L); yagarra (Le); yagar, yagara, yagarah, yagana (Lg); yaggār; Yuggera (M); guggaar 'Turrubul negative' (P); yugar (R); yūg'ar (Wa)] *See:* **jandai¹**; **munjan¹**.

Yagara₂ *n.* Yuggera, language spoken from the Great Dividing Range to Stradbroke (Bell 1937). [yagar (E); jagara (H); yuggera (Ha); yugar, yagar (Ja); yagara (L); yagarra (Le); yagar, yagara, yagarah, yagana (Lg); yaggār, Yuggera (M); guggaar (P); yugar (R); yūg'ar (Wa)] *See:* **Durubal¹**; **yagara¹**; **Yagarabal**.

Yagarabal *n.* Yuggerabal, speakers of Yagara. [Yugararpul (Bell 1934); Yurruah Pull, Yurrual Pul (Bn); jagarabal (H); Yug-ger-a-bool (Harper 1894); Yugarabul (Wa)] *See:* **-bal**; **Durubal¹**; **Yagara²**; **yagara¹**.

yagarabu *neg.* never, not at all. *lit.* yagara=bu 'definitely not'. [yagarapoo, yagarapo (Lg); yugarpo, yugārpo (R)] *See:* **=bu²**; **yagara¹**.

Yagubui *n.* man's name. [Yagoboi (N)]

yagui *n.* bandicoot. [yaggo-i (Ja); yaye (Le); yagoe (Lg); yackiel (Ln); yagooi (M); yagooi (W); yāgoi (Wa)]

Yagujai *n.* woman's name. [Yaggojay (W)]

yaja *quant.* first. [yutta (Ja); yutta (R); yul'la (Wa)] *See:* ganyara¹.

yalabin *n.* native raspberry. *Anth:* edible (FNSI). [yalabin (MMEIC)] *See:* gubu-guburan; malgam.

Yalaga *n.* place on Stradbroke between Dunwich and Wallen Wallen Creek. [Yulogga (Bn)] named by Balun.giny (Bn). *See:* Balun.giny.

yalingbila *n.* whale. [yullingbillar (We)]

Yali-yali *n.* man's name. [Yulliyally (M)]

yamal *v. Variant:* **yama.** scold. [yammul (Lg)]

Yamyi *n.* woman's name. [Yumb-yee (CW)]

yandany *Variant:* **yanda.** *v.* fear. [yandahnya (M); yandain, yundum (R)]

yandina *n.* small place of water. [yandinna (M)]

yangan₁ *n.* dugong. *[Dugong dugon]*. *Anth:* dugong rib bones were used as clapping sticks to accompany songs (MMEIC). [joungan (B); yungan, yūngun (Ja); jaŋan (H); yūngun (R); yungan (W); yun'gŭn (Wa); yungun, zungun (We)] *See:* bagirang; bujumbiriba¹; guranban; gurubul.

Yangan₂ *n.* Yangan, Logan's Vale. [Yangan (Yerrilee 1927)]

yangbang *adv.* afar. [yūngbāng (Ja)] *See:* daba.

yanggabara *n.* hostel, place where you may stay. [jaŋgabara (H)]

yanggar *n.* south. [yung-gar (M); yun'gŭr (Wa)] *See:* buran; mamuum.

yanggu *adj.* stiff. [yanku (L)]

yan.gua *adj; adv.* slow, slowly. [yancoa (M)] *See:* gandandi.

yaniri *v.* want. [yanēri (Ja); yanēri (R); yan'erī (Wa)] *See:* maun.ga; naruida; wangal.

yanmana *v.* run (of water), flood. [hoomah (Lg); yanmunna (M)] *See:* dabilyanmana; ngumar.

Yanmandany *n.* possibly Lawnton Pocket. [Yun Munday (Bd)] *lit.* yanmana-dany 'where it floods' or 'where (water) runs'. *See:* -dany; yanmana.

yara₁ *n.* spotted gum. *Anth:* growths contain water (DF); when in flower, possums are fat; burnt wood produces smoke that menstruating women should avoid (Wi). *[Corymbia sp.]*. [yura (M); yurra (R); yur'a (Wa)] *See:* gurdir; ngurgurga.

yara₂ *v.* swim, fly. [yeri (Ha); yūru, urooela (Ja); yūru (R); yur'a (Wa)] *See:* bugi.

Yara₃ *n.* Redcliffe area with spotted gums. [Yura (Bd)] *lit.* 'spotted gum'. *See:* yara¹.

yaraba *adv.* eventually. [yarrepo (Ja)] *See:* barany; juwanin.

yarabaan *n.* sea. *incorporates* baan 'salty'. [yarrabane (Ln)] *See:* baan; bamirigari; burugara; dabilbaan; dagan¹; wara¹; yara².

Yaraga *n.* man's name. [Yarraka (S)]

yaragal *n.* evening, sunset. [yurragul (Be); yaragal (L)] *See:* biigibiribi; jalu-jalu; ngunu; nulbu-nulbu.

Yaral *n.* Yerrol Creek at Two Mile. [Yarral (CW)]

yaraman *n.* horse. from NSW language; may mean 'big teeth'. *[Equus ferus caballus]*. [yarraman (Bl); erymun (Fi); jaraman (H); yarra man (Ha); yereman, yerenam (L); yarraman (Ln); yaraman (R)]

yaran *n.* beard. [yeren (Cl); yerang (Fi); jaran (H); yeren (Ja); yeren (L); yerreng (La); yaren (Lg); yeraan (Ln); yarran-yarran (M); yeran 'whisker' (N); yeren, yarran, yurra (R); yarren (Su); yeren (Th); yeren (W); yer'an (Wa)]

yarang₁ *n.* sand. [yarrone (Cl); yarun (E); yarun (E); jarun (H); yārūn 'dust', yarun 'hunting ground', yarrone, yarung 'sand' (Ja); yeranga (L); yarun (Lg); yārūn, yarung 'dust' (R); yār'ŭng (Wa); yarrong (We)] *See:* **mulula.**

Yarang₂ *n.* Yeronga. *lit.* 'sand'; possibly named by whites. [yarung (Ba); yarrone (Cl); yarun (E); jarun (H); Yeranga (L); yarun (Lg); yārūn, yarung (R); yār'ŭng (Wa); yarrong (We)] *See:* **yarang**¹.

Yarangbaan *n.* sandy stretch between Brisbane and Ipswich. *possibly lit.* yarangbaan 'hot sands'. [Yerongpan (L); Yarangpan (Wa)] *See:* **baan; -bany; yarang**¹.

yarangmulu *n.* sandstone. *lit.* yarangmulu 'sand stone'. [yarongmulu (Ca)] *See:* **mulu**¹; **yarang**¹.

yarang-yarang *n.* gunpowder. *lit.* 'sand-sand'. [yerang yerang (Lg)] *See:* **yarang**¹.

yaran-yaran *adj.* weak. [yarran-yarran (M)] *See:* **budung; manmal.**

yarara *n.* forest oak. *[Allocasuarina sp.].* [yarara (Ha)] *See:* **buranda; gundiba; ganjil.**

yari *n.* water herb. *[Nelumbo nucifera].* [yurri, yerra (R)] *See:* **jinbura; yigibin**¹; **yigilu.**

yaribu *n.* canoe. [yarrepo (Cl)] *See:* **dingga; gundul²**.

yaring *n.* crayfish. [yerring (Ln)]

Yarrawonga *n.* Yarrawonga. from English 'yarran' and 'wonga' borrowed from W Qld languages; named by whites. [Courier-Mail (1936)]

yarul₁ *n.* false rattan, supplejack. *[Flagellaria indica].* *Anth:* slender tough vine used for climbing (FNSI) [yurol (B); yurol (Ca); yerol 'malacca cane' (Ja); yurol (M); yurol (Ro); yerool (W); yū'ral (Wa)]

Yarul₂ *n.* creek at Myora. *lit.* 'false rattan'; named by Balun.giny (Bn). [yurol (B); yarul (Ba); Urul 'Two Mile' (Bn); yerrool (CW); yurol (M); yurol (Ro); Yerrol, Yerrool (S); yerool (W); yū'ral (Wa)] *See:* **Balun.giny; yarul**¹.

Yatala *n.* Yatala. *lit.* 'swampy' from a S Aus language; named by whites. [Courier-Mail (1936)]

yaugira *n.* lace monitor. from Yugambeh yawgar (Sh). *[Varanus varius].* [yawkerra (Ln)] *See:* **bara**¹; **giwa; walmuram**¹.

yawai₁ *excl.* yes. [yauai (Bd); yowi (Bl); ya-why (Cl); yawoi (E); ɟawai, jawa, juai, jawai (H); yo (Ha); yoai, ya-why, wawoy (Ja); yo (L); yawoi, yaou, yarowai, euingha, iugah (Lg); ya-wai, yo yoi (M); yoai (R); ya-why (Su); yawoi (W); yāwai (Wa)]

yawai₂ *excl.* goodbye. [yauai (Bd); yowi (Bl); yawoi (E); ɟawai, jawa, juai, jawai (H); yo (Ha); yoai, ya-why, wawoy (Ja); yo (L); yawoi, yaou, yarowai, euingha, iugah (Lg); ya-wai, yo yoi (M); yoai (R); ya-why (Su); yawoi (W); yāwai (Wa)] *See:* **guba²**.

yawani *adj.* hot. [yawahnee (Cl); yawahnee (Ja)] *See:* **nyangga.**

yibaru *n.* face. [eeboroo (M)] *See:* **ngangalinga; nguwar.**

yibiri₁ *v.* put something down, lay something down. [yebri (Ja); yebery (Ln); yibri (M); yeb'ri (Wa)] *See:* **wura**¹.

Yibiri₂ *n.* Yebri Creek. *lit.* 'put something down'. [Yibri (S)] *See:* **yibiri**¹.

yigi *n.* also, too. [ikki (Ja); ikki (R)]

yigibin₁ *n.* freshwater reed. *[Phragmites australis].* [yīkkibbin (Ja); yikibbin, yekkabin (M); yīkibbin (R)] *See:* **-bin; jinbura; nambur**¹; **yigilu; yari.**

Yigibin₂ *n.* Ekibin. *lit.* 'freshwater reeds'. [Yekkabin (S)] *See:* **yigibin.**

yigil *adj; n; v.* cold, ice, be cold. [yigill (Be); ĕtōndo (G); yeegil (Ha); yeegil (Hi); igil (Ja); yigil (L); wiggil 'ice, cold' (Lg); īgil, ikki (R); i'gil, yi'gil (Wa)] *See:* **dan-dan.**

yigilgan *n.* winter. *lit.* 'cold time'. [yeegilcun (Hi); yigilkan, yigilgan (L); younggurba (Lg)] *See:* **-gan; yigil.**

yigilu *n.* water reed. *[Phragmites australis].* [yigilu (Ba)] *See:* **jinburu**; **nambur**; **yari**; **yigibin.**

Yigumbumba *n.* district near Alex McKay's settlement, Upper Teviot. [Yeegum-bumpa (Ha)] *See:* -ba⁴.

yila *n; v.* smell, stench. [ialoh (Lg); eelim (M); yiluh (N)] *See:* **buga**¹.

yilal *n.* crystal. [yellal (Lg)] *See:* **daginy**; **gundir.**

Yilgunun *n.* woman's name. [Yeelgunun (Ha)]

yilim *n.* forehead. [yīlim (Ja); elim (Lg); eelim (M); yelimm (N); yilim, yīlim (R); yelim (W); yi'lam (Wa); yillim (We)] *See:* **mijiri.**

yilung *adj.* straight. [yeloong (Lg)] *See:* **jubui**; **nganiyiba.**

yima *n.* grey kangaroo (female). *[Macropus giganteus].* [yima, yimma (R)] *See:* **gara**²; **giriwan**; **guruuman**; **mari**¹.

yimban₁ *n.* bulrush. *[Typha sp.].* [yimbun (Ja); yimboon 'edible fern' (Lg); yimbun (M)] *See:* **yimbanban.**

Yimban₂ *n.* lagoon on Yebri Creek east of Redcliffe Rd. *lit.* 'bull-rush'. [Yimbun (S)] *See:* **yimban**¹.

yimbanban *n.* edible part of bulrush. [yinbunban (Bd)] *Anth:* edible; perhaps made into damper (Bd); *lit.* yimban-ban 'from bulrush'. *See:* -**ban**; **yimban**¹.

Yindili *n.* woman's name. [Yeendellie (M)]

yingang *adj.* new. [yingang (T)] *See:* **baranyba**¹.

yini *v.* bring. [yenee (Ha)] *See:* **ga**; **wujan.**

yinil *n.* small creek, gully. [yeana (Ca); eagnell (Ln); yinnil (M); yin-nell (P); yin'nel (Wa)] *See:* **bili**; **bijara**; **waril**¹.

yinjagu *interrog.* where to? [jinɡagu (H)] *See:* =**gu**; **wanyagu.**

yiran *n.* hoar frost. [ieeren (Lg)] *See:* **miwil**; **wala.**

Yiria *n.* man's name. [Yer rare (Ha)]

yirimau *n.* mouth of bees' nest. [yeridmou 'wild bees' nest' (Bd); yeridmou (Ja); yer'idmou (Wa)]

yirimbin *n.* basket. [yirimbin (Ja); yirimbin (M); yirimbin (R)] *See:* **banggam.**

yirin *n.* sand crab, mud crab. [yirin (Ja); erin (Lg); yeerin (W); yir'in (Wa)] *See:* **winyam.**

Yirubin *n.* King Island. [Yerubin (CW); Yeroobin (M); Yerubin, Erobin (S); Yerubin (W)] *See:* -**bin.**

yirul₁ *n.* branch, branches. [yerool (Lg)] *See:* **dal**²; **nguruwa.**

Yirul₂ *n.* Hamilton. *lit.* 'branches'. [Yerool (M)] *See:* **yirul**¹.

yirunbal *Variant:* **yirunba.** *v.* whistle. [yeroonbul (Lg)]

yiyara *n.* corroboree. [yiyara (J)] *See:* **ganjiil**; **gawabiri**; **ngari**²; **yuwar.**

yugai₁ *Variant:* **yugai-yugai.** *n.* fern-like herb. *[Astrostichum sp.].* [yugi-yugi (Ha); eugoi 'fern' (Lg); yūgai (R); yug'ai (Wa)] *See:* **durbin**¹.

Yugai₂ *n.* Yugar railway station. *lit.* 'fern-like herb'; possibly named by whites. [Yugar (Q)] *See:* **yugai**¹.

yugam *n.* seaside sword bean. *[Canavalia rosea].* [yugam (Ja); yugam (M); yūg'am (Wa)] *See:* **bulumbir**; **giji**; **magarabal.**

yugari *n.* eugarie, donax. *[Plebidonax deltoides].* *Anth:* very sweet shellfish, traditional food (MMEIC). [nugire (E); juguri (H); yugari (Ja); yugari (Ro); yūg'ārī (Wa)] *See:* **gijigagari.**

yugu₁ *demonstrative.* there (medial). [jugu (H)] *See:* **gaa**; **naam.**

yugu₂ *Variant:* **yugu-yugu.** *n.* fish, pike. [yooko-yooko, yoocoh (M)]

yuguny *Variant:* **yugunybin.** *n.* father's father. [juguɲ (H); yu-gun-ting (Ha); yungunpinn (N); yūinginpin 'grandfather' (Wa)]

Yulanggin₁ *n.* Carney's Hill and Creek, south of Boonah. [Yu-lungin (Ha); Yoolanggan (M)]

Yulanggin₂ *n.* woman's name. [Yu-lungin (Ha); Yoolanggan (M)]

yulany *n.* feathers. from Yugambeh yulany 'hide' (Sh). [eulwen (Lg)]

Yulubarabi *n.* Yoolooburrabee, hill behind Myora. *lit.* 'people of the sand and the sea' (QYAC). [Yoolooburrabee (Redland City Council 2023a)]

yunggariiba *n.* flood tide. *incorporates* gariiba 'tide'. [younggurba (E); younggurba (Ja); yungoorpa (Lg); yoong-goorpa (M)] *See:* **gariiba**; **jargariiba**.

yunggiri *n.* reeds for weaving. [yungere, yunggaire (MMEIC)] *See:* **mun.ga**.

Yuninya *n.* woman's name. [Yooneenya (M)]

yunma *v.* sleep. [yunma (MMEIC)] *See:* **bugany**; **waja**.

yun-yun *n.* skin, fat. [yoonyoon (M)] *See:* **damil**; **dinggal¹**; **gali²**; **mii²**; **mugan¹**.

yura *excl.* hello, welcome. [jura (H)] *See:* **wi balga**.

yuragin *n.* dingo. [euragin (Ln)] *[Canis familiaris]*. *See:* **miri**; **ngagam²**; **ngal-ngal**.

yuri₁ *n.* meat. [juri (H)] *See:* **jam**; **murang**.

yuri₂ *n.* totem. [juri (H)] *See:* **jurbil**.

yuwan *n.* snake, serpent. [juan (H); yuun (Ja); yuen 'small snake-like lizard' (Le); yioogurra, joanchee (M); yūun, yūwung (R)] *See:* **bui²**; **guda²**; **juumgu**; **mulumgal**.

yuwanji *n.* scrub ghost. [juangɟi (H)]

yuwar *n.* corroboree. [you-ara (Ha); yowar (Ja); yanerwille (Lg); yowar (M); yowar (R); yōw'ar, yau'ar (Wa)] *See:* **ganjiil**; **gawabiri**; **ngari²**; **yiyara**.

Yuwargara *Variant:* **Yuwar.** *n.* corroboree ground near Breakfast Creek. *Anth:* source of English 'Enoggera'; *lit.* yuwar-gara 'celebrate corroboree'. [yuwar (Ba); yow-eggara, yooggera (CW); karlippa you-ara (Ha); Yowaggara (M); yowar (R)] *See:* **ngari²**; **yuwar**.

2.3. English–Yagara Finder List

Notes on the finder list

Most of the information in the Yagara–English dictionary in Section 2.2 is not repeated in the finder list in Section 2.3. The finder list consists only of English words with their best-attested Yagara close equivalents. For more information on a Yagara word located using the finder list, the user is advised to look up the word in the Yagara–English dictionary.

Words with only one attestation, or which appear to be recent borrowings from other languages, are generally excluded from the English-Yagara finder list. They are, however, included if they are the only recorded word for a concept. If the user is interested in the less well-attested and borrowed words, these have their own entries in the Yagara–English dictionary and are additionally cross-referenced under the better-attested words for a concept. Words with uncertain definitions, such as placenames that designate unknown places, are not included in the finder list, but are listed in the Yagara–English dictionary. Suffixes and clitics are not included in the finder list. Yagara nominal suffixes are discussed in Sections 1.5.2–1.5.4, verbal suffixes are listed in Sections 1.6.2–1.6.3, and clitics are described in Section 1.8.

Some finder list entries include subentries, as in the entry for 'boy':

boy, **bujiri**
  baby, **mulam**
  uninitiated, **gumingguny**

Here, the general term for 'boy' is *bujiri*, whereas the subentries denote subcategories of 'boy'. For example, 'baby boy' is specifically *mulam*.

A – a

Aboriginal, **guri**
above, **wangandi**
across, **giram**
afar, **yangbang**
Albert River group, **Bunurajali**
alcohol, **gung**
alive, **milbul**, **milbulbu**
all, **ngambila**
almost, **jigandi**
also, **yigi**
always, **nulu**
Amity-area hill, **Miriginba**
Amity-area location, **Biran-biranba**, **Jabaninba**
Amity Point, **Bulan**
Amity Point language, **Gambalgari**
Amity Point location, **Daguwi**
ancestor, mythical, **bajiram**
and, **nga**
angry, **gula**, **wagara**
ankle, **wulu**
annoyed, **nubal**
another, **garuba**
ant,
    bulldog, **mugara**
    green-headed, **murin**
    jack jumper, **baigan**
    white, **giwarang**
anthill, **danmurin**
ant's nest, **bigunjur**
anus, **mabi**
appear, **nambany**
area, in the, **ngurdi**
arm,
    forearm, **daaran**, **wayaba**
    upper, **nyama**
around, **wandal**
ashamed, **mangin**

ashes, **buba**
Ashgrove, **Galindabin**
astonished, **baguru**
aunt,
    maternal, **bujang**
    paternal, **maran**
Aunty, **Maran**
awake, **milbanya**
axe, **gulmang**, **mugim**

B – b

baby, **jajam**, **nyamal**
bachelor, **buwadiya**
back of body, **dugal**, **mabara**
bad, **wali**, **warang**
Bald Hills, **Wiyanba**
bandicoot, **yagui**
    type of, **gima**
Banyo, **Banyu**
Barambin-area glade, **Walan**
bare, **win-win**
Bartley's Hill, **Gara-garanganbili**
basket, **yirimbin**
    small, **banggam**
bat,
    flying fox, **giraaman**
    microbat, **biling**
bathe, **garanba**
Batjala, **Bajala**
battle, **dulan**
    ritualised, **bulan-bulan**
bay, **budiri**
beard, **yaran**
Beaudesert, **Diraranbal**
beautiful, **bujari**, **marumba**
bed, **wura**
bee,
    carpenter, **jalaman**
    English, **nagi**

large dark, **gila**
little black, **mabi**
native, **banjin**
small black, **guja**
smallest, **gabai**
beer, **bira**
bees' nest, mouth of, **yirimau**
beetle, **bingging**
behind, **gurabi**
believe, **ngui**, **winanga**
belly, **digiri**
belt, possum, **magamba**
Ben Lomond, **Banbara**
bend, **bulimari**
between, **birin**
beyond, **jalagada**
big, **gurumba**
Bippo Penbean, **Bibu Binbiyan**
Bird Island, **Mabinbila**
bird, **daunbin**
  beach stone-curlew, **garal**
  bellbird, **jam-jam**
  big black cormorant, **bigargin**
  bittern, little, **winyiba**
  black cockatoo, **garara**, **balan**
  black swan, **muruguji**
  boobook, **gum-gum**
  Brahminy kite, **bugawan**
  brolga, **gariyagan**, **gundurgan**, **junggi**
  brown hawk, **gulurur**
  bush stone-curlew, **buwalgan**
  butcher, **bilba**
  channel-bill cuckoo, **durar**
  cockatoo's crest, **bila-bila**
  collared sparrowhawk, **minggal-minggal**
  crow, **waa-waa**, **wagam**
  curlew sandpiper, **gubalbin**
  duck, Australian wood, **ngau**

  duck, Pacific black, **naara**
  dusky moorhen, **jamgam**
  eastern koel, **duuwung**
  eastern osprey, **gangga**
  emerald dove, **gun-gunwan**
  emu, **nguruny**
  Eurasian coot, **ginbin**
  flycatcher, **duilgal**
  forest kingfisher, **dinin.giri**
  friarbird, **galgulang**
  frigate, **gijaambalgin**
  ibis, **murumurul**
  jabiru, **gilil-gilil**
  king parrot, **bilin-bilin**, **ngangan**
  kookaburra, **gaguwan**, **ganggun-gun**
  large kingfisher, **gargun**
  lyrebird, **galbuny**
  magpie, **jarwang**, **mirum**
  magpie goose, **wularaba gariyagan**
  musk lorikeet, **bir**, **mirin**
  nankeen kestrel, **gababanguru**
  owl, night, **gingga**
  owl, powerful, **nyinggal**
  owl, type of, **duribang**
  owlet-nightjar, **wumanggan**
  oystercatcher, **gibing-gibing**
  pallid cuckoo, **galambin**
  peewee, **balim**
  pelican, **buluwalung**, **gulugan**
  pheasant coucal, **bun-bun**
  pied currawong, **gulambarun**
  quail, **duwir**
  rainbow lorikeet, **bilin**
  regent bowerbird, **biigi-biigi**
  rose-crowned fruit dove, **baraabun**
  rosella parrot, **diluny-diluny**
  scarlet robin, **gin-gin**

sea eagle, **din.gal**, **miriginba**
seagull, **diriiri**
sulphur-crested cockatoo,
gaiyara
swallow, **bingal-bingal**
swamphen, **wagi-wagi**
turkey, **wagun**
type of seabird, **mamugamugan**
wedge-tailed eagle, **duwai**, **jibal**
willie wagtail, **jin.giri**
wompoo fruit-dove, **mamugal**
wonga pigeon, **gulun**
birdsong, **gunganya**
bite, **baada**
black, **gurung**
blacken one's face, **gaji**
blade, bone, **walangan**
blind, **milbang**, **milngundu**,
milwali
blind people, **walibajin**
blood, **gawan**
blubber, **biran**
Blue Lake, **Gabura**
blunt, **ngundu**
blunt-edged, **dambil**
Boggo, **Bulagu**
boil v., **duburugang**
boiling, **waliba**
bone, **jirban**
book, **muyum**
boomerang, **jirabang**
  returning, **baragany**
  toy, **birban**
Boonah location, **Buraadangal**
Boondall, **Bundal**
Booroodabin, **Burudabin**
boot, shoe, **jinagaba**
bora, **burul**
both, **bulabu**
bowels, **danggan**

Bowen Bridge Road hill,
Gilbumba
boy, **bujiri**
  baby, **mulam**
  uninitiated, **gumingguny**
boys, **duwangjin**
Bracalba, **Baragalba**
branch, **yirul**
branches, small, **nguruwa**
bread, **buridan**
break v., **banggany**, **gama**
Breakfast Creek-area corroboree
ground, **Yuwargara**
Breakfast Creek Point,
Ganinbinbila
breast, **ngamu**
breath, **nguru**
breathe, **bui**
Bremer River, **Ngararar**
Bribie Island, **Burabi**, **Jundubira**
Bribie Island group, **Dulangbari**,
Ningi-Ningi
bring, **balgal**, **yini**
bring back, **malbaribu**
Brisbane, **Miyanjin**, **Ngumbi**
Gurumba
Brisbane River,
  lower part, **Buruguwa**,
  Jirwamban
  upper part, **Maiwar**
Broadwater, **Miganaba**
broken, **girawali**
brother,
  elder, **ngabang**
  in-law, **gabagiri**
  younger, **duwanggal**
Brown Lake, **Bamira**
Bruckner's Mt, **Jagiri**
bucket, **nyugum**
Bulimba-area hill, **Namgaran**

Bulimba Creek, **Dabai**
Bulimba ferry, west, **Jin.gilingbin**
Bulimba river, **Dagalaba**
bullroarer,
  large, **bagaram**
  small, **wabalgan**
Bundamba Creek, **Bandaanba**
Bunjurgen, **Banjurgan**
Bunya group, **Waba**
bunyip, **jaagany, warajam**
burn, **ngunguma**
Burnett's Creek-area location,
Duwunan
bushes, **gudal**
bushfire, **warabana**
busy, **baragal**
butterfly, **balimbir**
buttocks, **jumar, naral**

C – c

Cabbage Tree Creek, **Digam**
Caboolture, **Gabuljar**
call off, **banggabadi**
camp, **dimany, giba, ngagamwaga**
camping place, **jalubaluba**
Canaipa, **Ganaiba**
Canaipa Point, **Dagabin**
Canalpin, **Ganalbin**
candle, **nagum-nagum**
Canning Downs, **Guragubi**
canoe, **gundul**
Canoe Creek group, **Garbanban**
Capalaba, **Gabalaba**
Cape Moreton, **Gunimba**
Capemba, **Gabingba**
Carney's Creek-area bush pub,
Dariganygali
Carney's Creek-area location,
Guburabil

Carney's Creek crossing, **Dirim**
Carney's Hill and Creek,
Yulanggin
carry, **burgunda**
cart, **wiilbara**
cat, **milgal**
celebrate, **ngari**
Cemetery Creek, **Birindaliba**
central, **jiladu**
charcoal, **gurung**
chase, **gawany**
cheek, **jaagul, wanggal**
chest, **dandara**
chew, **daldu**
Chiggil Chiggil Creek, **Jigal-jigal**
childless, **bujiriyagara**
children, **gin-gin**
chin, **waul**
Chinatown, **Gamgagulum**
chisel, **jindan**
cicada, **dinbir**
clam, **gijigagari**
clay,
  red, **guji**
  wet, **dalang**
  white, **bandu**
clean, **miliri**
Cleveland, **Nyandili**
Cleveland Point, **Ban.ginbany**
climb, **wandima**
cloak, **garang-garang**
  possum, **gubi garang-garang**
clock, **biigigaba**
clothes, **garang-garang**
cloud, **galan, guwaa**
coat, **biba**
cockle, **nurung**
cohabitation, **bulagan, mibanja**
cold, **dan-dan, yigil**
  overly, **gaura-gaura**

come, **balgal**
come here!, **ngagam-ngagam**
comfortable, **mangun**
completely, **jagu**
Condamine River group, **Gambal**
consent, **nganbadagu**
Coochin Coochin Homestead,
Bulban
Coochin Station, **Gujin-gujin**
Coomera group, **Balun.giny**
Coopooroo, **Gubuuru**
coral, **gajur**
corpse, **bijar**
corner, **waya**
corroboree, **yuwar**
cough, **galubal**
country, **gira**, **jara**
cousin, cross,
   female, **wumanggarigan**
   male, **wumanggari**
cousin, parallel,
   female, elder, **jajing**
   female, younger, **manganggal**
   male, elder, **ngabang**
   male, younger, **duwanggal**
cover something, **gunggal**
cow, **bula**
crab, **naluru**
   sand or mud, **yirin**
   soldier, **winyam**
crayfish, **yaring**
crazy, **binawali**
creek, **bili**, **waril**, **yinil**
crocodile, **ganyara**
crooked, **barang**, **bunbar**, **wandan**
crowd, **garubabany**
crumb, **dalgal**
crystal, quartz, **daginy**, **gundir**
Cubberla Creek, **Gabala**

Cuchiemudlo Island, **Guji-gujiba**,
Gujimulu
Currigee, **Garaji**
cut, **galgal**

D – d

Dakabin railway station, **Dagabin**
dance *v.*, **gali**
dare, **gujan**
darkness, **gurung-gurung**
daughter, **nyaringgan**
   in-law, **nguwan.gingan**
dawn, **barabil**
daytime, **wugalibila**
dead, **bang**, **ganggiri**
deaf, **binangundu**
deck of boat, **guraguda**
Deebing Creek, **Dibing**
desire, **muyan**
devil, **jagun**
die, **baluny**, **ganggirbany**
dilly bag, **bunbi**, **dili**, **gulai**
dingo, **ngal-ngal**
distant, **wurar**
dive, **buwaiya**
Dividing Range, **Ganul**
do, **yaga**
dog, tame, **miri**
don't!, **wana**
don't!!, **wanarara**
door, **bangaba**
downhill, **wigaliba**
dragonfly, **ngurin-ngurin**
dream, **baibun**
drip *v.*, **gajiru**
drop of liquid, **galga**
drought, **ganajara**
drown, **wanangin**
drunk, **jarangbina**

Dugandan camping ground, **Bibu-bibu**

Dugandan lagoon, **Buriimbam**

Dugandan railway station, **Gugin. gambal**

dugong, **yangan**

  intestines and skirt, **guranban**

  tasty part of, **gurubul**

  young female, **bujumbiriba**

Dunwich, **Guumbi**

Durubal-speaking group, **Bibuban**

E – e

Eagle Farm location, **Buduwar, Damgaiba**

Eagle St area, **Narang**

Eagle St-area hill, **Bilagal**

ear, **bina**

earnest, **digan**

earth, **jara**

  white, **buba jara**

eat, **dal**

eats a lot, **digirgali**

echidna, **gagara**

eel, **jagan**

  coral, **jigagara**

  sand, **jila**

  silver, **juruny**

egg, **gang-gang**

eh?, **wigu**

Ekibin, **Yigibin**

elbow, **gundi**

Elder, **darwan**

  female, **maran.gan, Maran**

  male, **Gaming**

employed, **burumbigan**

empty, **dulugamari**

end, **dabi**

enjoy, **dujin**

Enoggera, **Bulurjambin**

enter, **gurin**

erect *adj.*, **banda**

eugarie, **yugari**

evening, **biigibiribi, nulbu-nulbu**

eventually, **juwanin, yaraba**

excrement, **guna**

  dog's, **duwal**

  infant's, **majira**

excrete, **gunamali**

  uncontrollably, **gunabila**

eye, **mil**

eyeball, **danggal**

eyebrow, **midildin**

eyelash, **milbi**

eyelashes, **jinduru-jinduru**

F – f

fall *v.*, **ban.gin, garany**

family, **babimin**

far, **daba**

fart, **bujing**

fat, **dinggal, mugan**

father, **bing**

  in-law, **wumang**

fear, **jabu, yandany**

feathers, **yulany**

female *adj.*, **ngawur**

fence *n.*, **waru**

few, **dinari**

fibula, **girgal**

fight, **baga**

fight each other, **bagali**

finger, **galil**

fingernail, **gilan**

fire, **jalu**

fire starter, **burumbin jalu yaga**

fire time, **jalu-jalu**

firefly, **dalgi**

firestick, **jaludiya**
firewood, **diniri**
first, **yaja**
fish *v.*, **gilan-gilan**
fishhook, **gilan-gilan**
Fisherman Island, **Ngandagal**
fish, **guiyar, juwan**
  black bream, **dun.gala**
  bony bream, **ngalan**
  bream, **ginbun, man.gal**
  bullrout, **bilunga**
  catfish, **wargan**
  catfish, freshwater, **bigun, ngamarigara**
  cod, **duguu**
  diamond, **dulbang**
  eastern sea garfish, **juunburu**
  fantail mullet, **dilgam**
  john dory, **gunambarang**
  like a trevally, **gulbural**
  meal made of mullet, **gabujan**
  mullet, **ngandagal**
  mulloway, **buigum**
  parrot, **bulwar**
  part of mullet, **gumbal**
  perch, **migim**
  pike, **yugu**
  ray, **banggu**
  rock cod, **gujung**
  saltwater, type of, **bilanbin, guru-guru**
  snapper, **bimba**
  sole, **nugunja**
  tailor, **bunba**
  trevally, **janbilbin**
  whiting, **burang**
  yellowtail kingfish, **dirambila**
  yellowtail scad, **dulbi-dulbi**
five, **majanbula**
flame, **gujam**

flea, **gujiwang**
flesh, **baigal-baigal**
Fletcher's waterhole, **Garanbang**
Flinders Peak, **Baranggul**
Flinders Peak group, **Mawung**
flood, **yanmana**
Flying Fox Creek, **Juruny-jurunyba**
fly, **dudambara**
  bee fly, **gunidar**
  common, **bululum**
  sandfly, **ginin**
food, **dalgaba**
foot, **jina**
footprint, **jarajina**
forbidden, **danbal**
forehead, **yilim**
forest, **gadigal**
forested country, **widan**
Fortitude Valley, **Namirala**
Fortitude Valley creek, **Garabi**
Fortitude Valley lagoon, **Daran**
Fortitude Valley waterhole, **Galinggral**
four, **bula-bula**
friend, **gimunggan, nyungin**
  female, **jimbaljin**
  male, **banji**
frog,
  bullfrog, **wagal**
  green and yellow, **jaraagil**
  type of, **gubang, naji**
frost, **wala**
  full, **biduru, bila, ngumburu**
  hoar, **miwil, yiran**
full to the mouth, **damburu-bila**
fungus, yellow, **burganbalam**

G – g

game,
   cat's cradle, **waru-waru**
   played with a ball, **bara-bara**
   played with blunt spears,
   dambil-dambil
   played with boomerangs, **birban-birban**
   played with spears, **mari-mari**
   played with throwing sticks,
   muruny-muruny
gammon, **gujal**
Garden Island, **Dindaba**
Geebung, **Dalandala**
get *v.*, **many**
get out of the way!, **nya nya**
ghost, **magui**
girl, **gin**
   baby, **nyaramgan**
   little, **gilalan, gingali**
   no-good, **wanga**
give, **ga, wujan**
glider, **banggu**
   sugar, **jiburu**
go, **nyan**
go home, **ganyagu**
go on, **guba**
go round about, **gulgilun.gin**
go up, **wanda**
Goat Island, **Guwaawiniwa**
God, **Bayami**
gold, **jan-jan**
gone, completely, **maladiri**
good, **marumba**
goodbye, **yawai**
Goodna, **Guna**
Gowanbal people, **Guwanbal**
go!, **nyala**
Grampian Hills, **Gajira-gajira**

Grandchester, **Gujabila**
grandfather,
   maternal, **najang**
   paternal, **yuguny**
grandmother,
   maternal, **baabang**
   paternal, **gaminggan**
Grantham-area location,
Guwaangumbi
greedy, **jan**
   very, **jan.gali**
Green Island, **Danggari, Milwaba**
grey headed, **guibila magul**
grind, **gina**
grow, **balgama, daran**
grub,
   cobra, **gambu, ganyi**
   witchetty, **jabam**
gum,
   from the spotted gum, **nguwuny**
   from wattle, **jirai**
gums of mouth, **diyagarany**
gun, **dululbin**
gunpowder, **yarang-yarang**

H – h

hailstone, **daraubang,
mugaramulu**
hair, **bundal**
   black, **magul gurung**
   body, **dinibau**
   head, **gabui**
   red, **magul gawan-gawan**
   white, **magul buba bundal**
half full, **dulu**
Hamilton, **Yirul**
Hamilton-area sandbank,
Murumurulbin
Hamilton location, **Miyanda**

hand, **mara**
hand signs, **mirimbal**
handle, **darun**
hang something, **duran**
Harper's Hill,
    high part, **Giwabin**
    lower part, **Juwanbin**
hat, **magulgaba**
Hay's Inlet, **Danggulba**
head, **bum-bum, magul**
headache, **malunda**
headband,
    dingo's tail, **gila**
    ornamental, **dinggil**
    vine, **baraban**
    yellow reed, **gaiyarbin**
heal, **yagany**
hear, **wunyi**
heart, **dagal**
Heaven, **Wangandi Biradi**
heavy, **nganan**
Helidon, **Yabarba**
Helidon spring, **Wunarajimi**
hello!, **wi balga, yura**
Hemmant, **Guwirmandadu**
here it is!, **gamagu**
here, proximal, **ngagam**
hey!, **wi**
he/she/they,
    ergative, **ngunyalu**
    nominative, **ngunyal**
hide, **damil**
hide oneself, **nguruman**
Highgate Hill, **Binanggurung**
high, very, **wangan-wangan**
hill, **duun**
hill water cataract, **bibuji**
him/her/them,
    accusative, **ngunyana**
    dative, **ngunyanu**

hip, **guni**
his/her/their, **ngunyanuba**
hit, **buma**
hole, **miir, wangga**
holes, full of, **miir-miir**
holy, **bani**
honorific, **bandar**
hornet, **marura**
horn, of cow, **nilga-nilga**
horse, **yaraman**
hostel, **yanggabara**
hot, **nyangga**
house, **ngumbi**
how many?, **minyambu**
how?, **ngan.gu**
Humpybong, **Ngumbi Bang**
hungry, **wayara**
hurry up!, **dabarama**
husband, **nyubanyja, nyugunbing**

I – i

I, **ngaja**
immediately, **baranybu**
impudent, **bagangali**
Indooropilly, **Nyindurubili**
Indooroopilly site, **Mirbaba**
in-law, **bugui**
inside, **dungala, ganul**
Ipswich, **Dalmar, Gujira**
Ipswich group, **Nunilbira, Warbai**
island, **jarbany**
itch, **ging-ging**

J – j

Jandai speaker(s), **Jandaiwal**
jawbone, **wanggaljirban**
Jeebropilly, **Jiburubili**
join, **madi**
joking around, **gindigan**

jump, **dalbany**
Jumpinpin Channel, **Jambinbin**

K – k

Kangaroo Mt, **Jarajil**
Kangaroo Point, **Ngulawara**
kangaroo rat, **wugalban**
  rufous, **barung**
kangaroo,
  grey, **mari**
  grey creek, **giriwan**
  old man, **guruuman**
  tree, **mabi**
Karragarra Island, **Gara-gara**
Kedron,
  lower, **Bindari**
  upper, **Bilijara**
Kenmore area, **Magil-magil**
Keperra, **Gibara**
Kerwin Swamp, **Balinabal**
kill, **ganggirma**
King Island, **Yirubin**
kiss, **nyubi**
Knapp's peak, **Migan**
knee, **buun**
kneecap, **walar**
knife, **junguru**
  edge, **barang**
  back of, **bumbal**
koala, **dumbiribi**, **marangbi**
Kobble Creek, **Gabul**
Kooralbyn, **Guralbang**
Koureyabba Creek, **Gurijaba**

L – l

lagoon, **wira-wira**
Laidley, **Milgaro**
Laidley Creek, **Gunanjigirara**
Lamb Island, **Ngujuru**

last, **ngadaliba**
laugh, **gindin**
Lawnton Pocket, **Yanmandany**
lazy, **gawanwalunbina**, **giyagara**
lead *v.*, **gubama**
leaf, **bunggara**, **gajal**
  dry, **wang**
leave behind, **galabi**, **ngura**
leech, scrub, **nyinduru**
left-handed, **waram**
leg,
  lower, **buyu**
  thigh, **darany**
let go, **wiya**
liar, **nyalanggali**
lie down, **dany**
lies, tell, **nyalang**
lies, telling of, **nyalanggan**
lift, **juwan**
light, **gidibila**
  artificial, **jalungai**
  mysterious, **jagi**
lightning, **danagany**, **maral**
lightweight, **dang-dang**, **wirui**
like (similar to), **ngamba**
like this!, **ganangur**
little, **biribi**, **narang**
Little Peak, **Jin-jinba**
live *v.*, **digi**, **ngun**
liver, **guna**
lizard,
  bearded dragon, **binanggurung**, **nyara**
  blue-tongued, **gubargan**
  frilled, **ginairanda**
  goanna, small type of, **bara**
  'goorka lizard', **biran**
  lace monitor, **giwa**
  marbled gecko, **dalbara**
  sand goanna, **walmuram**

water dragon, **magil**
lobster, **ngajagarara**
log, **bural**
Logan River-area confederacy,
Jibara
Logan's Vale, **Yangan**
long, **buruuwal**, **murul**
long ago, **galuma**
Long Pocket, **Duuwung**
Long Pocket caretakers, **Buwubira**
look, **mil-mil**
look after, **bajii**
lose, **baludiriyari**
lost, **dalang**
loud noise, **dulul**
louse, **ngul-ngul**
love, **gawan**
Luggage Point, **Burangba**
lung, **buguru**, **dalu**
lustful, **giyi**
Lytton, **Ngalungbin**

M – m

Macleay Island, **Jin.gumirja**
maggot, **danbar**
male *adj.*, **budai**
mantis, **ngaraang-ngaraang**
many, **milin**
man,
  Aboriginal, **jaan**
  black, **malara**
  full, **maja**
  gentleman, **garangam**
  white, **dagai**
  white men, **daranyjin**
  white, evil, **majari**
  with white beard, **dagai jaan**
  young, **mulagu**
  young, white, **baling**

youth, initiated, **giba**
marriage, **ganinjibuwari**
  'straight', **gilbumba**, **gilgamari**
married couple, **nyubany**
marrow, **jang-jang**
marry, **buwa**
masturbation, **nigi-nigi**
Mater Hospital-area bora site,
Waraba
Mathieson Park-area inlet,
Gibamandin
me,
  accusative, **ngana**
  dative, **ngari**
meat, **murang**, **yuri**
medicine, **banygaba**
meet, **dandiiri**
message stick, **gabagabal**
midday, **biigigurumba**
mighty, **warunggul**
Milbong waterhole, **Wanaigubung**
milk, **ngamuban**
  nursery word, **nyamany-
  nyamany**
Milton, **Ngurujung**
Minto Crag, **Winbulin**
Minto Crag-area crossing,
Garwang
mischief, **gujalgan**
make, **walima**
mist, **dagan**
Moggill Creek, **Magil**
moiety, **Gabai**, **Gamil**
money, **baling**
Moodlu railway station, **Mulu**
moon, **baabun**
  crescent, **gilan**
Mooroondu Point, **Murunydu**
more, **damburu**
Moreton Bay, **Quandamooka**

Moreton Bay confederacy,
Burugingmiri
Moreton Island, **Ganginyangin**,
Murgambin
Moreton Island-area hill, **Ganara**,
Gindara, **Ngajagarara**, **Ngalda**
Moreton Island location, **Bamari**,
Durbin
Moreton Island people, **Ngugi**
morning, **gujundabu**, **ngunugaba**
mosquito, **dibing**
moss, **gabim**, **murung**
mother, **bujang**
   in-law, **wumanggan**
   step, **maril**
mountain, **bibu**
   large, **dalgambar**
mountainous country, **bibubin**
mouth, **damburu**
Mt Alford and its caretakers,
Gilajin
Mt Alford-area Scenic Rim
Brewery, **Ngariigambila**
Mt Alford-area swampy place,
Wurangbila
Mt Alford pillar box stone,
Bindinba
Mt Ballow, **Walmuram**
Mt Barney, **Bugara-bugara**
Mt Beerwah, **Birwa**
Mt Brisbane-area swamp by Lake
Wivenhoe, **Wunaring**
Mt Castle, **Baja**
Mt Clunie, **Muumgara**
Mt Coonowrin, **Gunburiyan**
Mt Coot-tha, **Guja**, **Mabi**
Mt Cotton, **Janggilbin**
Mt Dugandan, **Dugandan**
Mt Edward, **Wamam**
Mt French,

north peak, **Mibaram**
south peak, **Banjurgan**
Mt French spring, **Bilira**
Mt Gravatt, **Gagaramalbil**
Mt Greville, **Mugara**
Mt Gulman, **Gulmang**
Mt Hardgrave, **Bibu Nguyirbunya**
Mt Lindesay, **Dalgamban**
Mt Mitchell, **Daan**
Mt Moon, **Muum**
Mt Peak, **Baramba**
Mt Pleasant, **Wanagin**
Mt Roberts, **Ban.gu**
Mt Samson, **Baran**
Mt Tambourine, **Dambirin**
Mt Tibrogargan, **Jiburugargan**
Mt Toowoonan, **Biriga**
mud, **bangan**, **wabum**
Mud Island, **Bangamba**
mug, **banduny**
Mununjali, **Mananjali**
Murphy's Creek, **Damamarin**
Murrarrie, **Madari**
Murrumba, **Marumba**
Murrumba Downs, **Gulugan**
mussel, **muyum**
Mutdapilly, **Madabili**
my, **ngariba**
Myora, **Mun.galba**
Myora-area creek, **Gurung-
gurungba**, **Yarul**
Myora-area hill, **Bimbiyan**
Myora Mission, **Murigan**

N – n

nail, **gi**
name, **nai**, **nari**
name, boy's, **Gilba**

name, man's, **Baguuruyalju,
Banbunya, Baraami, Bibinira,
Bimbiyan, Binabira, Birali,
Biran, Biran-biranba, Bubal,
Bujarbin, Bujumbiri, Bulalbul,
Burul, Dagalandin, Dagaru,
Dagura, Dalaibi, Dalangmul,
Dalawana, Dalipi, Dalu
Diyamariba, Danburi, Dandali,
Dan.gum, Digaga, Dilgan,
Dimgil, Diyali, Dudari, Dumali,
Dumbani, Dumbar, Durbin,
Duru, Galanggaba, Galimbain,
Gambula, Ganarumba, Ganju,
Gari, Gariwariba, Gidilbin,
Gilil-gilil, Ginbul, Ginda,
Gindariba, Gira, Guburabil,
Gudagiri, Gudanu, Gumbiliba,
Jambuwa, Jan.gali, Jarjidanariba,
Jilba, Jirigai, Jiriran, Jububajur,
Juga, Junggai, Mirabul,
Muburum, Mugan, Mulbaju,
Mulumba, Mulurubin, Muralu,
Nagin, Naimany, Nanggu,
Ngamba, Ngaraju, Ngilarun,
Ngiri, Ngumgaru, Ngunubi,
Niral, Nugimba, Nunungga,
Nuranyum, Nuwaju, Nyanbabari,
Wagun, Wajabau, Walbaligu,
Walbul, Wanangga, Wandaru,
Wangga Ngarabin, Wanigani,
Wumbunggaru, Yagubui, Yali-
yali, Yaraga, Yiria**

name, man's, or boy's, **Dunbiyan,
Gimbujil**

name, person's, **Bugu, Dan.gardu,
Gamunyari, Guda, Malgaram,
Mini-mini, Miwa, Munipi,
Ngaraiyu, Ngimiba, Nguwararu,
Nidurwal, Waimba**

name, woman's, **Baali, Banjai,
Banjin, Banjui, Bayiba, Bayimba,
Bidiirabul, Bidiiri, Biinbira,
Bilunga, Bimi, Biya, Murunyba,
Bujumbiriba, Bula, Bulan, Bulina
Bilina, Bumirum, Bunbinbin,
Bunduba, Danggu, Dimali,
Dimbal, Dimbiny, Dimbuuna,
Dululbin, Duribang, Gaandin,
Gabalaba, Galangga, Galbin,
Galgali, Gamu, Garanbin,
Gijiri, Gindara, Ginggal Munyi
Biriba, Gin.gibin, Girila,
Gubi, Gugingbul, Gulum,
Gumbumba, Gunduwali, Gura,
Gurawi, Guru, Guwalbiyan,
Jalba, Jaragawan-gawan,
Jargiran, Jarlamban.gan, Jayam,
Jiduugun, Jilbangbin, Jilmari,
Jiniba, Junabin, Jununggan,
Juruny, Mambayiba, Mibiran,
Miji, Milinggiri, Mugulngura,
Nanjili, Ngajagarara,
Ngamingba, Ngunabi, Ngundu,
Ngunuranbin, Nuninya,
Nyaminba, Wabuunariba, Walin,
Wijambarigun, Wilangga,
Wilgunariba, Winyiba, Wiyan,
Yagujai, Yamyi, Yilgunun,
Yindili, Yulanggin, Yuninya**

Narangba, **Narangba**

navel, **mabiri**

near, **bidung, danyung**

nearly, **baranyba**

neck, **ngaran**

nape of, **dur-dur**

needle, **during**

Nerang group, **Dalgibira, Jabubira**

net, **bayal, durur**

    fishing, **mandin**

kangaroo, **mirbang**
large fishing, **dama**
never, **yagarabu**
new, **baranyba**, **yingang**
New Farm, **Bin.gingba**
Newmarket, **Buyuba**
Newstead Park point,
Garanbinbila
nice, **nyiwang**
night, **ngunu**
no, **jandai**, **munjan**, **yagara**
noise, **gulwal**
Noonuccal people, **Nunagal**
Norman Creek Damala,
Gulbuurum
north, **bajaragu**
North Ipswich convent,
Juriyandaju
North Pine, **Mandin**
North Pine lagoon, **Milin Yimban**
North Pine River-area group,
Bundurbira
nose, **muru**
nostril, **murumiir**
not yet, **nanjara**
now, **barany**
Nudgee, **Naarda**
Nudgee Waterhole Reserve, **Baama**
nulla-nulla, **bagan**, **jabiri**
heavy, **mar**
Nundah, **Ngumbi Dagai**, **Nyanda**
Nundah racecourse, **Gilwanba**

O – o

Oaky Creek area, **Waringari**
oar, **dabilgan**
Observatory Hill in Spring Hill,
Wilwinba
octopus, **maranjal**

often, **jigan**
old, **baji**
one, **ganyara**
One Mile, **Mabi-mabiba**
One Mile creek, **Ngara-ngaragai**
only, **gumbal**, **ngundu**
open, **bujurna**
our, **ngalbanuba**
outlaw, **dalabila**
overnight, **ngunubu**
owner, **jimbalang**
female, **jimbaljin**
Oxley Creek, **Mula**
Oxley Creek-area location,
Dulmur
Oxley Creek, mouth of, **Bimiraba**
oyster, **ginyinggara**
pearl, **guumbi**

P – p

pademelon,
red-necked, **bandung**
type of, **gumang**
paid, well, **marumbadi**
pants *n.*, **daranygaba**
path, **bambar**
Peel Island, **Jargariiba**
pelvis, **ngadang**
penis, **dugai**
glans, **gumi**
people, small mythical, **janjari**
period, menstrual, **dunguru**
person of power, **gayabandar**
person, pathetic, **bujal**, **gunin-
gunin**
person who won't listen, **binang
guri**
Petrie Bight, **Damaman**
Petrie location, **Dambaal**

Petrie pocket, **Banggil**
Petrie's Pocket hill, **Mulu-mulu**
Petrie spring, **Biranba**
pick out, **banman.gilin**
pierce, **bimba**
piercing, nose, **bulwalam**
pig, **biing-biing**
Pine Mt, **Gambarjubin**
Pinkenba, **Dunbam**
pipe, **bubalam**
pity, **dagal**
plains, **gunigal**
plant,
  arrowroot, **ganjabai**
  bean, type of, **bulumbir**
  berry, type of, **dabal**
  blackberry, **bundai**
  black-mouth bush, **nijigum**
  blackthorn, **gaiban**
  bottlebrush flower, **bindigam**
  brushwood, **darum**
  cane, **darganbin**
  castor oil, **guji**
  crab's eye, **giji**
  cunjevoi, **bundal**
  dracaena, **dindili**
  fern, bird's nest, **daragan**
  fern, bracken, **durbin**
  fern, root, **bangwal, danguwan**
  fern, staghorn, **dunbam**
  fern, tree, **barunyuba**
  finger lime, **marbana**
  five corners, **Gadara**
  flowers, **banggilgada**
  fruit, black, **damin**
  fruit, red, **bara**
  fruit, red scrub, **gurindin**
  fruit, scrub, **bumangbin**
  fruit, type of, **dirwa, mujiru-mujiru**

  fruit used as chewing gum, **bumbal**
  gooseberry, native, **malgam**
  grass, **banggil**
  grass, cogon, **baralbin**
  grass, long, **daga**
  grass, long coarse, **wali-waligarang**
  grass, seed ground into flour, **gula**
  grass, spiny-head mat-rush, **dili**
  grass tree, **garguru, winbulin**
  grass tree flower spike, **burumbin**
  grass tree, forest, **ngilarun**
  grass tree, large, **bulirbin**
  grass tree, swamp, **dagabin**
  guava, native, **guji-gujin.gal**
  heather, **ngara-ngaragai**
  herb, creeper, **dam**
  herb, fern-like, **yugai-yugai**
  herb, type of, **gigirilbin**
  herb, water, **yari**
  hibiscus, **gaya guriliyidal**
  hops, native, **ganingira gidar, gin-ginga**
  lawyer cane, **ngabu**
  lily, blue flax, **ngimbun**
  mallee scrub, **ngunadada**
  melon, native, **juwum**
  midyimberry, **mijim**
  moss, **gabim, murung**
  orchid, ground, **jingam**
  pigface, **babiragawi**
  plum, native, **mandany**
  potato, **gulgal**
  raspberry, native, **gubu-guburan, yalabin**
  red-leafed shrub, **gawanduwanbin**
  reed, bulrush, **yimban**

reed, bulrush, part of, **yimbanban**

reed, honey bulrush, **ginggal munyi biriba**

reed, for dilly bags, **mun.ga**

reed, for weaving, **yunggiri**

reed, freshwater, **yigibin**

reed, freshwater, roots, **jinbura**

reed, grass-bugle, **galgaribin**

reed, rushes, **ganarin**

reed, soft twigrush, **nyunggiya**

reed, water, **yigilu**

scrub, **gabany**

scrub wood, type of, **nuralgir**

sea grass, **gulbulburbin**

seaside sword bean, **yugam**

seaweed, **narung**

sedge, **burara**

settler's flax, **ngurgurgaban**

shrub, type of, **dirbang**

small scrub frequented by flies, **dudambarajuwal**

sugar cane, **dubaru**

taro, **dadam**

Tibouchina, native, **najigam**

used for ointment, **bundur**

vine, coastal, **garan**

vine, creeping, **majan. gundanbin**

vine, goat's foot, **darung**

vine, lawyer, **daigam**

vine, supplejack, **yarul**

vine with yellow berries, **bara**

water pepper, **danggul**

water plant, type of, **dandibin**

water weed, **nambur**

waterlily, **jinggalgal**

waterlily root, **muyu**

yam, **dam**

yam, large white, **guba**

yam, native root, **diga**

platform, ceremonial, **gaga**

platypus, **wajin**

Pleiades, **maran-maran**

plenty, **manyal**

pluck, **banman**

pockmark, **nuram**

Point Lookout, **Mulumba**

point of land, **dundu**

Point Talburpin, **Dalwalbin**

policeman, **dabingbila, gamadan, mug-mug**

polite, **nangalbanga**

poor thing!, **gunman**

porpoise, **buwanggan, dalubila**

 black, **baibi**

possum,

 bobuck, **gabala**

 brushtail, **gubi**

 ringtail, **miburu**

power, **gaya**

pox, **bagaram**

prawn, **buding**

pregnant, **nyamalbila**

pregnant person, **ngaragan**

press, **mama**

properly, **gurbi-gurbi**

Pullen Pullen Creek, **Bulan-bulan**

pulverise, **mamura mana**

punch, **mamgal**

punish, **galimal**

put, **wura**

put out a fire, **baluba**

put something down, **yibiri**

Q – q

quick, **burima**

quickly, **jubuiban**

quick-tempered, **baranygali**

quoll, **banjim**

R – r

Raby Bay, **Dubawa**
rain, **jurum-jurum**, **nyurung**
rainbow, **gayawur**
rainforest, **din-din**
rain-making ceremony, **waninga**
rat, **mubar**
   water, **guril**
read, **nguwinginin**
ready, **gawibiba**
red, **gawan-gawan**
   brownish, **guji**
Red Hill, **Buna**
Redcliffe area, **Yara**
Redcliffe-area site, **Gawan-gawan**
Redcliffe point, **Waram**
remember, **biyara**
return, **wira**
rib, **gudajirban**
ridge, **banyu**
rifle, **ganaral**
rise, **wandi**
river, **burugara**
   mouth, **nyanda**
   saltwater, **bamirigari**
road, **gulgan**
roll *v.*, **gurawin**
rope, **baguuru**
Rosewood, **Bunuru**, **Gaubanbi**
rough, **mulgara-mulgara**
round, **dagung**
Royal Brisbane Hospital site,
Ngalan
rum, **gira**
run, **buwarawa**, **nyigiran**

S – s

sacred, **dimanggali**
saltwater people, **bagarnuba**

salty, **baan**
Samford, **Gubidabin**
Samsonvale, **Dagawamba**
sand, **yarang**
Sandgate, **Wara**
sandstone, **dalangjili**, **yarangmulu**
Sandy Mt, **Biga Banga Jimba**
scarification, **mulgara**
   Amity Point pattern, **gambangga**
   shoulder, **dabir**
scold, **yamal**
scorpion, **duiwai**, **gandarba**
Scotts Point, **Banda Madu**
scrotum, **bulu**
sea, **yarabaan**
season
   summer, **nyanggagan**
   wet, **jan.gan**
   winter, **yigilgan**
second *adj.*, **bularam**
see, **nyaany**
seek, **ngangaba**
sell, **ngujubugu**
send, **waya**
set up, **gubilban**
sew, **galiba**
   with needle, **duringgaliba**
sexual activity, engage in,
gumuwara
sexual intercourse, **bam-bam**, **jim-jim**, **wiruwira**
shade, **gunggal**
shake, **jiga**
shape *n.*, **nguru**
shark, **buwai**
   banded wobbegong, **gunbing**
   shovel-nosed, **nirang**
sharp, **galin**
sheep, **manggi**
shell, **walamgan**

nautilus, **jaliny**
razorback, **magul**
type of, **dinggal**
shield, **dabira, gundan**
shipworm, **gambu, ganyi**
Shorncliffe, **Mura**
high part, **Girawali**
short, **jalgal**
shoulder, **giga**
shout, **gungany**
show *v.*, **nangiba**
sick, **bany**
side *n.*, **guda**
sing, **giya**
of birds, **gungany**
sing together, **giyali**
sir, **biru**
sister,
elder, **jajing**
younger, **manganggal**
sit, **nyinyi**
sit down, **nyinyili**
six, **majan-majan**
skin group,
female, **Banjurgan, Baranggan, Bundagan, Jarawanygan**
male, **Banjur, Barang, Bunda, Jarawany**
skin group, acceptable for marriage, **gilbumba, gilgamari**
skinny, **baragan**
skin, **damil**
removed from corpse, **gali**
skull, **gani, magulugul**
sky, **biram, wangan**
sleep, **bugany**
sleep, go to, **jiraba bugany**
sleep, put to, **buganyma**
slow *adj.*, **gandandi**
smell, **yila**

smile, **mabalbana**
smoke, **jumu**
smoke tobacco, **jalu mali**
snail, periwinkle, **nigar**
snake, **yuwan**
brown, **guralbang**
brown tree, **jari**
carpet python, **gabul**
death adder, **mulumgal**
red-bellied black, **juumgu**
small-eyed, **galinda**
yellow-faced whip, **diruny**
sneeze, **nuun.gali**
soft, **dan.gabing, gamdung**
son, **nyaring**
songs, composer of, **mayabiya**
sorcerer, **nan.gur**
sorry to hear that!, **walibina**
sour, **duurjagum**
overly, **duurwali**
south, **yanggar**
South Brisbane group, **Girgamban, Gubuuru-Jagin**
South Pine River mouth, **Nyandaba**
Southern Cross, **Mirabuga**
spear, **ganai**
fishing, **jibalang**
reed, **galgaribin ganai**
regulation, **bulan**
war, **bilara**
Spicer's Peak, **Bin.gingjuwa**
spider, **muga-muga**
spike, **migan**
spiral shape, **nguna-ngunan**
spirit land, **maguijan**
spit, **gijubal, mali**
spring, **gumabila**
Spring Hill, **Maril, Wumbunggaru**
Spring Hill area, **Dalawala**

Spring Hill camp, **Wurabinda**
St Helena Aboriginal group, **Gunul Gabalju**
St Helena Island, **Nugun**
stand up, **jilai**
star, **mirigin**
starving, **wayaragali**
　to death, **wayarabang**
stay, **dalan**
stay away!, **bugara-bugara**
steal, **mara**
stick, **dal**
　for throwing, **muruny**
sticky, **mada**
stiff, **yanggu**
stinky, **buga**
stone, **mulu, nalanggira**
　flint, **jindabang**
　for axes, **bandaan gulmang**
　for making buckets, **nyugum mulu**
　loose, **darau**
stop, **gagalum**
stopper, **dalan**
storm, **muburum**
Stradbroke creek, **Baralbinbila, Bigunjur, Gibiba, Wali-waligarang**
Stradbroke group, **Daranggari Gabalju, Guwanbal, Jujimayali, Nunagal**
Stradbroke language, **Jandai, Munjan**
Stradbroke location, **Bandan.gambaba**
Stradbroke wetlands, **Waran Gamari**
Stradbroke, part of, **Daranggari, Minjiriba**
straight, **jubui**

strike *v.*, **baji**
string, **nanyam**
striped, **wangalban**
strong, **bandara**
stubborn, **binawanga**
sugar, **dagi**
Sugar Loaf Mt, **Ngaijiraba**
summer, **nyanggagan**
sun, **biigi**
sunburnt, **biigibu**
sunset, **biigibang, biigigarany**
swallow *v.*, **nabidi**
Swan Bay, **Wiji-wijibin**
swear word, **bujingbila**
sweat *n.*, **nangal**
Sweeney Reserve bora site, **Nyindurunyinyidu**
sweetheart, **milgiri**
swim, **yara**

T – t

table, **birabun**
tail, **wanggin**
take care of oneself, **bajiili**
talk, **wulara, wularama, yaa**
talkative, **wularagali**
tall, **buruuwal**
Tangalooma, **Dungaluma**
Tarampa, **Darumba**
Taringa, **Daringga, Wumunyguru**
Taylor's Ridge group, **Gumbaban**
temples of forehead, **dala**
tent, **ganya**
Tent Hill group, **Majanbili**
testes, **mujin**
Teviot Falls, **Juwalga**
Teviot Range route, **Gulgan**
Teviot Range caves, **Dangarbin**
than, **ngi**
that way!, **jangil junggu**

that,
    distal, **danga**
    medial, **gaa**
their, **ngunyalinuba**
them, **ngunyalina**
there is/was, **ngaranga**
there,
    distal, **naam**
    medial, **yugu**
they, **ngunyali**
thief, **ngurun.gali**
thing, **daun**
thingamajig, **minyalang**
things, **nanajin**
think, **buga**
thirsty, **gana**
this, proximal, **diranga**
three, **bulaganyara**, **majan**
throat, **dalany**
throw, **biya**
throw away, **biyamal**
thumb, **mugul**
thunderstorm, **mugara**
thunder, heavy, **mumbal**
tick, scrub, **giran**
tide, **gariiba**
    ebb, **jargariiba**
    flood, **yunggariiba**
tie *v.*, **nany**
Tingalpa, **Dinggalba**
tired, **garulban**
toad, **wugulumba**
tobacco, **jumu**
today, **diyiin**
together, **ganyardi**
tomahawk, **nanggan**, **wagara**
tomorrow, **mulagu**, **ngunuwara**
tongue, **jugung**
too much, **ngagali**
Toorbul Point, **Durubal**

tooth, **diya**
    back, **diyabula**
    front, **diyaganyara**
toothache, **dagi**
Toowong, **Banyaraba**
Toowong area, **Juwai-juwai**
totem, **yuri**
totem-centre, **jurbil**
touch, **ngadan**
tree, **baguuru**
    acacia, **namui**
    apple box, **bubu**
    banksia, **mindi**
    banksia, type of, **danggal**
    beach tamarind, **dagaru**
    black ironbark, **jum-jum**
    black oak, **buruda**
    black wattle, **gagargal**
    blackbutt, **girigan**
    blood-gum, **binimda**
    bloodwood, **bana**
    blue gum, **manggara**
    blue quandong, **galamang**
    bottle, **guldan**
    brigalow, **banuru**, **duriny**
    Brisbane box, **dabilbala**
    broad-leafed tea, **ngujuru**
    brown mahogany, **ngurbin**
    brushwood, **dila**
    bunya, **buunyi**
    cabbage, **mungurgal**, **binygar**
    coachwood, **ngaruwing**
    cockspur briar, **jalbang**
    corkwood, **gundan**
    cotton, **dalwalbin**
    crow's nest ash, **balbara**
    cypress pine, **burugari**
    dead, **dalgai**
    dogwood, **dana**
    fig, **murabal**

fig, big-leafed, **jambal**
fig, large, **gurai**
fig, sandpaper, **nguwanga**
fig, small, **ganin, nyada**
forest oak, **buranda, gundiba**
geebung, **dalandala, gumbara**
grey gum, type of, **dambiri**
grey ironbark, **jana**
gum-top box, **ngarang**
gum, type of, **gar-gar**
hoop pine, **gambarju**
ironbark, type of, **ganaibira**
jackwood, **baanang**
juniper, **mi-mi**
kurrajong, **yabar**
Leichhardt bean, **magarabal**
mahogany, type of, **bundul**
maiden's blush, **gariing**
milky mangrove, **yabun**
Moreton Bay ash, **garan**
Moreton Bay chestnut, **mai**
myall, **dalaga**
narrow-leafed ironbark, **janduru**
orange mangrove, **gawan-gawan**
orange, native, **dangan**
pandanus, **junggul, winam**
piccabean palm, **bigi**
pine, **dandardam**
pine, small, **bugal**
prickly stem, **jirabang**
red bottlebrush, **gura**
red cedar, **mamin**
red ironbark, **bigara**
red mangrove, **gawan-gawan**
red-bark, **garuda**
red-stemmed gum, **ngararar**
rosewood, **bunuru, wajari**
sassafras, **jandigung**
saw banksia, **bambara**
scrub bottle, **jinbigari**

she-oak, **bandibar, bila**
silky oak, **jagin-jagin, ngarabin**
silver-leafed ironbark, **nyandala**
softwood with hard red berry,
gagal
spotted gum, **yara**
stinging, **baragany, gimbi**
stringybark, **gundul**
stringybark, type of, **jura, diyi**
swamp mahogany, **bularju**
Sydney blue gum, **bulagi,
durambai**
tea tree bark, **nambur**
tea tree, flaky-barked, **jiman-
jiman**
tulip satinwood, **garamgalgal**
tulipwood, **guwaramduwanbin**
turpentine, **bulurjambin,
gilawara**
type of, **jigal-jigal**
vitae, **jalgara**
wattle, **jiraigar**
white cedar, **daigil**
white mangrove, **janji**
white wood, **munura**
tree log, **maling**
tree root, **waran**
tree stump, **bilayir**
truth, **nguibina**
Tuleenderly Creek, **Dalangjili**
tummy, **binji**
turn, **gilangan**
Turrbul, **Durubal**
turtle, **mibaral**
eastern snake-necked, **mujing**
hawksbill, **dagibagam**
humpback, **naguba**
sea, **bubiya**
short-necked, **bin.ging**
two, **bula**

U – u

unable, **giyagarabany**
uncle,
  maternal, **gaming**
  paternal, **bing**
Uncle, **Gaming**
Upper Teviot-area district,
Yigumbumba
urinate, **gil**
urination, of women, **jalang**
us,
  accusative, **ngalbana**
  dative, **ngalbanu**
  you and me, accusative,
  ngalinyana
  you and me, dative, **ngalinyanu**

V – v

vagina, **nyaral**
vein, **gaiyang**
venereal disease, **wambany**
very, **biribanga**
very many, **milin.gali**
vest, made of skin, **wanganba**
Victoria Park gully, **Barambin**
Victoria Point, **Wara-wara**
Vulture St location, **Gambugiba**
vulva, **gaji, jurung**

W – w

waistcoat, **bibaba**
wait *v.*, **nyundal**
wait!, **gau**
wake, **mayalba**
walk to and fro, **ban.gawani**
wallaby,
  black-striped, **jamban**
  brush-tailed rock, **magun**
  female, **bangui, garil**
  old man, **wangun**
  pretty-face, **gibiri**
  swamp, **wangari**
  swamp, female, **bugul**
wallaroo, **dandurir**
Wallen Creek, **Walan**
Wallen Wallen Creek, **Walan-walan**
want, **maun.ga, naruida, wangal, yaniri**
Warrill Creek, **Waril**
wasp, **burin**
waste away, **mambarabany**
water, **dabil, gabing**
  open, **wara**
  running, **dabilyanmana**
  salt, **dabilbaan**
water cataract, **gurgundal**
water hole, **winil**
watercourse, **warambul**
watershed, **naga**
waves, **dagan**
we, **ngalba**
  you and I, **ngaliny**
weak, **budung, manmal, yaran-yaran**
wear, **wamba**
weep, **dungi**
Wellington Point, **Galan-galan**
west, **wiyan, yabarin**
West End, **Gurilba**
wet *adj.*, **jan**
whale, **yalingbila**
wharf, **mamba**
what for?, **minyanggu**
what?,
  accusative, **minyana**

nominative, **minya**
possessive, **minyangnuba**
when, **wina**
when?, **wanji**
where at?, **wanyadi**
where to?, **wanyagu**, **yinjagu**
where?, **wanya**
which?, **nguna**
whirl, **wulun**
whirlpool, **wugaru**
whistle, **yirunbal**
white, **buba**
Whites Hill, **Balimba**
whose?, **ngananuba**
who?,
ergative, **ngandu**
nominative, **ngan**
why?, **minyangdi**
wicked, **wurungali**
wide, **barwan**
widow, **ganibawininigan**
widower, **burgun**
wife, **nyubanyjalgan**,
nyugunbinggan
Wild Horse Mt, **Galimbin**
Wilson's peak, **Jiraman**
wind, **gubi**
east, **burging**, **dun.gai**, **winjia**
north, **dimbiny**
south, **buran**
west, **junggai**
whirlwind, **buwal**
wing, **maidamari**
winter, **yigilgan**
withered, **dawajangar**
woman, **jundal**
Aboriginal, **nginggaran**
fancy young, **balinggan**
gentlewoman, **garangamgan**

old, **waliinggara**
white, **waimirigan**
young, **mirung**
womb, **junu**
wood, **bumal**
Woodford, **Durandur**
Woodford-area group, **Gigabira**
Woogaroo, **Wugaru**
Woolloongabba, **Wulun.gaba**
Wooloowin, **Guluwin**
word, **wula**
worm, **nginjuru**
wow!, **gurii**
wrist, **mamun**
wrong, **bidamjaran**, **nguniwali**
Wynnum, **Winam**

Y – y

yabby, slender, **gambugi**
yam-stick, **galguru**
Yarrawonga, **Yarrawonga**
Yatala, **Yatala**
yawn, **nganbil**
Yebri Creek, **Yibiri**
Yebri Creek lagoon, **Yimban**
Yeerongpilly, **Nyurungbili**
yellow, **biigi-biigi**
Yeronga, **Yarang**
Yerrol Creek, **Yaral**
yes, **yawai**
yesterday, **garwaligu**
Yooloooburrabee, **Yulubarabi**
you,
accusative, **ngina**
ergative, **nginu**
nominative, **nginda**
you all,
accusative, **ngilbulana**
nominative, **ngilbula**

you two, **ngilbang**
your, **nginuba**
Yugar railway station, **Yugai**
Yuggera, **Yagara**
Yuggerabal, **Yagarabal**

Z – z

Zillmere Water Holes,
Dalandalayinil

Part 3. Texts

3.1. The contents of Part 3

Part 3 of this volume includes all known instances of written Yagara attributed to native speakers, consisting of individual sentences, three brief songs (Section 3.3) and several Bible stories (Sections 3.4–3.6). For all texts, the original unaltered transcriptions are here provided alongside standardised analysed versions. The inclusion of the original source material ensures that the reader has access to the full set of data that was available to the volume's authors. The analyses in this volume can therefore be easily reanalysed or updated if new Yagara data or other relevant information becomes available.

In general, individual words are listed in Part 2: Dictionary whereas longer sequences are included in Part 3: Texts, but the division between words and texts is not always obvious. For example, instances of multiple words are listed in Part 2: Dictionary when they (1) do not appear to constitute a complete utterance and (2) seem likely to be a fixed expression or recurring collocation. For example, *wularaba gariyagan* 'brolga that talks; magpie goose' (Meston 1867–1960) is listed in the dictionary rather than the texts even though it includes multiple words.

On the other hand, individual words are listed here in Part 3 if they appear to constitute a complete utterance. Some instances therefore appear in both Part 2 and Part 3. For example, Watkin (1887) lists the command *Galga* 'Cut it' as an utterance, so this is listed in Part 3 in addition to the dictionary entry for *galgal* 'cut' in Part 2.

3.2. Background to the texts

The texts in Part 3 are probably not the stories and sentences that anyone would have chosen as a record of Yagara. They were not selected for preservation by Yagara language owners and are not representative of the language or culture. Rather, the texts were requested and recorded by white men between 1841 and 1983 for reasons of their own.

These men's motivations, like their linguistic and cultural backgrounds (see Section 1.1.4) should be borne in mind when reading the texts. For example, most of the longer texts were obtained by a series of missionaries with little respect for Indigenous culture or beliefs. Lutheran missionary Christopher Eipper, for instance, was recruited by JD Lang, who was of the opinion that 'Aborigines' were 'a debased and degenerate people' (*Cooksland* 1847). Eipper found his purpose – to convert the 'heathen' – challenging, recording in his text *Observations Made on a Journey to the Natives at Toorbal August 2, 1841*:

> ... when beholding and hearing (the natives) thus engaged to contend with Satan, as they were doing for nearly the two hours which this total eclipse of the moon lasted, (it was) in vain to endeavour to convince them of their error by a rational explanation of the phenomenon; this was, they said, what the white man believed, but it was not for the black man. (Eipper 1841b, 10)

The Rev. Ridley, also recruited by JD Lang, took on the role of itinerant evangelist. His imperative was to translate Bible stories into local languages. In 1855 he convinced 13-year-old Tom Petrie to translate several stories into the Yagara dialect spoken by the Durubal people (see 3.4–3.6). Ridley then enticed young Petrie to lead him to where several hundred Durubal individuals were camped, at which point Rev. Ridley read his stories until the Durubal listeners tired and wandered off to bed. The Durubal listeners did not seem particularly impressed with Rev. Ridley. As recounted in *Tom Petrie's Reminiscences* (Petrie 1904, 143),

> Next day some of the young blackfellows turned up at the Petries' home, and they said to (Petrie) they knew who had told that man all his rubbish, and picking up a piece of paper started mimicking Mr. Ridley.

Most of the non-missionaries who collected Yagara texts never imagined that their work ever would be read by a First Nations audience. Indeed, they often showed little regard for the language owners' customs or desires. For example, the sentences in Section 3.3.4 were collected by JW Gibson of 'Stanmore' sugar plantation at Yatala. Gibson was connected by marriage to William Sloane, who operated as stock and station agent from 1858 and formed the company William Sloane & Co. in 1861, renamed the Union Mortgage & Agency Co. of Australia Ltd in 1884 and Australian Estates & Mortgage Company Limited in 1894 (Smith 2010). Gibson became familiar with local languages through everyday interactions with the First People of the Country whose land had been acquired through the colonial practice of squatting. When anthropologist and English Quaker AW Howitt approached Gibson to complete his language survey, Gibson not only provided Howitt with word lists supplied by his 'native' consultant Diafur, but also sent Howitt a sacred *bagaram* 'bullroarer', which he mistakenly termed a 'Bribbun' (*birban* 'boomerang') (Howitt 1904). Howitt then delivered this 'mystical object' to a fellow Quaker in England, and published Gibson's word lists in *The Native Tribes of South-East Australia* (1904). Both the *bagaram* and the word list had passed out of First Nations control and access.

Watkin (1887), a pharmacist at the Dunwich Benevolent Asylum, presented 'scientific' papers that incorporated sentences he learned during his placement there. Meston (1890), while Chief Protector of Aborigines for Southern Queensland, took the opportunity to record notes and publish newspaper articles on the languages of 'a dying race' during his visits to 'The Moreton Bay Tribes'. The purpose of Lauterer, a German-born medical practitioner who practised in South Brisbane, was predominantly ethno-botanical, though his work was still produced for a white audience. He was reported to have read a paper 'with great effect, and sang the aboriginal songs' in his February 1891 presentation to Royal Society of Queensland. Long-time Boonah farmer Hardcastle shared his knowledge of vocabulary and activities of local tribes through a presentation to the Geographical Society in 1949.

While these and other early collectors had varying motivations for collecting Yagara texts, all had white audiences in mind. There is no evidence that any of the collectors asked their Indigenous consultants what materials were important or ought to be recorded. As a result, the texts in this section fail to include the traditional stories and other culturally relevant texts in language that are frequently found in grammars.

3.3. Sentence lists

3.3.1. Eipper 1841a

nginda **ngan**
2SG.NOM who
Who are you?
Intangan?

wanya **nya-ra-nya** **malar**
where go-DEST-PRS black.man
Where are the black people going?
Wunna yarun mabar?

nginda **wanya** **nyan-ma-nya**
2SG.NOM where go-CAUS-PRS
Where are you going?
Inta wunna yanmana?

ngalan=gu **jar=gu** **dabil=gu**
bream=PURP earth=PURP water=PURP
To catch bream, to work the earth, to get water.
Woulanco, darco, dabilco.

nyandagal **nginda** **many**
mullet 2SG.NOM catch
Did you catch any fish?
Andeikal inta manan.

nyandagal **yagar** **ngalan** **yagar**
mullet no bream no
There is no mullet, nor bream
Andeikal yagar, woulan yagar,

dabil **wayara**
water be.hungry
the water is hungry.
dabil waiaroo.

minya **nginda** **mara**
what   2SG.NOM   get
What will you get?
Menäh inta marra?

nginda **bina**
2SG.NOM   know
You know.
Inta pitney.

biru **ngaja** **wayara** **ngariba** **'five island'**
sir   1SG.NOM   be.hungry   1SG.POSS   five island
Sir, I'm hungry, give me 'five island' (bread).
Biro, atta waiaroo, ariba five island.

3.3.2. Lang 1846

dulan=gu **gawibiba**
battle=PURP   ready
Are you ready to fight?
Doolungco cohipeppa

ngaja **ngun** **Eagle Farm-di**
1SG.NOM   live   Eagle Farm-LOC
I live at Eagle Farm.
Utter oon Eagle Farm de

ngi **buga**
Q   think
Do (I) think so?
Inpoggo 'I think so'

gindin-ba
laugh-SBJV
Laugh, if you like.
Kindapur 'Why laugh?'

gunga-Ø **giya-la**
shout-IMP   call-OBLG
Call out!
Kung-giela

minya-na
what-ACC
What is that?
Minyana

ngan   ngina
who   2SG.ACC
Who (will stay) with you?
Ngan gnina 'Who will stay at home?'

ngan   nguwar
who   face
Who is that?
Ngawngur

wanya   gawa-ra
where   chase-DEST
Where is he going off to?
Oonagoware

jarajina   yaga-dunga
footprint   make-IPFV
(He is) leaving footprints.
Tarachinda yagaltunga 'Change into a white fellow'

wulara   ngina
talk   2SG.ACC
Speak to you.
Wullara eana 'Teach me your language'

wana   ga-ra
refuse.to   give-NEG
I will not give.
Wonagra

wi   balga-Ø
hey   come-IMP
Hello! / Hey, c'mere!
Winbulca 'out-of-doors'

nya-ra **barany**
go-DEST now
Go now.
Yera bowya

nya-li-ba
go-FUT-SBJV
(You) should go.
Yellabah 'Keep/go away'

nya-li-ba=gu
go-FUT-SBJV=PURP
(He) intends to go (to do something)
Yeallibaggo 'He is going'

garuba=gu **baru** **yaa-li-ba**
another=PURP later speak-FUT-SBJV
I want to say something more later on.
Carao boggo parroo yealiba 'I will speak by and by'

barany **ngaja** **magul** **baragal**
now 1SG.NOM head busy
I am busy now.
Purren utter moggool burragol

yagara=gu **ngaja**
none=PURP 1SG.NOM
I have none.
Yagarago ngutter

ngaja **danga** **wana**
1SG.NOM that.DIST refuse
I do not want that.
Ngutter ding-a winnan

danga **ngaja** **many-ba** **marumba**
that.DIST 1SG.NOM take-SBJV good
I will take that good one.
Dinga ngutter maheba maroomber

ngari   **biribi**   **wuja-Ø**
1SG.DAT   little   give-IMP
Give me a little.
Ngare perpa oodar

nginda   **minyangdi**   **winanga-ri**   **yagarabu**
2SG.NOM   why   hear-PST   not.at.all
Why haven't you heard at all?
Inter mingemtur winnangere yagarapoo 'Do you know, or not?'

ngaja   **yagarabu**   **winanga-ri**
1SG.NOM   not.at.all   hear-PST
I have no idea. (lit. 'I haven't heard anything.')
Ngutter yagarapoo winnangere 'I do not know'

yagarabu   **ngaja**   **winanga-ri**
not.at.all   1SG.NOM   hear-PST
I have no idea. (lit. 'I haven't heard anything.')
Yagarapo ngutter winnangere 'I have not known'

ngunyalu   **nguna**   **ngina**
3SG.ERG   which   2SG.ACC
Which person (has told) you?
Ngoonloo ngoon-ngina 'No person has told me.'

nginda   **biyara-nya**   **yaa-ri**
2SG.NOM   remember-PRS   say-PST
You remember, you told (me).
Inter piorren yeare 'You tell me how.'

nginda   **ngaja**   **yaa-ri**
2SG.NOM   1SG.NOM   say-PST
You told me.
Intur ngadna yeare 'You tell me.'

minyangdi   **nya-ma-nya**
why   go-CAUS-PRS
Why are you going?
Minyanta yadmunna 'Where are you going?'

minyangdi **nya-ra** **England**
why go-DEST England
Why are you going off to England?
Minyanta yera England 'When are you going to England?'

ngura-ba **ngari** **jin-jin** **damburu**
leave-SBJV 1SG.DAT food more
Leave me more food …
Oorapa nare dindien tambroo …

labiya-labiya **maga-ba**
quickly eat-RTP
to eat quickly.
labbia labbia moggower

damburu **yaga-Ø**
more work-IMP
Work more.
Tambroo yacca

biya-ma **buga**
throw-CAUS stinky
Throw it away, it stinks.
Beheme booga

wula-gali **nginda**
word-VERY 2SG.NOM
You talk too much.
Wulle aculle intur

muyan-gali **nginda**
ask-VERY 2SG.NOM
You ask too much.
Mooe aculle intur

minya **nginda** **yaga-dunga**
what 2SG.NOM make-IPFV
What are you making?
Minya agoonter yagadua

nyinyi-nya
sit-PRS
(You) are sitting.
Nginana

jira-ba   **bugany**
go.to.sleep-SBJV   sleep
Go to sleep.
Dieraper boogon

wanya   **nginda**   **dalang**
where   2SG.NOM   lost
Where have you been?
Wunya inter tullung

ngaja   **giram**   **dabilbaan**
1SG.NOM   across   salt.water
I go across the salt water.
Ngutter kireum doolpan 'I go across the river'

nginda   **gindi-gali**
2SG.NOM   laugh-VERY
You laugh too much.
Nginter kindurculle

ngaja   **nyaany**
1SG.NOM   see
I see.
Ngutter nan

nginda   **nyaany**
2SG.NOM   see
You see.
Nginter nan '

ngandu   **ganai**   **wujan**
who.ERG   spear   give
Who gave you that spear?
Ando connoi oo dan

nginda   **yaga-ri**
2SG.NOM   make-PST
You made (it).
Inter yagadde

ngandu   **galga**   **baguuru**
who.ERG   cut   wood
Who cut the wood?
Ando calca boggoroo

ngari   **biribi**   **galga**   **wuja-Ø**
1SG.DAT   little   drop   give-IMP
Give me a little drop.
Nare perpa culga oodar

ngilbang   **nya-ra**
2DU.NOM   go-DEST
You two go there.
Ngilpung yera

ngari   **dabil**   **gana=gu**   **wuja-Ø**
1SG.DAT   water   thirsty=PURP   give-IMP
Give me water, I am thirsty.
Ngare tabil cadnango oodar

yamal-gali
scold-VERY
(You) scold (me) too much.
Yammulculle

nginda   **yaa-dunga**
2SG.NOM   say-IPFV
You're always telling me.
Inter yadlunga

wanya   **nyinyi-nya**
where   dwell-PRS
Where do you live?
Ooute naninga

yilung nyan-ma-nya
straight go-CAUS-PRS
Going straight forward.
Yeloong yadnunna 'Go straight forward.'

wanya galabi knife
where leave knife
Where did I leave the knife?
Wunra gallabi knife?

3.3.3. Gibson 1863

nginda wali
2SG.NOM bad
You're lying.
ēēn wattāry

wi many
hey give
Hey, give me (a light).
wēē mănim

ngama mugim balga nginda
hey stone.axe come 2SG.NOM
Hey, bring the tomahawk, …
Umma! Mogim balgandy: … 'Come. Bring the tomahawk. …

burima nginda
quickly 2SG.NOM
be quick!
borēēma indo. 'Look sharp!'

3.3.4. Ridley 1875

minya nginda yaga-ri
what 2SG.NOM do-PST
What have you done?
Minya inta yuggari?

minya   **nginda**   **barany**   **yaga-li-ba**
what   2SG.NOM   now   do-FUT-SBJV
What are you going to do now?
Minya inta berren yuggaliba?

gau-Ø   **ngaja**   **galga-li-ba**   **diranga**   **baguur**
stop-IMP   1SG.NOM   cut-FUT-SBJV   this.PROX   tree
Stop! I'm going to cut this tree.
Kaahuu! Ngutta kulkulliba diranga bagur.

ngaja   **yaga-ri**   **barany**
1SG.NOM   do-PST   now
I've finished (it) now.
Ngutta yuggari berren.

naam   **ngandu**
there.DIST   who.ERG
Who is that?
Naam ngandu?

ngari   **balga-Ø**   **minyalang**
1SG.ACC   come-IMP   thingamajig
Bring me that whatever-it-is.
Ngurri bulkai minyaluung?

ngunyalu   **yaraman**   **balga-ri**
3SG.ERG   horse   bring-PST
He brought the horse.
Wŭnyalu yaraman bulkaiari.

ngunyalu   **nyaring**   **waya-ri**
3SG.ERG   son   send-PST
He sent his son.
Wunyalu nurriŋ waiari.

3.3.5. Watkins and Hamilton 1887

wanya   **malar**
where   black.men
Where are the black people?
Wunnia malar?

ngaja   **jugu-ra**
1SG.NOM   know-NEG
I don't know.
Atcha djookoora.

guba-nya   **nginda**   **ngaja**   **bara**   **balgalbiny**
go.on-PRES   2SG.NOM   1SG.NOM   soon   return
You're going ahead, I'm coming back soon.
Cobana-inter, utcha baro balgalpin.

ngaja   **ngina**   **baibun-ma-ri**
1SG.NOM   2SG.ACC   dream-CAUS-PST
I dreamed about you.
Utcha ine biboon mare.

ngandu   **ngina**   **yaa-ri**
who.ERG   2SG.ACC   say-PST
Who told you?
Ando ine yare?

minyanggu   **nginda**   **gindin**
why   2SG.NOM   laugh
Why are you laughing?
Minango inter gindan?

wanya   **nginda**   **nya-ra-nya?**
where   2SG.NOM   go-DEST-PRS
Where are you going?
Wunya inter yeranya?

ngaja   **ngina**   **galgal-ba**
1SG.NOM   2SG.ACC   cut-SBJV
I'm going to cut you.
Utcha-ine kabal-wa.

ngandu   **ngina**   **galgal?**
who.ERG   2SG.ACC   cut
Who cut you?
Ando-ine-kabal?

galga-Ø
cut-IMP
Cut it.
Kapa.

nyinyi-la
sit-OBLG
Sit down.
Yin-ila.

balga-Ø
arise-IMP
Get up.
Bal-ka.

da-ri	**nginda**
eat-PST	2S.NOM

Have you eaten?
Tchare-inter?

bing	**nginda**	**yaa-la**
father	2SG.NOM	say-OBLG

Tell your father.
Bing-inter-yalwa.

nyalanggan	**nginda**
telling.lies	2SG.NOM

You're lying.
Nylan-ang-ken-inter.

minyambu	**nginda**	**many**
how.many	2SG.NOM	catch

How many did you catch?
Minyambo-inter-maan?

wiya-Ø
let.go-IMP
Let go.
Wia.

milbanya   nginda
be.awake   2SG.NOM
Are you awake?
Meal-panye-inter?

gindin   ngaja   ganggiri   buga
laugh   1SG.NOM   dead   stinky
I laughed until I was dead and stinky.
Gindan utcha kangere booghor.

3.3.6. Meston 1890

biya-ma   buga
throw-CAUS   stinky
Throw it away; it stinks.
Beeamah booga.

balga-Ø   ngaliny   nyan-ma   waril=gu
come-IMP   1DU.NOM   go-CAUS   river=PURP
Let's go to (cross) the river.
Bulka gnalleen yamee warrilcoo.

ngaliny   wira-ra-biny
1DU.NOM   return-DEST-BACK
We came back home.
Gnalleen weerareppee.

nyan-ma-ba   ngagam
go-CAUS-SBJV   here.PROX
Let's go away from here.
Yanmerpa nahga.

garulban   ngaja   diranga   jar-di
tired   1SG.NOM   this.PROX   Country-LOC
I'm tired of being in this Country.
Caroolcan gnatja teeran jargee.

gira   bularam   nyan-ba   ngaja
Country   another   go-SBJV   1SG.NOM
I want to go to another Country.
Geera boolieram yieeba gnatya.

ngaliny　　**juruny=gu**　　**nyan-ba**
1DU.NOM　　eel=PURP　　go-SBJV
Let's go to fish eels.
Gnahleen joanko yieeba.

wanya　　**nginda**　　**nya-ra-nya**
where　　2SG.NOM　　go-DEST-PRS
Where are you going?
Wan yan inta yaranya.

wanji　　**balgal**　　**wira-biny**
when　　come　　return-BACK
When are (you) coming back?
Wanchee bagga weereppee.

nya-la
go-OBLG
Go away!
Yallah!

ngaja　　**nginu**　　**gawan**
1SG.NOM　　2SG.DAT　　love
I love you.
Gnatcha gninoo cowan.

ngariba　　**milgiri**
1SG.POSS　　sweetheart
(He is) my sweetheart.
Gnareeba milkirrie.

wuja-Ø　　**ngari**　　**minyalang**
give-IMP　　1SG.POSS　　thingamajig
Give me that.
Widja ngarie meenyalla.

ngan.gu　　**nginda**
how　　2SG.NOM
How are you?
Gnanahgo yinta?

minya   nginda   gindin-nya
what   2SG.NOM   laugh-PRS
What are you laughing at?
Minta inta gindahnya?

winanga-li-ba   giya-li-ba   ngaliny
hear-FUT-SBJV   sing-FUT-SBJV   1DU.NOM
Let's listen and sing.
Winangalliebah kiarriebah gnaleen.

ngari   nyubi-Ø
1SG.DAT   kiss-IMP
Give me a kiss.
Gnarree yoobee.

wanya   malara
where   black.man
Where are the black people?
Wanya mullara?

wanya
where
I don't know (lit. 'where').
Wanya.

wi   ngaliny   nyan-ba   da-li-ba
hey   1DU.NOM   go-SBJV   drink-SBJV
Hey, let's go have a drink.
Wee gnahleen yieeba jaleeba.

nginda   magiiba
2SG.NOM   friend
You're a friend.
Gninda mag'ieeba.

ngaliny   nyan-ba   da-li-ba   marumba
1DU.NOM   go-SBJV   drink-FUT-SBJV   good
Let's go and we'll have a nice drink.
gnaleen yieeba jaleeba maroomba

3.3.7. Star Song (Lauterer 1891)

mirigin	**mirigin**	**many**
star	star	catch

Catch a star, a star!
Mirrigen, mirrigen marn.

barany	**barany**	**barany**
soon	soon	soon

Soon, soon, soon!
baru, baru, baru!

mara	**yanggu-ma**	**ngan.gu**
hand	stiff-CAUS	like.this

Make your hands stiff like this
Mara yankuma ngangpo

nyawang	**many**	**barany**	**wai**
nicely	catch	soon	SONG

Catch nicely, soon, *wai!*
Nyiewang manpawo wae

mara	**yanggu-ma**
hand	stiff-CAUS

Make your hands stiff!
Mara yankuma!

3.3.8. White Woman Song (Lauterer 1891)

giya-la	**ngariba**	**waimirigan**	**nyawang=gu**
sing-OBLG	1SG.POSS	white.woman	nice=PURP

Sing my (song), to be nice to the white woman,
Gayalo ngarampa whymerigan nowago; 'Song very nice white lady with.'

giya-la	**ngariba**	**waimirigan**	**nyawang=gu**	**wai**
sing-OBLG	1SG.POSS	white.woman	nice=PURP	SONG

Sing my (song), to be nice to the white woman, *wai!*
gáyalo ngarampa whymerigan nowago wae!

3.3.9. Lauterer 1891; 1895

minyambu	**gubi**		**baji**	**barany**
how.many	brushtail.possum		kill	today

How many possums did you kill today?
Menyembu kupi putni peren?

yagara	**ngaja**	**nyan-ma-nya**
not	1SG.NOM	go-CAUS-PRS

I'm not going.
yagara ngacia yadmanya.

nyan-ma-nya	**ngi**	**nginda**
go-CAUS-PRS	Q	2SG.NOM

Are you going?
Yadmanya ngi nginte? 'Dost thou come?'

wanya=gu	**nyan-ra-nya**	**ngi**	**nginda**
where=PURP	go-DEST-PRS	Q	2SG.NOM

Where are you going?
Wunyángo yadnanya ngi nginte?

bany	**ngi**	**ngagam**	**jundal**
sick	Q	here.PROX	woman

Is the woman here sick?
Bayi ngi ngalam ds'undal 'Is she sick?'

wayara	**ngi**	**nginda**
be.hungry	Q	2SG.NOM

Are you hungry?
Wuaera ngi nginte?

wayara	**ngi**	**ngagam**	**jundal**
be.hungry	Q	here.PROX	woman

Is the woman here hungry?
Wuaera ngi ngalam ds'undal 'Is she hungry?'

ngan	**nginda**
who	2SG.NOM

Who are you?
Ngan nginte?

wanya   jalu   nginuba?
where   fire   2SG.POSS
Where are you staying? (lit. 'Where is your fire?')
Wunya tārlo nunwa?

wanya=gu   nyan-ra-nya   ngi   nginda
where=PURP   go-DEST-PRS   Q   2SG.NOM
Where are you going?
Wunyango yadnanya ngi nginta?

wali=gu   nginda
bad=PURP   2SG.NOM
Are your intentions bad?
Wadlin-gu nginda? 'Are you bad?'

wali   ngi   nginda
bad   Q   2SG.NOM
Are you bad?
Wadlingi nginte? 'Are you bad?'

marumba   ngaja
good   1SG.NOM
I am good.
marumba ngaoia.

marumba-bany   ngaja
good-INCH   1SG.NOM
I have become good.
marumbabanyingats'a. 'I was good'

marumba   ngaja   ngi   nginda
good   1SG.NOM   than   2SG.NOM
I'm better than you.
marumban gaoia ngigninte.

marumba   marumba
good   good
Very good.
marumba marumba

wali   wali
bad   bad
Very bad.
wadly-wadly

wi   balga-Ø
hey   come-IMP
Hello! (lit. 'Hey, come')
we balka 'come here! (welcome)'

guba-Ø
go.on-IMP
Goodbye! (lit. 'go on')
go wa

3.3.10. Donovan 1895

wali   nginda   mujari   bina   nginda
bad   2SG.NOM   liar   hear   2SG.NOM
You are no good, I hear you are a liar
Wodley gintay muggery pyne gintay 'You are no good, you are a liar'

3.3.11. Bobbiwinta's Song (Petrie 1904)

dabilgan   wali
oar   bad
My oar is bad
Dabalgan wadli

nga   gundul   ngari   waya-Ø
and   canoe   1SG.DAT   send-IMP
and send me a boat,
nga kundul ngari waiyar

ngaja   nyinyi   wigu
1SG.NOM   sit   Q
I'm waiting, right?
ngatta inen wiga

dalan-gan-bu   **ngaja**   **nyinyi-dunga**
close-CHARACT-DUR   1S.NOM   wait-IPFV
As (the water) closed over, I was waiting
Tallo canbu ngatta yiri duwa

dalbany-la   **ngari**   **gimuman**
jump-OBLG   1SG.DAT   friend
Jump over for me, friends
Dulpaiila ngari kimmoman

3.3.12. Hardcastle 1946–7

gilan-gilan   **jagan**   **nyan-ma-nya**
fish   eel   go-CAUS-PRS
I'm going to fish eels.
Gilen-Kilen-Dargun-Yenmino.

wanya-nga   **nginda**
where-ALL   2SG.NOM
Where are you going?
Woon-nanta-Intair?

mara-ba   **jagan**
catch-SBJV   eel
I want to catch eels.
Myriva dargun.

minya   **nginda**   **yaa-nya**
what   2SG.NOM   talk-PRS
What are you saying?
Minyar-Intair-yunna.

wali   **wagara**
bad   angry
Very angry.
waldee wuggera.

milin-gali   **mulam**
many-VERY   baby.boy
Plenty of babies.
Millen kully moolum.

ngaja   **wayara**
1SG.NOM   be.hungry
I'm hungry.
Nutchair Wher-ar.

wayara   **ngaja**
be.hungry   1SG.NOM
I'm hungry.
Wher-ar Nutchair.

nyan-ra-nya   **?**
go-DEST-PRES   ?
Going.
Yurunner Wooairinn 'Going.'

nyigira-Ø   **nginda**
run-IMP   2SG.NOM
You run.
Yee-gear-rinna.

naam   **nginda**   **nya-ra-nya**
there.DIST 2SG.NOM   go-DEST-PRS
Go over there.
Nun Nair Yur-on-ner.

yagarabu   **jan-bany-nya**
not.at.all   wet-INCH-PRS
You haven't washed up at all.
Yuggera-pul-Jun-bunga.

ngi   **nginda**   **yaga**
Q   2SG.NOM   work
Are you working?
Uney-Intair yeaca?

dabil   **mara-Ø**
water   get-IMP
Bring water.
Tabbil Marra.

ngagam **ngaja** **yaa-li-ba** **ngina**
here.PROX 1SG.NOM say-FUT-SBJV 2SG.ACC
Come here; I want to talk to you.
Gorgoy-Nutchair-Yarlivar Intair.

ngagam **ngina** **ngaja**
here.PROX 2SG.ACC 1SG.NOM
Come here; I (want) you.
Gorgoy-Intair-Nutchair

ngan **ngina** **ngaja**
who 2SG.ACC 1SG.NOM
Who are you, I (wonder)?
Arn-Intair-Nutchair

nyan-ma-nya
go-CAUS-PRS
Go.
Yen mino

wanya **nya** **nginda**
where go 2SG.NOM
Where are you going?
Woonnanta-Intair

minya **nginda** **yaa-nya**
what 2SG.NOM say-PRS
What are you saying?
Minyar-Intair-yunna

yagara **winanga-ri**
not hear-PST
I don't know (lit. 'I didn't hear.').
Yuggera-Wunnair Unnair.

wuja-Ø **?** **ngana** **nginda**
bring-IMP ? 1SG.ACC 2SG.NOM
You bring it for me.
Woo-die-gerla-Nanee-Intair.

nginda   **mara-Ø**   **ngari**
2SG.NOM   get-IMP   1SG.DAT
Get it for me.
Intair-Mara-Naree.

baan-ma-nya   **milin-gali**
nasty-CAUS-PRS   many-VERY
Someone's making a lot of noise
(lit. 'Someone is causing a lot of unpleasantness').
Barn-munna millen kully.

ngan   **gungany**   **ngunu**
who   shout   night
Who's shouting at night?
Arn-Koorgun-Oon-nunga?

buwa-nya   **barany**
marry-PRS   soon
Getting married soon.
Boo-un-na-burro.

nginda   **wulara-gali**
2SG.NOM   talk-VERY
You talk a lot.
Intair Wullera kully.

barany   **nguun**   **gurumba**   **ngaja**
now   hot   greatly   1SG.NOM
Very hot now, I (think).
Birran Norn Kooroomba Nutchair

ngan   **dungi-nya**
who   weep-PRS
Who is crying?
Arn Dunginna?

nyaany=gu   **nginda**
see=PURP   2S.NOM
Have a look.
Nanga Intair.

ngagam   **nginda**   **yaga-li-ba**
here.PROX   2SG.NOM   do-FUT-SBJV
Here, you do it.
Gorgoy Intair Yuggar Liviar.

da-ma-nya   **malar-jin-du**
eat-CAUS-PRS   man-PL-ERG
People are eating it.
Junmino Ma-lardino.

ngaja   **yigil-nya**
1SG.NOM   be.cold-PRS
I'm cold.
Nutchair Yeelginn.

jan-gali-bany
wet-VERY-INCH
I've become thoroughly wet.
Jungul-pun. 'I'm a wet fellow.'

nginda   **nyalang-gali**
2SG.NOM   tell.lie-VERY
You're a liar. (Lit. 'you lie a lot')
Intair Un-un-kully.

3.3.13. Holmer 1983

wanya   **nginda**   **nya-ra-nya**
where   2SG.NOM   go-DEST-PRS
Where are you going?
waɲa ɲinda (ɲinda) jaraɲa

Miganjin   **ngaja**   **nya-ra-nya**
Brisbane   1SG.NOM   go-DEST-PRS
I'm going to Brisbane.
megenɟen ŋaja jaraɲa

nginda   **ngariba**   **milgiri**
2SG.NOM   1SG.POSS   sweetheart
You're my sweetheart.
ɲinda ɲariwa milgari

ngari   **nyubi-Ø**
1SG.DAT   kiss-IMP
Give me a kiss.
ɲari ɲubi

minyanggu   **nginda**   **ngariba**
why   2SG   1SG.POSS
Why are you talking to me?
miɲaŋgu ŋinda ŋariba

nyubany   **baga-li-nya**
married.couple   fight-REFL-PRS
A married couple is fighting (each other).
ɲubaɲ bagaliɲa

bujirang   **jabu-ra**
boy   ·   be.frightened-NEG
Don't be frightened, boy.
buɟiraŋ ɟabur(a)

biigi   **jabu**
sun   be.frightened
It's late (lit. 'the sun is frightened').
bigi ɟabu

nginda   **ngariba**   **giba**
2SG.NOM   1SG.POSS   initiated.youth
You're my young man.
ŋinda ŋarijuba gibar

yugu   **dabingbila**   **digi**
there.MED   policeman   white.man
There, a policeman, a white man.
jugu dabiŋbila, dege

gujalgan   **digi-jin**   **nginda**   **mara-ba**
mischief   white.man-PL   2SG.NOM   steal-SBJV
As mischief, you could steal (oysters) from the white people.
guɟalgan: degeɟin ŋinda mariba

3.3.14. Omitted sentences

The following sentences could not be glossed in Yagara and are not included in the above lists. Sentence (1) may be Badjala. Sentence (2), *Nunka Mubbil Birrain* translates as 'sun blind today' in Yugambeh, and sentence (3) is likely Yugambeh as well.

1. *Camia cajamia oonganna* 'I don't like you.' (Meston 1986a)
2. *Nunka Mubbil Birrain* 'No sun to-day.' (Hardcastle 1946–7)
3. *Kereena-Ker-reepa-Nulpa.* 'We go swim.' (Hardcastle 1946–7)

Other texts are omitted from the lists because they do not appear native-like. These consist of the sentences invented by Lauterer for purposes of grammatical explanation (Lauterer 1891); the versions of the Lord's Prayer by Lauterer and Meston (Lauterer 1891; Meston 1986b); the sentences Meston (1894) quotes himself as saying at an Aboriginal man's trial (1894, 549); and the phrases and sentences by an unknown speaker of limited fluency in Wurm (1960).

3.4. The Resurrection (Ridley 1875)

ngana	bangga	winanga-Ø
1SG.ACC	quickly	hear-IMP

Listen to me for a bit,
Ŋunna bukki wīnunga;

ngaja	ngilbulana	yaa-li
1SG.NOM	2PL.ACC	say-FUT

I'll talk to you.
ŋutta ilpūllāna yāli

ngaja	yagar	mujari-bany	nga
1SG.NOM	no	liar-INCH	and

I won't become a liar, and
ŋutta yugār mudyeri punna;

yaa	marumba	ngambila-nga
talk	good	everyone-ALL

talk is good for everyone.
ya murrūmba ŋāmbilleŋu

235

imanuwal   **ngunyal**   **mumbal-nuba**   **nyaring**
Immanuel   3SG.NOM   thunder-POSS   son
Immanuel, he was the son of God.
Immanuel wunnal Mūmbālnūbba nurriŋ;

ngunyal   **dagai-bany**
3SG.NOM   white.man-INCH
He became a white man;
Wunnal duggai punni

ngunyal   **baluny**   **ngalbanu**
3SG.NOM   die   1PL.DAT
he died for us.
wunnal bāllūn ŋulpunna.

ngaliny   **ngambila=bu**   **wali**
1DU.NOM   all=EMPH   bad
We are all bad;
Ŋulle ŋāmbillebu waddeli;

mumbal   **baan-du**   **ngalinyana**   **mumbal**   **yaa-ri**
thunder   be.angry-ATEL   1DU.ACC   thunder   say-PST
God is angry with us. God said,
Mūmbāl bāndu ŋulleŋunna. Mumbal yari:

ngambila=bu   **dagai-jin**   **wali**
all=EMPH   white.man-PL   bad
'All white men are bad;
'Ŋāmbillebu duggatin waddeli;

ngaja   **galima-li**   **ngunyalina**
1SG.NOM   punish-FUT   3PL.ACC
I will punish them.'
ŋutta kālimurri wunnālina.'

imanuwal   **yaa-ri**
Immanuel   say-PST
Immanuel said,
Imanuwal yari:

wana   **nginda**   **galimal**   **ngunyalina**
do.not   2SG.NOM   punish   3PL.ACC
'Don't punish them;
'Wunna ŋinta kālimul wunnalina;

ngana   **nginda**   **galimal**
1SG.ACC   2SG.NOM   punish
you punish me.
ŋunna ŋinta kalimul

ngana   **nginda**   **buma-Ø**   **ngaja**   **baluny-ba**
1SG.ACC   2SG.NOM   smite-IMP   1SG.NOM   die-SBJV
Strike me, let me die.'
ŋunna ŋinta būmma, ŋutta bāllūpa.'

imanuwal   **ngunyal**   **marumba**
Immanuel   3SG.NOM   good
Immanuel, he was good;
Immanuel wunnal murrumba;

ngunyal   **baluny**   **ngalinyanu**
3SG.NOM   die   1DU.DAT
he died for us;
Wunnal bāllūn ŋulleŋunnu;

ngaliny   **ngambila=bu**   **wali**
1DU.NOM   all=EMPH   bad
we are all bad.
ŋulle ŋāmbillebu waddeli;

ngaliny   **milbulbu-bany**
1DU.NOM   be.alive-INCH
We are alive;
ŋulle mibulpubun;

ngalinyana   **yagar**   **galima-nya**
1DU.ACC   not   punish-PRS
he is not punishing us.
ŋulleŋunna yugar kalimunna.

imanuwal   marumba
Immanuel   good
Immanuel is good;
Immanuel murrumba;

yagar   wali   ngunyal-ba-di   nyinyi-du
no   bad   3SG-ABL-LOC   dwell-ATEL
there is no evil in him.
yugar waddeli wunalpuddi ŋinēdu.

ngunyal   bany-bila-jin   yagany
3SG.NOM   sick-STATE-PL   heal
He heals the sick;
Wunnal paīmbiladin yuggān:

ngunyal   nga   binangundu   yagany
3SG.NOM   also   deaf   heal
he also heals the deaf;
wunnal ŋa pidnaŋūntū yuggān;

ngunyal   ganggir   balgal-ma-ri
3SG.NOM   dead   arise-CAUS-PST
he made the dead rise
Wunnal kungīr bulgunmurri,

nga   milbulbu-ma-ri
and   be.alive-CAUS-PST
and made them be alive.
ŋa milbulpumurri.

barany   wali   dagai-jin   imanuwal   many
then   bad   white.man-PL   Immanuel   take
Then bad white men seize Immanuel
Burru waddeli duggatin Immanuel māni,

nga   ganggir-ma-ri
and   dead-CAUS-PST
and killed him.
ŋa kungīrmurri.

ngunyali baguur jubui galga-ri
3PL.NOM tree straight cut-PST
They cut a straight tree;
Wunnale bāgūr tūbuī kulkurri;

ngunyali garuba baguur galga-ri
3PL.NOM another tree cut-PST
they cut another tree,
wunnale kurruba bagur kulkurri

nga wangan-ma-ri
and place.above-CAUS-PST
and put it on top.
ŋa wŭnkamurri;

ngunyali bulabu baguur-na nany
3PL.NOM both tree-ACC tie
They tied both trees.
wunnale būdelabo bagūrna nŭnni.

ngunyali imanuwal many
3PL.NOM Immanuel take
They seized Immanuel.
Wunnale Immanuel māni;

miir mara-di bimba-ri
hole hand-LOC pierce-PST
They pierced holes in his hands
mīr murradi bimberri;

nga miir jina-di bimba-ri
and hole foot-LOC pierce-PST
and pierced holes in his feet,
ŋa mīr tjidnendi bimberri.

nga ngunyali imanuwal baguur-di wura
and 3PL.NOM Immanuel tree-LOC put
and they put Immanuel on the trees;
Ŋa wunnale Imanuel bāgūrti wune:

ngunyal   **duran**   **baguur-di**
3SG.NOM   hang.something   tree-LOC
they hung him on the trees
Wunnal duran bāgūrti:

nga   **ngunyal**   **ganggir-bany**
and   3SG.NOM   die-INCH
and he died.
Ŋa Wunnal kungīrpun.

ngunyali   **balgal-ma-ri**   **baguuru-ba**
3PL.NOM   arise-CAUS-PST   tree-ABL
They lifted him from the trees
Wunnale bulgunmurri bagūrubba;

jar-di   **dany-ma-ri**
earth-LOC   lie-CAUS-PST
(and) laid him in the ground.
tarti daiemurri.

imanuwal   **ngunu-bu**   **ganggir**   **dany-dunga**
Immanuel   night-DUR   dead   lie-IPFV
That night Immanuel lay dead,
Imanuel ŋūnūmbo kungīr daieduŋa;

mulagu   **ngunyal**   **ganggir**   **dany-dunga**
next.day   3SG.NOM   dead   lie-IPFV
and the next day he lay dead,
mūdelago Wunnal kungīr daieduŋa;

nga   **ngunu**   **garuba**   **ganggir**   **dany-dunga**
and   night   another   dead   lie-IPFV
and another night he lay dead,
ŋa ŋūnnu kurruba kungīr daieduŋa:

garuba   **mulagu**   **ngunyal**   **balga-ra**
another   next.day   3SG.NOM   arise-DEST
and the next day he rose up,
kurruba mudelago Wunnal bulkurrun

milbulbu-bany
be.alive-INCH
(and) became alive.
milbulpubun.

barany	**imanuwal**	**biram-di**	**wandi-ri**
then	Immanuel	sky-LOC	rise-PST

Then Immanuel rose to the sky.
Burru Immanual birradi wundāre;

barany	**ngunyal**	**biram-di**	**nyinyi-nya**
now	3SG.NOM	sky-LOC	dwell-PRS

Now he lives in the sky.
berren Wunnal birradi ŋinnenna.

ngunyalu	**ngalbana**	**nyaa-nya**
3SG.ERG	1PL.ACC	see-PRS

He sees us.
Wunnalu ŋulpāna nanna.

3.5. From Genesis 1, 2, and 3 (Ridley 1875)

mumbal	**ngambila=bu**	**nana-jin**	**yaga-ri**
thunder	all=EMPH	thing-PL	make-PST

God made everything.
Mūmbāl ŋāmbillebu nunāntjin yugāri.

galuma	**biigi**	**yagar**
long.ago	day	not

Long ago, the sun didn't exist,
gālūma bīgi yugār,

nga	**gilan**	**yagar**	**nga**	**mirigin**
and	moon	not	and	star

and the moon didn't exist, nor the stars;
ŋa killen yugār ŋa mirregin;

nga	**daun**	**yagar**	**milbulbu**
and	creature	not	be.alive

nor any living thing.
ŋa daoŭn yugar milbūlpū.

yigi   **jar**   **ngalba**   **nyinyi-du**
also   earth   1PL.NOM   dwell-ATEL
Also the earth we live on,
Ikki tār, ŋulpa ŋinēdu

jar   **yagar**
earth   not
the earth didn't exist.
tār yugār.

gurumba   **mumbal**   **ngambila=bu**   **yaga-ri**
great   thunder   all=EMPH   make-PST
Great God made everything.
Kurumba Mūmbāl ŋambillebu yugāri.

jar   **barany**   **gurung**
earth   then   black
The earth was then black
Tār berren kūrūn,

yagar   **ngur**   **nyinyi-du**
not   shape   exist-ATEL
and shapeless.
yugar ŋōr ŋīnēdu

gurung-gurung   **wangandi**   **dabil**   **nyinyi**
darkness   above   water   sit
Darkness lay over the water.
Kūrunkūrun wuŋunti tabbil ŋinne.

baguur   **yagar**   **duru-dunga**   **jar-di**
tree   no   grow-IPFV   earth-LOC
There were no trees, growing in the earth,
Bāgūl yugār, dūrūthūŋa tārti,

gudal   **yagar,**   **dagai-jin**   **yagar**
bushes   not   white.man-PL   not
no bushes, no white men,
kuddal yugār, duggatin yugar

yaraman   yagar   nga   mari   yagar
horse   not   and   kangaroo   not
no horses and kangaroos,
yaraman yugar ŋa murri yugar,

nguruny   yagar
emu   not
no emus.
ŋurun yugar.

mumbal   ngambila=bu   yaga-ri
thunder   all=EMPH   make-PST
God made everything
Mumbal ŋambillebu yugāri,

majan   nga   majan   biigi
three   and   three   day
(in) three-and-three days.
muddān ŋa muddān bīgi.

yaja   biigi   mumbal   yaa-ri
first   day   thunder   say-PST
The first day, God said
Yutta bīgi; Mumbal yāri;

gidibila   balga-Ø   barany   gidibila   balga-ri
light   come-IMP   then   light   come-PST
'Light, come!' and the light came.
'Kittbilla bulka!' Berren kittibilla bulkurri.

mumbal   gidibila   banman.gilin   gurung-gurung-di
thunder   light   pick.out   darkness-LOC
God separated the light from the darkness.
Mumbal kittbila pūnmāngillin kūrunkūrunti.

mumbal   gidibila   nai-ba-ri   biigi
thunder   light   name-INCH-PST   day
God named the light 'day';
Mumbal kittibilla naiiburri bigi;

ngunyal   **gurung-gurung**   **nai-ba-ri**   **ngunu**
3SG.NOM   darkness   name-INCH-PST   night
he named the darkness 'night'.
wunnal kurunkurun naiiburri ŋūnnū.

biigi-biribi   **nga**   **ngunugaba**   **biigi**   **ganyar**
evening   and   morning   day   one
Evening and morning, day one.
Bīgibīrpi ŋa ŋūnnūŋubbu bigi kunnar.

biigi   **garuba**   **mumbal**   **biram**   **yaga-r**
day   another   thunder   sky   make-PST
Second day, God made the sky.
Bigi kurruga; Mumbal birra yugari.

biigi   **majan**   **mumbal**   **yaa-ri**
day   three   thunder   say-PST
Day three, God said,
Bigi muddān, Mumal yari;

ngambila=bu   **dabil**   **ganyardi**   **wandi**
all=EMPH   water   together   lift
'All waters, lift together,
'Nambillebu tabbil kunnarti wuni;

nga   **jara**   **nambany**
and   earth   appear
and earth, appear'.
ŋa durrun nūmbāni.

barany   **ngunyal**   **dabil**   **nai-ba-ri**   **dabilbaan**
then   3SG.NOM   water   name-INCH-PST   salt.water
Then he named the water 'sea',
Burru wunnal tabbil naīburri Tabbilbon;

nga   **jara**   **nai-ba-ri**   **jar**
and   earth   name-INCH-PST   earth
and named the earth, 'land'.
Ŋa durrun naīburri Tār.

ngunyal **baguur** **yaga-ri** **nga** **bunggil**
3SG.NOM   tree   make-PST   and   grass
He made trees and grass;
Wunnal bāgūr yugari ŋa bungil;

bunggil **daran** **jar** **gungama-ri**
grass   grow   earth   make.cover-PST
the grass grew and covered the earth.
bungil dūrūn, tār kūnkamurri.

bula **nga** **bula** **biigi**
two   and   two   day
Two-and-two day,
Būdela ŋa būdela bīgi;

mumbal **biigi** **nga** **gilan** **yaga-ri**
thunder   sun   and   moon   make-PST
God made the Sun and the Moon;
Mumbal bigi ŋa killen yugari;

ngunyal **yaa-ri** **biigi** **nambany-ba=gu**
3SG.NOM   say-PST   sun   shine-SBJV=PURP
he said, 'let the Sun shine,
Wunnal yari; bigi nūmbaipuggu;

barany **ngunyal** **gara-ba=gu**
then   3SG.NOM   go.down-SBJV=PURP
then let it set.'
burru wunnal kurraipuggu.

yigi **ngunyal** **mirigin** **yaga-ri**
also   3SG.NOM   star   make-PST
Also, he made the stars.
Ikki Wunnal mirregin yugari.

bula **nga** **majan** **biigi**
two   and   three   day
Two-and-three day,
Budela ŋa muddan bigi;

mumbal   daunbin   yaga-ri
thunder   bird   make-PST
God made birds;
Mumbal taoŭnpin yugari;

daunbin   wangandi   yara-dunga
bird   above   fly-IPFV
birds were flying up above;
taoŭnpin wungunti yūrūdunga.

ngunyal   gurumba   dalubila   yaga-ri
3SG.NOM   great   whale   make-PST
he made the mighty whales
Wunnal kūrūmba tāllūbilla yugari,

nga   buwai   nga   yangan
and   shark   and   dugong
and sharks and dugong
ŋa baoai ŋa yungun

nga   ngambila   guiyar   yaga-ri
and   all   fish   make-PST
and made all the fish;
ŋa ŋambille kuïyur yugari;

guiyar   yara-dunga   dabil-di
fish   swim-IPFV   water-LOC
fish were swimming in the water.
kuïyūr yūrūdunga tabbilti.

majan   nga   majan   biigi
three   and   three   day
Three-and-three day,
Muddān ŋa muddān bigi;

mumbal   yaraman   bula
thunder   horse   cattle
God … horse, cows,
Mumbal yaraman, bulla,

mari	**yuwan**	**gubi**	**miri**	**ngal-ngal**
kangaroo	snake	possum	tame.dog	dingo

kangaroos, snakes, possums, dogs, dingos,

murri, yūwun, kuppi, mirri, ŋulgul,

manggi-manggi	**ngambila=bu**	**milbulbu**
sheep	all=EMPH	be.alive

sheep, all living things

munkimunki, ŋambillebu milbūlpu

jar-di	**nyinyi-du**	**yaga-ri**
earth-LOC	dwell-ATEL	make-PST

dwelling on land, made.

tarti ŋinedu yugari.

barany	**mumbal**	**yaa-ri**	**ngaliny**	**yaga-li**
then	thunder	say-PST	1DU.NOM	make-FUT

Then God said, 'We will make

Burru Mumbal yari; 'ŋulle yugale

dagai	**ngamba**	**ngaliny**
white.man	like	1DU.NOM

white man like us

duggai ŋamba ŋulle;

nga	**ngunyal**	**bandar**	**ngambila=bu**	**jar-di**
and	3SG.NOM	honorific	all=EMPH	earth-LOC

and he will be lord of everything on Earth

ŋa Wunnal bundūr ŋambillebu tarti,

nga	**ngambila=bu**	**nana-jin**	**nyinyi-du**
and	all=EMPH	thing-PL	dwell-ATEL

and all the creatures dwelling there.

ŋa ŋambillebu nanantjin ŋinēdu.'

barany	**mumbal**	**dagai**	**yaga-ri**
then	thunder	white.man	make-PST

Then God made white man

Berren Mumbal duggai yugari

247

ngamba   ngunyal   marumba
like   3SG.NOM   good
like him, good.
ŋamba Wunnal murrumba.

yigi   mumbal   jundal   yaga-ri
also   thunder   woman   make-PST
He also made woman
Ikki Mumbal jŭndal yugari

ngamba   ngunyal   marumba
like   3SG.NOM   good
like him, good.
ŋamba Wunnal murrumba.

mumbal   yarang-di-ba   dagai-na   yaga-ri
thunder   sand-LOC-ABL   white.man-ACC   make-PST
God made white man out of sand.
Mumbal yārūntibēr duggana yugari.

ngunyal   nguru   bui
3SG.NOM   spirit   breathe
When he breathed spirit
Wunnal ŋuru puï

guri-ba-ma-ri   muru-di
enter-RTP-CAUS-PST   nose-LOC
into the nose,
kurribunmurri murudi;

barany   dagai   milbulbu-bany
then   white.man   be.alive-INCH
at once the white man came to life.
berren duggai milbūlpūbun;

mumbal   dagai-na   nai-ba-ri   adam
thunder   white.man-ACC   name-INCH-PST   Adam
God named the white man 'Adam'.
Mumbal duggana naïburri 'Adam.'

mumbal yaa-ri
thunder say-PST
God said,
Mumbal yari

yagar marumba dagai ganyar nyinyi
not good white.man alone dwell
'It's not good that the white man lives alone.
'Yugar murrumba duggai kunnar ŋinnen.

ngaja jundal ngunyanu yaga-li
1SG.NOM woman 3SG.DAT make-FUT
I'll make a woman for him.
Yutta jūndāl wunnaun yuggāle.'

mumbal adam bugany-ma-ri buiyala dany
thunder Adam sleep-CAUS-PST for.a.long.time lie
God put Adam to sleep, to lie for a long time.
Mumbal Adam būggānmurri puïyala daïn.

mumbal jirban guda-di-ba banman
thunder bone side-LOC-ABL pluck
God plucked a bone from his side;
Mumbal tirben kūttādibēr pūnmān;

ngunyal bangga baigal-baigal dalan ngadan-ma-ri
3SG.NOM quickly flesh close meet-CAUS-PST
He quickly closed the flesh and made it join.
Wunnal banka paigulpaigul dūllūŋūntūmurri.

barany ngunyal jirban guda-di-ba banman-ba
then 3SG.NOM bone side-LOC-ABL pluck-RTP
Then, plucking a bone from the side,
Berren Wunnal tjirbēn kuttadiber pūnmānibēr

junda-na yaga-ri
woman-ACC make-PST
he made woman.
jūndāna yugāri.

barany	mumbal	junda-na	balga-ri	dagai-na
then	thunder	woman-ACC	bring-PST	white.man-ACC

Then God brought the woman to the white man.
Burru Mumbal jundāna bulkairi duggānu.

adam	yaa-ri
Adam	say-PST

Adam said,
Adam yari,

gaa	jundal	jirban	jirban-di	ngariba-di
that.MED	woman	bone	bone-LOC	1SG.POSS-LOC

'This woman is bone of my bone,
'Ka jundal tjirben tjirbenti ŋurribāti,

nga	baigal-baigal	baigal-baigal-di	ngariba-di
and	flesh	flesh-LOC	1SG.POSS-LOC

and flesh of my flesh.
ŋa paigulpaigul paigulpaigulti ŋurribāti:

ngunyal	jundal	ngariba
3SG.NOM	woman	1SG.POSS

She is my wife.
wunnal jundal ŋurriba.

nai-ri	dagai	adam
name-PST	white.man	Adam

The white man was named Adam;
Nurri duggai Adam;

nai-ri	jundal	iva
name-PST	woman	Eve

the woman was named Eve.
nurri jundal Iva.

mumbal	dagai-na	nga	junda-na	yaa-ri
thunder	white.man-ACC	and	woman-ACC	say-PST

God said to the white man and the woman,
Mumbal duggana ŋa jundana yari,

nginda	**junggul**	**nguwanga**	**ganin**	**buunyi-buunyi**
2SG.NOM	pandanus	large.fig	small.fig	bunya

'You – the breadfruit, fig, small fig, bunya,
Ɲinda tjungūl, ŋōaɲā, kunnin, boinyi boinyi,

ngambila=bu	**baguur-di**	**da-la**
all=EMPH	tree-LOC	eat-OBLG

all the trees – may eat;
ŋāmbillebu baguti tulla:

ngundu	**ganyar**	**baguur**	**ngurdi**	**jiladu**
only	one	tree	in.the.area	in.the.middle

only the one tree in the middle,
ŋūndū kunnar bāgūr ŋūrti jillērdu

nginda	**wana**	**danga-na**	**baguur-na**	**da-la**
2SG.NOM	do.not	that.DIST-ACC	tree-ACC	eat-OBLG

do not eat from that tree.
inta wunna dungama bagurna tulla.

nginda	**wina**	**danga-na**	**baguur-na**	**da-li**
2SG.NOM	when	that.DIST-ACC	tree-ACC	eat-FUT

If you eat from that tree,
Ɲinda winna dungama bagurna tulli,

nga	**nginda**	**ngundu**	**baluny**	**biigi-bu**
and	2SG.NOM	surely	die	day-DUR

on that day you will surely die.
ŋa ŋinda ŋūndu balluia bigibu.

wali	**magui**	**yuwan-di**	**balga-ri**
bad	devil	serpent-LOC	come-PST

An evil spirit entered a serpent;
Waddeli maguï yūunti bulkurri;

ngunyal	**yaa-ri**	**mumbal**	**yaa-ri**
3SG.NOM	say-PST	thunder	say-PST

he said, 'God said,
wunnal yari, 'Mumbal yari,

nginda	**wana**	**ngambila=bu**	**baguur-di**	**da-la**
2SG.NOM	do.not	all=EMPH	tree-LOC	eat-OBLG

you may not eat from all the trees?'
ɲinta wunna ŋābillebu bagulti tulla?'

iva	**yaa-ri**	**mumbal**	**yaa-ri**	**ngalinyana**
Eve	say-PST	thunder	say-PST	1DU.ACC

Eve said, 'God said to us,
Iva yari: 'Mumbal yari ŋulleŋunna;

nginda	**junggul**	**nguwanga**	**ganin**	**buunyi-buunyi**
2SG.NOM	pandanus	large.fig	small.fig	bunya

'you, the breadfruit, fig, little fig, bunya,
Ɲinta, tjungūl, ŋōaŋā, kunnin, boinyiboinyi,

ngambila=bu	**baguur-di**	**da-la**
all=EMPH	tree-LOC	eat-OBLG

all the trees, may eat;
ŋāmbillebu bāgūlti tulla;

ngundu	**ganyar**	**baguur**	**ngurdi**	**jiladu**
only	one	tree	in.the.area	in.the.middle

only the one tree in the middle of the area,
ŋūndū kunnar bagur ŋūrti jillērdu,

nginda	**wana**	**danga-na**	**baguur-na**	**da-la**
2SG.NOM	do.not	that.DIST-ACC	tree-ACC	eat-OBLG

you may not eat from that tree.
inta wunna dungama bagūrna tulla.

nginda	**wina**	**danga-na**	**baguur-na**	**da-li**
2SG.NOM	when	that.DIST-ACC	tree-ACC	eat-FUT

If you eat from that tree,
Ɲinta winna dungama bagurna tulli,

nginda	**ngundu**	**baluny**	**biigi-bu**
2SG.NOM	surely	die	day-DUR

that day you will surely die.
ŋinta ŋundu balluïa bīgibu.

baguur **ngurdi** **jiladu** **dunbal**
tree in.the.area in.the.middle forbidden
The tree in the middle is forbidden.'
Bagur ŋurti jillerdu tūnbul.'

magui **yuwan-di** **nyinyi-dany** **yaa-ri**
devil serpent-LOC dwell-RNP say-PST
The demon that dwelled in the serpent said,
Maguï yūunti ŋīnēdu yari,

nginda **yagar** **baluny** **barany** **nginda**
2SG.NOM not die then 2SG.NOM
'You will not die. As soon as you
'Ŋinta yugar balluï. Burra ŋinta

wina **baguur-na** **ngurdi** **jiladu** **da-li**
when tree-ACC in.the.area in.the.middle eat-FUT
eat from the tree in the middle,
winna bagurna ŋurti jillerdu tulli,

mil **nginda** **yagany-ba**
eye 2SG.NOM heal-SBJV
your eyes will be healed;
mil ŋinta yuggaipa;

nginda **ngamba** **mumbal**
2SG.NOM like thunder
you will be like God.'
ŋinta ŋamba Mumbal.'

jundal **ngui-ba-nya** **nga** **yuwan** **winanga-ri**
woman believe-RTP-PRS and serpent hear-PST
The woman, believing, listened to the serpent;
Jūndāl ŋuïpunāŋ yūunwīnuŋurri;

guna **muya** **danga** **baguur-na**
heart desire that.DIST tree-ACC
her heart desired that fruit.
kudna muïya dūŋa bagūrnu.

barany **ngunyal** **banman**
then 3SG.NOM pluck
Then she plucked;
Burru wunnal pūnmān;

nga **da-ri** **nga** **dagai-na** **wujan**
and eat-PST and white.man-ACC give
and ate, and gave to the white man.
ŋa turri, ŋa dugganu widdan;

dagai-du **da-ri** **ngunyali** **mil** **yagany**
white.man-ERG eat-PST 3PL.NOM eye heal
The white man ate. Their eyes were healed.
duggaidu turri. Wunnale mil yuggān;

ngunyali **mangin-bany**
3PL.NOM be.ashamed-INCH
They became ashamed.
wunnale mūŋinpunni;

ngunyali **nguruman** **gudal-di** **mumbal-na-di**
3PL.NOM hide.oneself bushes-LOC thunder-ACC-LOC
They hid in the bushes from God,
wunnale ŋuruman kuddalti Mumbalnundi,

nyaany **ngundu** **ngunyal=gu**
see lest 3PL.NOM=PURP
so he wouldn't see them.
naiya ŋunda ŋullin.ga.

mumbal **gungany** **adam** **wanya** **nginda**
thunder shout Adam where 2SG.NOM
God called, 'Adam, where are you?'
Mumbal kuŋaïn: 'Adam, winna inta?'

adam **yaa-ri** **ngaja** **yandany**
Adam say-PST 1SG.NOM fear
Adam said, 'I was afraid;
Adam yari, 'ŋutta yundum;

ngaja   **mangin-bany**   **ngaja**   **nguruman**
1SG.NOM be.ashamed-INCH 1SG.NOM hide.oneself
I became ashamed; I hid.'
ŋutta mūɲinpunni, ŋutta ŋuruman.'

mumbal **yaa-ri**
thunder say-PST
God said,
Mumbal yar:

nginda   **minyangdi**   **mangin-ba-nya**
2SG.NOM why   ashamed-INCH-PRS
'Why were you ashamed?
Inta minninji mūɲinpunna?

nginda **baguuru-na** **ngurdi** **jiladu** **da-ri**
2SG.NOM tree-ACC in.the.area in.the.middle eat-PST
Have you eaten from the tree in the middle?'
Inta bagurna ŋurti jillerdu turri?'

dagai **yaa-ri**
white.man say-PST
The white man said,
Duggai yari:

jundal **nginda** **ngari** **wujan-ba**
woman 2SG.NOM 1SG.DAT give-RTP
'The woman that you gave me,
Jundal Inta ŋurri widdanibēr,

ngunyal **jundal** **ngari** **baguur-di** **wujan**
3SG.NOM woman 1SG.DAT tree-LOC give
the woman, she gave me fruit from the tree;
wunnal jundal ŋurri bagurti widdan;

nga **ngaja** **da-ri**
and 1SG.NOM eat-PST
and I ate.'
ŋa ŋutta turri.'

mumbal	**junda-na**	**yaa-ri**
thunder	woman-ACC	say-PST

God said to the woman,
Mumbal jundana yari,

nginda	**minya**	**yaga-ri**	**jundal**	**yaa-ri**
2SG.NOM	what	do-PST	woman	say-PST

'What have you done?' The woman said,
'Inta minya yugāri?' Jundal yari:

yuwan-du	**ngana**	**nyalang-ma-ri**	**yaa-ri**
serpent-ERG	1SG.ACC	tell.lie-CAUS-PST	say-PST

'The serpent told lies to me and spoke,
'Yūndu ŋunna nulluŋmurri yari;

nga	**ngaja**	**da-ri**
and	1SG.NOM	eat-PST

and I ate.'
ŋa ŋutta turri.'

mumbal	**dagai-na**	**nga**	**junda-na**	**yaa-ri**
thunder	white.man-ACC	and	woman-ACC	say-PST

God said to the white man and the woman,
Mumbal duggana ŋa jundana yari:

ngilbang	**bulabu**	**baluny**
2DU.NOM	both	die

'You both will die.
'Ilpūŋ budelabu ballui.

ngilbang	**yarang**	**gumbal**
2DU.NOM	sand	merely

You are only sand,
Ilpūŋ yārūng kūmbal,

nga	**yarang**	**gumbal**	**ngilbang**	**wira**
and	sand	merely	2DU.NOM	return

and you will return to sand.'
ŋa yarung kūmbal ilpūŋ wirrē.'

256

3.6. From Luke 7 and 8 (Ridley 1875)

imanuwal milindu yaa-nya
Immanuel long talk-PRS
Immanuel was speaking for a long time,
Imanuel millendu yana:

nga ngunyal nyan-dunga gabarnaum
and 3SG.NOM travel-IPFV Capernaum
and he was travelling to Capernaum.
ŋa Wunnal yeatuŋa Kapernaŭm;

gabarnaum Miyanjin ngaranga gamandan
Capernaum Brisbane there.is/was Commandant
Capernaum was a city. There was a Commandant,
Kapernaŭm mīantjun; ŋuruŋa Kommandant:

ngunyanuba dagai bany=gu da-nya
3SG.POSS white.man sick=PURP lie-PRS
his white man was lying sick;
wunnanŭbu duggai paingo daina;

ngunyal jigandi baluny
3SG.NOM almost dead
he was almost dead.
wunnal tjigenti bāllūni.

gamandan imanuwal winanga-ri
Commandant Immanuel hear-PST
The Commandant heard that Immanuel
Kommandant Immanuel wīnaŋurri

Miyanjin nyinyi-du
Brisbane dwell-ATEL
was staying in the city.
iantjun ŋīnadu:

ngunyal dagai-jin muyan=gu waya-ri
3SG.NOM white.man-PL entreat=PURP send-PST
He sent white men to entreat,
wunnal duggatin moyumko waiari:

257

dagai	**ngariba**	**bany=gu**	**nginda**	**balga-Ø**
white.man	1SG.POSS	sick=PURP	2SG.NOM	come-IMP

'My white man is sick; come,
'Duggai ŋurriba paingo; inta bulka;

bany	**yaga-li-ba**	**dagai**	**balga-ri**
sickness	heal-FUT-SBJV	white.man	come-PST

please heal the sickness. The white men came;
paī yagulliba.' Duggai bulkurri;

jigan	**yaa-li**	**imanuwal**	**balga-li-ba**
insistently	say-FUT	Immanuel	come-FUT-SBJV

insistently they tell Immanuel that he should come.
tiggen yali Immanuel bulkullibi

ngunyali	**yaa-li**	**gamandan**	**marumba**	**dagai**
3PL.NOM	say-FUT	Commandant	good	white.man

They say, 'The Commandant is a good white man.'
Wunnale yāli, 'Kommandant murrūmba duggai.'

imanuwal	**nyan-dunga**	**ngunyali-ba-nga**
Immanuel	travel-IPFV	3PL-ABL-ALL

Immanuel was travelling with them.
Imanuel yeatūŋa ŋulle buggā.

ngunyali	**jigandi**	**balga-ri**	**ngumbi-nga**
3PL.NOM	almost	come-PST	house-ALL

They had almost arrived at the house.
Wunnale tjigenti bulkari ūmpiŋga.

gamandan	**ngunyanuba**	**ngabang-na**	**waya-ri**
Commandant	3SG.POSS	elder.brother-ACC	send-PST

The Commandant sent his elder brother
Kommandant wūnnanūba ŋubbuŋa waiāri;

ngunyal	**yaa-li-ba**	**wana**	**balgal**
3SG.NOM	say-FUT-SBJV	do.not	come

to say, 'Don't come
wunnal yālibe, 'Wunna bulkul

ngaja   **yagar**   **marumba**
1SG.NOM   not   good
I am not good;
ŋutta yugar murrumba;

wana   **nginda**   **balgal-du**   **ngumbi**   **ngariba**
do.not   2SG.NOM   come-ATEL   house   1SG.POSS
don't come to my house.
wunna ŋinta bulkultu ūmpi ŋurribā.

nginda   **wula**   **ganyar**   **yaa**
2SG.NOM   word   one   say
You say one word,
Ninta wulla kunnar yā;

nginda   **yaa**   **ngunyal**   **yagany-ba**
2SG.NOM   say   3SG.NOM   heal-SBJV
you say "let him heal,"
Ninta yā, 'Wunnal yaraipa';

barany   **ngunyal**   **marumba**   **bany**
then   3SG.NOM   well   sickness
and at once he is well of sickness.
berren wunnal murrumba bai.

ngaja   **baigal**   **gayabandar**
1SG.NOM   man   man.of.power
I am a powerful man;
Nutta baigal kaiabunda:

milin   **dagai-jin**   **ngana**   **gurabi-nga**   **gawa-nya**
many   white.man-PL   1SG.ACC   behind-ALL   follow-PRES
many white men follow behind me.
millen duggatin ŋunna gūrpiŋga kāwunna:

ngaja   **ganyar**   **yaa**   **nginda**   **nya-ra**
1SG.NOM   one   say   2SG.NOM   go-DEST
I say to one, "Go there!"
Nutta kunnar yā, 'ŋinta yerra';

barany   ngunyal   nya-ri
at.once   3SG.NOM   go-PST
At once he went;
berren wunnal yerri:

ngaja   garuba   yaa-li
1SG.NOM   another   say-FUT
I say to another,
Ɲuttakurruba yāli,

nginda   balga-Ø   barany   ngunyal   balga-ri
2SG.NOM   come-IMP   at.once   3SG.NOM   come-PST
"Come!" At once he came.
'ɲinta bulka'; berren wunnal bulkurri;

ngaja   garuba   yaa-li
1SG.NOM   another   say-FUT
I say to another,
ɲutta kurruba yali,

nginda   danga   yaga-li
2SG.NOM   that.DIST   do-FUT
"You will do that!"
ɲinta duɲa yuggali';

barany   ngunyal   yaga-ri
at.once   3SG.NOM   do-PST
and at once he did.'
berren wunnal yuggāri.'

imanuwal   danga   bina
Immanuel   that.DIST   hear
Immanuel hears that.
Immanuel duɲa pīnaŋ.

biribanga   baguru-ba-ri
greatly   be.astonished-RTP-PST
Being greatly astonished,
Birribuŋ bugguru buddai:

gilangan **ngunyal** **yaa-ri**
turn 3SG.NOM say-PST
he turned and he said,
gillūŋin ūnal; yari,

ngaja **yagarabu** **nyaany**
1SG.NOM never see
'I never see
ŋutta yugārpo nānni,

dagai **ngamba** **ngunyal**
white.man like 3SG.NOM
white men like him.
duggai ŋāmba wunnal.

ngan-jin **ngana** **yagar** **winanga-nya**
who-PL 1SG.ACC not believe-PRS
Nobody else believes me.
Ńūndin ŋunna yugar wīnuŋunna.

gaa **gamandan** **ngana** **winanga-nya**
that.MED Commandant 1SG.ACC believe-PRS
That Commandant believes me.'
Kār Kommandant ŋunna wīnuŋunna.'

dagai-jin **gamandan-nuba** **wira** **ngumbi-nga**
white.man-PL Commandant-POSS return house-ALL
The Commandant's men returned to the house
Duggatin Kommandantnūbba wirreni ūmpiŋa;

nyaa-nya **dagai-na** **bany=gu** **dany-dany**
see-PRS white.man-ACC sickness=PURP lie-RNP
He sees the man who is lying sick.
nānna duggana paingo daīda

marumba **ngunyal** **yagany**
well 3SG.NOM heal
He heals him.
murrūmba wunnal yuggān.

261

imanuwal   **jar-di**   **balga-ri**
Immanuel   country-LOC   come-PST
Immanuel came to a land,
Immanuel tarti bulkurri,

gadara   **jigandi**   **galili**
Gadara   near   Galilee
Gadara, near Galilee.
Gadara tjingenti, Galili.

dagai   **balga-ri**   **Miyanjin-di**   **ngunyana**   **ngadan**
white.man   come-PST   Brisbane-LOC   3SG.ACC   meet
A white man came from the city to meet him.
Duggai bulkurri miantunti wunnana ŋadūn.

magui-du   **bargil**   **ngunyal-ba-di**   **nyinyi-du**
devil-ERG   a.long.time   3SG-ABL-LOC   dwell-ATEL
An evil spirit had been living in him for a long time.
Maguïkū barkil wunnalpuddi ŋinedu;

ngunyal   **binawali**
3SG.NOM   crazy
He was crazy.
wunnal pidnwuddeli.

garang-garang   **yagarabu**   **wumba-dunga**
clothes   not.at.all   wear-IPFV
He didn't wear any clothes;
garanggarang yagarabu wumbadūnga

ngumbi-nga   **yagarabu**   **nyinyi**
house-ALL   never   dwell
never lived in a house.
ngūmbinga yagārbu nyinyin:

ngunyal   **ganggir-di**   **nyinyi-dunga**
3SG.NOM   dead-LOC   dwell-IPFV
He lived amongst the dead.
wunnal kuŋgirti ŋinne dūŋa.

ngunyal **imanuwal** **nyaany**
3SG.NOM Immanuel see
He noticed Immanuel
Wunnal Immanuel nānni;

gungany **garany** **ngunyal-ba-di** **yaa-ri**
shout fall 3SG-ABL-LOC say-PST
He shouted and fell at him. He said,
kuŋgaï karan wunnalpuddi; yari,

minyanggu **ngana** **nginda**
what.is.the.matter 1SG.ACC 2SG.NOM
'What do you want with me,
'Minyaŋoŋunna ŋinta,

imanuwal **nyaring** **mumbal-nuba**
Immanuel son thunder-POSS
Immanuel son of God?
Immanuel nurriŋ Mumbālnūbba?

nginda **wana** **ngaja** **muyan**
2SG.NOM do.not 1SG.NOM beseech
Do not, I beseech you,
Inta wunna, ŋutta muīan,

nginda **wana** **ngana** **galimal**
2SG.NOM do.not 1SG.ACC punish
do not punish me.'
inta wunna ŋunna kālimul.'

imanuwal **yaa-ri** **magui**
Immanuel say-PST devil
Immanuel said, 'Demon,
Immanuel yari, 'Maguï,

balga-li **dagai-ba-di**
come-FUT white.man-ABL-LOC
you will come out of the white man.'
bulkurri duggai puddi.'

jigan   **ngunyana**   **many**
often   3SG.ACC   take
Often it seized him,
Tjigen wunnana māni,

ngunyanuba   **ngabang**   **jina**
3SG.POSS   elder.brother   foot
his older brother (tied) his feet
wunnanuba ŋubbuŋ tjidne

nga   **mara**   **nany**
and   hand   tie
and tied his hands;
ŋa murra nūnni;

ngunyal   **baguuru**   **gama-ri**
3SG.NOM   rope   break-PST
he broke the ropes
wunnal būggūru kamāri.

nga   **magui-du**   **ngunyana**   **gawany**   **gadigal-di**
and   devil-ERG   3SG.ACC   drive   forest-LOC
and the demon drove him into the forest.
Ŋa maguïdu wunnana kawāne kūdigulti.

imanuwal   **yaa-ri**   **nai**   **nginda**   **minya**
Immanuel   say-PST   name   2SG.NOM   what
Immanuel asked, 'What's your name?'
Immanuel yari, 'Naī ŋinta minya'?

magui-du   **yaa-ri**   **gurumba**   **milin**
devil-ERG   say-PST   great   many
The demon said, 'We are a great many.'
Maguïdu yari, 'Kurumba mulla.'

milin   **ngunyal-ba-di**   **gurin**
many   3SG-ABL-LOC   enter
Many demons were inside him.
Millen maguï wunnalpuddi kurrin.

ngambila   magui   muyan
all   devil   beseech
All the demons beg,
Ŋāmbille maguï muïan,

wana   ngalinyana   waya-ba   wungga
do.not   1DU.ACC   send-SBJV   hole
'Don't send us into the pit!'
'Wunna ŋulleŋunna waialta wunku.'

biing-biing   milin-gali   bibu-di   dal-ma-nya
pig   many-VERY   hill-LOC   eat-CAUS-PRS
Many pigs are feeding on the hillside.
Pigpig millenkolle bippudi tanmunna.

magui   muyan   yaa-ri
devil   beseech   say-PST
The demons beg, they say,
Maguï muïan, yari

ngaliny   nya-ra   biing-biing   wigu
1DU.NOM   go-DEST   pig   Q
'We can go to the pigs, yes?'
'Ŋulle yerrā pigpig, ēko?'

ngunyal   yaa-ri   nya-ra
3SG.NOM   say-PST   go-DEST
He said, 'Go there!'
Wunnal yari 'Yerra'

barany   ngambila   magui   nyan-dunga   dagai-ba
at.once   all   devil   go-IPFV   white.man-ABL
At once all the demons are leaving the white man
Berren ŋāmbille maguï yeatunga duggaipa

biing-biing-di   gurin
pig-LOC   enter
and enter the pigs;
pigpigti kurrin;

barany **ngambila** **biing-biing** **jubuiban** **nyigiran**
then   all   pig   quickly   run
then all the pigs quickly run
berren ŋamille pigpig tubbōrpun īgēren

jubui-di **bibu-di** **ban.gin**
straight-LOC   hill-LOC   fall
straight down the hill, fall
tubburti bipudi bunkin,

nga **dabil-di** **wanangin**
and   water-LOC   drown
and drown in the water.
ŋa tabbilti wūnuŋin.

dagai-jin **biing-biing** **nyundal-dany**
white.man-PL   pig   keep.animals-RNP
The pig-keeping men
Duggatin pigpig inēlta

nyigiran **Miyanjin-di** **ngambila** **yaa-ri**
run   Brisbane-LOC   all   say-PST
run to the city; they told everything.
īgeren mientjinti; ŋambilla yari.

dagai-jin **Miyanjin-di-ba** **nyan-dunga**
white.man-PL   Brisbane-LOC-ABL   travel-IPFV
The white men in the city were going
Duggaitin miëntjintiber yeatuŋa,

nyaany-ba **minya** **yaga-ri**
see-SBJV   what   do-PST
to see what (someone) did.
nānnibēr minna yugari.

ngunyal **balga-ri** **imanuwal** **nyaany**
3SG.NOM   come-PST   Immanuel   see
They came; they notice Immanuel.
Wunnal bulkurri; Immanuel nānni;

dagai **magui** **nyundal-du** **nyaany**
white.man   devil   keep.animals-ATEL   see
They see the white man with a demon living in him;
duggai maguï inēltu nānni

jina-di **imanuwal-nuba** **nyinyi-du**
foot-LOC   Immanuel-POSS   sit-ATEL
he is sitting at Immanuel's feet.
jidnendi Immanuelnūbba ŋinēdu,

garang-garang-bila
clothes-STATE
He is wearing clothes
geraŋ geraŋ pilla,

bina **yagany** **ngunyal** **ngunyali** **yandany**
mind   heal   3SG.NOM   3PL.NOM   fear
and his mind is healed. They are afraid.
pidna yuggan wunnal. Wunnale yandain.

dagai-jin **imanuwal-ba-di** **nyinyi-du**
white.man-PL   Immanuel-ABL-LOC   dwell-ATEL
The white men staying with Immanuel
Duggatin Immanuelpuddi ŋīnēdo

yaa-ri **ngambila**
say-PST   all
tell the whole story.
yari ŋāmbilla.

ngambila **dagai-jin** **jar-di-ba** **gadara**
all   white.man-PL   country-LOC-ABL   Gadera
All the white men in the land of Gadera
Ŋabille duggatin tartibēr Gadara

balga-ri **imanuwal** **nga** **muyan**
come-PST   Immanuel   and   beseech
came to Immanuel and beseech,
bulkurri Immanuel ŋa muïan;

nya-ra   **nginda**   **nya-ra**   **nginda**
go-DEST   2SG.NOM   go-DEST   2SG.NOM
'Go away, go away!'
'Yerrā ŋinta, yerrā ŋinta';

ngunyal   **gurumba**   **yandany**
3SG.NOM   greatly   fear
They are very afraid.
wunnal kurumba yandain.

imanuwal   **nyan-dunga**   **gundul-di**   **giram-di**   **wira**
Immanuel   travel-IPFV   canoe-LOC   across-LOC   return
Immanuel was travelling in a canoe, returning across.
Immanuel yeatuŋa kūndūlti, kīrgūmti wirren.

barany   **dagai**   **magui**   **ngunyal-ba-di**   **nyan-dany**
then   white.man   devil   3SG-ABL-LOC   go-RNP
Then the man, whom the demon had possessed,
Burru duggai, maguï wunnalpuddi yādeni,

balga-ri   **imanuwal**
come-PST   Immanuel
came to Immanuel.
bulkurri Immanuel;

yaa-ri   **ngaja**   **nginda-ba-di**   **nyinyi**
say-PST   1SG.NOM   2SG-ABL-LOC   dwell
He said, 'I'm staying with you.'
yari, 'ŋutta ŋintapuddi ŋinne.'

imanuwal   **ngunyalu**   **yaa-ri**
Immanuel   3SG.ERG   say-PST
Immanuel, he said,
Immanuel wunnalu yari,

nya-ra   **wira**   **ngumbi=gu**   **nginuba**
go-DEST   return   house=PURP   2SG.POSS
'Go, return to your house;
'yerrā; wirrēr umpiŋgo ŋinnuba;

nambany	**dagai-jin**	**daun**	**nginu**	**yaga-ri-ba**
show	white.man-PL	thing	2SG.DAT	do-PST-SBJV

show the white men the things (I) did for you.'
numpa duggaitin taoŭn ŋinnu yugariba.'

ngunyal	**nyan-dunga**	**nga**
3SG.NOM	travel-IPFV	and

He was travelling and
Wunnal yeatuŋa, ŋa

dagai-jin	**ngambila=bu**	**yaa-ri**	**daun**	**gurumba**
white.man-PL	all=EMPH	talk-PST	thing	great

told the white men all the great things
duggatin ŋambillabayari toŭn kurumba

ngunyalu	**imanuwal**	**yaga-ri**
3SG.ERG	Immanuel	do-PST

he, Immanuel, did.
wunnalu Immanuel yugari.

barany	**imanuwal**	**giram-di**	**wira-nya=bu**
then	Immanuel	across-LOC	return-PRS=EMPH

Then Immanuel is finally returning across
Burru Immanuel kīrumti wirē nēbu;

dagai-jin	**dujin**	**nyaany=gu**
white.man-PL	enjoy	see=PURP

and the white men are rejoicing to see him.
duggatin dūtin nānniŋo;

ngambila=bu	**ngunyana**	**nyundal-dunga**
all=EMPH	3SG.ACC	wait-IPFV

Everyone is waiting for him.
ŋambillabu wunnana ūndaltūŋa.

dagai	**nai**	**yairu**
white.man	name	Jairus

A white man named Jairus
Duggai, naiī Yāiru,

balga-ri	**ngunyal**	**ban.gin**	**jina**	**ngunyal-ba-di**
come-PST	3SG.NOM	fall	foot	3SG-ABL-LOC

came. He fell at his feet.
bulkurri; wunnal bunkin tjidna wunnalpuddi;

muyan	**yaa-ri**
entreat	say-PST

He pleaded,
muïan, yari;

nginda	**balga-Ø**	**ngumbi-nga**	**ngariba**
2SG.NOM	come-IMP	house-ALL	1SG.POSS

'Come to my house.
'ŋinta bulka umpiŋga ŋurriba:

ngariba	**nyaringgan**	**ganyar**	**gumbal**
1SG.POSS	daughter	one	only

My only daughter,
ŋurriba nuriŋgun kunnar kūmbal,

biribi	**gin**	**ngunyal**	**baranyba**	**baluny**
little	girl	3SG.NOM	nearly	dead

a little girl, she is almost dead.'
berpi kīn; wunnal barumpa balūni.'

imanuwal	**yaa-ri**	**ngaja**	**nginda-ba**	**nya-ra**
Immanuel	say-PST	1SG.NOM	2SG-ABL	go-DEST

Immanuel said, 'I will follow you there.'
Immanuel yari 'ŋutta ŋintaba yurrī.'

dagai-jin	**garubaba-ri**	**ngunyuna**
white.man-PL	crowd-PST	3SG.ACC

White men crowded him.
Duggatin kūrūkabari wunnana.

jundal	**bany-bila**
woman	be.sick-STATE

A woman was sick
Jūndāl paiïmbila;

yagar **ngunyana** **marumba** **yaga-li**
not   3SG.ACC   well   heal-FUT
and nothing would heal her.
yugar wunnana murrumba yuggali;

ngunyal **gurabi-nga** **balga-ri**
3SG.NOM   behind-ALL   come-PST
She came behind
wunnal gūrpinje bulkurri;

ngadan **garang-garang** **imanuwal-nuba**
touch   clothes   Immanuel-POSS
and touched Immanuel's clothing.
ŋādün geraŋgeraŋ Immanuelnübba.

barany **gawan** **dalan**
then   blood   stop
At once the blood stopped.
Berren kaoun dullan;

jundal **marumba** **bany** **imanuwal** **yaa-ri**
woman   well   sickness   Immanuel   say-PST
The woman was well of disease. Immanuel said,
jūndal murrumba baïn. Immanuel yari

ngandu **ngana** **ngadan**
who.ERG   1SG.ACC   touch
'Who touched me?'
'ŋāndu ŋunna ŋadūn?'

ngambila **yaa-ri** **yagar** **ngaja**
everyone   say-PST   not   1SG.NOM
Everyone said, 'Not I.'
Ŋambille yari 'yugar ŋutta.'

bidar **yaa-ri**
Peter   say-PST
Peter said,
Peter yari;

bandar	**dagai-jin**	**nginda**	**garubaba-ri**	
honorific	white.man-PL	2SG.NOM	throng-PST	

'Master, white men were crowding around you
'Bunjeru duggatin ŋinta kurukabari

nga	**nginda**	**mama**	**nginda**	**yaa-ri**
and	2SG.NOM	press	2SG.NOM	say-PST

and pressing you. You say,
ŋa ŋinta mumma: Ŋinta yari

ngandu	**ngana**	**ngadan**	**imanuwal**	**yaa-ri**
who.ERG	1SG.ACC	touch	Immanuel	say-PST

"Who touched me?"' Immanuel said,
ŋāndu ŋunna ŋadun?' Immanuel yari;

ganyara	**ngana**	**ngadan**
someone	1SG.ACC	touch

'Someone touched me.
'Kunnara ŋunna ŋadūn;

gaya	**ngaja-ba-di**	**nyigiran**	**jundal**	**nyaany**
power	1SG-ABL-LOC	run	woman	see

Power is gone from me.' The woman sees
kaia ŋuttabuddi īgeren.' Jūndal nāni

yagar	**ngunyal**	**marumba**	**nguruman**
not	3SG.NOM	well	hide.oneself

that she cannot hide from him
yugar wunnal murrumba ŋurumun;

ngunyal	**jiga-ba-li**	**balga-ri**
3SG.NOM	shake-RTP-REFL	come-PST

She shook as she came
wunnal jikkebele bulkurri;

garany	**jina-di**	**ngunyal-ba-di**
fall	foot-LOC	3SG-ABL-LOC

and fell at his feet.
karan tjidnendi wunnalpuddi;

nga   dagai-jin-ba-di   **ngambila=bu**   **yaa-ri**
and   white.man-PL-ABL-LOC   everyone=EMPH   say-PST
and in front of all the white men, said,
ŋa duggatin buddi ŋambillabo yari;

ngaja   nginuba   garang-garang   ngadan
1SG.NOM   2SG.POSS   clothes   touch
'I touched your clothing.'
'ŋutta Ŋinnuba geraŋgeran ŋadun,

barany   ngaja   bany   yagany
at.once   1SG.NOM   sickness   heal
At once I was healed of sickness.'
berren ŋutta paï yuggān.'

imanuwal   yaa-ri
Immanuel   say-PST
Immanuel said,
Immanuel yari;

ngariba   nyaringgan   marumba   nginda
1SG.POSS   daughter   good   2SG.NOM
'My daughter, you are good!
'ŋurriba nuriŋgun murrumba ŋinta!

nginda   ngana   ngui-ba-nya   winanga
2SG.NOM   1SG.ACC   believe-RTP-PRS   hear
Believing, you heard me.
Ŋinta ŋunna ŋuipunā ŋwīneüŋga;

dujin-nya   nginda   marumba
enjoy-PRS   2SG.NOM   well
Enjoy it well.'
dujinna inta murrumba.'

barany   dagai-jin
then   white.man-PL
Then the white men
Berren duggatin

ngumbi-nga   yairu-nuba   balga-ri
house-ALL   Jairus-POSS   come-PST
came to the house of Jairus.
umpiŋga Yāirūnubba bulkurri;

yaa-ri   nyaringgan   nginuba   baluny
say-PST   daughter   2SG.POSS   die
He said, 'Your daughter is dead.
yari 'nuriŋgun ŋinnuba balūni;

wana   ngandu   yaa-du
do.not   who.ERG   say-ATEL
Nobody say anything more.'
wunna ŋundin yāldu.'

imanuwal   winanga-ri   yaa-ri   yandany   wana
Immanuel   hear-PST   say-PST   fear   do.not
Immanuel heard, and said, 'Fear not.
Immanuel wīnaŋurri; yari; 'yandai wunna;

ngundu   ngana   ngui-ba-nya   winanga
only   1SG.ACC   believe-RTP-PRS   hear
Only hear me, believing:
ŋūndu ŋunna ŋuipunāŋ wīneūŋga;

nyaringgan   nginuba   marumba   bany   yagany-ba
daughter   2SG.POSS   well   sickness   heal-SBJV
Your daughter may be healed of sickness.'
nuiŋgun ŋinnuba murrumba paī yugaipa.'

barany   ngunyali   ngumbi-nga   balga-ri
then   3PL.NOM   house-ALL   come-PST
Then they came to the house.
Burru wunnale ūmpīŋga bulkurri.

imanuwal   wana   dagai-jin-na
Immanuel   forbid   white.man-PL-ACC
Immanuel forbade the white men
Immanuel wunna duggatina

balgal-du ngumbi-nga
come-ATEL house-ALL
going into the house;
bulgutu ūmpiŋga;

ngundu bidar nga yaguba
only Peter and Jacob
only Peter and Jacob
ŋūndu Peter ŋa Yakoba

nga yan nga bing
and John and father
and John and the father
ŋa Yohan, ŋa biŋ

nga bujang gin-nuba
and mother girl-POSS
and mother of the girl.
ŋa pudjaŋ kīnnūbba.

ngambila=bu dungi-nya yaa-ri gin baluny
everyone=EMPH weep-PRS say-PST girl die
Everyone was weeping, and said, 'The girl is dead,
Ŋambilladu dūŋinnā; yari; 'kīn balluni;

gin baluny imanuwal yaa-ri
girl die Immanuel say-PST
the girl is dead.' Immanuel said,
kīn balluni.' Immanuel yari

wana dungi-du yagar ngunyal baluny
do.not weep-ATEL not 3SG.NOM dead
'Don't weep; she is not dead,
'wunna dūŋidū; yugar wunnal ballun,

ngundu bugany gumbal
but sleep only
but only sleeping.'
ŋundu bugankūmbal.'

ngambila=bu   **gindin**   **winanga-ri**   **baluny-ba**
everyone=EMPH   laugh   believe-PST   dead-RTP
Everyone laughed, believing her dead.
Ŋambilladu ginden; wineūŋari balunibēr.

imanuwal   **ngambila=bu**   **gawany**
Immanuel   everyone=EMPH   drive
Immanuel drove everyone out.
Immanuel ŋambillebu kawāne;

ngunyal   **gin**   **mara-di**   **many**
3SG.NOM   girl   hand-LOC   take
He grasped the girl's hand,
wunnal kīn murradi māni;

ngunyal   **yaa-ba-ri**   **ngunyana**   **gin**   **balga-ra**
3SG.NOM   say-RTP-PST   3SG.ACC   girl   come-DEST
while saying to her, 'Girl! Come here!'
wunnal yambari wunnana; yari; 'kin! Bulkurai!'

nguru   **wira-biny=bu**
spirit   return-BACK=EMPH
The spirit returns!
ŋūru wīrepinebu;

ngunyal   **bangga**   **dalbany**
3SG.NOM   quickly   sit.up
She quickly sits up.
wunnal banka dulpain.

imanuwal   **yaa-ri**   **dalgaba**   **ngunyanu**   **wuja-Ø**
Immanuel   say-PST   food   3SG.DAT   give-IMP
Immanuel said, 'Give her food.'
Immanuel yari; 'tākūba wunnanu widda.'

bing   **nga**   **bujang**   **gurii**
father   and   mother   be.astonished
The father and mother marvelled.
Bīŋ ŋa pujaŋ kurrī.

References

Ah Kee, Vernon. 2012. *Transforming Tindale: Digital Stories*. State Library of Queensland. Available at: www.slq.qld.gov.au/discover/past-exhibitions/transforming-tindale/digital-stories (Accessed 10 November 2022).

Aird, Michael. 2012. *Transforming Tindale*. Photographic and art exhibition. State Library of Queensland. Available at: www.slq.qld.gov.au/discover/past-exhibitions/transforming-tindale/gallery (Accessed 10 November 2022).

Aird, Michael. 2020. 'From Illustration to Evidence: Centring Historical Photographs in Native Land Claims'. *Kronos* 46, no. 1: 148–71.

Aird, Michael, Joanna Sassoon, and David Trigger. 2020. 'From Illustration to Evidence: Historical Photographs and Aboriginal Native Title Claims in South-East Queensland, Australia'. *Anthropology and Photography* 13: 1–27.

Allen, John and John Lane. 1914. 'Grammar, Vocabulary and Notes of the Wangerriburra Tribe'. *Annual Report of the Chief Protector of Aboriginals for the Year 1913*. Available at: aiatsis.gov.au/sites/default/files/catalogue_resources/63892.pdf (Accessed 6 July 2022).

Baker, Ali Gumillya. 2019. 'Camping in the Shadow of the Racist Text'. *The National 4. Australian Art Now*. Available at: www.the-national.com.au/essays/camping-in-the-shadow-of-the-racist-text/ (Accessed 10 November 2022).

Ballard, Kath. 2007. *Brisbane the Beginning*. Enoggera: Snap Printing Enoggera.

Bannister, Dennis Daniel. 1982. 'Guwar: The Language of Moreton Island'. In *Collection – Papers on the Aboriginal Languages of Queensland*, edited by Dennis Daniel Bannister. Brisbane: University of Queensland Press.

Bannister, Dennis Daniel. 1986. *Sources of Information on the Durubul Language of Brisbane 1838–1975*. AIAS Library.

Bell, Enid. 1934. 'Dialects of the Vanished Tribes'. *The Queenslander* (Brisbane, Queensland), 18 January 1934 (p. 13) and 25 January 1934 (p. 13).

Bell, Jeanie. 1994. *Dictionary of the Gubbi-Gubbi and Butchulla languages.* Self-published.

Bell, Jeanie. 2003. 'A Sketch Grammar of the Badjala Language of Gari (Fraser Island)'. Masters thesis, University of Melbourne.

Bensted, Phillip. 1924. Memorandum dated 12.5.24 to the Deputy Chief Protector of Aboriginals, South Brisbane. Correspondence from the Home-Secretary, Home Department to all protectors of Aboriginals. PR489478. Queensland State Archives.

Birch, Gustavus. 1873. Unpublished diary, transcribed by Heather Frankland. John Oxley Library, State Library of Queensland.

Blackman, FA. 1900. 'Linguistics'. *Science of Man and Journal of the Royal Anthropological Society of Australasia* 3, no. 4: 60–61.

Borey, Bernice and Peter K Laurer. 1984. *Myora Aboriginal Cemetery.* Brisbane: Anthropology Museum, University of Queensland.

Bowern, Claire and Quentin Atkinson. 2012. 'Computational Phylogenetics and the Internal Structure of Pama-Nyungan'. *Language* 88: 817–45. doi.org/10.1353/lan.2012.0081.

Bunce, Daniel. 1846–7. *Journal of Daniel Bunce, Botanist to Leichhardt's Expedition, 1846–7.* Unpublished.

Bunce, Daniel. 1859. *Language of the Aborigines of the Colony of Victoria and Other Australian Districts.* Thomas Brown: Geelong.

Butcher, Andrew and Deborah Loakes. 2008. 'Enhancing the Left Edge: The Phonetics of Prestopped Sonorants in Australian Languages'. *The Journal of the Acoustical Society of America* 124, no. 4: 2527. doi.org/10.1121/1.4782973.

Cadell, William Thomas. c.1900. *From WT Cadell (authorised surveyor).* Meston papers, OM 64-17, Box 1, Item 16, Box 8431, State Library of Queensland.

Charlton, Kerry and Barry Brown. 2019. *An Introduction to the Languages of Moreton Bay: Yagarabul and its Djandewal Dialect, and Moreton Islands Gowar.* Self-published.

Clark, Walter. 1916. 'The Aborigines: Their Manners and Customs'. *The Queenslander* (Brisbane), 16 September 1916, p. 8.

Clunie, James Oliphant. 1839. 'Moreton Bay'. In *Journal of Three Expeditions,* edited by Thomas Mitchell. London: T and W Boone.

Colliver, Frederick Stanley and Frank Palmer Woolston. 1975. 'The Aborigines of Stradbroke Island'. *Proceedings of the Royal Society of Queensland* 86, no. 16: 91–104.

Colliver, Frederick Stanley and Frank Palmer Woolston. 1978. 'Aboriginals in the Brisbane Area'. *Archaeology Papers No. 6*, 1–24. Brisbane: Brisbane Library Board of Queensland.

Corbett, Greville G. 2000. *Number.* Cambridge: Cambridge University Press.

Courier-Mail. 1936. 'Nomenclature of Queensland', 8 October 1936.

Courier-Mail. 1947. 'Keen Student of Aborigines Dead', 17 April 1947.

Cowell, Mark W. 1964. *A Reference Grammar of Syrian Arabic, Part 1.* Washington DC: Georgetown University Press.

Cunningham, MC. 1969. *A Description of the Yugumbir Dialect of Bandjalang.* Faculty of Arts Papers Volume 1, No. 8. Brisbane: University of Queensland.

Curr, Edward Micklethwaite. 1887. *The Australian Race, Vol. III.* Melbourne: John Ferres, Government Printer.

Darragh, T and R Fensham (eds). 2013. *The Leichhardt Diaries: Early Travels in Australia During 1842–1844.* Memoirs of the Queensland Museum – Culture 7, Parts 1 and 2. Brisbane: Queensland Museum.

Dawson, Christopher. 2011. 'What's in a Name? The Rise, Fall and Comeback of Boggo'. *Queensland History Journal* 21, no. 4: 227–34.

Delaney, Sandra. 1994. 'The Brown Family's Association to the Quandamooka Area'. MA thesis, University of South Australia.

Donovan, Dan. 1877. 'Our Native Timbers'. 23 November 1877. *Brisbane Courier,* p. 3.

Donovan, Dan. 1888a. 'Our Native Timbers'. 16 January 1888. *Brisbane Courier,* p. 6.

Donovan, Dan. 1888b. 'Our Native Timbers'. 17 January 1888. *Brisbane Courier,* p. 3.

Donovan, Dan. 1888c. 'Our Native Timbers'. 27 March 1888. *Brisbane Courier,* p. 6.

Donovan, Dan. 1888d. 'Our Native Timbers'. 10 July 1888. *Brisbane Courier,* p. 6.

Donovan, Dan. 1895. 'The Bora at Gatton'. 30 November 1895. *The Queenslander.* (Brisbane), p. 1034.

Dousset, Laurent. 2008. 'The "Global" Versus the "Local": Cognitive Processes of Kin Determination in Aboriginal Australia'. *Oceania* 78 no. 3: 260–79. doi.org/10.1002/j.1834-4461.2008.tb00041.x.

Dousset, Laurent. 2011. *Australian Aboriginal Kinship: An Introductory Handbook with Particular Emphasis on the Western Desert.* Marseille: Pacific-Credo Publications. doi.org/10.4000/books.pacific.556.

Eipper, Christopher. 1841a. *Statement of the Origin, Condition, and Prospects, of the German Mission to the Aborigines at Moreton Bay.* Sydney: James Reading.

Eipper, Christopher. 1841b. 'Observations Made on a Journey to the Natives at Toorbal, August 2, 1841'. *Colonial Observer* (Sydney), 14 October 1841, p. 10.

Eipper, Christopher. 1841c. 'Observations Made on a Journey to the Natives at Toorbal, August 2, 1841'. *Colonial Observer* (Sydney), 21 October 1841, p. 23.

Eipper, Christopher. 1986 [1841]. 'The Following Vocabulary Appeared in Mission to Aborigines by Rev. E. C. Eipper, 1841'. In *Sources of Information on the Durubul Language of Brisbane 1838–1975*, edited by Dennis Daniel Bannister, 1–2. AIAS Library.

Fensham, Roderick J. 2021. 'Leichhardt's Ethnobotany for the Eucalypts of Southeast Queensland'. *Australian Journal of Botany* 69: 185–214. doi.org/10.1071/BT21007.

Finch, Charles Wray. 1842. Charles Wray Finch Papers, OM92-176. John Oxley Library, State Library of Queensland.

Fison, Cecil S. 1889. *Report on the Oyster Fisheries of Moreton Bay and The Great Sandy Island Cape, 12 August, 1889.* Available at: archive.org/stream/reporton oysterfi00fiso/reportonoysterfi00fiso_djvu.txt (Accessed 7 July 2022).

Flint, Elwyn H. 1960. Recordings. Queensland Speech Survey of Aboriginal English, Group 64. Elwyn Flint Collection, UQFL 173, University of Queensland.

Foley Fiona L. 2019. *Badtjala–English English–Badtjala Word List.* Brisbane: Pirri Productions.

Gardner, William. 1854. *Volume 01: Production and Resources of the Northern and Western Districts of New South Wales, 1854* [ca. 1850–1857]. A 176/Vol 1, State Library of New South Wales.

Gibson, James. 1863. Letter to Annabella Sloane, 24 April. AIATSIS (catalogue entry in process: details forthcoming).

Gibson, James. 1882. Letter to AW Howitt, 27 May. MS 69, Howitt Papers, Box 5, folder 2; 2p, 233191-1001. AIATSIS.

Hale, Kenneth L. 1976. 'The Adjoined Relative Clause in Australia'. In *Grammatical Categories in Australian Languages: Proceedings of the 1974 AIAS Conference*, edited by RMW Dixon, 78–105. Canberra: Australian Institute of Aboriginal Studies.

Hall, Thomas. 1928. *The Early History of Warwick District and Pioneers*. Toowoomba: Robertson & Proven Ltd.

Hanlon, WE. 1931. 'Aboriginal Place Names'. *The Brisbane Courier*, 6 June 1931.

Hardcastle, Thomas W. 1946–7. 'A Vocabulary of the Yuggarabul Language Spoken in the Boonah District 1900–1904'. In *Queensland Geographical Journal 51*, edited by DA O'Brien: 21–28.

Harper, Edward. 1894. 'Early Days on the Tweed'. *The Queenslander* (Brisbane). 1 September 1894, p. 410.

Harward-Nalder, G and M Grenfell. 2012. 'Learning from the Quandamooka'. In *A Place of Sandhills: Ecology, Hydrogeomorphology and Management of Queensland's Dune Islands*, edited by AH Arthington, T Page, CW Rose and R Sathyamurthy, 495–501. Proceedings of the Royal Society of Queensland Vol. 117.

Haworth, Sylvia. 2011. Affidavit Of Syliva (sic) Haworth. Affidavit to *Sandy on behalf of the Yugara People v State of Queensland (No 3)* [2015] FCA 210. Federal Court file no. QUD6196/1998.

Hinchcliffe, Frederick William. 1890. 'The Aboriginal Language'. *The Queenslander* (Brisbane). 27 December 1890, p. 1218.

Hockings, HJ. 1884. 'Notes on Two Australian Species of *Trigona*'. *Transactions of the Royal Entomological Society of London* 32, no. 1: 149–57. doi.org/10.1111/j.1365-2311.1884.tb01606.x.

Holmer, Nils M. 1983. *Linguistic Survey of South-Eastern Queensland*. Pacific Linguistics Series D, No. 54. Canberra: Department of Linguistics, Research School of Pacific Studies, The Australian National University.

Howitt, Alfred William. 1904. *The Native Tribes of South-East Australia*. London: Macmillan and Co., Ltd.

Jackson, George Kenneth. 1937. *Turubul Tribe: Typed Vocabulary*. PMS 5354, 0036153. AIATSIS.

Jefferies, Anthony. 2011. 'Guwar, the Language of Moreton Island, and its Relationship to the Bandjalang and Yagara Subgroups: A Case for Phylogenetic Migratory Expansion?' MPhil Thesis, The University of Queensland.

Kidd, Ros. 2001. 'Aboriginal History of South Brisbane'. *Journal of the Royal Historical Society of Queensland* 17, no. 11: 463–80.

Kite, Suzanne and Stephen Wurm. 2004. *The Dūɲidjawu Language of Southeast Queensland: Grammar, Texts and Vocabulary.* Canberra: Pacific Linguistics.

Kombumerri Corporation for Culture (eds). 2001. *The Language of the Wangerriburra and Neighbouring Groups in the Yugambeh Region: From the Works of John Allen and John Lane.* Self-published.

Lang, John Dunmore. 1846. Australian Aboriginal Vocabulary. B396 Mitchell Library.

Lang, John Dunmore. 1847. *Cooksland in North-Eastern Australia.* London: Longman, Brown, Green and Longmans (republished 1970).

Latham, RG. 1852. 'Remarks on the Vocabularies of the Voyage of the Rattlesnake'. In *Voyage of HMS Rattlesnake Vol 2*, by John Macgillivray. London: T & W Boone.

Lauterer, Joseph. 1891. 'Scientific and Useful: An Aboriginal Language'. *The Queenslander* (Brisbane). 21 February 1891, p. 555.

Lauterer, Joseph. 1895. 'Outlines of a Grammar of the "Yaggara", the Language of the Yerongpan Tribe on the "Sandy Country" between Brisbane and Ipswich'. *Report of the Australasian Association for the Advancement of Science* 6: 619–24.

Lauterer, Joseph. 1897. 'The Aboriginal Languages of Eastern Australia Compared: A Philological Essay'. *Proceedings of the Royal Society of Queensland* 12: 11–16. doi.org/10.5962/p.351257.

Leichhardt, Ludwig. 1842–1844. *The Leichhardt Diaries: Early Travels in Australia During 1842–1844.* Edited by Thomas A Darragh and Roderick J Fensham. Memoirs of the Queensland Museum: Cultural Heritage Series 7(1). Brisbane: Queensland Museum.

Lenet, George W. 1904. 'Aboriginal Dialects and Place Names (Queensland)'. *Science of Man and Journal of the Royal Anthropological Society of Australasia* 7, no. 5: 72–76.

Macarthur, William and Charles Moore. 1867. *Catalogue of the Natural and Industrial Products of New South Wales Forwarded to the Paris Universal Exhibition of 1867 by the New South Wales Exhibition Commissioner.* Sydney: Thomas Richards Government Printers.

Macdonald, Gaynor. 2010. 'An Anthropological Assessment of Turrbal Connection'. Assessment made as part of case *Sandy on behalf of the Yugara People v State of Queensland (No 3)* [2015] FCA 210. Federal Court file no. QUD6196/1998; QC98/026.

MacKenzie, Annie. 1992. *Memories along the Boggo track.* Brisbane: Boolarong Publications.

Mathew, John. 1910. *Two Representative Tribes of Queensland.* London: T Fisher Unwin.

Mathews, Robert Hamilton. 1898. 'Australian Divisional Systems'. *Journal and Proceedings of the Royal Society of NSW* 32: 66–255.

McClurg, John HC. 1975. *Historical Sketches of Brisbane.* Brisbane: Library Board of Queensland and Royal Historical Society of Queensland.

McConvell, Patrick. 2018. 'The Birds and the Bees: The Origins of Sections in Queensland'. In *Skin, Kin and Clan: The Dynamics of Social Categories in Indigenous Australia*, edited by Patrick McConvell, Piers Kelly and Sébastien Lacrampe, 219–70. Canberra: ANU Press. doi.org/10.22459/SKC.04.2018.08.

Meston, Archibald. 1867–1960. Archibald Meston Papers. OM64-17. John Oxley Library, State Library of Queensland.

Meston, Archibald. 1893. A. Meston to Howitt 23 April 1893. Howitt Papers. XM259. *From the Page.* Available at: fromthepage.com/tyay/howitt-and-fison-papers/xm259-icdms-lowres (Accessed 20 February 2023).

Meston, Archibald. 1894. 'Old Harper's Yarns'. *The Queenslander* (Brisbane). 22 September 1894, p. 549.

Meston, Archibald. 1895. *Geographic History of Queensland.* Brisbane: Edmund Gregory, Government Printer.

Meston, Archibald. 1896. *Report on the Aboriginals of Queensland.* Brisbane: Government Printer.

Meston, Archibald. 1923a. 'Old Moreton Bay Tribes: Their Lost Languages'. *The Brisbane Courier.* 25 August 1923, p. 19.

Meston, Archibald. 1923b. 'Old Moreton Bay Tribes: Their Lost Languages'. *The Brisbane Courier.* 20 October 1923, p. 18.

Meston, Archibald. 1923c. 'Old Moreton Bay Tribes: Their Lost Languages'. *The Brisbane Courier.* 1 December 1923, p. 19.

Meston, Archibald. 1984. 'Entries in Jandai Vocabulary'. In *Aboriginal Pathways in Southeast Queensland and the Richmond River*, edited by John Gladstone Steele, 114–20. St Lucia: University of Queensland Press.

Meston, Archibald. 1986a [1890]. 'Sentences. Coobenpil Dialect. Coonool Cabalcho Tribe. Lytton, A. Meston, 1890'. In *Sources of Information on the Durubul Language of Brisbane 1838–1975*, edited by Dennis Daniel Bannister, 1–2. AIAS Library.

Meston, Archibald. 1986b [1895]. 'Lord's Prayer in the Lytton Dialect (Coopenbil). A. Meston, January, 1895'. In *Sources of Information on the Durubul Language of Brisbane 1838-1975*, edited by Dennis Daniel Bannister, 1–2. AIAS Library.

Meston, Leo A. 1931a. 'Aboriginal Place Names'. *The Brisbane Courier*, 23 May 1931.

Meston, Leo A. 1931b. 'Tallebudgera and Tamborine'. *The Brisbane Courier*, 22 June 1931.

Minjerribah Moorgumpin Elders in Council (MMEIC). 2011. *Jandai Language Dictionary*. Self-published.

Monaghan, Paul. 2003. 'Laying Down the Country: Norman B. Tindale and the Linguistic Construction of the North-west of South Australia'. Doctoral Thesis, University of Adelaide. Available at: digital.library.adelaide.edu.au/dspace/bitstream/2440/21991/2/02whole.pdf (Accessed 10 November 2022).

Moreton Bay. 1838. *The Australian*, 22 December 1838. p. 3. Available at: nla.gov.au/nla.news-article36859622 (Accessed 1 February 2023).

NNW. 1868. 'Vocabulary of the Thoerwel Dialect from N.N.W.'. *Our Paper No. 7* (Brisbane), 12 September 1868.

Oates, Lynette. 1975. *The 1973 Supplement to a Revised Linguistic Survey of Australia*. Armidale: Christian Book Centre.

O'Grady, Geoffrey, CF Voegelin and FN Voegelin. 1966. *Languages of the World: Indo-Pacific Fascicle 6*. Indiana University Press.

Petrie, Constance Campbell. 1904. *Tom Petrie's Reminiscences of Early Queensland*. Brisbane: Watson, Ferguson & Co.

Petrie, Thomas. 1901. 'The Old Brisbane Blacks: Mr Tom Petrie in Reply to the Editor'. *The Brisbane Courier*. 2 September 1901.

Petrie, Thomas. 1902. 'Native Name of the Brisbane River'. *Science of Man and Journal of the Royal Anthropological Society of Australasia* 4, no. 12: 203.

Pitt Rivers Museum. 2012. Transcription of Box 12: Howitt Correspondence. Tylor papers, Pitt Rivers Museum Manuscript Collections Part 1. Available at: web. prm.ox.ac.uk/sma/index.php/primary-documents/primary-documents-index/ 414-howitt-tylor-papers-prm.html (Accessed 28 April 2023).

Quandamooka Yooloourrabee Aboriginal Corporation (QYAC) and Queensland Parks and Wildlife Service and Partnerships (QPWS&P). 2021. *Naree Budjong Djara Resource Information*. Available at: parks.des.qld.gov.au/__data/assets/ pdf_file/0028/237466/naree-budjong-djara-resource-information.pdf (Accessed 8 May 2022).

Radcliffe-Browne, AR. 1930. 'The Social Organization of Australian Tribes. Part 2'. *Oceania* 1, no. 2: 206–46. doi.org/10.1002/j.1834-4461.1930.tb01645.x.

Redland City Council. 2023a. 'Quandamooka'. *Redlands Coast Timelines*. Redland Libraries. Available at: www.redland.qld.gov.au/download/downloads/id/3982/ quandamooka_timeline.pdf (Accessed 27 April 2023).

Redland City Council. 2023b. 'Thorneside'. *Redland City Council*. Available at: www.redland.qld.gov.au/info/20125/our_suburbs_and_islands/179/thorneside (Accessed 27 April 2023).

Ridley, William. 1855. Notebook and Report to the Moreton Bay Aborigines' Friends Society Wednesday 21st November. OM79-32/17, Collection of the State Library of Queensland.

Ridley, William. 1875. *Kamilaroi and other Australian Languages*. Sydney, New South Wales: Thomas Richards, Government Printer.

Ridley, William. 1887. 'North Side of Moreton Bay'. In *The Australian Race, Vol. III.*, by Edward Micklethwaite Curr, 130–33. Melbourne: John Ferres, Government Printer.

Ridley, William. 1986. 'The Following Vocabulary is Collated from all Word Lists and Textual Material Published in the Various Works of Rev. William Ridley between 1855 and 1877'. In *Sources of Information on the Durubul Language of Brisbane 1838–1975*, edited by Dennis Daniel Bannister, 2–9. AIAS.

Rigney, Lester-Irabinna. 1997. 'Internationalisation of an Indigenous Anti-colonial Cultural Critique of Research Methodologies: A Guide to Indigenist Research Methodology and Its Principles'. *HERDSA Annual International Conference Proceedings: Research and Development in Higher Education: Advancing International Perspectives* 20: 629–36.

Roth, Walter Edmund. 1897. *Ethnological Studies among the North-West-Central Queensland Aborigines*. Brisbane, Qld: Edmund Gregory, Government Printer, William Street.

Roth, Walter Edmund. 1910. 'North Queensland Ethnography. Bulletin No. 18. Social and Individual Nomenclature'. *Records of the Australian Museum* 8, no. 1: 79–106. doi.org/10.3853/j.0067-1975.8.1910.936.

Round, Erich. 2014. 'Prestopping of nasals and laterals is only partly parallel'. In *Language Description Informed by Theory*, edited by Rob Pensalfini, Myfany Turpin and Diana Guillemin, 81–95. Amsterdam: John Benjamins Publishing. doi.org/10.1075/slcs.147.05rou.

Sharpe, Margaret. 1998. *Dictionary of Yugambeh Including Neighbouring Dialects*. Canberra: Pacific Linguistics.

Sharpe, Margaret. 2020. *Gurgun Mibinyah: Yugambeh, Ngarahngwal, Ngahnduwal: A Dictionary and Grammar of Mibiny Language Varieties from the Tweed*. Canberra: AIATSIS.

Smith, Bruce A. 2010. 'William Sloan & Company (1861–1884)'. *Guide to Australian Business Records*. Available at: www.gabr.net.au/biogs/ABE0818b.htm. (Accessed 10 November 2022).

State of Queensland. 2022. *Queensland Place Names Database*. Available at: www. qld.gov.au/environment/land/title/place-names. (Accessed 29 October 2022).

Steele, John Gladstone. 1984. *Aboriginal Pathways in Southeast Queensland and the Richmond River*. St Lucia: University of Queensland Press.

Stephens, Kathy M and Donovan Sharp. 2009. *The Flora of North Stradbroke Island*. Brisbane: Queensland Herbarium, Environmental Protection Agency.

Suttor, John Bligh. 1897. 'Linguistics'. *The Australasian Anthropological Journal* 30 April: 106–07.

Tennant-Kelly, Caroline. 1935. 'Tribes on Cherburg Settlement, Queensland'. *Oceania* 5, no. 4: 461–73. doi.org/10.1002/j.1834-4461.1935.tb00165.x.

Tennant-Kelly, Caroline. 2011. 'The Caroline Tennant-Kelly Ethnographic Collection: Fieldwork Accounts of Aboriginal Culture in the 1930s'. Electronic resource. Brisbane: University of Queensland.

Threlkeld, Lancelot. 1846. Provided the Moreton Bay data in 'The Languages of Australia'. In *Ethnography and Philology*, edited by Horatio Hale, 479–81. Philadelphia: C Sherman.

Tindale, Norman Barnett. 1974. *Results of the Harvard–Adelaide Universities Anthropological Expedition, 1938–1939: Distribution of Australian Aboriginal Tribes: A Field Survey*. Collected papers (University of Adelaide), Issue 376. Adelaide: University of Adelaide.

Turner, George (Rev). 1861. *Moreton Bay Vocabulary in Nineteen years in Polynesia: Missionary Life, Travels and Researches in the Islands of the Pacific.* London: John Snow, Paternoster Row.

Walker, Kath 'Oodgeroo Noonuccal'. 1972. *Stradbroke Dreamtime.* Sydney: Angus and Robertson.

Walsh, Michael. 1981. 'Australia' section. In *Language Atlas of the Pacific Area*, edited by Stephen Wurm and Shirô Hattori. Canberra: Australian Academy of the Humanities.

Watkins, George. 1891. 'Notes on the Aboriginals of Stradbroke Island'. Read before the Royal Society of Queensland, 17 April 1891.

Watkins, George. 1984. Entries in 'Jandai Vocabulary'. In *Aboriginal Pathways in Southeast Queensland and the Richmond River*, edited by John Gladstone Steele, 114–20. St Lucia: University of Queensland Press.

Watkins, George. 1986. 'Sentences from Mr George Watkin. Djandai Dialect'. In *Sources of Information on the Durubul Language of Brisbane 1838–1975*, edited by Dennis Daniel Bannister, 11. AIAS Library.

Watkins, George and JE Hamilton. 1887. 'Stradbroke and Moreton Islands'. In *The Australian Race Vol. II*, by Edward Micklethwaite Curr, 222–31. Melbourne: John Ferres, Government Printer.

Watson, Frederick James. 1941. FJ Watson Papers 1941 OM73-20. State Library of Queensland.

Watson, Frederick James. 1943. *Vocabularies of Four Representative Tribes of South Eastern Queensland.* Supplement to the Journal of the Royal Geographical Society of Australasia (Queensland) 48, no. 34. Brisbane: Royal Geographical Society of Australasia (Queensland).

Welsby, Thomas. 1916. *Recollections of the Natives of Moreton Bay.* Delivered before the University Historical Society, 27 September 1916.

Winterbotham, Lindsey Page. 1950. Recordings. OH128, Dr LP Winterbotham oral history. John Oxley Library, State Library of Queensland, Australia.

Winterbotham, Lindsey Page. 1957. Gaiarbau's Story of the Jinibara Tribe of South East Queensland (and its Neighbours). MS. Reprinted in 1982 in *Some Original Views Around Kilcoy. Book 1: The Aboriginal Perspectives.* Transcription and notes by G Langevad, with editorial assistance of B Langevad. Brisbane: Department of Aboriginal and Islanders Advancement.

Wurm, Stephen Adolphe. 1960. Recordings. WURM_S03-002885A. AIATSIS.

Wurm, Stephen Adolphe. 1972. *Languages of Australia and Tasmania*. Janua Linguarum: Series Critica, 1. The Hague/Berlin: Mouton de Gruyter. doi.org/10.1515/9783110808292.

Wurm, Stephen Adolphe. 1994. 'Australasia and the Pacific'. In *Atlas of the World's Languages*, edited by Christopher Moseley and Ron E Asher, 93–130. London/New York: Routledge.

Yerrilee. 1921. 'An Enchanting Scene. The Hills Near Emu Vale. The Queen of All Views'. *Warwick Daily News*. 12 April 1921, p. 2.

Yerrilee. 1927. 'Aborigines. Early Tribes'. *Richmond River Express and Casino Kyogle Advertiser*. 6 May 1927, p. 5.

Yosso, Tara J. 2005. 'Whose Culture Has Capital? A Critical Race Theory Discussion of Community Cultural Wealth'. *Race, Ethnicity and Education* 8, no. 1: 69–91. doi.org/10.1080/1361332052000341006.

www.ingramcontent.com/pod-product-compliance
Lightning Source LLC
Chambersburg PA
CBHW071906090426
42811CB00004B/759